ISBN: 978129009096

Published by:
HardPress Publishing
8345 NW 66TH ST #2561
MIAMI FL 33166-2626

Email: info@hardpress.net
Web: http://www.hardpress.net

acd. Oct 4/11.
to the Bristol Museum

CATALOGUE OF ENGLISH COINS

IN THE BRITISH MUSEUM

A CATALOGUE

OF

ENGLISH COINS

IN THE

BRITISH MUSEUM

THE NORMAN KINGS

BY

GEORGE CYRIL BROOKE, B.A.

IN TWO VOLUMES

WITH AN INTRODUCTION AND 62 PLATES

VOLUME I

(INTRODUCTION, TABLES AND PLATES)

LONDON

PRINTED BY ORDER OF THE TRUSTEES

SOLD AT THE BRITISH MUSEUM, AND BY

Longmans & Co., 39 Paternoster Row
Bernard Quaritch, 11 Grafton Street, New Bond Street, W.
Asher & Co., 13 Bedford Street, Covent Garden
Humphrey Milford, Oxford University Press, Amen Corner, E.C.
And Rollin & Feuardent, 69 Great Russell Street, W.C., and 4 Rue de Louvois, Paris

1916

PRINTED IN ENGLAND
AT THE OXFORD UNIVERSITY PRESS

v. 1

PREFACE

THE second volume of the Catalogue of English Coins in the British Museum, completing the Anglo-Saxon Series, was published in 1893. The retirement of Mr. Keary from the service of the Trustees, and the employment of Mr. Grueber on other parts of the Collection, explain the delay of twenty-three years between that publication and the appearance of the present two volumes. These are entirely the work of Mr. George Cyril Brooke, B.A., Assistant in the Department. They cover the period of the Norman Kings.

Comparison with earlier volumes will show that considerable modifications have been made in the methods of arranging and describing the coins. Special attention has been paid to the epigraphical details of the inscriptions, the importance of which will be manifest upon a glance at the Epigraphical Table which accompanies the work. Special founts have been prepared for the inscriptions. Descriptions and illustrations of important coins which are not represented in the National Collection have been included from other collections, public or private, making the volume for practical purposes a fairly complete work of reference on Anglo-Norman coins. In order to add to the clearness of the descriptions all extraneous information, relating to provenance and similar matters, has been relegated to foot-notes.

Most important of all is the subordination of the mints to the types in the classification; an arrangement which is justified by the great advance which has been made of recent years in fixing the chronology of the types.

The work has been printed by the Clarendon Press, and the collotype plates executed by the London Stereoscopic Company. I have read the proofs of the whole, and compared the descriptions with the coins.

English coins were represented in the collections of Sir Robert Cotton and Sir Hans Sloane, which formed the nucleus of the British Museum at its foundation in 1753. For half a century little addition seems to have been made to the collection. The coins from the Tyssen collection purchased in 1802 did not include his Norman pieces, but many of these found their way into the Museum through the hands of Barré Charles Roberts. The magnificent series of English coins belonging to this collector was purchased in 1810 for 4,000 guineas. No other acquisition approaching this in importance as regards the English series was made for more than a century. The collection of King George III, acquired in 1825, contained a few Norman coins, and purchases were made from time to time at the sales of collections such as those of the Duke of Devonshire (1844), the Earl of Pembroke (1848), James Dodsley Cuff (1854), Hyman Montagu (1896–7), E. W. Rashleigh (1900), and P. W. P. Carlyon-Britton (1913). At the last moment it has fortunately been possible to include in an Appendix fifty-six coins from the cabinet of the late Sir John Evans, although the Norman series was not strongly represented in that collection.

Hoards acquired in part or in their entirety under the law of Treasure Trove have also contributed to the Collection. As these are fully discussed in the Introduction, it suffices to mention here the hoard of many thousand coins found at Beaworth in 1833; nearly seven hundred of these appear in this Catalogue.

The present volumes will, it is hoped, be followed in a few years by a Catalogue of the early Plantagenet series.

G. F. HILL,
Keeper of Coins and Medals.

CONTENTS

VOLUME I

VOLUME II

CATALOGUE OF COINS:—

LIST OF PLATES

ERRATA

p. 22, no. 114 ; p. 36, no. 187 ; p. 41, no. 219 ; p. 67, no. 359 (*not* Sir Hans Sloane coll.) ; p. 86, no. 464 ; insert as provenance *'Cotton Collection, 1753'*.

p. 38, no. 200, insert as moneyer's name ' Godwi '.

p. 52, no. 274, insert as moneyer's name ' Sæwi (Sæwine ?) '.

p. 59, no. 307, for ' Druman ' read ' Dirman '.

pp. 64, 65, nos. 340–2, for moneyer's name read ' Eadwi '.

p. 66, no. 349, insert as moneyer's name ' Godwi '.

p. 68, no. 362, for '(Ælfh[en ?)' read '(Ælfh[eh] ?)'.

p. 71, no. 384, remove to WINCHCOMBE (cf. coin from same obv. die in T. Bliss coll. on which mint reads PILL).

p. 72, no. 385, for ' Sæwi[ne] ' read ' Sæwi (Sæwine ?) '.

p. 130, no. 693, for ' Ciwince ' read ' Cipince '.

p. 162, no. 868, for ' Ælfhen ' read 'Ælfheh '.

p. 170, no. 912, for ' Ælfen ' read 'Ælfeh '.

p. 221, no. 41, for ' N ' in reverse inscription read ' H ', and for ' Ælfhen ' read ' Ælfheh '.

p. 228, no. 79, for moneyer's name read 'Æ[l]fsi '.

p. 230, no. 96, for '·ÐIDRIL' read '·ÐIDRII' (cf. p. 403, no. 96 A).

p. 232, no. 104, insert in provenance ' *W. Allen sale, 1898, lot 321* '.

p. 233, no. 111, for ' Edwine ' read ' Edwi '.

p. 235, no. 125, insert in provenance ' *W. Allen sale, 1898, lot 327* '.

p. 237, no. 138, insert as moneyer's name ' Sewi (Sewine ?) '.

p. 246, no. 190, for ' Swirlinc ' read ' Spirlinc '.

p. 253, no. 227, for ' Sæwine or Sewi ' read ' Sewi (Sewine ?) '.

p. 256, no. 237, for ' Swerlinc ' read ' Sperlinc '.

p. 279, no. 40, for ' Swerlig ? ' read ' Sperlig '.

p. 351, no. 104, for ' S DB ' read ' SVDB '.

Plate LX, for ' Queen Matilda and Eustace ' read ' Stephen and Queen Matilda ', and *dele* ' Eustace, son of Stephen (?) ; '.

INTRODUCTION

THE coinage of the Norman kings of England[1] follows in unbroken sequence that of the Anglo-Saxon kings; no change is introduced in denomination, standard, weight, or form, and even officials who held office in the mints of the Confessor continued to be responsible for the coinage of the Conqueror. In Normandy William had been alive to the distress caused by the continual debasement of the feudal coinages, but his attempts to remedy the evil—by substituting a triennial tax for the revenue which accrued to him from lowering the standard of the coinage—were a failure owing to the heavy loss consequent upon the natural outflow of his own better coinage and inflow into his dukedom of the baser deniers of neighbouring lords, a loss so serious that it quickly led to the closing of his mints. Finding in England a currency of high standard, long established and well accepted, he had good reason to adopt this, as he did most Anglo-Saxon institutions. The only denomination[2] still struck for currency was the penny weighing $22\frac{1}{2}$ grains Troy of silver of the standard of 11 oz. 2 dwt. of fine silver to 18 dwt. of alloy,[3] and fractions of this were still obtained by the elementary method of cutting the coin into halves and quarters. The type remained as in Anglo-Saxon times: on the obverse was the bust, or sometimes the figure, of the king, variously rendered on different

---

[1] The coinage of the first two, or four, years of Henry II, if any was struck, is included, as it seems that Stephen's name continued in use on the coins until the reforms of the year 1156 (or 8?).

[2] For other monetary denominations in use as moneys of account see below, p. clix.

[3] There is some doubt about the standard weight and fineness of the penny of this and earlier periods; see below, pp. cli ff. Mr. H. Symonds kindly informs me that a double assay of a penny of William I (from same dies as no. 815 below) has produced the results (1) 10 oz. 19 dwt. 18 grs., and (2) 10 oz. 18 dwt. 22 grs. For this double result from the same coin cf. *Num. Chron.*, 1915, pp. 201-2.

types, with his name and title round it; on the reverse was one of
the many designs, usually with some form of cross as their main
feature, which seem to have been used without any particular
meaning and to have been selected at random from the regular
trade stock of the engraver; round the design were the name of
the official called *monetarius* or 'moneyer',[1] who was responsible
for the good weight and purity of the coin, and the name of the
mint at which he worked, the word ON (*i. e.* at) coupling the two
names.

These obverse and reverse designs form together what is
technically known as a 'type'; that is to say, one particular form
of obverse is always found, except on irregular coins known as
'mules',[2] with one particular reverse design. These 'types' used to
be considered by some authorities as contemporaneous issues,[3] but
it is clear, not only from the evidence of finds of the coins, but also
from the passages in Domesday[4] relating that payments were made
by moneyers on receipt of their dies *quando moneta vertebatur,*
quando moneta renovatur or *moneta vertente,* that the types were
successively issued. The object of this change of types is not
known. From the passages in Domesday mentioned above we
know that the change of type was made the occasion of a payment
to the king by his moneyers and to bishops by their moneyers, but
to suppose that a scheme of taxation was the origin of the changes
of type is to confound cause and effect. To change the types in
order to make moneyers pay the purchase-money of new dies and
a tax at the same time would be an extremely expensive form of

---

[1] See below, pp. cxli ff.   [2] See below, pp. xxxvi ff.

[3] See, for example, *Num. Chron.*, 1893, pp. 129 ff. A statement made *ibid.*,
p. 131, is worth mentioning as it involves a very common and very misleading
form of error. Packe there says, 'The argument for a successive issue of
each type requires that those similar to each other should be near together in
point of time'. As changes of type are quite clearly due not, as in Continental
coinages, to mere development or degradation of design, but to intentional
changes for some specific purpose, it is quite evident that the contrary is the
case; the *intention* being to distinguish one type from another, we must
expect closely similar designs to be separate in point of time. This error is
pointed out in *Num. Chron.*, 1901, p. 35, but on a theory of legal tender.

[4] *Domesday*, I, ff. 172, 179, 252. See below, p. cxxxv.

tax-collecting, nor could there be any necessity for changing the
type in order to mark a period of taxation; on the other hand,
given a periodical change of types necessary for some other purpose,
then the purchase of the new dies was a natural and convenient
opportunity at which to collect the moneyers' fees. It seems
possible to explain these successive types as marking periods of
control of the output of the mint, that is to say, to find a parallel
in the change of mint-marks of a later date, and to assume a
periodical Mint Assay, similar to the Trial of the Pyx, which
would necessitate some mark on the coinage, if not a complete
change of type, for the purpose of certifying to the Assayers that
the coins they assayed were those of the latest issue and not of an
issue already tested. This was the purpose of the mint-marks
which were changed at the Trials of the Pyx.[1] The date of the
institution of the Trial of the Pyx is not known, the earliest
recorded trial being of the fifth year of Edward I;[2] a similar
trial, though not actually called a Trial of the Pyx, is described
of the thirty-second year of Henry III, which shows that an assay
of this sort was in existence, while it was still the practice to
put the moneyers' names on the coins. Some such trial seems to
have been necessary to complete the control of the mint. The issue
of dies from London to the moneyers guarded against the cutting
of false inscriptions on the dies though it did not prevent some
moneyers from changing or erasing inscriptions on their dies,[3]

---

[1] Cf., in Ruding, *Annals*, vol. ii, p. 262, the indenture of Edward IV showing
the object of the mint-marks. In the period intervening between the regular
change of type and the issue of mint-marks, the reigns of Henry II to Henry VI
inclusive, it is possible that small privy marks were used. Thus on the gold
coinage of Edward III (see *Num. Chron.*, 1911, pp. 313-9) annulet or saltire
stops, a barred or unbarred A and similar small differences were evidently
used as definite marks to distinguish issues of different periods, and may
perhaps have had the same significance as the types of the Norman period and
the mint-marks of the fifteenth to the seventeenth centuries; similarly in the
short-cross coinage of King John Mr. Lawrence has shown, in a paper to be
published shortly in the *British Numismatic Journal*, that the letter S was
reversed on all coins of a certain period (Mr. Lawrence's classes IV and V a),
evidently with some deliberate purpose on the part of the mint authorities.

[2] See H. Symonds, *Mint-marks, &c., of James I* (*Brit. Num. Journ.*, vol. ix),
p. 209.   [3] See below, pp. cxlix ff.

and the engraving of the reverse die with the moneyer's name
must have led to the conviction of the moneyer on the discovery of
a coin of impure standard or low weight; but that would be no safe-
guard without some method of finding untrue coins. Legislation
against striking coins outside a town [1] probably served the double
purpose of defence against an enemy and control over the coinage.
The supposition of a periodical Mint Assay would explain a
periodical change of types; but this is mere supposition, and the
organization of the mint at this early period must remain obscure.
It is not possible to see in the change of types any connexion
with legal tender.[2] It would only be possible for the types to
mark legal tender if one type only were allowed in currency.
But this was clearly not the case, for in hoards large numbers
of coins of more than one type are very frequently found: in
the Tamworth find, for example, coins were found of three consecutive types to the number of 30, 97, and 164 respectively, that is
to say, if one type only were legal tender, the owner of the hoard
while collecting his 164 current pennies was impoverishing himself
by keeping in his possession 127 coins which were no longer legal
tender. If a definite number of types, more than one, were
allowed in currency and previous types declared false tender, the
public would be assumed to have the almost impossible knowledge
of the order in which the types had been issued.[3] Similarly, the

---

[1] Greatley Synod, Liebermann, *Gesetze*, vol. i, pp. 158-9 (14).

[2] *Num. Chron.*, 1901, pp. 35-6, and *Brit. Num. Journ.*, vol. viii, pp. 113-4.
On Mr. Andrew's showing the Shillington find would prove that the tender,
having been limited by the first type of William II and again by the second of
Henry I, was later thrown open, and types as far back as the last of William I
—types, that is, which had already been withdrawn and had therefore,
presumably, ceased to exist—were restored to circulation. The fact that no
two profile types occur in finds of Norman coins may be explained by the
rarity of profile types in periods of which finds are common (e. g. William I),
and the rarity of finds of periods in which profile types are common (e. g.
Henry I).

[3] For example, assume that at the end of the reign of William I types V,
VI, VII and VIII of his reign were legal tender, then the man in the street
receiving a penny of type IV would have to know by instinct that it was
struck before the last four types of the reign, for there is nothing on the coin
to show it.

suggestion that the issue of a type with the bust in profile marked a limit of legal tender is untenable for the same reason. A profile type, for example, is the second (or possibly third) of the reign of Henry I, and the next profile issue is his sixth type; on the issue of type VI, therefore, type I would be no longer legal tender, yet a man receiving a coin of type I could not be expected to know whether it was issued before or after type II; there is nothing on the coin to show the period of its issue, and man's memory can hardly cover a period of ten years or more in a subject of the technicalities of which he is quite ignorant, to say nothing of the difficulty arising on the issue of a type in three-quarter face such as the second and fifth types of Stephen. Finds of coins seem to show that there was no limit of tender at this period, or, if any, a very long one; the St. Mary Hill Church find, for example, contained no fewer than eleven types, and the Shillington find covered an even longer period (see pp. lii–liii). Nor could there be any reason for limiting the legal tender at a period when the purity and good weight of the coinage was maintained, unless it were to stop the circulation of worn and clipped coins; but these would probably find their way automatically to the melting-pot even if measures were not taken, as they may have been, to get them returned. At periods when we know the legal tender to have been limited, we also find that the frequent changes of type were abandoned; thus, on the issue of the 'short-cross' coinage by Henry II all previous issues were put out of currency, and this 'short-cross' type continued until it was in its turn put out of currency at the introduction of the 'long-cross' type by Henry III.

The approximate arrangement of the types in the order in which they were struck is possible by means of the combined evidence to be obtained from Finds of coins, 'Overstruck' coins, 'Mules', and Epigraphical data.

In the following pages the types are described by the numbers in the plates of Hawkins's *Silver Coins* (Hks. 233, &c.) and by descriptive names ('Profile—Cross fleury' type, &c.).

FINDS OF COINS.
(See Table of Finds.)

The importance of finds lies in the grouping of types which occur in the same find; but for the evidence thus obtained to be of primary value it is necessary for the hoard to contain a considerable number of coins and for the whole hoard to have been adequately described at the time of its discovery. A glance at the Table of Finds will show that the Malmesbury find of 1828 is an example of a thoroughly unsatisfactory find; we do not know of how many coins it consisted, but thirteen only are described, twelve of which belong to one type and one to another; similar is the Shillington hoard, of which we have the most meagre information. A contrast is seen in the Beaworth, Tamworth, and Watford finds, in which there is no doubt that the vast majority, probably all, of the coins discovered belong to the types described; in these examples, therefore, one cannot lightly abandon the evidence of the grouping of types which they afford, whereas in the former examples the evidence of the finds can only be accepted in confirmation of evidence from other sources or at least in the absence of any conflicting evidence. Again, if a hoard contains a large number of coins, and every coin discovered in it is known to have been described, the evidence, though very strong, is not absolutely conclusive that the types of the hoard form a group; a stray coin or two of an earlier period than the rest is quite likely to be present, as was the case in the Colchester find of 1902, which contained two pennies of Henry I and one of Stephen, with about 11,000 of the 'short-cross' issue (Henry II to Henry III); but such stray coins are not usually very apt to mislead. The more dangerous form of hoard, which is fortunately rare, is a hoard which has lain dormant for a time and been increased at a later period. There are obvious reasons why such a hoard may be made: a man may bury his savings before going away for military service or on any other business, recover his hoard on his return, add to it and bury it again on leaving home a second time; or a portion of a dowry may be kept and additions made to it after a lapse of years, when the financial position of the owner has improved. An instance of some such find as this is doubtless seen in the Shillington find of 1871, which contained coins of William II and four or five coins of Henry I's seventh type and at the most one coin of the intervening types; it is unlikely that the portion not seen by the recorder of the hoard included all the missing types.

Though as many as two dozen finds have been recorded which contain coins of the Norman period, the evidence to be obtained from them is hardly so satisfactory as might be expected. This is chiefly due to the fact that the finds are very unevenly distributed; of the types between the third of William II and the fourteenth of Henry I there have been very few coins found and no satisfactory hoards recorded, and similarly of the types between the second and last of Stephen's reign; on the other hand, finds of the early types of William I and of the last two types of Henry and the first two of Stephen have been comparatively numerous, though mostly small, and good corroborative evidence is thus obtained. Some finds have contained but few coins, and in many cases hoards have been quickly dispersed and their description consequently incomplete.

The recorded finds which contained coins of Edward Confessor or Harold II with coins of William are six in number:

Soberton, 1851;
York, 1845;
York, 1882;
Whitchurch (Oxfordshire?), date uncertain;
St. Mary Hill Church, London, 1774;
City of London, 1872.

The *Soberton (Hampshire) Find* [1] (1851) consisted of 259 coins and two gold rings, which were found in a vessel of dingy red ware in a field near Wickham Lodge, Soberton. The coins were:

---

[1] *Num. Chron.*, 1852, Proceedings, p. 17. Several of the coins from this find are in the British Museum; an account of the find in *Arch. Journ.*, viii (1851), p. 100, is wrong in describing all the 78 coins of the Confessor as Hks. 223 and all the 159 of Harold as Hks. 231.

Edward Confessor, Hks. 219, P. C. B.[1] VI . . 1

„   „   Hks. 223, P. C. B. XI . . 77

Harold, Hks. 230 152

„ Hks. 231 7

William I, Hks. 233, 'Profile—Cross Fleury' type . 22

Total 259

The complete hoard seems to have been described.

York Find (1845).[2] Discovered in digging out the foundation of a house near Jubbergate. About 600 coins were said to have been found, of which Hawkins saw 167; these were:

Edward Confessor, type not described . . . 1

William I, Hks. 234, 'Bonnet' type . . . 165

„ 'with profile head' 1

Total 167

He says that there was one penny of William with a profile head, but he did not see it and was not able to say what was its type; from a comparison with all the other finds in which coins of William were discovered with coins of the Confessor we may fairly conclude that this coin was of Hks. 233, the 'Profile—Cross Fleury' type.

York Find (1882).[3] No description of this find was made at the time of its discovery. Coins of uncertain number of Edward Confessor and William were found in Bishophill; the types of William represented in the hoard were Hks. 233, 'Profile—Cross Fleury' type, and 234, 'Bonnet' type, and the mule of these two types, Hks. 235. The bulk of the hoard seems to have been of the 'Bonnet' type.

Whitchurch (Oxfordshire?) Find[4] (date unknown). Not described at time of discovery. It is said to have contained many coins of Edward Confessor, Hks. 225 and 223 (P. C. B. X and XI), possibly some of Harold, and coins of William I, 'Profile—Cross Fleury',

[1] Major Carlyon-Britton's classification in *Num. Chron.*, 1905, pp. 179 ff.

[2] *Num. Chron.*, 1846, pp. 123-5.

[3] *Brit. Num. Journ.*, vol. ii, p. 115.

[4] *Num. Chron.*, 1902, p. 219, and *Brit. Num. Journ.*, vol. ii, pp. 115-6.

'Bonnet', and 'Canopy' types (Hks. 233, 234, 236); Hks. 234 and 236 predominating.

St. Mary Hill Church Find[1] (1774). Near the church of St. Mary Hill, London, was found at about fourteen or fifteen feet below the level of the street an earthen vessel containing coins, and within the vessel was another smaller one of crucible shape which also contained coins and a gold brooch. The number of the coins that were found is not known; between 300 and 400 were examined, and of these the majority were of Edward Confessor (P. C. B. VI to XI inclusive and a mule of VII × VIII); of Harold II thirty-one moneyers and twenty-two mints were represented, some coins having the sceptre and others not; of William I the 'Profile—Cross Fleury', 'Bonnet', 'Canopy' and 'Two Sceptres' types (Hks. 233, 234, 236, 237) were present, and also a curious mule with obverse of an unusual variety of the 'Canopy' type and reverse of the 'Two Sceptres' type;[2] there were many cut half-pennies and farthings.

City of London Find[3] (1872). Said to have contained about 7,000 coins, of which over 2,800 were examined and described by E. H. Willett in *Num. Chron.*, 1876, and nearly 500 were described later in *Num. Chron.*, 1885, by Sir John Evans. The hoard contained a few coins of Æthelred II, Cnut, Harold I, and Harthacnut; a very large majority of the coins described (2,798 out of 2,829 in Willett's and about 450 in Evans's list) were of Edward Confessor, including all the types of his reign except the rare so-called 'Harthacnut' type;[4] the few remaining English coins of the find were of Harold II and William I; two foreign coins, both figured in *Num. Chron.*, 1876, Pl. X. 8, 9, are described, one as a coin of Magnus, which should be attributed to Svend Estridsen (1047–1075),[5] the other as an uncertain eleventh-century German coin,

---

[1] *Archaeologia*, vol. iv, pp. 356 ff.

[2] Now in the Hunterian Collection. See below, pp. xxxix, 43, and Pl. VIII. 11.

[3] *Num. Chron.*, 1876, pp. 323 ff., and *op. cit.*, 1885, pp. 254 ff.

[4] *Num. Chron.*, 1905, Pl. VII. 1.

[5] Cf. Hauberg, *Myntforhold og Udmyntninger i Danmark*, Pl. VIII. 6.

which may probably be identified as a coin of Celle of Heinrich III (1039–56).[1] The coins of William I represent three types: 'Profile —Cross Fleury', 'Bonnet', and 'Two Sceptres' (Hks. 233, 234, and 237).

Two other finds which may be mentioned here are those of York in 1704 and Dyns Marsh in 1739. The former[2] contained 250 coins, of which Thoresby saw fifty or sixty, and describes them as mostly, if not all, of William; fifteen of these, in Thoresby's collection, were: two of the 'Profile—Cross Fleury' type (Hks. 233), and thirteen of the 'Bonnet' type (Hks. 234). The find in 1739 at Dyns Marsh,[3] between Dungeness and Lydd, receives a passing mention in *Archaeologia* as having contained above 200 pennies of Edward Confessor, Harold II, and William.

To summarize, the Soberton find, of which all the coins were examined, shows the 'Profile—Cross Fleury' type (Hks. 233) to be the first type of William I, and this is confirmed by the appearance of this type in all the other finds[4] which contain coins of the Confessor and Harold. The York finds show that the 'Bonnet' type (Hks. 234) follows this as the second type. From the St. Mary Hill Church find it is clear that the 'Canopy' and 'Two Sceptres' types (Hks. 236, 237) must immediately follow the 'Bonnet' type, but the evidence of the Whitchurch and City of London finds is conflicting as regards the question which is the earlier of these two types, and our knowledge of these finds is very scanty.

Malmesbury Find[5] (1828) contained some coins, the number of which is uncertain. They were found under the foundations

---

[1] Cf. Dannenberg, *Deutsche Münzen*, Pl. VIII. 185.

[2] Thoresby, *Ducatus Leodiensis*, p. 349.

[3] *Archaeologia*, vol. iv, p. 358. Described as 'Dymchurch' in *Brit. Num. Journ.*, vol. ii, p. 97.

[4] Except the York find, 1845, in which, however, a profile coin is said to have been seen but not described.

[5] Akerman. *Num. Journ.*, vol. ii, 1837, p. 106; Sainthill, *Olla Podrida*, vol. i, p. 189.

of the chapel built at Malmesbury by William the Conqueror. A few coins of the 'Two Sceptres' type (Hks. 237) are described and one of the 'Bonnet' type (Hks. 234) is said to have been present. The incomplete account, which states that 'many pennies were found' and describes only about a dozen, makes the find useless as evidence of the order of the types.

York Minster Find. In the York Museum are eleven coins which are there described as having been found together in York Minster; of these coins six belong to the 'Two Stars' type (Hks. 238), and five to the 'Sword' type (Hks. 243).[1] Though the coins are too few to supply any definite conclusion, this find creates a probability of these two types being consecutive.

Beaworth Find[2] (1833). More than 6,500 coins were found in a leaden box,[3] under the surface of a wagon track, in pasture land attached to the Manor House, Beaworth (Hampshire). Hawkins, in his account of the find, says that most, if not all, of the coins were examined and described, but later withdraws the statement. There was a general scramble for the coins at the time of the discovery and, though at the request of the owner of the land very many were returned, a large number seem to have escaped description. Four types only, and one mule, were represented in the hoard:

'Two Stars' type (Hks. 238)	31	pennies
'Sword' type (Hks. 243)	34	,,
'Profile—Cross and Trefoils' type (Hks. 239) .	11	,,
Mules of preceding and following types (Hks. 240)	6	,,
'Paxs' type (Hks. 241, 242)	6,439	,,
Total	6,521	,,

There were also eighteen cut halfpennies of the 'Paxs' type.
Hawkins gives the definite number of coins which he examined

---

[1] The coins are described in *Brit. Num. Journ.*, vol. ii, p. 115. The information of the find was given me at the York Museum.

[2] *Archaeologia*, vol. xxvi, pp. 1-25. Reprinted in Ruding, *Annals*, vol. i, pp. 151-61.

[3] The box is illustrated in *Brit. Num. Journ.*, vol. ii, p. 102.

of the 'Paxs' type only; of the other types he gives the varieties
of readings on the coins, from which it appears that he only saw
one coin of each variety; the numbers given above are based
on this supposition, which is confirmed by his statement that the
total number of coins was about 6,500. Mr. Andrew,[1] following
Major Carlyon-Britton's local information that the box contained
from 8,000 to 9,000 pennies, conjectures from this and other
arguments that the hoard was originally one of the donations of
six marks of gold,[2] which, the Anglo-Saxon Chronicle tells us,
William II in 1087 distributed to monasteries for his father's
soul. The condition of the coins and the unusually high proportion
of coins of the latest of the types (the type presumably in issue
at the date of the burial of the hoard) seem to show that the
hoard came straight from a mint or treasury. But Hawkins, in
his *Silver Coins*, p. 168, says that some thousands more coins from
this hoard found their way to London and were examined by him
and his friends later, and he there estimates the total number
at scarcely less than 12,000. Though the Anglo-Saxon Chronicle
tells us of the donations to monasteries we do not anywhere hear
of the loss of any one of them, nor is there any reason for connecting this hoard with these donations even were the amount of
the find equivalent. There is no reason to suppose the sum so
exceptional that a cause must be found for it being amassed.

Tamworth Find [3] (1877). Discovered during work in connexion
with the Board Schools at Tamworth. In a leaden box of triangular
shape were found about 300 coins. Four or five only are said to
have been dispersed, the remainder are described as:

'Paxs' type (Hks. 241)	30 coins
'Profile' type (Hks. 244)	97 ,,
Mules of preceding and following types (Hks. 245)	3 ,,
'Cross in Quatrefoil' type (Hks. 246) . .	164 ,,
Total	294 ,,

---

[1] *Brit. Num. Journ.*, vol. i, pp. 26 ff.
[2] A mark of gold = £6; six marks would therefore contain 8,640 pennies.
[3] *Num. Chron.*, 1877, pp. 340 ff.

The two following finds contain coins of William with coins of Henry:

Shillington Find[1] (1871). Discovered by workmen in the neighbourhood of Shillington (Bedfordshire). Probably upwards of 250 coins were found, contained in a small jar with herring-bone ornament. About one-third of them were examined; the types represented were, of William: 'Paxs' (Hks. 241) one coin only, 'Profile' (Hks. 244), 'Cross in Quatrefoil' (Hks. 246), 'Cross voided' (Hks. 250), and 'Crosses Pattée and Fleury' (Hks. 247);[2] and of Henry: 'Quatrefoil and Piles' (Hks. 252) and one other type undescribed.

Bermondsey Find[3] (c. 1820). Thirteen pennies found by workmen sinking for the foundation of a house:

William, 'Cross in Quatrefoil' type (Hks. 246) . . .	3	coins
,, 'Cross Voided' type (Hks. 250 and 249) . . .	5	,,
Henry I, 'Annulets' type (Hks. 251, one omitting the annulets)	5	,,
Total	13	,,

This set of finds, which comprises discoveries of coins of William alone and of coins of William with coins of Henry, contains two hoards of considerable importance found at Beaworth and Tamworth. These two hoards overlap each other in the 'Paxs' type, which represents a very large proportion of the Beaworth and a small proportion of the Tamworth. As this is the only overlapping type, it must be considered as the latest type represented in one hoard and the earliest in the other; from the proportionate number of coins of the type in the two finds, it should probably be placed as the last type of the Beaworth and as the first of the Tamworth find. The 'Two Stars' (Hks. 238) and 'Sword' (Hks. 243) types

---

[1] *Num. Chron.*, 1871, pp. 227-8. See above, p. xvii, and below, pp. xxiv, lii.

[2] Not described in *Num. Chron.*, 1871, but this type is represented among the coins of this find which were presented to the Library of Trinity College, Cambridge. See *Brit. Num. Journ.*, vol. ii, pp. 108-9.

[3] *Num. Chron.*, 1846, p. 170.

therefore precede the 'Paxs' type, and from the evidence of the York Minster find these two types should probably be placed together, but there is no evidence to show whether the 'Profile—Cross and Trefoils' type [1] (Hks. 239), the remaining type found at Beaworth, should precede or follow them. The remaining two types of the Tamworth Find, 'Profile' type (Hks. 244) and 'Cross in Quatrefoil' (Hks. 246), are therefore concluded to be later than the 'Paxs' type; this conclusion is confirmed by the Shillington and Bermondsey finds, where one or both of these types are found with coins of Henry. With regard to these two finds it is necessary to anticipate evidence from other sources so far as to say that the evidence of the Shillington find concerning coins of Henry I is untrustworthy; [2] as mentioned above, this find is of a complicated nature and evidently represents an owner's savings of two distinct periods. In further anticipation, it may be noted that the Bermondsey find, of which all the coins are said to have been examined and described, omits the last two types of William II, and therefore shows with what caution so small a find must be treated.

Bari (*Italy*) *Find* [3] (*c.* 1891). In a large hoard of continental coins mostly of the eleventh and twelfth centuries, which are not further described, were found upwards of twenty-five pennies of Henry I. These coins are of two types only; twenty-seven coins are described:

'Annulets and Piles' type (Hks. 257)	. .	3 coins
'Voided Cross and Fleurs' type (Hks. 267).	.	24 „
	Total	27 „

---

[1] From the numbers, one would suppose that Hks. 239 was the earliest type of the find, but it must be remembered that the total find numbers over 6,500 coins, and that therefore thirty coins must, equally with ten, be treated as stray specimens. Hawkins, in his account of the find, shows reason for supposing that it came straight from the mint, owing to the fact that in so large a hoard almost all the coins are of one type only.

[2] See pp. lii, liii.

[3] *Num. Chron.*, 1892, pp. 83 ff.

This seems to show that these two types were issued consecutively, but the evidence of so small a number of coins, as mentioned above, is by no means conclusive, especially in a large hoard of continental coins.

Canterbury Find[1] (*c.* 1901 ?). No record of this find has been published; the coins were said to have come from Bournemouth, but there is reason to suppose that they were discovered at Canterbury during work at the Archbishop's Palace, and conveyed to Bournemouth before distribution. Many of the coins were seen by Major Carlyon-Britton and notes were made by him, but it is impossible to say how many coins were in the hoard; all seem to have been of Henry I, and the following have been noted:

'Full face—Cross Fleury' type (Hks. iv) . .	3 coins
'Lozenge Fleury enclosing Star' type (Hks. 265)	1 ,,
Mule of preceding and following types . .	1 ,,
'Pellets in Quatrefoil' type (Hks. 262) . .	353 ,,
Total	358 ,,

Lowestoft Find[2] (1905). Twelve pennies of Henry I are described as having been found together on the beach at Lowestoft, probably carried down by a fall of the cliff. Whether these constituted the whole hoard is not known. They are of two types:

'Pellets in Quatrefoil' type (Hks. 262) . .	6 coins
'Quadrilateral on Cross Fleury' type (Hks. 255)	6 ,,
Total	12 ,,

Battle (Sussex) Find[3] (1860 ?). Twelve coins of Henry I, found near Battle, were of the following types:

'Full face—Cross Fleury' type (Hks. iv) . .	1 coin
'Double Inscription' type (Hks. 258) . .	1 ,,
'Quadrilateral on Cross Fleury' type (Hks. 255).	10 ,,
Total	12 ,,

---

[1] I am indebted to Major Carlyon-Britton for the loan of his private notes on this find; also to Mr. Baldwin for further information of the provenance.

[2] *Num. Chron.*, 1905, p. 112.

[3] *Ibid.*, 1873, p. 175.

The following hoards contained coins of Henry I and Stephen together:

Watford Finds[1] (1818). Some labourers digging in a field near Watford found a few silver coins, and, on further search being made, a rude clay jar was discovered, broken, about ten or twelve inches below the surface of the ground, containing a large hoard of coins. Rashleigh, in his account of the hoard in *Num. Chron.*, 1850, states that the total number of coins was 1,094 pennies and 33 halves of pennies. These coins were kept together in the possession of the original owner until at his death they passed into the hands of Rashleigh, who wrote a full account of them. He says that he thinks this number is nearly all that were found, a few probably having been picked up and sold by the workmen. The following coins are described:

	Pennies	Half-pennies
William, 'Two Stars' type (Hks. 238) . . .	—	1
Henry I, 'Pellets in Quatrefoil' type (Hks. 262) .	58	—
„ 'Quadrilateral on Cross Fleury' type (Hks. 255)	398	21
Stephen, 'Watford' type (Hks. 270)	632	11
„ Variety II, with obverse inscription PERERIC (Pl. LVII. 9–15)	2	—
Empress Matilda (MATILDI COI)	1	—
Uncertain coins (Baronial?)	3	—
Total	1,094	33

This long survival of a halfpenny of the middle of William I's reign (about 60 years) is remarkable.

In the Appendix to *Archaeologia*, vol. xxi, pp. 539 ff., is an account laid before the Society of Antiquaries by Taylor Combe, in January 1822, of a find in April 1818 of a quantity of silver coins, in number above a hundred. They were found by labourers hoeing in a field of beans near the site of the ancient manor-house of Oxhey Place, in the parish of Watford; the coins were lying scattered upon the surface of the ground, together with a fragment of an earthen

---

[1] *Num. Chron.*, 1850, pp. 138 ff.

vessel in which they had probably been deposited. Clutterbuck, on inquiry in the neighbourhood, could only procure nine specimens, but on further digging found thirty more coins. The types represented by the coins are the same three as were found in the Watford hoard above described, Hks. 262, 255, and 270, with the addition of the coin described below as variety III 6, p. xci, Pl. LVIII. 6 (Hks. 273). Whether this small find should be considered as part of the larger hoard it is impossible to say. The discovery of these coins, with a fragment of an earthen vessel, on the surface of the ground points rather to this being a residue not found in the search which resulted in the discovery of the large hoard and broken vessel. But, on the other hand, were this find later than the larger one, Clutterbuck could hardly have failed to obtain information of it when he made inquiries in the neighbourhood; nor do we know that both finds were in the same field, though both occurred in or near Watford and both in the year 1818. There would be nothing surprising in two separate hoards being buried at the same time and in the same neighbourhood, for the same cause might well induce two neighbours to take similar action.

These two finds are distinguished in the Catalogue as 'Watford Find' and 'Smaller Watford Find'.

Nottingham Find[1] (1880). This hoard was discovered on Jan. 5, 1880, at the back of old property in Bridlesmith Gate, Nottingham. The coins were quickly dispersed, the original number being more than three hundred;[2] comparatively few are described; they consist of:

Henry I, 'Annulets' type (Hks. 251) . . . . 1 coin
„ 'Full face—Cross Fleury' type (Hks. iv) . . 1 „
„ 'Quadrilateral on Cross Fleury' type (Hks. 255)
                                        at least 7 „
Stephen, 'Watford' type (Hks. 270) . . upwards of 150 „
„ Variety I, with erased obverse die (see below,
        pp. lxxvi ff.). . . . . uncertain number

---

[1] *Num. Chron.*, 1881, pp. 36 ff.
[2] I am indebted to Mr. Andrew for this information.

Stephen, Variety II, with inscription PERERIC
        (see below, pp. lxxxii ff.)   .   .   1 coin described
   ,,   Variety IV A (*a*) (see below, p. xcv) .   1 coin described
Empress Matilda (see below, pp. cxviii ff.)   .   at least 1 coin

Mr. Andrew connects the burial of this hoard with the fire at Nottingham on Sept. 8, 1141.[1]

Dartford Find[2] (1825). Found at Dartford in Kent; said to have contained about 65 pennies, of which the following are described:

Henry I, 'Quadrilateral on Cross Fleury' type (Hks. 255).   4 coins
Stephen, 'Watford' type (Hks. 270)   .   .   .   44 ,,
   ,,   Variety I, with erased obverse die (see below,
        pp. lxxvi ff.) .   .   .   .   .   1 ,,
   ,,   Variety IV B (*a*) (see below, p. xcvi) .   .   3 ,,
Empress Matilda (see below, pp. cxviii ff.)   .   .   5[3] ,,
Scottish, David I (?), of Carlisle (?) .   .   .   .   1 ,,

Sheldon Find[4] (1867). A hoard of 95 pennies and 7 halfpennies found at Sheldon in Derbyshire. The following are the types described:

	Pennies	Half-pennies
Henry I, 'Quadrilateral on Cross Fleury' type (Hks. 255)	3	—
Stephen, 'Watford' type (Hks. 270)[5]	73	3
,, Mule, Hks. 270 × 269 (*Brit. Num. Journ.*, vol. vii, p. 44, nos. 69–70)	1	1
,, Hks. 269, contemporary forgeries?[6] (*ibid.*, p. 85, nos. 101, 102)	2	—

---

[1] *Brit. Num. Journ.*, vol. i, pp. 30 ff.

[2] *Num. Chron.*, 1851, pp. 186 ff.

[3] One of these is described as an Oxford coin of Stephen, in *Num. Chron.*, 1851, p. 188; the coin was in Rashleigh sale, lot 630, and later in Mr. H. M. Reynolds's collection.

[4] *Brit. Num. Journ.*, vol. vii, pp. 27 ff.

[5] These are the coins in Mr. Andrew's list numbered 4–68, 73, 77 (from same dies as coin described below, p. 356, no. 137), 78, 79–83, 96, 97, 99.

[6] There seems to me insufficient reason for the attribution of the coins to Matilda; even the letters IMP on no. 101 are extremely doubtful. Their very rough work and light weight incline me to consider them contemporary forgeries of Hks. 269.

	Pennies	Half-pennies
Stephen, Variety I, with erased obverse die[1] (*ibid.*, p. 55, no. 76, pp. 60 ff., nos. 84–95, 98) .	11	3
„ Variety II, with inscription PERERIC[2] (*ibid.*, p. 81, no. 100)	1	—
„ Variety III 8 (*b*)[3] (*ibid.*, p. 51, no. 74) . .	1	—
„ Variety IV B (*a*)[4] (*ibid.*, p. 53, no. 75) . .	1	—
Scottish, David I (*ibid.*, p. 46, nos. 71, 72) . . .	2	—
	95	7

Linton (Maidstone) Find[5] (1883). The total number of coins in this find is said to have been about 180; they were found in an earthen jar, about fifteen inches below the surface of the ground; nearly a hundred of the coins are described:

	Pennies	Half-pennies	Farthings
Henry I, 'Quadrilateral on Cross Fleury' type (Hks. 255)	6	1	—
Stephen, 'Watford' type (Hks. 270) . .	32	4	4
„ 'Cross Voided and Mullets' type (Hks. 269)	24	14	1
„ Variety II, with inscription PERERIC (see below, pp. lxxxii ff.) . .	2	—	—
„ Variety III 7 (see below, pp. xci ff.)	4	2	—
Total described	68	21	5

Of these finds, in which coins of Henry I are found mixed with coins of Stephen, the Dartford and Sheldon hoards contained only one true type of each reign; in each case these two types are Hks. 255 and 270, which may therefore be placed as the last of Henry and the first of Stephen. The Nottingham find confirms this, but has also two stray coins of Henry (Hks. 251 and iv) in addition. The Watford finds have coins of Hks. 262 with coins of Hks. 255 and 270, and therefore confirm the slight evidence of the Lowestoft find in placing the two types, Hks. 262 and 255, together. The

---

[1] See below, pp. lxxvi ff. [2] See below, pp. lxxxii ff.
[3] See below, p. xcv. [4] See below, p. xcvi.
[5] *Num. Chron.*, 1883, pp. 108 ff.

Linton find is the latest of this group of finds, and gives us as the second type of Stephen's reign Hks. 269, which is confirmed in the Sheldon hoard by the mules of 270×269 and also by the two contemporary forgeries, or whatever they may be, of this type. These finds are of further importance as containing various irregular issues, such as coins of Matilda, coins with obverse inscription PERERIC, coins with obverse type erased, and other varieties; all of which are thus shown to have been issued before the issue of the second regular type of the reign (Hks. 269); these coins are treated separately below (pp. lxxi ff.).

Bute Find [1] (1863). At the south end of the island, about 300 yards from the ancient Chapel of Saint Blane, were found 27 silver coins (some in fragments) with two gold rings, three gold bands, and one silver bar. The following coins are described:

Stephen, 'Watford' type (Hks. 270)	3 coins
Scottish, David I	14 „
„ Earl Henry (see below, p. xcviii) . . .	1 „
Uncertain (type as Hks. 270)	9 „
	Total 27 „

Winterslow Find [2] (c. 1804). In *Gentleman's Magazine*, vol. lxxiv (1804), p. 15, is a notice of a coin (the Dimsdale specimen) ' lately found, with several of Stephen, in the vicinity of Salisbury '. In the MS. Catalogue of the B. C. Roberts collection some coins are noted as having been found in a chalk pit at Winterslow, near Salisbury; many halfpennies are there said to have been found. The coins so noted in the Roberts Catalogue and elsewhere [3] are:

---

[1] *Num. Chron.*, 1863, p. 216; *ibid.*, 1865, pp. 57 ff.

[2] In his Introduction to Domesday Book, Sir Henry Ellis mentions this find as containing 'a large assemblage of pennies from the Saxon times to the reign of Stephen'; this improbable statement may be partly explained by the attribution at that time of coins of Henry of Anjou to Henry I, and of coins of William (of Gloucester?) to William I and William II.

[3] Catalogue of T. Dimsdale sale, 1824, lot 228. Hawkins (*Silver Coins*, p. 185) also mentions the find without giving any additional information.

	Pennies	Half-pennies
Stephen, 'Watford' type (Hks. 270) . . .	1	—
„ 'Cross Voided and Mullets' type (Hks. 269)	2	2
„ 'Cross and Fleurs' type (Hks. 276) . .	1	—
„ Variety III 4 (see below, p. xc) . . .	1	—
„ Variety IV D (b) (see below, p. cvi) . .	1	—
.Henry of Anjou, type I (b) (see below, p. cxxi) .	1	
„ „ type I (c) (see below, p. cxxii) .	3	—
„ „ type II (a) (see below, pp. cxxii f.).	1	—
„ „ type II (b) (see below, p. cxxiii) .	—	1
William (of Gloucester?), type II (b) (see below, p. cxxx)	1	—
Uncertain baronial, no. 1 (see below, p. cxxxii) .	1	—
„ „ no. 3 (see below, p. cxxxiii) .	1	—
Total	14	3

At *Catal*,[1] near Wetherby, were found a few silver coins in
1684, including one of Stephen, variety IV D (d) (see below, p. cvi),
one of Eustace FitzJohn, type B (see below, p. cxiv), one of
Robert de Stuteville (see below, p. cxvi), and another coin of
Stephen (type not described).

Awbridge Find[2] (c. 1902). About 180 coins of Stephen and
Henry II were found at Awbridge, near Romsey, Hampshire, all
close together at about 2½ feet below the surface of the ground.
The following are described :

Stephen, 'Awbridge' type (Hks. 268)	31	coins
„ Variety III 7 (see below, pp. xci ff.) . . .	3	„
Henry II, 'Tealby' type (Hks. 285)	110	„
Total	144	„

This find shows Hks. 268 to have been the last type issued by
Stephen. The finds give no evidence of the order, or even existence
as definite types, of any types between the second and the last of
this reign; one coin of Hks. 276 occurred in the Winterslow find,

---

[1] Thoresby, *Ducatus Leodiensis*, pp. 350, 351 ; Proc. of *Yorkshire Philosophical Soc.*, 1855, p. 216.
[2] *Num. Chron.*, 1905, pp. 354 ff.

with a few coins of the first two types of the reign and several coins of irregular issues.

To summarize the evidence obtained from finds, the following groups may be made with some probability (the numbers of Hawkins's figures are here used alone to denote the types):

WILLIAM I and II.

233 (first type) — 234 (second type) — $\begin{Bmatrix}236\\237\end{Bmatrix}$

$\begin{Bmatrix}238\\243\\239\end{Bmatrix}$ — 241 — $\begin{Bmatrix}244\\246\end{Bmatrix}$ — $\begin{Bmatrix}250\\247\end{Bmatrix}$

HENRY I.

251 or 252 (first type)

$\begin{Bmatrix}257\\267\end{Bmatrix}$

262 — 255 (last type).

STEPHEN.

270 (first type) — 269 (second type)
268 (last type).

OVERSTRUCK COINS.

Coins are commonly found in this, as in almost every series, on which the impression of the dies is superimposed upon an underlying impression of a different pair of dies; that is to say, coins having been struck, and, perhaps, passed into circulation, return to the mint and are re-struck without the previous impression having been removed. The two impressions on a coin may be from dies of the same type or from dies of different types; in the latter case it follows that, as the types were not struck contemporarily, the earlier, or obliterated, impression on the coin is that of the earlier of the two types; coins of the former class, where the two impressions belong to the same type, cannot easily be distinguished from double-struck coins, and are, in any case, unimportant. The coins re-struck with dies of a different type are commonly known as 'Overstrikes' and are very important as giving quite definite evidence that one type precedes another.[1] It cannot be concluded, though it frequently happens, that the later type *immediately* follows the earlier; in fact, in some cases, *e. g.* no. 10 on p. xxxiv, a considerable period intervenes before the re-striking of the coin.

It has been suggested that the coins known as 'Overstrikes' represent not re-struck coins, but coins struck from re-engraved dies from which the original design was not completely erased;[2] but it is clear from an examination of such coins that this is not the case. On these coins it will be found that the parts in high relief in the original have been flattened down by the second striking to the level of the field, and are marked out by an incuse outline which represents the part of the field of the original coin that has failed to rise into the later dies, owing to its protection by the original high relief beside it; this effect can only be produced by a blow which has hammered the high relief flat and sunk part of the flat surface into incuse. The reason for re-striking coins in this way is quite uncertain. It cannot have been done with the object of restoring to currency coins that were no longer current, for we have seen above[3] that one type cannot have gone out of currency on the issue of another. Nor, again, can it have been due to the coins being clipped or effaced by circulation; clipped coins would have to be returned to the melting-pot, as their weight would be untrue, and in some of the cases here quoted the original impression still stands out so clearly through the overstruck type that it is impossible to suppose the coins to have been much worn. It is possible, though there is no documentary support for the assumption, that officials of the exchange were prohibited from circulating coins of any type but that actually in issue at the mint;[4] in which case, re-striking might

---

[1] As overstriking might be supposed to guarantee the genuineness of a coin, it should perhaps be mentioned that some ingenious modern forgeries are struck on genuine mediaeval coins (see *Brit. Num. Journ.*, vol. iii, pp. 282 ff.).

[2] *Num. Chron.*, 1905, pp. 110-1.

[3] p. xiv.

[4] *Brit. Num. Journ.*, vol. viii, p. 123. Such a prohibition would presumably

be due to the necessity of circulating coins which remained in, or
came into, the mint or exchange after the issue of a new type.

The following are the overstrikes that have been noted in the
coinage of this period :

(1) William, 'Bonnet' type (Hks. 234) over type of Harold II (Hks.
230). A coin of Huntingdon in P. W. P. Carlyon-Britton
collection.

(2) William, 'Bonnet' type (Hks. 234) over 'Profile—Cross Fleury'
type (Hks. 233). Coin of Wallingford, p. 29, no. 154; also
Malmesbury (H. W. Morrieson collection) and Hereford (W.
Sharp Ogden collection).

(3) William, Mule (Hks. 237 × 238) over 'Two Sceptres' type (Hks. 237).
Coin of Hereford in P. W. P. Carlyon-Britton collection (see
below, p. 56).

(4) William, 'Two Stars' type (Hks. 238) over 'Two Sceptres' type
(Hks. 237). Coin of Cricklade, p. 60, no. 308; one of same
mint (Carlyon-Britton sale, 1913, lot 706) and another of
Winchester in P. W. P. Carlyon-Britton collection.

(5) William, 'Sword' type (Hks. 243) over 'Two Sceptres' type
(Hks. 237). Coin of London (Carlyon-Britton sale, 1913,
lot 712).

(6) William, 'Profile—Cross and Trefoils' type (Hks. 239) over 'Sword'
type (Hks. 243). Coin of uncertain mint (Carlyon-Britton sale,
1913, lot 717).

(7) William, 'Paxs' type (Hks. 241) over 'Profile—Cross and Trefoils'
type (Hks. 239). Coin of Southampton in P. W. P. Carlyon-
Britton collection.

(8) William, 'Profile' type (Hks. 244) over 'Paxs' type (Hks. 241).
Coin of London (Carlyon-Britton sale, 1913, lot 747).

(9) William, Mule (Hks. 245) over 'Profile' type (Hks. 244). Coin of
Leicester in Evans collection (see below, p. 403, no. 67 A).

(10) William, 'Cross in Quatrefoil' type (Hks. 246) over 'Canopy'
type (Hks. 236). Coin of Chichester, p. 227, no. 76.

(11) William, 'Cross in Quatrefoil' type (Hks. 246) over 'Profile'
type (Hks. 244). Coins of Hereford, p. 230, no. 93, and Worcester,

be intended to prevent the moneyers from evading the cost of new dies by
continuing to use dies of an old type. Perhaps such an evasion is meant by the
forisfacturæ veteris monetæ charged to Gilpatric in the Pipe Roll (see below,
p. cxlvi)

p. 242, no. 171; also of Oxford in P. W. P. Carlyon-Britton
collection.

(12) William, 'Crosses Pattée and Fleury' type (Hks. 247) over 'Cross
in Quatrefoil' type (Hks. 246). Coin of Rochester, p. 258,
no. 247.

(13) William, 'Crosses Pattée and Fleury' type (Hks. 247) over 'Cross
Voided' type (Hks. 250). Coin of Thetford, p. 258, no. 252.

No overstrikes are known of the reigns of Henry I or Stephen;
this is perhaps due partly to more careful striking of the coins,
partly to the greater rarity of coins of these reigns, and partly to
the obverse and reverse designs filling more completely the surface
of the field, so that any former impression is more thoroughly
obliterated.[1]

As regards the evidence afforded by the overstrikes towards
placing the coin-types, much confirmatory, and some additional,
evidence is thus given to the groups of the types that were formed
after examining the finds of the coins.

No. 2 confirms the placing of the 'Profile—Cross Fleury' type before
the 'Bonnet' type.

Nos. 4 and 5 show that the group 238, 243, and 239 is correctly placed
later than the group 236 and 237.

No. 6 places 239 later than 243, and thus, combined with the evidence
of the York Minster find, in which 238 and 243 were found
together, makes 239 immediately precede the 'Paxs' type (241).

---

[1] In *Brit. Num. Journ.*, vol. viii, pp. 125–6, too much stress is laid on the rarity
of both overstrikes and mules of these two later reigns. Overstrikes are of
course most common in periods of which the coins are most frequent—for
example, Hks. 234, 244, and 246; but it must also be remembered that overstruck coins have an unpleasing appearance, and therefore used not to be
preserved by collectors, which perhaps accounts for the rarity of overstrikes
of the 'Paxs' type (type VIII) of William in spite of the Beaworth hoard
having made this issue so common in the present day. They have probably
frequently been thrown out among the refuse of a find, which was certainly in
some cases (*e. g.* the Watford find) consigned to the melting-pot. Mules, too,
are naturally most common of the types of Hks. 240 and 245, owing to the
Beaworth and Tamworth finds. Rarity of coins at the present day is not
a safe reason for assuming few to have been in currency; it is usually due to
scarcity of finds of certain periods: the 'Paxs' type of William, for example,
was, before the Beaworth find, the rarest of his types.

Nos. 7 and 8 support the evidence of the Beaworth and Tamworth finds
in making the 'Paxs' type the latest of the Beaworth and earliest
of the Tamworth types.

No. 11 places the 'Cross in Quatrefoil' (Hks. 246) as the last of the
three Tamworth types, which are therefore 241—244—246.

No. 13 makes Hks. 247 later than Hks. 250.

The groups of types of William I and II on page xxxii may
therefore be extended, by adding the evidence of overstrikes, to
the following:

233 (first type)—234 (second type)—$\begin{Bmatrix}236\\237\end{Bmatrix}$—$\begin{Bmatrix}238\\243\end{Bmatrix}$—239—241—244
—246—250—247.

But the position of Hks. 248 is still left in complete uncertainty.
The groups of the two later reigns remain as before.

MULES.

The term 'Mule' is strictly applicable to all coins which are
struck from an incorrect combination of dies, that is to say, when
an obverse die is used with a reverse for which it was not originally
made, or *vice versa*; for example, on pp. 205-6, nos. 1107–13 are all
struck from the same obverse die, and therefore, though one of these
may be made with a true combination of dies, the remaining six,
although of the same type, must be, strictly speaking, 'mules'.[1] But
as 'mules' of this sort are very common and of minor importance,
the term 'mule' is here limited to the technical sense in which
it is commonly used in this coinage, to denote only those coins on
which are combined an obverse of one type and a reverse of another.

That these mules were authorized issues of the Crown introducing
a new type seems hardly possible. The so-called 'artificial mule'[2]
of the Confessor, connecting the last two types of his reign, is
quoted in support of this theory on the ground that the obverse
die must have been made specially for the mule issue. But the

---

[1] Unless, of course, it was the practice so early as this to issue two reverse
dies with one obverse, in which case five of these coins are 'mules'.

[2] *Num. Chron.*, 1905, Pl. VIII. 24; and *B.M. Catalogue, Ang.-Sax. Series*,
vol. ii, p. 352, no. 157, and Pl. XXIII. 8.

treatment of this coin as a mule is, I think, incorrect; the reverse
is indeed identical with the reverse of the later type, but the
obverse differs very widely from that of the earlier type (the ends
of the diadem hang straight down on either side of the head,
the draping of the bust is quite different, a sceptre is added, the
bust is continued to the edge of the coin and the inner circle
omitted). It seems more likely that this so-called 'mule' bears
the obverse originally designed for the last type of the reign, and
that its superficial resemblance to that of the preceding type led
to its withdrawal and the substitution of the more common profile
obverse; the comparative frequency of this 'mule' (see *Num.
Chron.*, 1905, pp. 196–7) seems to point to the same conclusion.

The improbability of the Crown confusing its issues by such
a coinage of mules is a serious obstacle to the theory that they are
regular issues, and presumptive evidence to the contrary is found
in the rarity of mules of the London mint. Of the Norman period
no London mules are at present known;[1] of the Confessor's reign
I know three only: *Num. Chron.*, 1905, p. 189 (= Carlyon-Britton
sale, 1913, lot 601), Carlyon-Britton sale, 1913, lot 590, and Montagu
sale, part I, lot 850. If mules were regularly issued for a short
period prior to the introduction of the new type, they, like the
ordinary issues, would probably be most frequently found of the
London mint, where the supply of bullion and the output of
coins may reasonably be assumed to have been most regular; that
they more frequently bear the names of lesser mints may perhaps
be due to moneyers at the smaller mints being more frequently
left, at the change of type, in possession of dies so little worn
as to tempt them, for the saving of the purchase-money of new
dies, to risk the penalties for the fraudulent retention of dies and
the issue of an unauthorized coinage.

This aspect of the 'mule' as an irregular issue, of which the object
must have been the saving of expense in the purchase of new dies,
is substantiated by the two mules which are described below as
nos. 3 and 4 (p. xxxix). Each of these mules has had the obverse

---

[1] Except the coin described in catalogue of H. H. Allan sale, 1908, lot 36.

die worked over in such a way as to make it approximately similar to that of the true obverse corresponding to the reverse type; on the 'Bonnet' obverse pillars have been placed beside the head to resemble those of the 'Canopy' type, and on the 'Canopy' obverse an inner circle has been drawn, cutting through the bust, and the pillars have been turned into the sceptres botonné and patté which are found beside the bust on the 'Two Sceptres' issue. The object of these alterations must surely have been to circulate the coins with less likelihood of detection. The issue of mules [1] must therefore have been fraudulent, but at the same time the risk of the fraud being exposed would in any case be slight, as the two sides of a coin cannot be seen at the same time and the inconsistency of obverse and reverse, either of which is with its proper fellow true currency, is not easily detected.

Mules are usually, as one would expect, made from dies of two consecutive types, but occasional examples occur (see no. 1, below) of a mule made from a die which has survived a longer period. As a general rule, therefore, a mule may be considered, in the absence of conflicting evidence, to connect two consecutive types. Also, as a general rule, the obverse of a mule will represent the earlier of the two types.[2] But this is not an absolute rule; two mules occur, for example, with the reverse of Henry I's 'Full face— Cross Fleury' type (Hks. iv), nos. 10 and 11 below, having different obverses. It is natural, therefore, to suppose that the reverse of Hks. iv is muled with both the preceding and subsequent obverses, and this supposition is confirmed by an examination of the later of these two mules, no. 11, the reverse of which is struck from the same die as a coin of the true type (Hks. iv) in Major Carlyon-Britton's collection. That the mule is the later of the two strikings is, I think, almost certain, for the roughness in the field of the reverse in the third quarter of the cross (see Pl. XLII. 5) is not corrosion,

---

[1] Using 'mule' here and throughout in the strictly limited sense of a coin combining two types.

[2] Because the obverse, or standard, die naturally outlives the reverse, or trussel, and is therefore the more likely to be left in good condition at the change of type.

but a roughness of the metal caused, no doubt, by rust on the die, and this is not visible on the true coin; the true coin was therefore struck earlier than the mule, and we may conclude that the obverse of the mule belongs to a type *later* than Hks. iv.

The following are the mules at present known of the Norman period:

(1) *Obv.* Edward Confessor, type XI (*Num. Chron.*, 1905).
   Rev. William, ' Bonnet ' type (Hks. 234).
   Coin of Shaftesbury (?), p. 13, no. 71 ; another of uncertain mint in York Museum. **Pl. III. 11, 12.**

(2) *Obv.* William, ' Profile—Cross Fleury ' type (Hks. 233).
   Rev.   „   ' Bonnet ' type (Hks. 234).
   Coins of Huntingdon and Stamford, p. 14, nos. 72, 73 ; others of Lincoln (P. W. P. Carlyon-Britton and H. M. Reynolds collections), Salisbury (Fitzwilliam Museum), Stamford (W. C. Wells collection), and Taunton (R. C. Lockett collection). **Pl. III. 13–15.**

(3) *Obv.* William, ' Bonnet ' type (Hks. 234).
   Rev.   „   ' Canopy ' type (Hks. 236).
   Coin of Ipswich, p. 33, no. 180. The obverse die from which this coin has been struck is altered evidently with a view to making it resemble the ' Canopy ' obverse ; a pillar has been cut on the die on each side of the bust ; possibly the double-striking is also intentional. See above, pp. xxxvii–xxxviii. **Pl. VI. 15.** Another of London (II. H. Allan sale, 1908, lot 36).

(4) *Obv.* William, ' Canopy ' type (Hks. 236).
   Rev.   „   ' Two Sceptres ' type (Hks. 237).
   Coin of Exeter in Hunterian collection. The obverse die of this coin is, similarly to the preceding, altered in order approximately to resemble the ' Two Sceptres ' obverse ; the inner circle has been continued through the bust, the pillars of the ' Canopy ' have been turned into the sceptres of the later type, though an ignorance of die-engraving has caused them to be reversed, the sceptre botonné being placed to left instead of right. This coin came from the St. Mary Hill Church find. See above, pp. xxxvii–xxxviii. **Pl. VIII. 11.**

(5) *Obv.* William, ' Two Sceptres ' type (Hks. 237).
   Rev.   „   ' Two Stars ' type (Hks. 238).

Coin of Hereford in P. W. P. Carlyon-Britton collection; two of Dorchester and one of Ipswich have also been published.[1] Pl. XI. 1.

(6) *Obv.* William, 'Profile—Cross and Trefoils' type (Hks. 239).
  Rev.   „   'Paxs' type (Hks. 241).
  Coins of Maldon, Malmesbury, Nottingham, Taunton, Thetford, Winchester. See pp. 91–3. Pl. XVII. 11–16.

(7) *Obv.* William, 'Profile' type (Hks. 244).
  Rev.   „   'Cross in Quatrefoil' type (Hks. 246).
  Coins of Dover and Gloucester, p. 225, nos. 66, 67; also of Chester and Leicester (Evans collection; see below, p. 403, nos. 65 A, 67 A), Oxford (Royal Mint Museum) and Winchester (H. M. Reynolds collection). Pl. XXX. 13–15.

(8) *Obv.* William, 'Crosses Pattée and Fleury' type (Hks. 247).
  Rev.   „   'Cross Fleury and Piles' type (Hks. 248).
  Coin of Canterbury (?) in L. E. Bruun collection. Pl. XXXVI. 15.

In Whitbourn sale, 1869, lot 148, is described a coin bearing obverse with bust to l., and reverse of Hks. 251. This may possibly be, as described in *Num. Chron.*, 1901, p. 48, a mule of Hks. 254 and 251, but is perhaps an error of the sale catalogue.

A coin described in *Num. Chron.*, 1901, pp. 59–60, as a mule of Hks. 257 and 267, is a contemporary forgery of a coin of Hks. 267; it is very base, weighs only 10·7 grs., and is of very rough work.[2] Fig. H on p. 60 (*op. cit.*) does not reproduce the very bad condition and rough work of the coin.

(9) *Obv.* Henry I, 'Voided Cross and Fleurs' type (Hks. 267).
  Rev.   „   'Pointing Bust and Stars' type (Hks. 266).
  Coin of Warwick in P.W.P. Carlyon-Britton collection. Pl. XL. 5.

(10) *Obv.* Henry I, 'Cross in Quatrefoil' type (Hks. 263).
  Rev.   „   'Full face—Cross Fleury' type (Hks. iv).
  Coin of Gloucester in Hunterian collection. Pl. XLI. 9.

(11) *Obv.* Henry I, 'Double Inscription' type (Hks. 258).
  Rev.   „   'Full face—Cross Fleury' type (Hks. iv).
  Coin of Thetford in Hunterian collection. Pl. XLII. 5.

---

[1] *Brit. Num. Journ.*, vol. ii, p. 151.
[2] I am indebted to Sheriff Mackenzie for kindly sending me the coin.

This coin is from the same reverse die as a coin of the true type (Hks. iv) in the Carlyon-Britton collection. Rust-marks in the field of the mule show it to be later than the true coin. Hks. 258 may therefore be assumed to be the later of the two types.

(12) *Obv.* Henry I, ' Lozenge Fleury enclosing Star ' type (Hks. 265).
    Rev.   ,,   ' Pellets in Quatrefoil ' type (Hks. 262).
        Coin of Romney in P. W. P. Carlyon-Britton collection. **Pl. XLIII. 15.**
(13) *Obv.* Stephen, ' Watford ' type (Hks. 270).
    Rev.   ,,   ' Cross Voided and Mullets ' type (Hks. 269).
        Penny and Halfpenny of Canterbury (?) from the Sheldon find (*Brit. Num. Journ.*, vol. vii, p. 44); another halfpenny (same dies as Sheldon penny) in B. Roth collection. **Pl. LIII. 1, 2.**

These mules not only confirm the evidence obtained from finds and overstrikes, but also complete the series of types of the reigns of the two Williams; the regular chain of mules, nos. 2–5, Hks. 233 × 234, 234 × 236, 236 × 237, 237 × 238, forms a convincing proof that these five types, 233, 234, 236, 237, 238, form in that order the first five types of the William coins; the sequence 239— 241—244—246 is also confirmed by the mules 239 × 241 and 244 × 246 (nos. 6 and 7). The eighth mule of this list brings Hks. 248 for the first time into the scheme and places it at the end of the William series. Of Henry I, mule 9, combined with the evidence of the Bari find, forms a series 257—267—266; mules 10 and 11 form another series 263—iv—258, and mule 12 shows that 265 is the type immediately preceding 262. The mule of Stephen only confirms the position of his first two types.

The additional evidence of mules, therefore, results in a very probable sequence of the types of the two Williams, and further groups of Henry I:

WILLIAM I and II.

233—234—236—237—238—243—239—241—244—246—250—247 —248.

HENRY I.

251 or 252 (first type)
257—267—266
263—iv—258
265—262—255 (last type).

STEPHEN.

270 (first type)—269 (second type)
268 (last type).

EPIGRAPHY.

(See Epigraphical Table.)

The form of the obverse and reverse inscriptions, which was in use on Anglo-Saxon coins of the eleventh century, continued in use throughout the Norman period; on the obverse was the king's name with or without the royal title,[1] on the reverse the names of the moneyer and the mint connected by the word ON ;[2] nor is there any reason to believe that any change took place in the means by which the inscriptions were cut on the dies. In *B. M. Catalogue*, 'Anglo-Saxon Coins', vol. ii, p. xcix, it is said that the letters are not cut with a graving tool, but punched into the die with tools of different shapes, a punch like a small blunt chisel forming the vertical strokes of such letters as B, E, M, &c., a small wedge-shaped punch forming the horizontal bars of E, F, L, the tail of R, &c., and crescent-shaped punches of larger and smaller size forming the curves of D, O, and P, B, &c. The disjointed forms of the letters, the strange character of some of them (notably A and C [3]),

---

[1] Exception must be made of the irregular issues (see below, pp. lxxi ff.). The varieties of obverse inscription used on the different types of the reigns of William I may be seen in Major Carlyon-Britton's description of the types in *Brit. Num. Journ.*, vol. ii, pp. 130 ff., and those of the reign of Henry I in Mr. Andrew's description of the types of that reign in *Num. Chron.*, 1901, pp. 38 ff.

[2] The Launceston coins of the fifth type of William I, described on p. 62, nos. 325-6, omit the moneyer's name. O (regularly on Norwich coins), N (p. 17, no. 81), and ONN (on Oxford and Thetford coins of William I, type II, in York Museum) occur for ON; on p. 75, no. 402, OF is used probably in error.

[3] See Epigraphical Table, Series I.

the close resemblance of the upright strokes and the strange mistakes that commonly occur [1] seem only explicable as the result of punch-work of this nature; this explanation has therefore been accepted without question and without serious investigation as regards, at least, the later Anglo-Saxon and Norman periods. A recent paper read by Mr. Hocking before the Royal Numismatic Society [2] has made it necessary to inquire more critically into the subject. This explanation of the engraving of dies by means of punches during the Norman period was there condemned on the grounds of the impossibility of hammering such broad blunt punches so close to the edge of a die without splitting it, [3] and of the great variety of shape, notably in breadth and in the finish of the fish-tail ends, that is usually exhibited in the upright strokes on the same coin and the same side of it—facts incongruous with the previously accepted theory.

A close examination of the lettering on the coins described in this catalogue results in the conclusion that (1) the inscriptions were cut on the dies by means of punches; (2) the punches, though similar in shape to those above described, were in most cases narrower and less blunt, and do not correspond exactly with the lettering seen on the coins; that is to say, after the engraver had hammered the punch into the die, he usually broadened the incision thus made and finished it off by means of a tool, presumably a graver's cutting tool; (3) the irregularity of shape and thickness exhibited by the lettering is explained partly by the finishing touches added with the graver's tool after punching, but partly also by unsuccessful striking of the coins themselves, the metal in many cases having failed to fill sufficiently the hollows of the die. These conclusions are based on the following points:

---

[1] See Epigraphical Table, Series I, letters C (2), F (2), L (2), S (6), and TH (5).

[2] *Num. Chron.*, 1913, Proceedings, p. 10.

[3] The turning up of the edge of the coins shows that the dies were not larger in diameter than the coins they struck; but this does not prove that the dies were not made of larger size and filed down after they were engraved.

(1) A certain flaw repeating itself in precisely the same position on different letters of a coin shows that these letters must have been made by punching the die with an instrument which itself contained this flaw. Instances of this are fairly numerous and in many cases easily visible. In the vertical strokes of the letters the following flaws have been noted :

(*a*) On the obverse of William II, no. 69, the letter **M** has a small flaw at the bottom of the left-hand corner of each vertical stroke, a small semicircular piece being broken off the corner of the punch from which these strokes were made; the same flaw may be seen, less clearly, on most, if not all, of the other letters on the obverse of this coin, notably on the three letters immediately preceding the **M**.

(*b*) A similar, slightly smaller, flaw appears in the same position on the vertical strokes of the obverse of William II, no. 81 (**Pl. XXXI. 7**).

(*c*) A similar flaw, in similar position, but rather smaller and less round in shape, on the letters **MRE** of the obverse of William II, no. 104 (**Pl. XXXI. 16**).

(*d*) A small hole in the left-hand corner of the bottom edge of the vertical strokes of **LELM** and **E** on the obverse of William II, no. 155 (**Pl. XXXIII. 7**).

(*e*) A small flaw in the lower left-hand fish-tail of the two strokes of **Λ** in the mint-name on the reverse of William II, no. 160 (**Pl. XXXIII. 9**); the V-shaped form of this flaw is noticeable in both strokes of the letter.

(*f*) On the reverse of Stephen, no. 157 (**Pl. LIII. 14**), a crack across the lower left-hand corner, just above the serif, of the second vertical stroke of the **N** of **ON** and of the **N** of the mint-name.

(*g*) A small hole in the centre of the top edge, just below the serif, of both vertical strokes of the letter **N** on the obverse of Stephen, no. 170 (**Pl. LIV. 8**).

(*h*) The obverse and reverse of a coin of William II, Hks. 250, of Salisbury (P. C. B. coll.), and of one of the same type of Wilton (H. W. M. coll.), and the reverse of one of the same type of Worcester (P. C. B. coll.), show a break across the centre of the vertical strokes; it stretches right through the verticals from side to side, and slopes slightly downwards from left to right; on the reverse of the Wilton coin the punch is sometimes inverted, on **NE**, for example, at the end of the mint-name. This group is important, not only as showing that the vertical strokes were made with one punch and not, as has been suggested, from piece-punches (one punch forming the upper half, and another, or the same punch again, forming the lower half of the stroke), but also as evidence of the dies having been made at London (see below, pp. cxxxv ff.). The close resemblance of the shape of the break in these strokes in all three coins leaves little room for doubt that the dies for the three coins were all made with the same punch.

In the horizontal wedge-shaped strokes forming the bars of E, F, &c., the following flaws have been noted:

(*i*) On the reverse of William II, no. 16 (Pl. **XXVIII.** 12), the wedge-shaped bars forming the tail of **R**, the lower bar of **F** and the three bars of **E** in the mint-name, show two holes, one near each end of the bar; it may be noted that the top bar of **E** is punched closer in to the vertical stroke than the other two bars, and on this bar the two holes are closer to the vertical, showing clearly that these two flaws were in the punch from which all these bars were made.

(*k*) On the reverse of William II, no. 94 (Pl. **XXXI.** 11), there is a similar flaw on the bars of **E** and **F** in the mint-name near the broad end of the bars.

(2) An examination of the strokes containing the flaws above mentioned, and shown therefore to be made from the same punch, reveals considerable variety of shape and breadth in the strokes which were themselves the work of the same punch; for example, on the coin mentioned above as flaw *d* (Pl. **XXXIII.** 7) the

strokes **LEL** on the obverse vary in breadth, the first **L** being narrower and more waisted than the other two letters; they vary also in the shape and length of their fish-tail ends. As these letters show the same flaw and are therefore made with the same punch, we must conclude that, after hammering the punch into the die, the engraver broadened the incision and finished off the ends with a tool. But the point is better shown by instances which have been noted of a portion of a letter being double-punched :

(*a*) On the reverse of William I, no. 292 (**Pl. X. 16**), the letter **I** in the moneyer's name shows a shaped piece protruding beyond its lower end, corresponding to it in shape but much smaller in size; also, near the top of the letter a fish-tail protrudes on either side corresponding to the fish-tails at the top of the letter.

(*b*) On a coin of London (moneyer Wulfword) of William II, type IV, in the York Museum, a similar projection may be seen above the vertical of **P** on the obverse, and a similar fish-tail protruding from the left side near the bottom of the letter.

These show clearly that the punch has been struck twice into the die and the marks of the mis-strike not obliterated; the narrower form of the projecting piece is no doubt partly due to the punch not being hammered so deeply as in the true impression, but also is probably in part due to the broadening of the true impression after punching. Many instances may be found of a similar protrusion above or below a letter ; for example, on the obverse of William I, no. 167, below the **R**, and on William I, no. 137 (**Pl. V. 12**), above the vertical of the initial cross of the reverse ; in these and similar cases the protrusion is invariably shaped similarly to the true strike of the vertical stroke, though thinner and smaller; it cannot therefore be due to the slipping of a graver's tool.

An example of similar double-punching of a horizontal bar may be seen on the obverse of William II, no. 262 (**Pl. XXXVII. 4**), where the bar of the third **L** has a wedge-shaped protrusion beyond its broad end. There are also cases where more than three bars are visible on an **E**,—on William II, no. 83 (**Pl. XXXI. 8**), the second **E** of the obverse inscription has the horizontal bar punched no fewer than five times. Similarly, on the reverse of William II, no. 202, the **B** of the moneyer's name has four instead of two crescent-shaped punch-marks; in these cases, again, the narrowness of the punch-marks, as compared with corresponding strokes of other letters, seems to imply that the usual practice was to broaden the letters after they were punched.

That a cutting tool was used for finishing off the fish-tail ends after punching is also shown by William I, no. 1029, on which the first stroke of **Λ** in the mint-name has the lower fish-tail on the left running right out to the vertical of the preceding letter **P**; this must have been due to a slip of the graver's tool.

The original form of the punches may probably be gathered from William I, no. 186 (**Pl. VII. 5**), on the reverse of which the letters **LI** of the moneyer's name present a somewhat unusual appearance. The upper surface of these letters is narrow and is sloped sharply off to the field of the die, forming a steep slope instead of the usual perpendicular setting of the letters to the field of the coin;[1] probably the engraver, after punching the strokes of the letters, cut the metal of the die in a sharp slope down to the deepest point of the punched impression, instead of cutting down perpendicularly and so broadening the impression. In section, the sides of the vertical strokes of these letters are of the shape ⟶, instead of the usual ⟶; the shape of the vertical strokes, showing in dotted lines their point of contact with the field, is thus: **Ⲩ**.

It is possible that the punches themselves sloped off in this way, and that these letters show the untouched punch-work.

Frequent varieties of the letter T, on which the horizontal bar has been so punched as to leave the top of the vertical visible

---

[1] Cf. also the lettering of the obverse of the coin of William I, no. 84 (**Pl. IV. 6**), where, however, it may be due to faulty striking; see below, p. xlviii.

above it, show similarly the shape of one end of the stroke. See Epigraphical Table, Series I, T (2).

We may therefore conclude that the punches were all narrower than the lettering seen on the coins, but probably of the same length,[1] and that the engraver, after hammering the punch into the die, broadened with a tool the incision thus made and finished off the corners, increasing the slope of the fish-tail ends of the uprights.

(3) The very thin lettering which is seen occasionally on coins is probably due in some cases to the omission of the engraver to broaden the punch-marks; but duplicates show that it is sometimes due to faulty striking of the coins, the flan failing to take the full impression of the die.[2] It is not, therefore, possible to conclude with certainty that the thin lettering gives us the untouched work of the punch. How nearly the lettering of the later coins, when serifs are added and the verticals are convex instead of concave, resembles the shape and breadth of the punches, it is impossible to say; in this later period the serifs are added with separate punches and are sometimes omitted.[3]

Two coins, William I, no. 329 (Pl. XII. 5) and William II, no. 184 (Pl. XXXIV. 4), have upright strokes in the obverse inscription without the horizontal strokes to complete the letters; on the former coin, between P and M, the inscription consists of nothing but vertical strokes, on the other coin the initial cross and P alone are complete, the remainder of the inscription being vertical strokes only. On both these coins the uprights seem to be carefully spaced out in such a way as to leave room for the horizontal strokes to be inserted; and they seem to show that, in making these two dies at least, the engravers punched first

---

[1] See below, p. l.

[2] Compare, for example, William I, nos. 1113, 1114, two coins struck from the same reverse die; the N of the mint-name has on no. 1113 this very thin appearance and on the other the normal thickness.

[3] See Henry I, no. 58 (Pl. XLI. 11), on the obverse of which some of the letters are without serifs.

the uprights and finished them off with the graving tool before punching the horizontal strokes. It seems natural to suppose that this was the regular practice, as it would be quicker in working with a punch to hammer into the die the strokes that one punch would make, rather than to keep changing tools in order to finish off one letter before beginning another.

Having arrived at the conclusion that punches were used in making the inscriptions on the dies, it is possible to find varieties of lettering which may be traced to a change in height or shape of the punches used at different times by engravers, and thereby to obtain further evidence of the chronological sequence of the coin-types of this period.[1] With the evidence that has been drawn from Finds, Overstrikes, and Mules, a considerable number of the types of these four reigns have already been placed in chronological sequence, and this order, which is shown on pp. xli–xlii, connects the various series of epigraphical groups which serve to allocate most of the types at present unplaced.

The most important epigraphical change of this period takes place in the reign of Henry I; on the coins of the two Williams, as on Anglo-Saxon coins, the uprights of the letters have concave sides and more or less fish-tailed ends without serifs; so, too, on four of the types of Henry I. The remainder of Henry's coins and those of Stephen belong to quite a new epigraphical class, having uprights with convex sides and serifs added by means of separate punches at both ends, serifs being also sometimes present at the ends of the horizontal strokes of **Ɛ**, **E**, &c.; improved (*i. e.* less rudimentary) forms of lettering, notably **A**, **Ꝁ**, **V**, are found on coins of this new class, and also on coins of one type[2] only of the old class, a type which may therefore safely be regarded as the last of the types which bear the old form of lettering.

The Epigraphical Table shows clearly the distinction between these two classes, Series I–IV comprising the earlier class, and

---

[1] See *Num. Chron.*, 1913, pp. 399 ff.

[2] 'Annulets and Piles' type of Henry I (Hks. 257).

Series V–IX the later. The nine series into which the epigraphical groups are there divided reflect the use of different forms of punches in the cutting of the dies; in each series the normal forms of all the letters and the most important varieties are figured. The drawings are to the scale of 2 to 1.

Of the four series of the old class, two are found on types of Henry I, the later of which must be that in which occur the new forms of **A**, **h**, **V**, *i.e.* Series IV; Series III will therefore be the other series of the old class which is found on coins of Henry I. Series I covers all the types of the two Williams with the exception of some coins of the 'Voided Cross' type (Hks. 250) and all of the 'Crosses Pattée and Fleury' type (Hks. 247), which have lettering of a larger type, Series II, and the coins of the 'Cross Fleury and Piles' (Hks. 248), which have lettering of Series III. The new class of lettering forms five series, of which two contain types of Henry I, and two contain types of Stephen; the remaining one contains types of both Henry I and Stephen, and may therefore be placed between the two series of Henry types and the two series of Stephen types; this middle series groups together, as would be expected, Hks. 262, 255, 270, and 269, which were found on other evidence to be the last two types of Henry and the first two of Stephen. Immediately preceding this series (no. VII) must be placed the series containing Hks. 265, the type that has been found to precede Hks. 262; this is therefore Series VI, and the other series of Henry types is Series V. Of the two series of Stephen types, the one containing Hks. 268, the last type of the reign, must be the later, and these series can therefore be numbered IX and VIII respectively.

The nine series are differentiated, after the main division of the old and new classes of lettering, chiefly by the height of the uprights; measurement shows so minute a variation in the height of lettering on coins of the same series that it is safe to assume that the engraver, in finishing off the letters with the tool, kept within the upper and lower limits of the punch-mark, broadening the strokes without increasing their height. The measurement is taken to the centre of the top and bottom of the uprights. There is also marked difference in finish and breadth of lettering in the different series. Probably the engravers copied a model set them by the chief engraver, so that the finish of the letter is not the original effort of the individual workman based on the traditions of the mint, but a close copy of the chief engraver's original design; otherwise it would be impossible to account for the very close resemblance of the finished lettering on the coins; presumably the workmen were usually unable to read or write, and ignorantly copied the model set them.[1] The variety of form and height of these uprights may be seen on the following diagram, on which the uprights are drawn to scale (three times the original size) upon a ground ruled with horizontal lines which mark halves of millimetres in the original:[2]

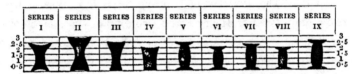

SERIES I	SERIES II	SERIES III	SERIES IV	SERIES V	SERIES VI	SERIES VII	SERIES VIII	SERIES IX

Series I is the lettering in use at the beginning of the reign of William I, and continues through ten types bearing the name of William; it includes also some of the coins of the eleventh William type (Hks. 250, 'Cross Voided' type). It is not, however, a strictly homogeneous series, but is comprised of three groups which differ slightly in finish but hardly enough to necessitate the creation of three separate series. The earliest of the three groups is seen on coins of the first four types of William I, and occasionally on coins of his fifth ('Two Stars'), and sixth ('Sword') types, and is of the form represented in the table; it is usually narrower and slightly smaller (2·2 mm.) than that which follows it (2·4 mm.). The second group with thicker uprights appears first on the fourth ('Two Sceptres') type and continues to the eighth ('Paxs') type. On Hks. 244 the third

---

[1] For intelligent attempts to copy a blundered model see below, p. cxxxvi.
[2] This block is reproduced from *Num. Chron.*, 1913, p. 404, by kind permission of the Council of the Royal Numismatic Society.

group appears—a lettering of the same height as the preceding, but having as its characteristic more marked fish-tail ends to the uprights; this continues on Hks. 246 and some coins of Hks. 250. Thus, with the exception of these slight varieties within the series (it must be remembered that the drawings of Series I represent rather the earlier than the later style of this series), Series I continues throughout the first ten types bearing the name of William and on some coins of the 'Cross Voided' type (Hks. 250).

The finish of the lettering of the first eight types is very good, and carefully worked, especially in types III to VIII, but after the 'Paxs' type there is a very marked decline both in the striking of the coins and in the finish of the dies.

Series II represents a much larger lettering (2·8 mm.) with coarser finish and more careless striking. It is used on some coins of the 'Cross Voided' type (Hks. 250) and all the coins of the 'Crosses Pattée and Fleury' type (Hks. 247[1]). The fact that Hks. 250 forms a transitional type containing lettering of both Series I and II confirms the previous evidence of its position between Hks. 246 and Hks. 247.

Series III (2·5 mm.) is of a narrower and less clumsy form; the lettering shows better finish and greater neatness, the uprights broaden at the top more than at the lower end. It is used on the coins of the 'Cross Fleury and Piles' type (Hks. 248) with the name of William, and on those of the 'Annulets' type (Hks. 251) with the name of Henry. An epigraphical connexion is thus formed between the William and Henry coins, confirming the placing of Hks. 248 as the last type of William II, and defining the first type of Henry I. The evidence of Finds left a doubt whether Hks. 252, which occurs in the Shillington find, or Hks. 251, which occurs in the Bermondsey find (see above, pp. xxiii–xxiv), was the first type of the reign of Henry I. The evidence of the Bermondsey find is therefore correct; in fact, the type of the Shillington find, Hks. 252, has

---

[1] The few exceptions mentioned in *Num. Chron.*, 1913, p. 404, are very doubtful.

lettering of the new class with serifs and convex uprights, and must therefore at the earliest come later than the four Henry types with lettering of the old class.

Series IV (1·8 mm.) is the last of the old concave style. The uprights are usually disproportionately broad, giving an ugly squat appearance to the letters. It covers three types of Henry I— the 'Profile and Cross Fleury' (Hks. 254), 'Pax' (Hks. 253), and 'Annulets and Piles' (Hks. 257) types; of the first two of these three types we have at present found no evidence of position, but the third (Hks. 257) has already been shown, from the forms **A, ᚺ,** and **V,**[1] to be the last type with lettering of the old class. In the word PAX in the field of Hks. 253 occurs the form of **A** found in the inscriptions of Hks. 257, sometimes with and sometimes without the upper bar. This first appearance of a true A form[2] may perhaps be taken as evidence that the 'Pax' type immediately precedes Hks. 257, but this conclusion is by no means a certain one, for the use of the letter in the word PAX may be conventional, as we find a similar true A form in PAXS on coins of Hks. 241 and also on the coins of Harold. The 'Profile and Cross Fleury' (Hks. 254) and 'Pax' (Hks. 253) types may therefore be placed provisionally as second and third types, with the 'Annulets and Piles' (Hks. 257) type as the fourth type of the reign. On the last of these three types there appears a slight tendency to make the lettering narrower and more legible, but the height is only very slightly increased, and the execution remains careless and ill finished.

Series V (2·5 mm.). This is the first series of the new class with serifs and convex uprights. It includes all the coins of :

'Voided Cross and Fleurs' type (Hks. 267),

'Pointing Bust and Stars' type (Hks. 266),

'Quatrefoil and Piles' type (Hks. 252),

'Larger Profile and Cross and Annulets' type (Hks. 256) ;

---

[1] See also notes on letter G below, p. lviii.

[2] With the exception of occasional forms on William coins; see Epigraphical Table, Series I, A. 4, 5, 6.

and some coins of:

'Cross in Quatrefoil' type (Hks. 263),

'Full Face and Cross Fleury' type (Hks. iv),

'Double Inscription' type (Hks. 258).

Of these types, Hks. 267 is connected by the Bari find with Hks. 257, which has been placed as the fourth of the reign, and Hks. 266 is connected by a mule with Hks. 267. The other two types, Hks. 252 and 256, which have this series of lettering only, must be placed as the seventh and eighth types, but there is no evidence to show which of the two is the earlier. The order of the three remaining types, which form transitional types from Series V to Series VI, is already fixed by the mules in the Hunterian collection (see above, pp. xl–xli).

The earliest form of lettering of this series, at the introduction of the serifs and convex uprights with type V (Hks. 267), differs slightly from the later forms; it is somewhat higher (2·7 mm.), rather less convex, and very much finer in execution.[1] The lettering assumes its more usual form on some coins of type VI and so continues throughout the series; this form is less neat in appearance and the finish less careful.

The introduction of pellets to divide the words of the legends begins in this series,[2]—on the fifth, sixth, and seventh types of Henry they are used occasionally, and on the eighth and later types almost invariably.

Series VI (2 mm.) is a smaller and more neatly finished lettering. It covers the remaining coins of types IX, X, XI (Hks. 263, iv, 258), and all the coins of the 'Smaller Profile and Cross and Annulets' (Hks. 264) and 'Star in Lozenge Fleury' (Hks. 265) types, the latter of which is connected by a mule with the 'Pellets in Quatrefoil'

---

[1] It was pointed out above, p. xxv, that the evidence of the Bari find was not by any means conclusive; but I am content to accept it in placing Hks. 267 as the first type of the new class of lettering, as I think that this different and much more finely executed form of lettering is likely to be the earliest work after the change.

[2] There are a few isolated instances on earlier coins.

type (Hks. 262); some coins also of Hks. 262 have lettering of this series. Hks. 264 is thus fixed as the twelfth type of the reign.

Series VII (2·3 mm.) includes coins of the last two types of Henry I and of the first two types of Stephen (Hks. 262, 255, 270, 269). It is a larger lettering and has uprights with less curved sides; the dies appear for the most part to have been carefully finished. A still larger style of lettering seems to have come into occasional use for obverse inscriptions during this series; this larger lettering (2·7 mm.) is found on the obverse of some coins of Stephen's first type (Hks. 270) which read STIEFNE, and also on a few coins of his second type (Hks. 269); examples of it may be seen on **Pl. L. 11, LI. 11, LIII. 4.**

Series VIII (2 mm.) is a small lettering with straighter sides to the uprights, their convexity being now scarcely visible. Some coins of Stephen's second type (Hks. 269) fall into this series,[1] which includes also the coins of the 'Cross and Fleurs' (Hks. 276) and 'Lozenge Fleury and Annulets' (Hks. xix) types, and some coins apparently of the type figured on **Pl. LV. 1.** Of this last type only two specimens are known to me; on one (see below, p. 367, no. 179, **Pl. LV.** 1) the lettering is of Series IX, on the other[2] the obverse is illegible and the reverse has lettering of Series VIII; this therefore seems to be the transitional type of Series VIII and IX, and Hks. 276 and xix may be placed immediately after Hks. 269 as the third and fourth types of the reign, though there is no evidence to show which is the earlier of the two.

Series IX (2·6 mm.) returns to a much larger lettering. The types falling into this series are, besides the transitional type just mentioned as the fifth of the reign, the remaining two types of Stephen, Hks. xviii b and 268, of which Hks. 268 is already placed as the last type by the Awbridge find. On this series there seems to be some irregularity of height, some of the uprights

---

[1] Also perhaps a few, but very few, of Stephen's first type (Hks. 270). See *Num. Chron.*, 1913, p. 409.

[2] B. Roth collection (the reverse is illustrated in *Num. Chron.*, 1913, Pl. XIX. 7 b).

measuring as much as 2·8 and others only 2·4 mm.; it may be that
here again a larger lettering was sometimes used for obverse
inscriptions, as on some coins of Stephen's first type.[1] The coins
have for the most part a coarse and unpleasing appearance, due
partly to the clumsiness of the lettering and partly to the roughness
in execution of the dies. This large lettering is also seen on some
coins of the first issue of Henry II (the so-called 'Tealby' type).

The results thus obtained from epigraphical evidence, and the
association of this evidence with that of Finds and Mules, may be
seen below, pp. lxvi–lxvii.

In the Epigraphical Table the ordinary forms of letters in use
in each series are figured, and also the chief varieties; from these
are omitted the forms on coins of very coarse and irregular work
which are mentioned below.[2]

A. The first two forms in the table are those in regular use, the
former being the earlier and more common on the early types of
William I; the inclination of the two strokes tends quickly to
diminish, and the form of the letter is reduced to the two parallel
strokes of the second form, which remains in use throughout
the reigns of William I and II, and the first three types of
Henry I.

The third form, similar to form 1 but with a cross-bar added,
occurs rarely: p. 7, no. 31; p. 10, no. 55; p. 22, no. 114; p. 46,
no. 234 (Pl. III. 4; V. 3; IX. 1). Similarly, with parallel uprights,
the letter H is substituted for Λ on p. 22, no. 117.

Form 4: p. 3, no. 9 (Pl. I. 8).

Form 5: p. 75, no. 402 (Pl. XIV. 8); p. 82, no. 445; a Stamford
coin of the second type of William I (York Museum); in the word
PꞀXS on all coins of the eighth type of William I.

Form 6: p. 37, no. 196 (Pl. VII. 11).

Series III, form 2, occurs on the obverse of a Winchester coin of
Henry I, type I, in Mr. Lockett's collection; this is a roughly-
formed letter engraved somewhat carelessly; the finish at the

---

[1] See above, p. lv.   [2] p. cxxxviii.

upper end is uncertain, nor is it quite clear whether there is a central cross-bar (see **Pl. XXXVIII. 16**).

In Series IV, forms 2 and 3 are found in the word **PⳫX** on type III of Henry I,[1] and are both in regular use on type IV, the old form being now abandoned.

The forms of this letter in the new class of lettering, Series V–IX, call for no comment; a large top bar with serifs is introduced in Series VII and continues to the end of the period. In Series IX both barred and unbarred forms are found on types VI and VII of Stephen.

B shows no varieties of importance. An interesting case of double-punching of this letter is seen on the coin of William II, p. 249, no. 202, and has already been mentioned.[2]

In Series II the crescents tend to be thinner and less curved; in Series III the second form, which occurs on p. 264, no. 273 (**Pl. XXXVII. 15**), is due to the limited space in which the engraver had to cut the letter.

C is regularly of the square form throughout the whole of this period; the second figure of Series I shows a very natural punch-worker's error which occurs occasionally. The round forms (Series I, form 3, Series V, form 3, and Series VII, form 2) occur on William I, p. 75, no. 402 (**Pl. XIV. 8**), Henry I, p. 288, no. 70, and pp. 323–4, nos. 231–4 (**Pl. XLVII. 16**).

D. The very straight form of loop which is figured in Series V, form 1, occurs on the earlier coins of the series which have the finer lettering.[3] Cf. p. 276, no. 33 (**Pl. XL. 1**).

E. The round form of Series I, form 2, is found on William I, p. 25, no. 132 (**Pl. V. 10**); the similar form, Series V, form 3, is on a London (Sigar) coin of Henry I, type VI, in the Hunterian collection. In Series V and VI the horizontal bars of **E**, as also of **Ⳑ** and **F**, are sometimes with, sometimes without, serifs; in Series VII they are more common without serifs, but are still

---

[1] See above, p. liii. [2] p. xlvii.
[3] See above, p. liv.

sometimes found with them; in Series VIII and IX the serifs are usually present.

F. Series I, form 2, shows a not uncommon error and one natural to punch-work; cf. William I, p. 28, no. 148 (**Pl. VI. 3**). Similar errors are Ⴑ, cf. William I, p. 117, no. 624 (**Pl. XIX. 11**), and Ⴑ for **F**, and Ⴅ for **E**.

G. The first two forms of Series I are both in regular use; form 3 shows a different shape of the top stroke, probably this is worked with a tool and not due to a punch of different shape. In Series II both forms are again commonly used, and in Series III and IV the form with the complete circle—**O** with a wedge-shaped bar at the top—is alone used, except on a Hunterian coin (Winchester) of type IV, where the new form of this letter, Series IV, form 2, is already introduced. Probably the letter was not made in the ordinary way with a punch, but, like O,[1] marked out on the die with a turning instrument like a pair of compasses, in some cases the circle not being completed and in others a complete circle being formed, and at the top of this circle or semicircle an incision was made with a wedge-shaped punch such as is used for the bars of E, &c. In the centre of the letter may sometimes be seen a raised pellet, cf. William I, p. 47, no. 239 (**Pl. IX. 4**); a similar pellet is commonly seen in the centre of the letter O, also frequently in the centre of the reverse of coins, notably in William I's first type. This pellet is probably due to the fixed foot of the compasses cutting a small hole in the die. The unevenness of the outline would be due to the engraver finishing off the letter free-hand after marking it out in this way. Series IV, form 2, is mentioned above; it is the earliest appearance of the form of G which is in use on the serifed classes (Series V–VIII) and supplies additional evidence of this type being the fourth of the reign.[2]

H. As already mentioned, the Roman form of this letter is invariable down to the third type of Henry I's reign; on his fourth

---

[1] See below, p. lx.   [2] See above, p. liii.

type the English form appears and is always used to the end of the period. The importance of this letter in determining the position of type IV of Henry I (Hks. 257) has already been noticed.

I. The only point with regard to this letter that need be mentioned is its frequent use instead of **Ⲁ**, **Ⲛ**, &c., at the end of an inscription where there is not room for the whole letter; thus **ⲢILLEM REⲬ I** (for **Ⲁ**) is of frequent occurrence, similarly **LVϺI** for **LVϺN**.

K. This letter is found on two coins in the York Museum of William I's first type (*var.* inscription beginning above head) which read **VLFKEⲤEL ON EOFOR** (same dies?). Also on Winchester coins of Henry I, type XV, and Stephen, type I, with the moneyer's name *Kippig* or *Ckippig*; see p. 332, nos. 296, 297, and pp. 353–4, nos. 120–3.

L. The second form in Series I is figured as one of the many examples of errors that are essentially due to working with punches. William I, p. 58, no. 297.

M. The intersecting lines of the letter seem to have been usually engraved with a tool; this, however, was not always the case, as some coins show clearly that wedge-shaped punches were used for this purpose, *e. g.* William I, p. 159, no. 856 (reverse), William II, p. 264, no. 271 (obverse). The varieties in Series I need no special comment; for form 3 see William I, p. 30, no. 162 (Pl. **VI.** 11); for form 4, William I, p. 12, no. 69 (Pl. **III. 9**). In Series V, form 2 occurs on Henry I, p. 280, no. 42 (Pl. **XL. 12**), and a similar spread form on Henry I, p. 291, no. 78 (Pl. **XLII. 9**). Series VI, form 2, is found on Henry I, p. 286, no. 62.

N. There are no varieties of particular interest. In Series I the reversely barred form, form 3, occurs on William I, p. 12, no. 67, and p. 117, no. 624 (Pl. **III. 7**; **XIX. 11**); for form 4 see William II, p. 219, nos. 29–31 (Pl. **XXIX. 5**). In Series IV the regular form, form 1, is alone in use on coins at present known of types II and III; on type IV is introduced a fashion of the reversely barred letter, form 2; all the known coins of type IV, with one exception,[1] having form 2, or, rarely, form 3. On some coins of type V which have the earlier style of Series V, the reversely barred form (form 1 of Series V) is still retained in use, but it disappears before the introduction of type VI.

o. Form 1 of Series I is that in regular use in the reign of William I; it seems not to have been punched into the die, but to have been marked out with compasses, and afterwards, like punched letters, thickened and finished with a tool;[2] as in the letter G, a pellet is frequently visible in the centre. The size varies considerably, a very small form (Series I, form 2) being sometimes seen.[3] The letter is not uncommonly found in the form of a large pellet, that is to say, the centre of the letter has been accidentally cut away on the die.[4] A double form sometimes occurs (Series I, form 3 [5]), which might be due either to double-punching or to marking out the circle in the wrong position and re-marking it, or by marking it doubly by swinging the compasses round on the wrong foot.

During the reign of William I is introduced a different form of the letter (Series I, form 4), which is made by two crescent-shaped punches; it occurs as early as type IV,[6] but is very rarely found before type VIII; on type VIII the two forms are equally common; on William II's first type the form made by two crescent punches is the one in regular use, the other form being not frequent on this type and rare on type II; on the introduction of Series II the round form returns into regular use, and is not uncommonly of small size (Series II, form 2); Series II, form 3, occurs occasionally on type III and rarely on type IV. In Series III a small round type is regular, form 2 occurring on William II, p. 264, no. 271,

---

[1] A coin in the Hunterian collection reading ✠GODPIN:ONPIN E:

[2] See on G above, p. lviii.

[3] William I, p. 97, no. 511 (Pl. XVIII. 6).   [4] William I, p. 16, no. 78.

[5] William I, p. 55, no. 289 (Pl. X. 14); William II, pp. 229-30, nos. 89, 90.

[6] See p. 54, no. 281 (Pl. X. 8).

and p. 265, no. 280 (Pl. **XXXVII. 11, 16**). The round type alone is found in Series IV, but with the introduction of the new style in Series V the form made with crescent punches is re-introduced, and the round form does not appear again.

Some strange forms of this letter have occasionally been noted, e.g. *Num. Chron.*, 1901, p. 288 (British Museum coin, p. 273, no. 27), due in this and some other cases to a flaw in the die, or, more frequently, to the letter being engraved over the impression of a vertical punch (see Pl. **XVI. 5**; **XIX. 14**).

P. There are no varieties of this letter, except such slight varieties as are due to the careless punching of the loop; an instance is shown in Series I, form 2 (cf. on William I, p. 137, no. 728, the last letter of the reverse inscription).[1]

R. This letter, similarly, has only varieties due to careless punch-work; a strange instance is shown in the Table (Series I, form 2), on which the loop has been punched away from the vertical stroke at the end of the tail, which is itself placed nearly at right angles to the vertical; see William II, p. 246, no. 187, the R in the moneyer's name (Pl. **XXXIV. 7**).

A coin of Henry I, p. 329, no. 276 (Pl. **XLVIII. 6**), has in the mint-name an instance of this letter with a true-formed tail with double curve (**R**), instead of the usual small crescent; traces of double-punching within the letter incline one to think that this must be made with a new tail-punch, but I have not met with this form elsewhere in this period.

S. How much of this letter was made by punches is not always quite clear; it shows considerable variety in form, due partly to difference in the finish of the central part of the letter, the usual practice being to form the letter of two small crescent and two small wedge punches. For lesser varieties see William I, nos. 11, 15, 45, 70 (Pl. **I. 10, 13**; **II. 16**; **III. 10**), also the **S** in **PꝤ✕S** throughout type VIII, where the crescent punch-marks overlap

---

[1] The fourth form of W should also be classed as P; see below, p. 246, no. 190, and *Errata*.

considerably owing to the small space within which the letter is enclosed. The following are the varieties figured in the Table:

Series I, form 2: not uncommon, *e.g.* William I, p. 16, no. 77, and p. 32, no. 175 (Pl. **IV. 3**; **VI. 14**).

form 3: William I, p. 136, no. 722 (a contemporary forgery).

form 4: William I, p. 18, no. 90 (Pl. **IV. 11**).

form 5: William I, p. 20, nos. 100, 101.

form 6: William II, p. 246, no. 190, a variety showing extreme carelessness of punch-work.

Series V, form 2: Henry I, type VII, London, Spirling (P. C. B. coll.).

form 3: Henry I, type IX, Sandwich, Wulfwart (W. C. W. coll.), Pl. **XLI. 8**.

Series VI, form 2: Henry I, p. 285, no. 58 (Pl. **XLI. 11**).

T. The upright of this letter appears as either a thin vertical punch, such as is used also for making initial crosses (Series I, forms 1, 2), or an ordinary thick vertical (Series I, form 3), or wedge-shaped (Series I, form 4); the cross-bar is commonly made by an ordinary vertical punch thickened and finished off in the usual way; sometimes by two wedge-shaped punches (Series I, form 4; Series II, form 2), a form which is in regular use in and after Series III. Series I, form 2, shows the way in which the top of the vertical is frequently left visible,[1] cf. William I, nos. 540, 559, 852 (Pl. **XVIII. 15**); form 4 may be seen on p. 4, no. 11 (Pl. **I. 10**); form 5 on p. 49, no. 251 (Pl. **IX. 8**), and William II, p. 222, no. 46 (Pl. **XXX. 2**).

The varieties of later series are due mostly to presence or absence of serifs to the upper bar, and the use of wedge punches for the bar or the engraving of a line. In Series V, form 3 shows again the top of the vertical punch, Henry I, p. 277, no. 36 (Pl. **XL. 4**).

V. At the beginning of the reign of William I the two strokes forming this letter are usually sloped towards each other at the lower end, but this letter soon becomes, like A, two parallel strokes, and therefore not distinguishable from A. The true V form (Series I, form 3) made with two long wedge-shaped punches

---

[1] See above, p. xlvii.

occurs on William I, p. 11, no. 62; p. 162, no. 869 (**Pl. XXIII.** 8), and a few other coins.

In Series IV form 1 is used throughout types II and III, and form 2, we have seen above,[1] is the true form which appears first on type IV, and continues (in variety with or without serifs) to the end of the period.

W. The Anglo-Saxon form, *Wen*, is used to express this letter throughout the whole period; for a short period in Series VI and VII the later English form, W, is introduced on the last two types of Henry I and the first type of Stephen, but the Anglo-Saxon form continues with it and survives it; the form W occurs only rarely on Stephen's first type, and apparently not at all on the remaining types of his reign.[2]

The form used for *Wen* is not different from that of P except on a few coins of the first two types of William I, on which a wedge punch is used instead of the crescent punch (Series I, form 2). See p. 9, nos. 45, 46 (**Pl. II. 16**); examples of this are rare, and are probably accidental rather than intentional. Form 3 shows the large crescent punch used by mistake for the small crescent, see William I, p. 2, no. 3 (**Pl. I. 3**), and p. 52, no. 273; in form 4 the loop has been punched too close to the vertical, and gives the appearance of a swelling on the side of the vertical, see William II, p. 246, no. 190.[3]

X. The regular form of this letter is made with wedge-shaped punches; occasionally a cross is used in its place, as on p. 10, no. 53 (**Pl. III. 3**), a form figured in Series I, form 2; this form made with an ordinary upright and two wedge punches is always used on the three types of Series IV. In the new class of lettering the form varies considerably; the limbs are usually straight, sometimes thick, sometimes thin, either with or without serifs.

---

[1] p. xlix.
[2] Except in irregular issues (see below, pp. xcii ff.).
[3] This letter should have been read as P, and not W; the name is evidently Sperling.

DH, TH. The Anglo-Saxon form, Đ, remains in use on coins nearly to the end of the reign of Henry I; its last appearance is on the Bath coin of Henry I, type XIII, p. 295, no. 87 (Pl. **XLIII. 2**). The earliest appearance of TH as separate letters is on the Bristol coin of Henry I, type X, p. 285, no. 57 (Pl. **XLI. 10**). In the name of the mint, Thetford, the form Đ is earlier abandoned for the letter T; on Henry I's third type the Đ form is used, but on the fifth[1] and later types the name of the mint appears as TETFO, &c.

The regular form of the letter is form 1, Series I; it is made as D with the addition of a wedge-shaped stroke on either side of the vertical, each pointed towards the vertical; form 2 shows a variety with the wedges punched with broad ends towards the vertical, p. 25, no. 133; in form 3 a longer wedge has been punched through the loop instead of two small wedges through the vertical, William I, nos. 80, 96-8, 150, 166, 167, 170, 171, 173, 177, 178 (Pl. **IV. 14**; **VI. 13**). Form 4 is made with a small instead of a large crescent punch, p. 28, no. 148 (Pl. **VI. 3**). Form 5 is a typical punch-worker's error: the engraver has used the straight punch instead of the large crescent punch; it occurs on p. 27, nos. 144-6[2] (Pl. **VI. 2**), and p. 220, no. 37 (Pl. **XXIX. 10**).

In Series II the regular form is as that of Series I; on p. 257, no. 245 (shown more clearly on a Hunterian coin from the same dies) form 2 of this series is used; instead of two wedge-shaped impressions one only is made, that within the letter, the outer one being omitted. This becomes the regular form of Series III and IV; on the introduction of the new class of lettering in Series V, the cross-bar is carried right through the vertical.

Æ. On the first three types of William I the diphthong form figured in Series I, form 1, is frequently used, e. g. p. 42, no. 224 (Pl. **VIII. 10**); this is made by attaching a long wedge-shaped stroke to the letter E; a similar diphthong form, but made with a short, instead of a long, wedge punch, is also used, Series I, form 2, e. g. p. 16, no. 78.[3] Series I, form 3, which occurs on some coins of

---

[1] Of his fourth type I know no Thetford coins.　　[2] See below, p. cxxxvi.
[3] These two forms are not distinguished in the text of the Catalogue.

the earliest types of William I, becomes the only form in use at the end of the reign; it consists of the bars of an E attached to the second vertical of an A, the verticals of A being little or not at all inclined towards each other at their upper end; in appearance, therefore, it does not differ from IE. This form continues to the end of the old class of lettering; it is found on Henry I's third type, and on a coin of his fourth type in Major Carlyon-Britton's collection,[1] if the moneyer's name on this coin reads, as I think, **SIEPINE**. In Series VII the diphthong appears in the natural form, the bars of an E being attached to the second stroke of an A. I have found no instance of the use of the diphthong during Series V and VI,[2] but as in every form that occurs, except the first two forms of Series I and that of Henry I, type IV (when a new A form had just been introduced), the bars of an E are added to the form of A at the time in use, it is reasonable to suppose that in Series V and VI the form would be similar to that of Series VII; the change of form (which is in reality dependent on the form of A) comes most probably with the change from the old to the new class of lettering.

✠. The custom of placing a cross at the beginning of both obverse and reverse legends is continued throughout this period with few exceptions.[3] This initial cross is formed of a vertical, usually thinner than that of the ordinary letters, with a wedge-shaped stroke on either side of it. Sometimes the cross-bar is formed by a single stroke similar to the vertical, Series I, form 2. Form 3 shows a common variety with broad vertical like that of other letters; this form is always used in Series IV instead of that with a thin vertical. In the new class of lettering the forms

---

[1] *Num. Chron.*, 1901, Pl. III. 10.

[2] In *Num. Chron.*, 1901, p. 53, it is stated that IE represents Æ on type VII (Hks. 252; W. J. A. IV), but I can find no instance of the diphthong occurring on this type in this or any other form except the one quoted (*ibid.*, p. 288) from a sale catalogue.

[3] William I, p. 27, nos. 144–6 (reverse); p. 150, no. 805 (obverse); William II, p. 222, no. 46 (obverse); Henry I, obverse of all coins of type XI; also p. 313, no. 177 (obverse), and p. 314, no. 181 (obverse).

vary with or without serifs, and with straight or wedge-shaped limbs.

The use of compound, or ligatured, letters seems to begin in the fifth type of William I; the only earlier instance that I have met in this reign is **NN** in type I (p. 8, no. 38, and p. 11, no. 59); in types V to VII they are not common, but in type VIII they are frequent, and continue in common use in the later reigns. They have no significance, and are evidently used merely for the saving of space or, sometimes, are due to an error of the die engraver. Occasionally as many as three letters are run together, e.g. **ER** on p. 223, no. 52, &c., **NM** on p. 153, no. 823.

Order of Types.

The following Table summarizes the evidence for the arrangement of the types. On the left, the types are bracketed by the Epigraphical Series, and on the right by Mules (with references to numbers on pp. xxxix ff.) and Finds. The numbers of Hawkins's plates are inserted between the brackets of Mules and Finds in order to render the table more clear. The Nottingham, Bute, Winterslow, and Colchester finds are omitted from this table (see pp. xxvii ff. and Table of Finds). The brackets of Finds are dotted to show types absent from the finds.

For the following notes see references on p. lxvii.

[1] Classification of types of William I and II in *Num. Chron.*, 1902, pp. 211 ff., and *Brit. Num. Journ.*, vol. ii, pp. 130 ff.; and classification of types of Henry I in *Num. Chron.*, 1901, pp. 42 ff., and of Stephen in *Brit. Num. Journ.*, vol. viii, p. 386.

[2] Overstruck on type I and on coin of Harold II (p. xxxiv, nos. 1, 2).

[3] Overstruck on type IV (p. xxxiv, no. 4).

[4] Overstruck on type IV (p. xxxiv, no. 5).

[5] Overstruck on type VI (p. xxxiv, no. 6).

[6] Overstruck on type VII (p. xxxiv, no. 7).

[7] Overstruck on William I, type VIII (p. xxxiv, no. 8).

[8] Overstruck on William I, type III, and on William II, type I (p. xxxiv, nos. 10, 11).

[9] Overstruck on William II, types II and III (p. xxxv, nos. 12, 13).

[10] Order of types II and III doubtful, see p. liii.

[11] Evidence of letters (**A, h, V**, &c.), see p. xlix.

[12] Order of types VII and VIII doubtful, see p. liv.

[13] Order of types III and IV doubtful, see p. lv.

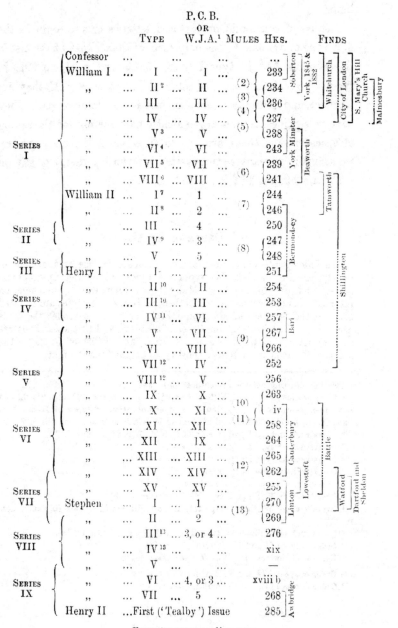

		TYPE	P.C.B. OR W.J.A.¹	MULES	HKS.	FINDS
	Confessor	...	...	...	...	
	William I	I	I	...	233	Soberton / York, 1845 & 1882 / Whitchurch / City of London / S. Mary's Hill Church / Malmesbury
	,,	II²	II	... (2)	{234	
	,,	III	III	... (3)	{236	
	,,	IV	IV	... (4)	{237	
	,,	V³	V	... (5)	{238	
SERIES I	,,	VI⁴	VI	...	243	York Minster / Beaworth
	,,	VII⁵	VII	...	{239	
	,,	VIII⁶	VIII	... (6)	{241	
	William II	I⁷	1	... 7)	{244	Tamworth
	,,	II⁸	2	...	{246	
SERIES II	,,	III	4	...	250	Bermondsey
	,,	IV⁹	3	... (8)	{247	
SERIES III	,,	V	5	...	{248	
	Henry I	I	I	...	251	Stillington
	,,	II¹⁰	II	...	254	
SERIES IV	,,	III¹⁰	III	...	253	
	,,	IV¹¹	VI	...	257	Bari
	,,	V	VII	... (9)	{267	
	,,	VI	VIII	...	{266	
SERIES V	,,	VII¹²	IV	...	252	
	,,	VIII¹²	V	...	256	
	,,	IX	X	... 10)	{263	
	,,	X	XI	... (11)	{ iv	
SERIES VI	,,	XI	XII	...	258	Canterbury / Battle
	,,	XII	IX	...	264	
	,,	XIII	XIII	...	{265	
	,,	XIV	XIV	... (12)	{262	Lowestoft
SERIES VII	,,	XV	XV	...	255	Watford / Dartford and Sheldon
	Stephen	I	1	... (13)	{270	Linton
	,,	II	2	...	{269	
SERIES VIII	,,	III¹³	3, or 4	...	276	
	,,	IV¹³	...	...	xix	
	,,	V	...	...	—	
SERIES IX	,,	VI	4, or 3	...	xviii b	
	,,	VII	5	...	268	Awbridge
	Henry II	First ('Tealby') Issue			285	

For notes see preceding page.

For this attribution of eight types to William I and five to William II there seems considerable probability, though there is no definite evidence. It rests mainly on the proportion of types to the years of the reign and a comparison with that of other reigns.[1] Many other arguments have been and might be produced in favour of this division, but they are all conjectural and open to serious objection. That the first type issued after the accession of a Norman king would necessarily be in profile[2] cannot be maintained in the face of the strong evidence in favour of placing the full-face type (Hks. 251) at the beginning of the reign of Henry I. It might be considered satisfactory to divide the types at a point where no mule exists, in which case the only variants to the present attribution are to draw the line before or after Hks. 243, or before or after Hks. 250, and none of these divisions gives so satisfactory a proportion; but, on the other hand, mules exist not only with an obverse of Edward Confessor and reverse of Harold II,[3] but even with an obverse of Edward Confessor and the reverse of William I's second type (see below, p. 13).

The 'Paxs' type has been assigned to a date within the period 1082-7 on the evidence of the Durham coinage (*Num. Chron.*, 1901, p. 183), but the charter by which the Durham coins were dated is spurious (see Davis, *Regesta*, vol. i, no. 148). If the use of the word *Pax* in the design of the coinage could be supposed to have any reference to the condition of the country, the only period in which the issue of the 'Paxs' type by either William could reasonably be placed would be during the last two years of the reign of William I, that is to say, after the Danes abandoned their scheme of invasion in the autumn of 1085. But no such meaning can be attached to the use of *Pax* as a design for the coinage when that design was the only one issued by the

---

[1] See *Num. Chron.*, 1912, pp. 103-4, where it is shown that there seems to be an average duration of between two and three years for each type.

[2] *Brit. Num. Journ.*, vol. ii, p. 137.

[3] *Num. Chron.*, 1905, Pl. VIII. 31.

unfortunate Harold II,[1] whose succession was so hazardous as to require indecent haste in the burial of the late king and in his own coronation ceremony; who came to the throne with an invasion already preparing in Norway, and in face of the certainty of armed opposition from Normandy and the probability of risings in Northumbria, if not in other parts of the country; who was no sooner crowned than he made ready for war, and defeated one enemy only to meet his death immediately after at the hands of another.

The dating of the types is also conjectural and can only be based on the proportion of types to the number of years of the reign. It is certainly noteworthy that these and other reigns seem to show an average duration of two to three years for each type,[2] and perhaps two or three years was the usual period for a type to run; but it is difficult to put so short a limit to the first type of Stephen, which there is good reason to suppose was in issue at the time of his captivity in 1141.[3]

A theory of the triennial issue of types has been based on the evidence of a tax called *Monetagium* or *Monedagium*, which is mentioned in Domesday[4] and in the Charter of Liberties of Henry I[5] (1100); a parallel has been found between this tax and the *Monetagium* of Normandy,[6] a triennial hearth-tax granted to the people by Duke William, probably in or shortly before 1080, as a concession in exchange for the ducal privilege of debasing

---

[1] See Ramsay, *Foundations of England*, vol. ii, pp. 2-3. But this type was not originated by the Confessor, for the coins with his obverse which bear this reverse type are clearly 'mules' struck in the reign of Harold. The type must have been issued by Harold.

[2] See *Num. Chron.*, 1912, pp. 103-4.

[3] See below, p. lxxv.

[4] 'Aluredus nepos Turoldi habet 3 toftes de terra Sybi, quam rex sibi dedit, in quibus habet omnes consuetudines praeter geldum regis de Monedagio' (*Domesday*, fol. 336 b (Lincoln)).

[5] 'Monetagium commune quod capiebatur per ciuitates et comitatus, quod non fuit tempore regis Eadwardi, hoc ne amodo sit, omnino defendo' (*Charter of Liberties of Henry I, 1100*).

[6] *Num. Chron.*, 1893, p. 131; 1901, p. 14; 1902, pp. 209 ff.; *Brit. Num. Journ.*, vol. ii, p. 92 (from Ruding, vol. i, p. 163, note 2); vol. viii, pp. 114-9.

the coinage ; and from this it is concluded that the English coin-types were issued triennially. But no parallel exists;[1] the Norman tax was viewed as a concession from Duke William to the people, the English tax was evidently one of King William's impositions, as its removal by Henry I was one of this king's concessions to the people ; the Norman tax was levied in exchange for the debasement of the coinage, a baronial privilege not exercised by the English kings ; the Norman tax was triennial and we have no reason to assume the same of the English tax ; the tax could not possibly be referred to the change of types of the coins, nor, if it could, would it make the change triennial, but, if a parallel with the Norman tax existed, it would stop the change of types altogether. The tax was, as Sir H. Ellis[2] says, probably identical with the payments *de Moneta* which are mentioned in Domesday at several mint-towns.

Coincidences of types with current events are also misleading, as has been shown above with reference to the 'Paxs' type; similarly, the 'Cross voided' type of William II, which usually has two stars on the obverse, has been connected with the appearance of a comet in the year 1097,[3] a date at which the fourth type was probably in issue, but this 'Two Stars' type has now been shown to be the third type of the reign,[4] and was therefore certainly out of issue before the comet appeared. The coinage, or absence of coinage, of any mints is quite untrustworthy as a means of dating the coins; at Bath, for example, no coins are known of the reign of William II, and it might naturally be supposed that the destruction of the city by fire in 1088 put an end to the working of its mint; but a notification of William II, which is assigned to the period 1089 to January 1091, grants to St. Peter of Bath, Bishop John and his successors, in alms for the augmentation of the see, the whole city of Bath, ' with all customs and a mint and

---

[1] See *Num. Chron.*, 1912, pp. 98 ff.

[2] *Introduction to Domesday Book*, p. lv (folio ed.), note 9.

[3] *Brit. Num. Journ.*, vol. ii, p. 179.

[4] See *Num. Chron.*, 1913, pp. 402 and 411. An arrangement since adopted by Major Carlyon-Britton in *Brit. Num. Journ.* (see vol. viii, p. 62).

toll';[1] clearly the mint was still in existence, probably too in operation. The dating of the types must therefore be left in uncertainty, admitting that an approximate period of two to three years is the probable duration of each type.

The monetary inquiries of 1108 and 1125 and the possibility of assigning certain types to these periods are discussed below, pp. cliv f.; there seems to be some support in these dates for the attribution of a period of about two and a half years to each type. Some additional evidence of the order of the types may be found in the statement of William of Malmesbury with regard to the incising of coins (see below, p. cxlviii).

IRREGULAR ISSUES.

The coins above described represent the regular issues of currency from 1066 to 1156 or 8;[2] such coins as can be shown to be forgeries of these regular issues, struck by the moneyers in base metal or of light weight for their own profit, are reserved for consideration in connexion with the control and organization of the mint (see below, pp. cxlix ff.). The coins here described as 'Irregular Issues' comprise special issues of particular mints which differ, for some known or unknown reason, from the regular types of the reign; they may belong to the ordinary currency of the period or they may have been issued by some authority other than the king, whether privileged by royal grant or usurping the privilege unlawfully.[3] They differ from the regular issues in having the usual obverse or reverse design altered or vitiated in some way, or, while conforming to a regular type, bear an obverse inscription other than the name and title of the king. With one exception these all belong to the reign of Stephen.[4]

---

[1] Davis, *Regesta*, vol. i, no. 326.

[2] See above, p. xi, note 1.

[3] The privileged ecclesiastical issues of Canterbury, York, Bury St. Edmunds, &c., are not differentiated from royal issues, and have therefore not been reserved for separate treatment.

[4] The type used for inscriptions of irregular coinages does not always accurately represent the original.

One coin of the reign of William II needs special mention. It is published and illustrated in *Brit. Num. Journ.*, vol. viii, pp. 83 ff. In obverse and reverse design it conforms to the second type of William II ('Cross in Quatrefoil' type) but bears the following inscriptions:

Obv. ΠΕΡΙΓΓΕΝR✠ (or, as in *op. cit.*, ✠LΕΡΙΓΓΕΝR Ε✠ ?).

Rev. ✠HRVEOVONRV·ÐΓO

It weighs 18 grains and is apparently of good silver. Major Carlyon-Britton shows reason for attributing this coin to Llewellyn son of Cadwgan; the obverse inscription, though the first letter is not clearly legible, seems to be intended for Lewillen, or Lewelin, as the name is written in the *Annales Cambriae*, and there is likelihood in the reading of the mint-name RV·ÐΓO as Rhyd y Gors, or Ryt Cors, as it appears in *Brut y Tywysogion*.

From the Chroniclers we learn that in the reign of Stephen the barons had mints in their castles and issued their own money;[1] and that forgery produced a coinage so light and debased that in ten or more shillings the value of twelve pence could scarcely be found;[2] also, that in 1149 Henry of Anjou, when he invaded England, struck a new coin which obtained the name of the Duke's money, and that not only he but all the magnates, bishops, earls, and barons, made their own money, but when

---

[1] 'Castella quippe per singulas provincias studio partium crebra surrexerant, erantque in Anglia quodammodo tot reges, vel potius tyranni, quot domini castellorum, habentes singuli percussuram proprii numismatis, et potestatem subditis, regio more, dicendi juris' (William of Newburgh, Rolls Series, no. 82, vol. i, p. 69; sub anno 1149).

[2] The statement in W. Malm. is: 'Jamque caritas annonæ paulatim crescebat; et pro falsitate difficultas monetæ tanta erat ut interdum ex decem et eo amplius solidis vix duodecim denarii reciperentur. Ferebatur ipse rex pondus denariorum, quod fuerat tempore Henrici regis, alleviari jussisse; quia, exhausto prædecessoris sui immenso illo thesauro, tot militum expensis nequiret sufficere' (a. 1140; Stubbs (Rolls Series, no. 90), vol. ii, p. 562).

the Duke came (on which occasion it is not quite clear), he put down the coins of the greater part of them.[1]

There are many coins which vary in legend or design from the regular issues of the reign, and which from their occurrence in finds of the normal coinage or for other reasons must be assigned to this period. It is therefore natural to suppose that some of these represent the baronial issues above referred to, but there is great difficulty in so assigning them, owing partly to the indefinite information that is given us by the Chroniclers of the nature of this irregular coinage. In the first place it is evident from the passage in William of Newburgh quoted above that some barons *usurped* the privilege of coining and presumably made profit by issuing light and base coins; in this case we should expect their coins to imitate the types and inscriptions of the current coinage of the realm, and to differ from it only in quality and weight and perhaps in roughness of execution; for by altering the design they would defeat their object of passing their base issues into currency. It is therefore natural to look for baronial coins of this class among the coarse and light coins described under the regular issues of the reign, and perhaps they may be illustrated by such coins as nos. 142, 143, 144 of the Catalogue, pp. 356-7, and others (*e. g.* the coin attributed to Watchet, p. 352, no. 113) which combine with lightness of weight a coarseness of fabric and an irregularity of lettering which seem to show that the die-engravers were not in possession of the punches which were used by the officials of the royal mint. But rom the coins themselves it is evident that not only did Duke Henry and his mother, the Empress Matilda, strike coins, as we should expect, bearing their own names, but others—bishops, barons, &c.—issued a named coinage; such, for example, are Bishop Henry (presumably of Winchester), Eustace FitzJohn, Robert(?), William (?), and others. As these coins bear the names of their issuers and usually differ in type from the regular currency, it is possible that the privilege of coining was actually bestowed by the King or the Empress on some of their followers; for a usurp-

---

[1] Roger of Hoveden (Rolls Series, no. 51), vol. i, p. 211.

ing authority would be likely to imitate the currency of the realm in order to command a wide currency for the imitations it issued. Further, the circumstances of the Civil War, and especially the events of the year 1141, make it probable that the authority of the royal mint was to some extent impaired, and that the control of some of the more distant provincial mints, especially in the North and West, lapsed during part of this reign.

The identification of the coins is very uncertain, and it seems therefore desirable, having determined, so far as possible, which coins belong to the regular currency and in what order they may be placed, to deal separately with all the coins that differ from these types, and arrange them so far as possible in groups, for the purpose of deciding the locality and authority that issued them. The order in which the varieties are described is one of convenience; it is impossible to make any scientific classification in our present lack of knowledge of the time and place of issue of the majority of them. They are grouped in the following classes :

    I. Coins struck from erased obverse dies.

    II. Coins with inscription PERERIL.

    III. Issues bearing the king's name, of uncertain attribution.

    IV. Issues bearing the king's name, of certain, or probable, localities: A. Midland Counties; B. Eastern Counties; C. Scottish or Border Counties ; D. York and district.

    V. Coins not issued under the king's name.

It has been assumed above that the currency of Stephen's reign may be divided into seven types, the order of which has been determined on the evidence of Finds, Mules, and Epigraphy (see p. lxvii), but some of these types, notably III, IV, V, are known to us by so few specimens that it is not possible to be certain that each one represents a distinct type rather than a variety of another. Of the first two types there can scarcely be any doubt, the evidence of finds and mules being sufficiently strong to define them as the first two types of the reign, and similarly the last type is assured by its occurrence with Henry II's coins in the Awbridge find; the intervening types are very uncertain.

There is reason to suppose that the duration of the first type of this reign was longer than usual. It was shown above that it was not unlikely that the types were changed on the occasion of some assay or examination corresponding to the Trial of the Pyx, and that this took place at more or less regular intervals of two or three years (see pp. xii ff.), but, though the imitation of the first type of Stephen by the Empress Matilda in her own coinage does not necessarily show that the issue of this type continued till 1139,[1] the fact that the majority of the irregular coinages of the reign copy the obverse or reverse design of the first type makes it probable that this type was still in issue, or at least prevalent in currency, as late as 1141, the time of the king's imprisonment and the greatest confusion in the country.[2] Nor is it unlikely that the civil wars threw the mint organization out of gear, and that an examination of the coinage was thus impossible, and the first type therefore issued for a longer period than usual. Nevertheless, the regular coinage of the reign retained its standard weight and fineness, and light or base coins are not more frequent in this than in the preceding reigns; such as there are may be explained as the fraudulent work of the mint officials, or in some cases as the imitations of baronial mints. The tradition quoted by William of Malmesbury (see p. lxxii, note 2), that Stephen reduced the standard of the coinage, is therefore not supported by the evidence of the coins.

---

[1] If the issue of the second type had commenced in the preceding year, coins of the first type would probably still be the prevailing currency, and would therefore be more likely to be imitated by Matilda than the type which was actually being issued at the time of her landing. The use of this type again by Henry of Anjou might be due to his continuing the type adopted by his mother.

[2] Cf. *Brit. Num. Journ.*, vol. vii, p. 42.

I. COINS OF TYPE I STRUCK WITH ERASED OBVERSE DIES.

The following coins are known :[1]

Mint.	Reverse Inscription.	Form of Erasure on Obverse.	Wt.	Provenance, &c Notes.
3ristol	**VRDAN BR S:**	Series of cuts, vertical and horizontal.	23·2	B. Roth (Ra sale, lot 602 Dartford find, **Pl. LVII.**
,,	..	,,	20·2	W. C. Wells same reverse perhaps obver as preceding).
orwich	**✠ALFPAR D:ON:NOR**	Plain cross from edge to edge.		B. Roth and I Carlyon-Britto merly Capt. D These two co from the sam
,,	**FPAR D:ON[**	Plain cross from edge to edge, and additional small cross in second and fourth angles.		Nottingham M (from Nott find, 1880).
,,	**✠OT A:O [ ]P:**	From same obverse die (with erasure) as preceding.	fragment	,,
,,	**✠EDS[ ] N:NOR**	Plain cross from edge to edge.	17·5	H. M. Reynold Nottingham 1880).
,,	**✠OT RE:O N:NOR**	..		P. W. P. C Britton (f Hilton-Price).

[1] This and subsequent lists omit coins of which the readings are quite un

Mint.	Reverse Inscription.	Form of Erasure on Obverse.	Wt.	Provenance, &c., and Notes.
Norwich	✠WALTIE R:ON:NO	Plain cross from edge to edge.	21·1	British Museum, no. 229. **Pl. LVII. 2.** Another from same dies in P. W. P. Carlyon-Britton collection. Others (from different dies) in Nottingham Museum (from Nottingham find, 1880) and B. Roth collection.
Norwich?	VSTAL E:ON:H	Plain cross from edge to edge, and additional small cross in second (?) and fourth angles.	15·0	H. M. Reynolds (from Nottingham find, 1880).
Nottingham	✠SPEIN:O N:SNOT:	Small cross on king's face. The cross varies in form and position, but usually has limbs more or less patté; sometimes a pellet is added in one angle.	14–17	Several specimens. Some from Nottingham and Sheldon finds. British Museum fragment, no. 229 A, and coin from Evans coll., p. 410, no. 229 B. **Pl. LVII. 3, 4.**
Stamford	✠LEFSI:O N:STAN: Pellet on each limb of reverse cross.	Small cross on king's shoulder and stroke through shaft of sceptre.	14·8	B. Roth (Rashleigh sale, lot 605). **Pl. LVII. 5.** Another from same dies (a fragment, 13·8 grs.) in W. C. Wells collection. Mr. W. C. Wells has also a coin (17·7 grs.) struck from the same dies before the erasure of the obverse die and another from same obverse and a reverse of ordinary type (15·2 grs.).

Mint.	Reverse Inscription.	Form of Erasure on Obverse.	Wt.	Provenance, &c., and Notes.
Thetford	✠B[ ]WI :ON:TEF	Plain cross from edge to edge.	15·7	British Museum, no. 230; and, from same reverse (and perhaps obverse) die, Sotheby sale, July 26, 1911, lot 553. **Pl. LVII. 6.**
York	✠MARTIN :ON:EVE Coin of very rough work; bust to l. without sceptre.	Two parallel cuts from upper to lower edge.		B. Roth. **Pl. LVII. 7.**
Uncertain Mint (Canterbury?)	✠ BE EAME	Cross on king's shoulder. The shaft of the sceptre is ornamented with two fleur-de-lys set end to end.	20·6	British Museum, no. 231 (Montagu sale, lot 335; from Toplis collection and Nottingham find, 1880). **Pl. LVII. 8.**

Coins of this type were in the following finds:

Nottingham (uncertain number).
Dartford (1 penny).
Sheldon (10 pennies, 3 halfpennies).

It was suggested by Archdeacon Pownall (*Num. Chron.*, 1862, pp. 189–90), when publishing a coin of Stephen struck with a defaced or erased obverse die, that it might be assigned to the Empress Matilda, assuming that for the purpose of saving time and expense in making new dies she made use of Stephen's dies that fell into her hands during the captivity of Stephen in 1141. Though we now know that coins were struck bearing the Empress's own name, this attribution might still be tenable except for the mints at which these defaced coins were issued; coins are described above of Norwich, Thetford, and York, places which did not fall into the hands of the Empress.

In *Num. Chron.*, 1881, pp. 42 ff., the same writer comments on a large number of these coins which were published by Toplis in his account of the Nottingham find (*ibid.*, pp. 37 ff.) and, abandoning his former attribution to the Empress, he finds in them the 'Duke's Money'[1] of the Chroniclers, that is, money struck by Henry of Anjou during one of his visits to England. This theory is open to the same objection as the previous one, namely, that they were issued from mints over which the Duke never had control.

In Hawkins's *Silver Coins* (p. 178) it is said that 'they were probably struck by a partisan of Matilda, who wished to use Stephen's dies, but not to acknowledge Stephen's title'; this is the view that has since been generally held, and in his account of the Sheldon find (*Brit. Num. Journ.*, vol. vii, pp. 59 ff.) Mr. Andrew adopts this view and attributes them to various barons, those of Nottingham to William Peverel, those of Thetford to Hugh Bigod, &c.

It is noteworthy, and is elsewhere observed, that the obliterating cross or lines are cut or punched on the die;[2] in proof of which several duplicates exist, and of the Stamford mint coins are known struck from the same obverse die both before and after the erasure was made upon it. It is not therefore a method of stamping coins of light weight or base metal in order to pass them for currency or reject them from it. That the object was to erase the king's figure from the die is not so clear; on the Nottingham and Stamford coins the erasing cross falls not on the king's face, but on his shoulder, and on the York coin the die is cut on either side of the king's bust. One may reasonably doubt whether any of the barons who usurped the privilege of coining would have hazarded the possibility of passing his coins into currency by deliberately obliterating the obverse die for the sake of marking his independence

---

[1] See above, p. lxxii.

[2] From the regular form of the cross on some coins, notably those of Nottingham and Thetford and some of Norwich, I am inclined to believe that a punch was used; on others the erasure has evidently been made with a cutting instrument.

of the king;[1] if he succeeded in capturing coining dies he would
be glad to make profit by issuing coins which could be easily
passed into currency. There seems more reason to suppose that
the object of obliterating the dies was to prevent their use in case
of their falling into unscrupulous hands, in just the same way as
dies at the present day, if kept, are obliterated by some mark upon
their surface in order to prevent their use for forgery.[2] I am
inclined to believe that it was by royal authority that the dies were
obliterated; the erasure of the obverse or standard dies would be
sufficient to put both obverse and reverse dies out of action, and
this may have been done at times when the mints were in danger
of falling into the enemy's hands. Nottingham, for example, was
in 1138 held by Peverel for the Empress, but he seems to have
come over to Stephen in 1139, at the time that Stephen ratified
Queen Matilda's treaty with Henry of Northumberland at Nottingham, for from this time until he surrendered his castle to the ·
Empress in 1141 as the price of his personal freedom, he is found on
the King's side.[3] The sacking of the town by Robert of Gloucester
in 1140 or 1141 might have caused the authorities of the mint to
obliterate their standard dies in fear of their falling into the Earl's
hands. Assuming the dies to have been obliterated for this purpose,
the question remains,—by whom were they put into use after the
obliteration? The majority of the coins are of low weight,
14–17 grains, and many certainly have the appearance of being
of base silver; but some are undoubtedly of good weight: a
Bristol coin, if the Rashleigh Sale Catalogue is correct, weighs
23·2 grs., the Norwich coin in the British Museum weighs 21·1 grs.,
and the British Museum coin of uncertain mint weighs 20·6 grs.; some,
too, are certainly of excellent silver, as, for example, the Norwich

---

[1] Mr. Andrew sees in the Nottingham crosses a personal badge; I think
that, even if this is not too early a date for such a use of heraldic devices,
a baron would not impose his badge upon a die in such a way as to deface the
coins which he hoped to pass into currency.

[2] See *Num. Chron.*, 1915, pp. 105 ff.

[3] Ramsay, *Foundations of England*, vol. ii, p. 394. But Peverel's position is
very difficult to follow (see *Brit. Num. Journ.*, vol. vii, pp. 61 ff.). The date
of the sacking of Nottingham is also uncertain; 1141 seems the more probable.

coin mentioned above, which weighs 21·1 grs. While one would naturally suppose that the dies fell into the hands of the king's enemies, and were turned to good account by the issue of light and base coins, in spite of the erasure of the standard dies, one can hardly believe that so good a coin as the British Museum piece of Norwich was issued by a usurping authority. It is not impossible that, the king's enemies having succeeded in passing into circulation the light coins in spite of their defaced obverses, the king's own moneyers at other mints which had not been captured, or on the recapture of their implements, saved themselves expense by following the example of their enemies and bringing back into use dies which they had themselves erased.[1] The uneven quality of the coins of this series increases the difficulty of its solution, which is at present merely conjectural.

In *Brit. Num. Journ.*, vol. vii, p. 66, Mr. Andrew describes coins of Nottingham which have the obverse inscription curiously stamped out. As he points out, the marks are not uniform on coins from the same die; the obliteration was therefore not on the die itself. It occurs occasionally on the reverse instead of the obverse, and may perhaps be attributed to uneven flans or faulty striking rather than a deliberate obliteration of the king's name on the coins.

I have inserted here a coin of York in Mr. Roth's collection (Pl. LVII. 7); this differs from the other coins in being struck from dies of extremely rough workmanship, and perhaps is the work of a forger's dies, which had been obliterated by the two lines cut on the obverse, and again used for striking false coins.

---

[1] Or the contrary may have been the case, *i. e.* the king having ordered his own obliterated dies to be used in spite of the obliteration, barons were able, on getting possession of obliterated dies, to issue coins struck from them. But this is obviously less likely.

II. COINS OF TYPE I WITH OBVERSE INSCRIPTION **PERERIC** ETC.

The following coins are known:

Mint.	Obverse.	Reverse.	Wt.	Provenance, &c.
Bristol	+PERER	+TVRE BRI		Montagu sale, lot 361.
Bristol?	+PERE[	+TVRELI[		B. Roth.
Canterbury	+PERERI C:	+PILLEM: ON:LANP:	21·1	Brit. Mus., no. 232 Pl. LVII. 9.
,,	From same dies	as preceding.		B. Roth. Pl. LVII. 10.
Lincoln	+PERERI C:	+RAPVLF :ON:NILO:	20·8	Brit. Mus., no. 233 Pl. LVII. 11.
,,	From same dies	as preceding.		B. Roth.
,,	From same dies	as preceding.	19·2	Rashleigh sale, lot 633.
,,	+PERERI LM:	+SIPARD: ON:NILO:	20·8 (Rashleigh specimen) 19·0 (Sheldon specimen)	B. Roth (2 coins), Rashleigh sale, lot 634, Sheldon find (these coins are all from the same dies). Pl. LVII. 12.
London	+PERE[RI L:]	+AL EJ: ON:LVN		B. Roth, from same obverse die as following coins of Godricus.

Mint.	Obverse.	Reverse.	Wt.	Provenance, &c.
London	**✠PERERI C:**	**✠GODRIC VS:ONL V**	22·4, 22·7 22·0, 22·6	Brit.Mus.,no.234, Evans collection (below, p. 410, no. 234 A), H. M. Reynolds, Rashleigh sale, lot 635 (all from the same dies). **Pl. LVII. 13, 14.**
Stamford	**✠PERERI C:**	**✠LEFSI:O N:STAN C:**		B. Roth. **Pl. LVII. 15.**
Winchester ?	**✠PE[**	**✠GEFREI: ON░░NC:**		B. Roth.

Mr. Andrew[1] also mentions coins of Bedford, Oxford, and Wareham.

Coins of this type were in the following finds:

> Watford (2 coins);
> Nottingham (1 coin described);
> Sheldon (1 coin);
> Linton (2 coins).

This series of coins was first described by Rashleigh in his account of the Watford find (*Num. Chron.*, 1850, pp. 165 ff.), and from the resemblance of the name to ' Werewic ', or Warwick, they were attributed by him to the Earl of Warwick; Packe (*Num. Chron.*, 1896, p. 64) pointed out the anachronism of this use of a territorial title by itself, and suggested that the final C might represent ' Comes ', and supposed ' PERERI ' to be a blundered inscription that might perhaps be appropriated to Robert Ferrers, Earl of Derby. But it is no less impossible to attribute to the

---

[1] *Brit. Num. Journ.*, vol. vii, p. 81. Mr. Andrew informs me that he was mistaken in attributing PERERIC coins to these mints.

Earl of Derby than to the Earl of Warwick coins struck at so many mints, including London and Canterbury.

In *Brit. Num. Journ.*, vol. vii, pp. 81 ff., Mr. Andrew says: 'Obviously the only person in whose name money could have been issued at mints spread nearly all over the country—and the list would probably be extended if we had not to rely for our information on the mere accident of discovery—was either Stephen himself or the Empress Matilda. Stephen is ruled out as impossible, for his name and title have no break in their sequence, and so Matilda remains.' In the inscriptions PERERIC and PERERILM[1] he reads a lopped form of the word IMPERATRICIS, commencing in front of the king's face with a cross inserted by the shoulder in imitation of the current coins of Stephen. Apart from the difficulty that I find in the evolution, ingenious though it is, of this puzzling inscription from the title 'Imperatricis', I am unable to agree with Mr. Andrew's original proposition that coins struck at all these mints can be attributed to the Empress. Her career in England was, in brief, this: she landed at Arundel in 1139 (Sept. 30) and was given by Stephen a safe-conduct to Bristol. On Oct. 15 she moved to Gloucester. Her movement from the west dates from the battle of Lincoln (Feb. 2, 1141); Robert of Gloucester brought Stephen a prisoner to her at Gloucester, she sent him on to Bristol; she then advanced to Cirencester (Feb. 13), where she negotiated with Henry, Bishop of Winchester, the Legate (Feb. 16). On March 2 she met the Legate again at Wherwell, near Andover, and made terms for securing the throne; the following day she arrived at Winchester and was there blessed, the crown was handed to her, and she had herself proclaimed 'Lady and Queen' of England. For Easter (March 30) she went to Oxford, where Robert d'Oilly surrendered the castle to her. On April 7–8 a Synod at Winchester declared her 'Lady of England and Normandy'. On April 9–10 the deputation of Londoners arrived at Winchester and demanded the release of their

---

[1] He also gives the reading PERERILI. It appears to be a misreading of a Lincoln coin, on which the final letter of the obverse inscription is shown to be M by another specimen from the same dies.

king without actually opposing the decision in favour of Matilda; Matilda proceeded to Reading and St. Albans, and in the meantime efforts were made to win the Londoners; in May she was joined by King David of Scotland (presumably to assist at her coronation). A few days before June 24, the Londoners at last gave in and were induced to receive her; they conducted her to Westminster. She demanded a subsidy from the Londoners, refused a request to grant the good laws of the Confessor, and by her general demeanour roused hostility; in the meantime, Queen Matilda and William of Ypres had been raising an army in Kent, and on their approach to the city the Londoners, now thoroughly hostile to the Empress, opened the gates to them on June 24. The Empress escaped to Oxford, having already alienated the Legate by refusing to secure Stephen's sons in their father's continental possessions. Earl Robert failed to reconcile the Legate, and the Empress entered Winchester with an armed force (July 31) and besieging the Bishop was herself besieged in turn by Queen Matilda and William of Ypres; the Empress escaped (Sept. 14) through Ludgershall and Devizes to Gloucester; Earl Robert was taken prisoner and exchanged for Stephen. Stephen, set free at Bristol on Nov. 1, went to Winchester and London (Dec.), and held the Christmas crown-wearing at Canterbury; in March–April, 1142, he made a royal progress to York *via* Ipswich and Stamford. The Empress spent the winter, 1141–2, at Oxford, going at the end of March, 1142, to Devizes, whence she sent an embassy to her husband, urging him to come over; he sent over the young Duke Henry, who landed at Bristol in the late autumn. From September to December, 1142, the Empress was besieged by Stephen at Oxford, and at Christmas escaped by night to Abingdon and thence to Wallingford. After this she returned to her old quarters at Bristol and Gloucester, and ceased to play a prominent part in the war, which dragged on for the next five years; it was carried on by Robert of Gloucester on behalf of Henry of Anjou.[1] In February, 1148, she left England for ever.

---

[1] See below, pp. cxxvi f.

This bald statement of the movements of the Empress is sufficient to show the difficulty of attributing this series to her.

It is noteworthy that these coins seem all to be of good weight and of good metal, thus differing from most of the irregular issues of the period and notably from the coins bearing the title of the Empress; also, they are struck from dies evidently made in the regular way with the official coining-irons. These points, together with the issue of the coins from the London mint, show that, if issued by the Empress, they were issued after March 3, 1141, when she proclaimed herself ' Lady and Queen of England' and received the crown at Winchester. Though she was only admitted to London for a very few days, it is not beyond the bounds of possibility that in that time the mint officials had come over to her and accepted her orders for her title to be placed on the coins; Bristol was her own stronghold, and though there is evidence that coins were struck there for Stephen (Catalogue, p. 335, no. 2), the mint is likely to have fallen into her hands. At Winchester, too, coins might conceivably have been struck in her name after her acceptance as ' Lady of England'. At Canterbury, Lincoln, and Stamford the case is otherwise. Though the castle at Canterbury was in 1135 in the hands of Robert of Gloucester's men and they refused admittance to Stephen on his arrival in England, the mint of Canterbury was evidently in his hands at this period (Catalogue, pp.336-7, nos. 9-16), and there is no reason to suppose that it ever fell into the hands of the Empress; she never went there, and it was this part of the country that was most loyal to Stephen's Queen and raised the troops which she led into London on June 24, 1141. Lincoln Castle was apparently seized by Ralph of Chester in 1140; the town was sacked and burnt after the battle of Lincoln, but the castle seems to have remained intact and was surrendered by Ralph to Stephen in 1146; Matilda never held Lincoln, and there is no reason to suppose that she could ever have struck coins there. Finally, so far as we know, Stamford was always in the King's hands, and only surrendered to Henry in 1153.

The quality and the extent of the issue of PERERIC coins seem to show that they must for a period have constituted the true coinage of the realm, though it is difficult to explain the unintelligible title on coins which are of good quality and no worse executed than any other of the reign. During Stephen's captivity there was much confusion and uncertainty throughout the country; the barons secured their position by supporting the side which fortune seemed to favour or which offered them the highest price for their support, and some at least of the ecclesiastics, if we can accept William of Malmesbury's statement, attached themselves to the Empress after obtaining Stephen's permission to temporize. The position of a moneyer was as difficult as anyone's; the coins themselves which he issued constituted a public declaration of the side which he supported; and as soon as the King's imprisonment and the Empress's recognition by the clergy made it clear that, for a time at least, she would be on the throne, the issue of coins with Stephen's name on the obverse and the moneyer's name on the reverse was irrefutable evidence of his disloyalty to the Empress. If, on the other hand, Stephen should later obtain his freedom and regain the throne, to have struck coins in the name of the Empress would equally convict a moneyer of disloyalty to the King. I am therefore inclined to believe that the moneyers temporized as the clergy did, and that the inscription PERERIC was deliberately substituted for the King's name and was intended to be unintelligible then as it is to us. The coins are well struck, of good weight and of good metal, their circulation among an illiterate public would therefore not be deterred by the change of the obverse inscription, whereas, on examination of the coins, either party could be satisfied that they were not struck in the name of the other. London would probably still impose the form of die adopted in some, at least, of the provinces; and that fact would account for the uniformity of this meaningless title, a thing very difficult to explain on the theory that it is merely a blundered form of *Imperatricis*. It is curious that in the Danish coins with the inscription IOANSTREX, issued apparently during the struggle between Magnus and Swein for the throne of Denmark in 1044–7, we have a possible parallel to this use of a meaningless inscription[1] (see Hauberg, *Myntforhold og Udmyntninger i Danmark*, p. 49, and Pl. VIII, 1–7).[2]

---

[1] Sir Arthur Evans, in his presidential address to the Royal Numismatic Society (*Num. Chron.*, 1915, *Proceedings*, p. 37), threw some light on the origins of the PERERIE and IOANSTREX inscriptions.

[2] See also *Num. Chron.*, 1915, pp. 109 ff. I have recently had an opportunity of obtaining a clearer view of Mr. Andrew's opinion and argument. He argues that the Archbishop of Canterbury, after declaring himself on the side of the Empress, would have issued his coins under her name, and that Lincoln under Ralph of Chester, then her partisan, was also likely to issue her coins; further, that no less difficulty lies in assuming, for example, that a Bristol moneyer of this date was time-serving than in assigning a coinage of the Empress to such mints as Canterbury, Lincoln, and Stamford. He does not, however, attach much importance to the mints and thinks that the issue may prove more extensive than is at present known. It seems that we are agreed as to the date of the issue and in considering it the regular coinage of the realm for a few months in 1141. Mr. Andrew holds that Matilda's position was at this time considered so strong and her attainment of the throne so certain that she was generally accepted throughout the country and her coinage therefore issued by most of the principal mints; he sees in the obverse legend a corruption due to a misunderstanding by the die-engraver of an original order in which the title was written in abbreviated script.

Though perhaps I should modify the conclusion that I have drawn above from the mints of this issue, I have left unaltered what I had written before I fully understood Mr. Andrew's argument or appreciated how nearly we were in agreement in some respects; for I feel that the attribution to Stephen or to the Empress must at present be left an open question, and that the decision depends mainly on the historical evidence. From the numismatic point of view I cannot persuade myself to accept Mr. Andrew's interpretation of the inscription, but my own suggestion is not free from difficulty. On the historical side I doubt whether Matilda was even at this time so universally accepted or her power so extensive as this coinage would imply if assigned to her authority. That all hope of the King's release was never abandoned is shown most clearly by the obstinacy of the Londoners and by the attitude of the men of Kent who, even when the Londoners accepted the Empress, were enrolling themselves under Stephen's Queen. I do not agree with Mr. Andrew that the 'temporizing' of the clergy was merely a question of obtaining release from their oath for conscience sake. I think that they and many of the barons were safeguarding themselves for the future in view of a possible return of the King to power.

III. Issues bearing the King's Name, of uncertain attribution.

1. Similar to type I, but very large head either to l. or r., and of very coarse work.

Obverse.	Reverse.	Provenance, &c.
✠STEFENE Bust l.	**✠DAGVN:ON**	Hunterian collection. **Pl. LVIII. 1.**
II✠IFENE Bust l.	Illegible.	B. Roth.
]ST[Bust r.	**]OBERTVS· ON[**	P. W. P. Carlyon-Britton.

The only reason for separating these coins from the other coins of type I, among which specimens of rough work and low weight or standard have been included, is that they approach each other in style, and therefore come perhaps from the same locality. The direction of the bust to right or left is unimportant, it merely marks the hand of an ignorant engraver who omitted to reverse his model in copying it upon the die. Their very coarse work suggests forgery, and it is not unlikely that they represent some of the many imitations issued during the period of anarchy.

2. As type I, but the shaft of the sceptre terminates in an annulet from which issue seven rays or spikes and which has a pellet in the centre.

Obv. **✠STIEFN**   *Rev.* **✠RO BERT:ON:CA**

Wt. 20·1 grs. British Museum, no. 235. **Pl. LVIII. 2.**

The object that replaces the sceptre has usually been described as a horseman's mace; it certainly has that appearance, supposing the pellet in the centre to represent a spike foreshortened. On the other hand, we do not know that a spiked mace of this sort was in use at so early a date; it certainly does not appear on the Bayeux Tapestry, where horsemen are armed with lances, spears, swords, or truncheon-shaped clubs. Mr. Andrew has suggested that it represents the Host, radiate, elevated on a monstrance, and this is perhaps a more probable interpretation. The coin, which I believe is unique, is of good weight, and apparently of good metal; one is at a loss to account for so strange a variety in place of the usual sceptre. As regards the lettering and style there is nothing unusual about the coin except the rounded form of the letter C on the reverse.

3. As type I, but with a large rosette of pellets at the end of the obverse inscription.

Obv.   **TIEFN**   *Rev.*   **✠BRILTPIN[**
Wt. 16·6 grs.   British Museum, no. 236.   **Pl. LVIII. 3.**

The style and lettering of this coin are similar to those of the ordinary issues, but the weight rather points to the coin being a forgery, perhaps made by a mint official. One can give no reason for the stamping of the rosette of pellets on the die; cf. following coin and p. xcv, no. III 8 (*b*), also p. cxxi, Henry of Anjou, type I (*b*).

4. *Obv.* Bust to r., rosette of pellets in front of forehead; inscription, beginning above crown : **]ᴓTEF[**

Rev. Cross pattée, three pellets at end of each limb, in each angle a mullet of six points; beaded inner circle; inscription **]VBERT:ON[**
Wt. 16·3 grs. (good metal?).   British Museum, no. 237.   **Pl. LVIII. 4.**

This coin seems to be a contemporary imitation, with its obverse type copied from the first type and the reverse from the second type of the reign. The lettering is somewhat coarsely worked. It was found in a chalk pit at Winterslow, near Salisbury, with a few coins of Stephen, types I (1), II (2 pennies, 2 halves), III (1), and some baronial and irregular issues (see above, pp. xxx–xxxi). It therefore probably belongs to a later period than most of the irregular coins here described.

5. As type I, but with an annulet enclosing a pellet in place of each fleur-de-lys on the reverse, and an annulet at the end of each limb of the cross. The obverse has an annulet on the shoulder. **✠ᴓTIE[**
Reverse inscription blundered and uncertain. Wt. 15·9 grs. British Museum, no. 238.   **Pl. LVIII. 5.**

This coin is of very coarse work (more especially the reverse), and is no doubt a contemporary forgery of some sort, perhaps one of the many that are said to have been struck by the barons at their castles.

6. *Obv.* As type I, but with plain domed crown without fleurs; an annulet on the shoulder. ✠STIE[

Rev. On a short cross voided a quadrilateral with incurved sides and a pellet at each angle and in the centre. Beaded outer and plain inner circle. ✠OSBER[   ]✗:

Wt. 17·6 grs. (clipped?). British Museum, no. 239. Pl. LVIII. 6.

This coin came from the smaller Watford find (see above, pp. xxvi, xxvii), and must therefore be contemporary with the first type of the reign. Apart from the peculiarities noted, the style is not peculiar, and the lettering, though small (corresponding to Series VIII), is apparently worked on the die with the ordinary punches. It is impossible to account for this deviation from the regular reverse type; it cannot be treated as a separate type of the reign, or as a mule of the first and an unknown second type, because the Watford, Dartford, and Linton finds prove unquestionably which are the first two types of the reign, and this coin, occurring in the smaller Watford find, must have been in currency contemporarily with the first type, and previous to the issue of the second type. It is certainly an irregular issue of some kind, but by whom it was issued, and where, it is impossible to say.

7. As type I, but on the obverse the collar is represented by annulets instead of pellets; on the reverse the cross moline is voided and has an annulet in the centre and at the end of each limb.

Obverse.	Reverse.	Wt.	Provenance, &c.
✠STEFNE·R Ex	✠SANSON: ONANT	16·7 17·4	British Museum, nos. 240, 241. Pl. LVIII. 7.

Obverse.	Reverse.	Wt.	Provenance, &c.
✠STEFNE·R E✗	[✠S]ANSON :ONAN:	17·3	British Museum, no. 242.
✠STE░N✗	✠SANSON: O[	16·2	British Museum, no. 243. Pl. LVIII. 8.
✠STEFNE·R E✗	✠SAN░ONI OAN	16·0	H. M. Reynolds.
✠STEFNERE	✠SANSVN OANTOI	14·0	,,
✠S[	]NSONI: ON[	cut half-penny	B. Roth.
░STEFNE░░	✠Ⱳ[ ]NA NT		T. Bliss.

These coins all appear to be of very base metal. Four pennies and two halfpennies were found at Linton,[1] and three at Awbridge. In describing the Awbridge find (*Num. Chron.*, 1905, p. 361), Mr. Grueber put forward a proposal of Mr. Walters that the **A**, having a large upper bar, might represent a combined **TA**, and the coins be attributed to Taunton; in a review of this article in *Brit. Num. Journ.*, vol. iii, p. 345, Mr. Andrew, without expressing his opinion, adds that 'there is documentary evidence to prove that Sansun, the moneyer, was a tenant of the Bishop of Winchester, who, of course, was closely connected with the town of Taunton'. I do not find that the **A** in the mint name has a larger upper bar than the letter has elsewhere on these coins,

---

[1] I am indebted to Mr. Andrew for this information; one penny only was described in the publication of the find.

or on other coins of this reign, and I see no reason to imagine so harsh a combination of letters, and so unparalleled an obscuring of the mint-name. The natural attribution of the coins is to Southampton, which is variously spelt 'Hamtune' or 'Amtune' (cf. William·I, nos. 138, 369), but the occurrence of so many dies on which the first three letters of the mint read invariably **ANT** causes considerable doubt whether so unusual a form as 'Anton' for Southampton can really be intended.[1]

A curious feature of these coins is that the finds in which they occur show that, though they obviously use Stephen's first type for their model, they were not only in issue with the early currency of Henry II but were first put into circulation after, or very shortly before, the first type of Stephen was superseded at the royal mints. The only finds in which they have been recorded are the Linton and Awbridge finds; at Linton four pennies and two halfpennies were found with seven coins of Henry I's last type, forty of Stephen's first, and thirty-nine of his second type, and two coins with the PERERIC inscription; in the Awbridge find three specimens are noted, with thirty-one of Stephen's last issue and 110 of Henry II's first ('Tealby') coinage. Their occurrence in so late a hoard may possibly be due to the locality of the find, but none are recorded in the Watford, Dartford, or Sheldon finds. It seems therefore that they first made their appearance during the issue of Stephen's second type, and that their circulation continued into the reign of Henry II, when no other coins of Stephen's reign except those of his last issue found their way into a hoard.

One can only conjecture that these coins are the work of one of the magnates who was powerful at the period of Stephen's captivity, and held his power down to the end of the reign; but in face of the difficulty of determining the mint at which they were struck, it is impossible to hazard even a guess at the issuer of this money. There were several barons who strengthened their castles in the time of the civil war, and held them until the peace of

---

[1] On the other hand, 'Northantona' occurs in the Pipe Rolls.

Wallingford in 1153, and even later, till Henry II put them down in 1155; such were Henry, Bishop of Winchester, William Peverel, Roger of Hereford, Hugh of Mortimer, whose castles were all taken or demolished by King Henry in 1155, Ralph of Chester, who died in 1153, and many others. These coins, more than any other distinct class, fulfil the conditions which we should expect in a coinage issued by a baron who took advantage of the confusion of the country to usurp this privilege; they were probably first issued by him when the first type of Stephen was the most frequent in circulation, and that type was adopted as a model,— or, possibly, the similar issue of Henry (cf. Henry of Anjou, type I (b))—;[1] they were issued of base metal and light weight, the dies being worked by an engraver who was not a very skilful workman, and evidently was not in possession of the instruments used by the officials of the royal mint. Having originated his type, he continued to employ it even after the original ceased to be . issued and was superseded in currency by later types. The method is simply one of organized forgery, and cannot be distinguished from the work of an ordinary forger, except that perhaps the baron's control of the neighbouring country put him in an advantageous position for the circulation of his coins, and his military power secured him from punishment in case of discovery. From this point of view it is apparent that, as the obverse type and legend use a genuine coin as a model, so too on the reverse the legend as well as the type may be copied and may not represent the actual place of issue.

8 (a). As type I, but with long cross fleury superimposed on the cross moline of the reverse, dividing the legend.

Obv. ▨S[ ]EFNER✕

Rev. SIM VN ONE ▨ E

B. Roth, two coins from the same dies. **Pl. LVIII. 9.**

Perhaps of Exeter. These coins are of good work made with the usual punches of the period.

---

[1] But in this case there seems no reason to change the obverse title to that of Stephen.

(*b*) Similar, but a small quadrilateral fleury takes the place of the original cross moline of the reverse type.   .

Obv.   ]NER⁛ (retrograde).

Rev.   ⬛ODⴸ INⴸS OO⊟✗[

Wt. 16 grs. Sheldon find (*Brit. Num. Journ.*, vol. vii, p. 51, no. 74).

Of very coarse work, not made with ordinary punches. For the rosette of pellets cf. p. xc, nos. III 3 and III 4, and p. cxxi, Henry of Anjou, type I (*b*).

IV. Varieties grouped geographically.

A. *Midland Counties.*

(*a*) As type I, but having long cross fleury superimposed on the cross moline of the reverse, dividing the legend. Similar in type to variety III 8 (*a*) above, but quite different in style.

Obv. ✚·ST RE ANG

Rev. C ICD ENⴸ ERC A·

Wt. 17·3 grs. British Museum, no. 244, and B. Roth (same dies). **Pl. LVIII. 10.**

See *Brit. Num. Journ.*, vol. v, p. 440, and vol. vii, pp. 54 and 82, where these coins are assigned to Alexander, Bishop of Lincoln; there can be little doubt that they were struck at Newark.

(*b*) *Obv.* Rude head r., sceptre in front. *Rev.* Short cross voided, in each angle a bird.

Obverse.	Reverse.	Wt.	Provenance, &c.
✚STEPHAN VSRE✗	✚ⴸALCHEL IⴸVSDERBI	20·9	British Museum, no. 245. Pl. LVIII. 11.
,,	,,	22·0	H. M. Reynolds.
,,	,,	20·5	Rashleigh sale, lot 618.
,,	,,	21·3	P. W. P. Carlyon-Britton. Pl. LVIII. 12. B. Roth.
,,	,,		

All from same dies.

Base metal? Walkelin, the moneyer of Derby, is referred to in contemporary deeds.[1]

---

[1] See *Brit. Num. Journ.*, vol. v, p. 439, and Rashleigh sale catalogue, note on lot 618.

(*c*) *Obv.* Rude head r., sceptre in front (very similar to preceding variety). *Rev.* Short cross voided, over it a saltire fleury.

Obv. **✠STEPHANVSRE✠**

Rev. **✠·RAINALD·ONSTO·**

Wt. 14·9 grs. British Museum, no. 246.

Pl. LVIII. 13.

The reading of the mint is uncertain; it may be either **STO** (Nottingham) or **STV** (Stutesbery or Tutbury?), see *Brit. Num. Journ.*, vol. v, p. 440.

Of the three varieties above described and attributed to the Midland Counties, the first bears the same type as a variety, III 8 (*a*), of the indeterminate issues, but it differs from it in the very coarse fabric and poor weight of the coins. The lettering is very similar in style to that of the other two Midland varieties. These other two varieties are even more closely connected, for they are identical in style of design and lettering on obverse and reverse, the only difference being the placing of a bird in each angle of the cross in the Derby coins, and a fleured saltire over the cross on the Nottingham or Tutbury coin; the attribution of this coin to Nottingham or Tutbury must be left uncertain.

B. *Eastern Counties.*

(*a*) As type I, but of very coarse work, and having on the reverse a broad cross with a pellet at the end of each limb and in each angle, superimposed on the cross moline.

Obverse.	Reverse.	Wt.	Provenance, &c.
✠STEPHAN VSRE✠	**AILR⬚⬚V∅✠ ONLIN**	22·1	British Museum, no. 247, and B. Roth (same dies). Pl. LVIII. 14.
]EPH⬚N[ ] R[	**GLADEVIN[**	22·0	Sheldon find.

Obverse.	Reverse.		Wt.	Provenance, &c.
EPHA[　]	·ROGE[　　　]N		21·5	H. M. Reynolds, from Rashleigh sale, lot 616, and Dartford find, 1825.
IANVS·	NIN[	]VS✠O	21·7	British Museum, no. 248. **Pl. LVIII. 15.**
]REx	]✠ONL[		22·0	Rashleigh sale, lot 615, from Dartford find, 1825.

e coins seem to be of good silver and good weight; they obably all be attributed to the Lincoln mint; for their :semblance necessitates the attribution of them all to the int, which the reading of the first coin and the moneyer of nd show to be Lincoln.

s type I, but with a small broad cross superimposed on the cross)f the reverse.

:. ✠STIEFNE:R
:. ✠BALDEWI:ON:T:

Wt. 17·2 and 17·0 grs.　British Museum, no. 249, and H. M Reynolds (same dies).　**Pl. LVIII. 16.**

e coins seem to be of base metal; the style is rather less than that of the Lincoln coins above described, with which ily connected by the imposition of the broad cross on the type.　It is presumably of Thetford, where the same r's name occurs on regular issues of this reign.

C. *Scottish or Border Counties* (?).

(a) *Obv.* As obverse of type I of Stephen, bearing title of Earl Henry.

Rev. Cross crosslet, in each angle a cross pattée suspended from a crescent resting on the inner circle.

See Catalogue, p. 397.

Obverse.	Reverse.	Wt.	Provenance, &c.
✠И·ЕИСI:СО N	✠:WILEL:M: O░I:░	22·8	British Museum, no. 287.
Same die as preceding.	✠:WILEL:M: ОИСI:B (or Đ ?):	20·5	H. M. Reynolds. Pl. LIX. 1.
]ЕИСI:░ОИ	✠:WILEL:M: O░CI:░	23·0 pierced 17·6 clipped	British Museum, nos. 288, 289, from same rev. (and obv. ?) die.
✠ИЕИСI:СО░	✠[ ]EL:M:O ИCI:B (or Đ ?)	15·6 broken	British Museum, no. 290.
✠И:Е[ ]И	✠WILEL:I░ ░ (or Đ ?):	14·8 clipped	British Museum, no. 291.

A coin of the type of Stephen's first issue of distinct Scottish style (thus differing from similar coins of Henry of Anjou) may also be attributed to the Earl; it is illustrated in Burns, *Coinage of Scotland*, Pl. III. 24 A. The inscriptions seem to be ✠ҺЕN RICVS and ✠ЕRЕB[   ]D: It should probably be attributed to Carlisle, and was presumably struck by Earl Henry in virtue of his possession of the town between 1136 and 1139. The coin was found in the Bute hoard.

(*b*) Same type as (*a*) above.

Obv. ✠STIFENEⱶE

Rev. ✠:ⱲI:LELM:OꞍ:OꝹ (or B?)CI

> Wt. 21·0 and 19·3 grs. H. M. Reynolds and Rashleigh sale,
> lot 613 (same dies). Pl. LIX. 2.
>
> Attributed by Mr. Lawrence to Outchester (2½ miles south-east of
> Belford), where the find of the Earl Henry coins occurred.

(*c*) As type I of Stephen, but on the reverse a long cross voided is
superimposed on the cross moline.

Obverse.	Reverse.	Wt.	Provenance, &c.
✠STIFENEⱶ E:	✠ꝷI: LЕO: Ꞧ :OꝹ CꞰIT	19·9	British Museum, no. 250. Pl. LIX. 3.
✠STIEENEⱶ E:	✠ⱲI: LEL: Ꞧ :OꞍ: CꞰST:	21·5	British Museum, no. 251. Pl. LIX. 4.
]NEEH·∞·	]ⱶꞰN ∞Œ· E Œ[	21·5	H. M. Reynolds.

(*d*) *Obv.* As type I of Stephen, with star in field to r. of sceptre.
     Rev. As type I, with annulet at point of each fleur and at end of
each limb of cross.

Obverse.	Reverse.	Wt.	Provenance, &c.
✠STIFENEⱶ E	✠FOB▨▨▨:OꞍ DⱯNI.E:	15·5	British Museum, no. 252. Pl. LIX. 5.
Same die as preceding.	✠FOBꞍD:OꞍ: DⱯNI:		B. Roth.

A coin of the ordinary type of Stephen's first issue, but resembling these in style, reads:

Obv. ✠STEᏞNEⵗI:

Rev. ✠FOB▨ND:ON.DⴸNI.ꙅℳ

Wt. 15·2 grs. S. M. Spink (Rashleigh sale, lot 608).

Another, similar, in Nottingham Museum, reads:

Obv.]NEᏞᴥE:

Rev.]ND:ON:DⴸN[

(*e*) Similar to preceding (var. *d*), but the annulets on reverse take the place of the spikes of the fleurs, and an annulet occurs at the base of each fleur as well as at the end of each limb of cross. No star on obverse.

Obv. Illegible.

Rev. ✠▨IᴙDIᴙEDON:EI

Wt. 18·6 grs. British Museum, no. 253, and Nottingham Museum (same rev. (and obv.?) die).

Pl. LIX. 6.

The bulk of Earl Henry's coins (variety *a*) were found in Outchester. There is an obvious temptation to see in all these mint-readings of the first three varieties (CI:TH, OTHCI, OCCAIT, CAST) different forms of the name of this same place, Outchester, near Belford. At least one may confidently attribute them to this neighbourhood.

There seems no reason to doubt the attribution of variety (*a*) to Henry, the son of King David of Scotland, who was created Earl of Northumberland by Stephen in 1139. The obverse resembles in style the Scottish coinage, and the irregular broad flans correspond more to the Scottish than the English fabric; but their probable issue in the north of England brings them within the scope of the English coinage, and they are here described among varieties bearing Stephen's name in order to show their connexion with the other varieties. Variety (*b*) has the appearance of a mule from a reverse die of Henry of Northumberland and an obverse die with name of Stephen which belongs to the coinage of either variety (*c*) or variety (*d*). Apart from the more general resemblance of the inscription and type of this obverse to that of the two later varieties, the peculiarity of the form used for the letter R (**lʍ**), which I have not found on any but these coins, shows an intimate connexion between them.

Varieties. (c) and (d) are closely connected by the style and lettering of the obverse and, as above mentioned, more especially by the peculiar form of the letter R. The mint-readings of variety (c) are suggestive of Outchester; all the coins of variety (d), including the coin described above which differs only in style from Stephen's first type, bear a mint-name DVNI——, which seems likely to be Durham; var. (e) is closely similar to var. (d); the mint reads EI, which is quite uncertain.

The curious feature about these coins is the connexion of the coins of the varieties (c), (d), (e), which bear the name of Stephen, with those of variety (a) which bear the name of Henry, son of David, by means of the intermediate issue described as variety (b).

In January, 1136, King David crossed the border and took Carlisle, Wark, Norham, Alnwick, and Newcastle, but failed to capture Bamborough. Stephen, arriving at Durham on Feb. 5, saved this city from falling into David's hands, and by large concessions made peace, conferring on Henry the earldom of Huntingdon with Doncaster and Carlisle, the rest of David's conquests being restored. Henry did homage to Stephen at York, presumably on behalf of his English estates; he then followed Stephen to London to assist at Queen Matilda's coronation, where the precedence which was assigned to him caused great indignation, and the Earl of Chester was so offensive that it was some time before David allowed his son to return to the English court. In 1138 Henry was with his father's army, which invaded England and was defeated at the Battle of the Standard, when Henry was cut off after a successful advance on the wing and had to make his way independently to Carlisle. In 1139 a peace was arranged at Durham by Queen Matilda and ratified at Nottingham by Stephen, and Henry received from Stephen the earldom of Northumberland, with the exception of Bamborough and Newcastle, he withdrawing his authority from the lands of St. Cuthbert and of St. Andrew's, Hexham. Henry remained for Easter with Stephen and accompanied him in an expedition against Ludlow, when the King saved his life. In the following year we hear on his return to Scotland of an attempt on his life by the Earl of Chester, which was frustrated by the escort given him by Stephen. In 1147 we are told that the only district of England in the enjoyment of peace was that beyond the Tees, which was under the sway of Earl Henry. He was with his father at Carlisle, at Whitsun, 1149,[1] at the knighting of Henry of Anjou. He died in 1153.

The intermediate issue (var. *b*) must have been struck either by Stephen or by the Earl Henry. If it was struck by Stephen, his adoption of the type of the Earl's coinage must imply the capture by Stephen of some place in which the Earl's coinage was previously issued or current.[2] This presents two difficulties:

(1) What object would Stephen have in using the type of the Earl's coinage? In the event of one of the King's mints falling into the hands of one of the barons, one would naturally suppose that the baron would turn it to his profit by striking base coin with the King's die; the King, on the other hand, could not have any reason for using the Earl's die or copying his type, unless the people of that district were more familiar with the Earl's coinage and would more readily accept it than the current coin of Stephen.

(2) Did Stephen at any time capture a town in which Henry of Northumberland had his mint or issued his currency? The first invasion, that of 1136, was met by the arrival of Stephen at Durham, which saved the fall of the city—peace was immediately concluded without any advance of Stephen into the country held by the Scottish. The second, at the beginning of 1138, was a plundering raid which advanced as far as the Tyne, but with-

---

[1] See below, p. cxxv.

[2] The opposite case (that the coinage was originally Stephen's, and that Henry captured a reverse die and made an obverse of his own to pair with it) does not seem possible, because the coinage is more akin to the Scottish than the English, and is therefore supposed to have been originated by the Earl.

drew to Wark on Stephen's approach; Stephen, instead of attacking the invading army, made a counter-raid into Berwickshire, and hostilities were abandoned at Lent. The third invasion, in July of the same year, pushed through Durham into Yorkshire and ended in the defeat of the Scots at Northallerton; the Scots retreated, some being cut off on the way, but there was no serious pursuit.

Thus it is clear that Stephen did not on any of these occasions push a serious attack into the territory of the Scottish king or his son; his raid into Berwickshire in reply to the second Scottish invasion seems to have been a mere raid and not to have involved the capture of any towns. At the truce of 1136 David, in return for Stephen's concessions, gave up the country conquered by him in the North of England; but the coinage of Earl Henry is almost certain to have been struck by him after the grant of the earldom of Northumberland in 1139.

I am inclined to believe that Earl Henry in the first place issued a coinage in the name of Stephen. We know that after he received his earldom of Huntingdon in 1136 he paid homage to Stephen at York, and again in 1139, as Earl of Northumberland, he was attached to Stephen's court and fought for him at Ludlow. It is impossible to say by what right he issued coins—perhaps in view of his earldom of Northumberland; but the occurrence of his reverse type with an obverse bearing Stephen's name and title seems to me, for the reasons given above, to indicate that he began his issue in the name of Stephen and later replaced that name by his own.

In consideration of the very close connexion which exists between the five varieties of Class C, I am inclined to attribute all the coins of this class to the Earl of Northumberland, though such an attribution is of course of a conjectural and tentative nature. In this case the first issue of the Earl will probably be the coins of varieties (d) and (e), which imitate the coinage of Stephen both in type and inscriptions; the second issue will be variety (c), which shows a variety of the type and style of lettering

which approximates more nearly to that of his named coins; the
third issue will be the variety (*b*), where an original reverse type
is first used and his dependency on the English king still acknowledged; and the fourth and last the variety (*a*), on which the Earl's
name is substituted for that of Stephen. The greatest difficulty
lies in the obscurity of the mint-names upon all these coins; even
the attribution to Durham of the coins which I have suggested may
be the earliest struck by the Earl is not by any means certain;
though he may possibly have struck coins at Durham about the
year 1141, when his presence there is proved by his charter to the
monks of Coldingham (Lawrie, *Early Scottish Charters*, cxxxiii)
and his influence by the part he played during William Cumyn's
attempt to seize the bishopric (cf. *op. cit.*, pp. 366–70). But too
much importance must not be placed on the inscriptions of the two
varieties (*d*) and (*e*). The coins are all of light weight and apparently of base metal; this coinage therefore, by whomsoever it was
issued, seems to have been a usurped privilege akin to forgery,
and, as I showed above (p. xciv), a baron who was issuing a base
coinage would have no reason to put the names of his mint and
moneyer upon the coins, and the reverse inscription of his model
would be as likely to be copied as that of the obverse. In the
present instance, some coins of variety (*d*) have what seem to
be either ornaments or meaningless letters at the end of the
reverse inscription, and this may perhaps be explained as an
attempt to fill up a space where the coin that served as a model
could not be read. With the other issues the case is different: the
coins of the second, third, and fourth issues of the Earl, varieties
(*c*), (*b*), (*a*), are of good weight and apparently of good metal; the
issuer had therefore established a mint or mints upon a proper
basis, presumably by grant of the king. Whether these coins may
all be assigned to one mint is not certain; but they must all
presumably have been struck in the same neighbourhood, probably
in Northumberland. This theory then assumes that Earl Henry
usurped the privilege of coining and thus issued varieties (*d*)
and (*e*), that he later received recognition of the privilege and

acknowledged the suzerainty of Stephen by placing his name on his next issues (c) and (b), and that finally he issued coins of variety (a), bearing his own name and title.

The coin figured in Burns, *Coinage of Scotland*, Pl. III. 24 A, which I mentioned above (p. xcviii), is not included in this series which I have tentatively assigned to the Earl. I regard it as belonging to the earlier period, 1136–9, and assume that he copied the type not directly from Stephen but from the issues of David, which are identical with this in style (cf. *op. cit.*, pl. III. 24). The series of Earl Henry coins and the cognate issues with which I am here concerned were presumably struck after 1139. The possibility of the attribution of so many of the series to Outchester, the place where the find of the named Henry coins took place, is of some importance. It seems to me that the coins of the three issues (a, b, and c) are all liable to this interpretation.

It is necessary to emphasize the fact that the attribution of these coinages to the Earl is conjectural, and based upon the close connexion of varieties bearing the name of Stephen with the issue which bears the Earl's own name (ᴎЕᴎCI CON = HENRICVS : COMES ?). Failing this attribution, it seems necessary to assume that a central authority in the North of England controlled or supplied the dies for the coinages issued in Scottish border counties by Stephen and the Earl of Northumberland, in order to account for the unity of style and of peculiarity in detail which appears in the coinages of the King and Earl; or we must abandon the accepted attribution of the ᴎЕᴎCI CON coins to Henry of Northumberland. In *Num. Chron.*, 1895, pp. 110 ff., Mr. Lawrence[1] gave reasons for attributing them to Henry of Anjou, but one can hardly assign a series which seems to be of northern origin to the Duke, nor does it in any way fit into the series which can with little doubt be attributed to him; nor, even so, would there be less difficulty in the close connexion of an issue of the Duke with issues bearing the name of Stephen.

---

[1] He has since abandoned this theory.

D. *York and District.*

(*a*) As type I of Stephen, but of curious workmanship similar to that of the following varieties; the beaded inner circle of the obverse runs through the king's bust.

Obv. ✠HSEPEFETI⋊

Rev. ✠⧢I⊠SᏰ·ᏩHET⊙⊃A

Wt. 20 grs. H. M. Reynolds. **Pl. LIX. 7.**

Obv. ✠STIEFHEP▨

Rev. ✠⧢I✝SᏰ·ᏩHOT▨A

B. Roth.

(*b*) As type I of Stephen, but having a representation of the Standard or a horseman's lance (?) in place of the sceptre in the king's hand. A star in field to r.

Obv. ✠STIEFNER·

Rev. ✠VI▨DHESIOHEV:

Wt. 19·5 grs. H. M. Reynolds. **Pl. LIX. 8.**

Various inscriptions and ornaments. Wt. 14·5–19 grs. See Catalogue, pp. 386–7, nos. 254–9. **Pl. LIX. 9–14.**

(*c*) *Obv.* As type I of Stephen, but voided lozenge containing pellet in place of spike of lys on sceptre. ✠STIEH and ornaments.

Rev. Saltire fleury on cross pattée. Ornaments in place of inscription.

Wt. 17·2 and 15·5 grs. (chipped). British Museum, no. 260, and P. W. P. Carlyon-Britton. **Pl. LIX. 15, 16.**

(*d*) *Obv.* Two figures, male and female, facing each other, supporting between them a long sceptre fleury.

Rev. Cross fleury over thin saltire pommée; annulets in field.

Obverse.	Reverse.	Wt.	Provenance, &c.
✠STE ⅁I⏀⊖	Ornaments (annulets omitted in field).	17·8	British Museum, no. 261. **Pl. LX. 1.**
✠⅁TIE ENER ⊖	Ornaments.	17·3– 20·5	British Museum, nos. 262, 263; H. M. Reynolds; P. W. P. Carlyon-Britton; B. Roth, &c. **Pl. LX. 2–4.**

Variety (a) seems to form a step from the ordinary first type of Stephen to variety (b), which is commonly known as the 'Flag type'. The object held in the king's hand on coins of variety (b) has been supposed to represent the Standard which was borne into the battle at Northallerton. The Standard was a heavy mast bearing the three flags of St. Peter of York, St. John of Beverley and St. Wilfrith of Ripon, crowned by a silver pyx containing the Host, and was borne on a four-wheeled waggon. Possibly this represents the standard in miniature, or it may be merely a horseman's lance (cf. Demay, *Le Costume au Moyen Age d'après les Sceaux*, p. 158, fig. 179).

The reverse inscriptions on these 'Flag' coins appear to be more or less degraded copies of some common original, and, from Mr. Reynolds's coin above described, it appears that the original bore the mint-name of York; the attribution of these coins to York or its neighbourhood is confirmed by their resemblance in style, and in the ornaments employed, to named coins of Eustace and of Robert de Stuteville, which seem certainly to have been struck in or near York. Ingenious attempts have been made (by Packe in *Num. Chron.*, 1896, pp. 59 ff., and others) to decipher these reverse inscriptions, but such attempts do not seem likely to prove successful. During the civil wars, and especially in the period immediately preceding and during the captivity of Stephen, communication between London and the North must have been difficult, and probably the central control from London of the northern mint organizations was temporarily suspended. This would lead not only to variation of the usual type but to laxity in local mint administration, affording easy opportunity for the issue of light or base coins without risk of detection; the dies must have been engraved locally, and the reverse inscription seems to have been not accidentally but intentionally blundered and rendered illegible, so that the moneyer responsible could not be convicted by the presence of his name on the coins. If the object in the king's hand is the Standard, the coins were presumably issued in 1138, or shortly after, but it is not possible to be certain of this or to

explain the appearance of the strange ornaments in the reverse
inscription ; but I am inclined to think that the latter was a device
of the issuer for satisfying an illiterate public with the appearance
of the coin without incriminating his moneyer by engraving the
usual legend on the die. Mr. Andrew (*Num. Circ.*, 1914, pp. 627–8)
attributes this coinage to the Archiepiscopal mint, and interprets
the legend :

$$\left.\begin{matrix}\text{VI}\\\text{MANu}\end{matrix}\right\}\text{PeTrI ECcleSiæ}\left\{\begin{matrix}\text{EBoRaci DomiNI}\\\text{ON EVerwic}\end{matrix}\right.$$

Variety (*c*) is probably a similar local production which is more
curious in that the reverse type, instead of following the usual
type of Stephen's first issue, is that which appears on the coins
of Robert de Stuteville (see below, p. cxvi), and the ornaments in
the obverse and reverse legends are also similar.

Variety (*d*) is one of the most curious issues of this reign;
to the left of a tall sceptre is represented a male figure in chain-
armour, wearing a peaked helmet and long trousers; to the right
is a female figure, her hair long and tied with ribbons, wearing
a bodice of mail and a stiff triangular skirt; both figures have
long manches; between them they support, each with one hand,
a tall fleured sceptre. The reason for the attribution of this
issue to the York district is the style of lettering and ornaments.
The design appears to be the original work of a northern engraver,
fancifully representing Queen Matilda assisting the king to support
the sceptre of the kingdom during the period of his captivity. The
male figure can hardly be Eustace, who was not knighted till 1147
or 1149.[1] The figure is a knight in full armour and may reasonably
represent the king, whose name forms the obverse legend. Various
suggestions have been made for the interpretation of these two figures;

---

[1] The coins of this York series are all placed about the year 1141, or slightly
earlier, owing to their close connexion with each other and, through the 'Flag
type' coins, with the first issue of Stephen, which presumably did not continue
after 1141. An interpretation of the 'Flag type' coins as commemorative of
the Battle of the Standard would place that issue in, or shortly after, 1138; the
'Double-figure' type, if attributed to the period of Stephen's captivity, would
be issued in the year 1141. On Pl. LX the coins are assigned to 'Queen
Matilda and Eustace'; this should be corrected to 'Stephen and Queen Matilda'.

some have even held that both figures are male, but this is clearly wrong—the different representation of the trousers of the male figure and the triangular skirt of the female figure can easily be seen by an examination of various specimens,[1] and the figure to the left wears a peaked helmet, while the female figure has the head bare, showing the long hair bound with ribbons or ornaments after the feminine fashion of the time.

Packe's theory (*Num. Chron.*, 1896, pp. 69–70[2]) that the figures are Queen Matilda and Prince Henry, and the occasion the convention of Durham in 1139, is most unconvincing; that a peace should be an occasion for putting one's former enemy side by side with the queen in place of the king's head upon the coins is hardly possible. The probable Yorkshire provenance of the issue renders the interpretation of the type as Duke Henry and his mother the Empress improbable, as also does the inscription, the name of Stephen. The issue belongs clearly, as Packe pointed out (*Num. Chron.*, 1896, pp. 65 ff.), to a large series of coins the provenance of which must be Yorkshire, if not the city of York itself. As well as the varieties above described, the series includes coins with the name of Eustace which represent a full figure in armour on the obverse, others bearing the same name with an animal as obverse design, and also coins of Robert with horseman type. The connexion of all these issues is not merely a superficial similarity in style, but a detailed identity both of lettering and of ornaments. This identity may best be seen by a comparison of the catalogue descriptions of the coins, where the ornamental borders and some inscriptions have been reproduced from drawings made as accurately as possible to scale; the form of lettering is not only common to all these issues but peculiar to this series—it is punched work of a neat though disjointed and rather meagre form, the length of serifs and horizontal strokes dwarfing the uprights; the ornaments are

---

[1] But it is curious that Eustace, on the full-figure coins which bear his name, is clad in just such a skirt as the female figure is wearing on these coins.

[2] Mr. Andrew (*Num. Circ.*, 1914, p. 628) also takes this view, and supposes the coins to have been struck at York in honour of this peace.

most curious and unintelligible, but it is important to notice how
the same ornaments reproduce themselves on all the issues of this
series with the exception of some of the 'Lion type' Eustace coins.
It is therefore impossible to believe that the coins do not all come
from the same mint, or, at least, the dies from the same local centre.
That this mint is York, or some place in the neighbourhood, is shown
by the 'Flag type' coin in Mr. Reynolds's collection (VIDNESI ON
EV), by the reverse inscriptions of the Eustace coins, and by the
obverse legend of the Robert coins, which seems certainly to denote
Robert de Stuteville, the Yorkshire magnate. The issues seem to
me to represent the efforts of the mint of York in the hands of
local administration thrown upon its own resources, and upon the
ingenuity of local engravers, owing to the severing of control from
the central authority at London. It appears that the control of the
mint or mints of Yorkshire was taken over at some period in the
reign (presumably about 1141, or perhaps slightly earlier) by the
Constable of York and other magnates, either on the king's behalf
or for their own profit; and most probably those who were friends
of the king, or the moneyers who acted for them, were not above
making some profit for themselves by issuing coins of low weight,
as most of these issues seem to be. To attempt any further
explanation of these strange types and inexplicable inscriptions than
as the original work of local genius must bring one into the
region of fanciful speculation. It has already been suggested that
the 'Flag type' perhaps represents the Standard that was taken
into battle at Northallerton, and the confused reverse inscriptions
perhaps show attempts to obscure the moneyer's identity; the
'Double-figure' type probably represents the Queen assisting the
King to support the royal power in his captivity; but whether
the coins were made by officers of the King or by independent
barons is mere conjecture.

V. Coins not bearing the King's Title.

Eustace FitzJohn (?)

Type A. 'Full-figure' type.

Obv. Full figure in armour, holding sword.

Rev. Cross pattée in quatrefoil.

Obverse.	Reverse.	Wt.	Provenance, &c.
1. **EVST ALI VS+** Pl. LX. 5, 6.	**+EBORACI⊙E D⊙TS**	18·5 19·0	British Museum, no. 264 and Hunterian coll. (same dies); H. M. Reynolds and B. Roth (same dies). All from same reverse die.
2. Same die as preceding coin in British Museum. Pl. LX. 7.	**+EBORACI⊙T DEFΓ**	18·3	British Museum, no. 265.
3. Similar to preceding; but no annulets in field. Pl. LX. 8.	**+ÞOMHSFI LIUSVLF**	19·0 18·9	British Museum, nos. 266, 267 and B. Roth (all from same dies).
4. **EVSTA LI VS** Type as preceding. Pl. LX. 9.	Ornaments.	16·1	British Museum, no. 268.

Coins of the full-figure type of Eustace are not recorded in any published finds; but their approximate date of issue is shown by their close association in style with issues, such as the Double-figure type and others, which have been found at Catal and elsewhere in company with coins of Stephen. They have usually been attributed to Eustace, son of Stephen. Ruding, *Annals of the Coinage*, vol. i, p. 169, states that Eustace probably struck these coins 'during his residence at York as governor';[1] he gives no authority for conferring this title on Eustace. Packe's reference to Stubbs's *Constitutional History* (see *Num. Chron.*, 1896, p. 67) is unintelligible; Stubbs has no such statement. I gather that it arises somehow from the account of Eustace's arrival at York and order for Divine Service to be held in spite of the Papal Interdict, in 1149. I can find in the Chronicles no reason for the conclusion that Eustace was Governor of York at the time; William of Newburgh (under the year 1147) says, 'adveniens Eustachius regis filius sacra officia celebrari præcepit'; John of Hexham (Symeon, *H. R.*, Cont.) says, 'post regis abscessum venit filius ejus Eustachius Eboracum, divinaque officia in eo cessare reperiens, clericos de divinis ministeriis nil omittere coegit'; these expressions rather give the impression that Eustace was not in any official position at York, but coming there on his father's departure took very strong action on finding that the Papal Interdict was being observed. Nor do I know any reason to believe that such an office as 'Governor' of York existed in the twelfth century.

The connexion of Eustace, Stephen's son, with the city of York seems to have been exaggerated. The passages quoted above tend rather to show that his arrival in 1149 was not in the capacity of an official of York; but, however that may be, there is no trace of his having had any connexion with the city at an earlier period. On the contrary, his age, which, though not definitely known, can be approximately deduced, is sufficient guarantee that he held no independent authority at the time that this coinage must have been issued. The coins bear a close resemblance in style and lettering to the irregular issues of York above described, which is strongly suggestive of work contemporaneous, or approximately contemporaneous, with those issues; and this connexion is greatly strengthened by a comparison of the ornaments of the Eustace coin, no. 268, on p. 390, with those of 'Flag type' coins on pp. 386–7 and of the 'Double-figure' coins on p. 388; some of these ornaments may even have been made with the same punches. The probability

---

[1] A similar statement occurs in Withy and Ryall (1756); I have not succeeded in tracing it further.

of the issue of all these coinages of York at an early date, hardly later than 1141, and in particular those of the 'Flag' and 'Double-figure' types, has been shown above (p. cviii, note 1). The Eustace coins of the 'Full-figure' type must therefore be assigned to a date hardly later, perhaps even earlier, than 1141. Eustace, son of Stephen, was knighted in 1147 or 1149;[1] hence he may be assumed to have been born about 1130 and to have been, at the most, very little more than ten years old when these coins were struck. The representation of a knight in full armour cannot depict the son of Stephen before 1147 or 1149. The coins[2] should, I think, be assigned to Eustace FitzJohn, to whom the 'Lion' issues, described below, are attributed on the evidence of the fragment in Mr. Lawrence's collection published by him in *Num. Chron.*, 1890, pp. 42 ff., where Mr. Lawrence also advocated the attribution of all the Eustace coins to FitzJohn. As Packe pointed out, the full-figure types are clearly struck at York city, for some bear an inscription which identifies the town name, though part of the inscription is unintelligible, and others bear the name of Thomas FitzUlf, whom he identified as 'Thomas FitzUlviet' of *Pipe Roll, Henry I*, ed. Hunter, p. 34, an alderman of York. FitzJohn was certainly a Yorkshire magnate, and lord of Malton and Knaresborough, but we cannot at present trace his connexion with the city of York. He was fighting for David at the Battle of the Standard in 1138, and seems from his signature to a charter to have been, at least temporarily, reconciled to Stephen by 1141–2.[3] That he issued coins in his own name somewhere in the neighbourhood of York is made certain by Mr. Lawrence's fragment described below. In our present scanty knowledge of

---

[1] Ramsay (*Foundations*, vol. ii, p. 437, note 4) follows Howlett's argument—the signature of charters of 1147–8 by Eustace with title *Comes*—for accepting 1147 of the *Gesta* against 1149 of Huntingdon and Hexham. Round (*Feudal England*, p. 495) denies that knighthood need precede the use of the title *Comes*, and places it in 1149.

[2] On Plate LX they are described as coins of 'Eustace, son of Stephen (?)'; but since the plate was printed I have felt more strongly the necessity of abandoning this attribution.

[3] See below, p. cxv.

h

this period it is impossible to say how he came to do so in York itself. It is important to note that the fragment which identifies the 'Lion' issues as a coinage of FitzJohn, though resembling the other 'Lion' coins in type, is in style more closely allied to the 'Full-figure' coins; this is most noticeable in the form of lettering and punctuation, but it is also noteworthy that what remains of its reverse inscription bears at least a superficial resemblance to the unintelligible part of the reverse inscription of the British Museum coin of Full-figure type, no. 265.

Eustace FitzJohn.

Type B. 'Lion' type.

Obv. A lion (?) passant to r., ornaments in field.

Rev. Cross fleury over saltire, each limb of which ends in small crosses pattées; annulets in field.

Obverse.	Reverse.	Wt.	Provenance, &c.
✠[ ]CII⊙ᚼII⊙ IOᚣᚺIS Pl. LX. 10.	✠IT⊙ᚱID✠BE[	frag-ment	L. A. Lawrence.
✠ᚽISTᚪOᚼIᚢ S: Pl. LX. 11.	Ornaments in place of legend (each limb of saltire ends in two crescents from which a chain issues to the edge of the coin(.	18·8 16·6 chipped 18·0 18·9 21·3	British Museum, nos. 269, 270, and other specimens from the same pair of dies.

Very little is known of Eustace FitzJohn during the reign of Stephen; his close intimacy with the court of Henry I naturally led him to favour the cause of the Empress, and in February, 1138, we hear of Stephen depriving him of the custody of Bamborough Castle, on the ground that he was plotting with Matilda; in July of the same year he joined David of Scotland, surrendering to him his castle of Alnwick, and, as we have seen, fought on his side at the Battle of the Standard. Between Christmas, 1141, and Easter,

1142,[1] he witnessed at Stamford a charter of Stephen to William, Earl of Lincoln. In the later part of the reign we only hear of him founding and endowing religious houses. His signature to the charter at Stamford seems to point to a reconciliation with Stephen between 1138 and 1142; but the witnesses of this charter are mostly local magnates or relations of the grantee, some (such as Randulf of Chester and Roger of Warwick) certainly in revolt both before and after this date, and perhaps the signatures only denote a temporary truce and not a definite transfer of allegiance. He witnessed Scottish charters at Scone in 1124, at York (?) in 1128, at place unknown *circa* 1136, at Carlisle *circa* 1139, at Durham *circa* 1141, at Huntingdon *circa* 1145 (perhaps earlier), at Corbridge in 1150-2 (Lawrie, *Early Scottish Charters*, liv, lxxv and lxxvi, cxv, cxxiii, cxxxiii, clxxvii, ccxlvii).

The fragment in Mr. Lawrence's collection must clearly be attributed to this Eustace, and the other coins naturally follow it. Mr. Andrew,[2] however, prefers to separate the ordinary Lion-type issue from that bearing the full name of FitzJohn, attributing the former to the son of Stephen, and assuming FitzJohn to have issued in his own name an imitation of this issue of Eustace, son of Stephen. But finding an issue in currency which would even in name serve as his own, he would surely not expose his abuse by adding to the name Eustace the additional 'Filius Iohannis'; nor is there any reason to suppose that the FitzJohn fragment is lighter or baser, or in any other way more like an imitation, than the ordinary Lion-type issue. The reason for the divorce of these two closely related issues seems to be the connexion with the issues of York, and the lack of any authority for assigning to FitzJohn power in the city of York. This difficulty is not, however, solved by this means, for of the two Lion-type issues the one bearing the name 'Filius Iohannis' is most certainly the nearer in style to the other Eustace coins of York, the style of lettering and of ornaments and design being

---

[1] Round, *Geoffrey de Mandeville*, pp. 157-9.
[2] *Num. Circ.*, 1914, pp. 629-30.

of the good workmanship of the York coins, whereas the more common Lion-type coins, which bear the name 'Eistaohius', though still similar in style, especially of lettering, differ from any other of the York issues in the form of the ornaments in the reverse inscription. If either, therefore, is to be regarded as an' imitation of the other, it should surely be the 'Eistaohius' issue.

ROBERT DE STUTEVILLE.

Obv. Armed figure on horseback to r. **✠RODBERTUSDE STV**

Rev. Cross pattée over saltire fleury. Ornaments.
British Museum, no. 271; Hunterian coll.; H. M. Reynolds; P. W. P. Carlyon-Britton; B. Roth. The British Museum, Hunterian, and Reynolds specimens are from the same dies.

Pl. LX. 12, 13.

All the specimens at present known of this coinage, except that in the Hunterian collection, are in a more or less fragmentary condition which renders the last part of the obverse inscription illegible; this has made possible the traditional attribution to Robert of Gloucester, an attribution which was, however, questioned by Packe in *Num. Chron.*, 1896, p. 70, on grounds of style and identity of reverse type with the coin of Stephen described above as variety IV D (c). Packe's suggestion of Robert de Stuteville as the issuer of this coinage is made almost certain by the Hunterian coin, on which the whole obverse inscription is clearly legible with the exception of the letters **DE**; these are read by comparison with the Reynolds specimen. Of this Robert de Stuteville we know nothing except that he was one of the Yorkshire magnates who met at York in 1138 to consider measures of defence against David of Scotland; he is supposed to have been the father of the sheriff of Yorkshire of 1170–5.

The similarity of the style of his coins to that of the other irregular issues of York points to an early date of issue, apparently within the period 1138–41.

HENRY, BISHOP OF WINCHESTER.

Obv. Bust r., crowned, holding crozier; star in field to r.
Rev. Cross pattée over cross fleury.

Obverse.		Reverse.	Wt.	Provenance, &c.
✠ᎰᏏᎬᏔ[₡ ᏙᏃᎬᏢᏟ Pl. LX. 14.		Ꮓ[ᏢᏏᎰᎯᏔᏙ Ꮓ·ᏒᎬᕽ	15·9 frag- ment	British Museum, no. 272.
✠ᎠᎬᏔᏒᏐᏟᏙᏃ ᎬᏢᎬ Pl. LX. 15.		Ꮓ░PPᎯᎰᏙ Ꮓ·ᏒᎬᕽ	18·0	P.W.P.Carlyon- Britton.

There seem to have been only two bishops of the name of Henry in English sees during the reign of Stephen—the Bishop of Winchester and Henry Murdac, Archbishop of York (1147–53).

Murdac, who was not recognized by Stephen till their reconciliation in 1150, is hardly a possible candidate for this coinage, and would doubtless have used the title *archiepiscopus* instead of *episcopus*.

The coinage is a very curious one and is a remarkable illustration of the extraordinary power of Henry of Blois. Like the late eighth-century coins of Canterbury, these coins couple the royal title on the reverse with the episcopal title on the obverse, showing probably that the coinage was issued by grant of, and not in defiance of, the King. Whether the story is true or false that Bishop Henry was actually elected to the archbishopric of Canterbury in 1136 but refused translation by the Pope, his legatine commission in 1139 gave him a position superior to the Primate; in 1142 he even urged the Pope to raise Winchester to metropolitan rank, and according to Ralph de Diceto the pall was actually sent him by the Pope; in 1143 he consecrated William as Archbishop of York, Theobald of Canterbury dissenting. One is naturally inclined to place his coinage in the period of his greatest ecclesiastical power, that is, between his appointment as Legate in March, 1139, and the expiry of his legatine commission with the death of Innocent in September, 1143; from this period may be deducted nearly the whole of the year 1141 (February to December), the period of Stephen's captivity, which leaves the alternative of the two periods March, 1139—February, 1141, and December, 1141—September, 1143. The later of these two periods is not a likely date for a coinage which adopts for the portrait that of the King's first issue. We may therefore take as a conjectural date of the issue the period March, 1139—February, 1141. This date is confirmed by the resemblance in style to the York issues, a resemblance so close as to suggest that the dies were made at York or even the coins struck there (Major Carlyon-Britton's specimen was found at York), but I cannot accept Mr. Andrew's theory [1] that they were issued by William Fitzherbert shortly after June, 1141, in honour of his uncle, the Legate. Fitzherbert was not consecrated till 1143, and an unconsecrated Archbishop of York is not likely to have issued a coinage bearing the names of the Bishop of Winchester and the King.

EMPRESS MATILDA.

Type as first issue of Stephen.

Obverse.	Reverse.	Wt.	Provenance, &c.
:IMPERATR: Pl. LXI. 1, 2.	TVR▨▨L·D E·BR▨▨	16·6 15·8	P. W. P. Carlyon-Britton (two coins from same die).
]ILDICOI:	✠ALFRED[ ] VD:	18·5	Rashleigh sale, lot 631.
:M[ ]LDIS· IMPER: Pl. LXI. 3.	✠ARFENI:▨ BRI▨T		B. Roth.

[1] *Num. Circ.*, 1914, pp. 628-9.

Obverse.	Reverse.	Wt.	Provenance, &c.
MATILDI:I⬛⬛	⬛⬛⬛DAN·DE·BR[	17·0	Rashleigh sale, lot 632.
:MATILLIS:I MF³ Pl. LXI. 4.	]ER:CA[		B. Roth (two coins from same dies).
⬛ATILDI:IM ⬛: Pl. LXI. 5.	✠SVE⬛⬛⬛:O N:O✗:	17·2 16·5	British Museum, no. 273, and H. M. Reynolds.
]ILDI·IMP Pl. LXI. 6.	✠RA⬛⬛⬛·DE·WAR⬛		B. Roth (two coins).
Illegible.	✠RAVL·ON· ⬛[		B. Roth (very similar to preceding).
⬛ATILDI:IM	⬛RA⬛⬛⬛F:D E:⬛VN⬛		B. Roth.
]C:IMP[	]VRIC:⬛N[		,,

A brief description of the Empress's movements in England is given above in the account of the coins inscribed PERERIC (see pp. lxxxiv f.). Her coins are all of the type of Stephen's first issue and bear as obverse inscriptions forms, more or less abbreviated, of *Imperatrix*, *Matildis Comitissa*, and *Matildis Imperatrix*. The dies were of rough work and were hand-engraved with the exception of the reverse of the Oxford coin, which is made with the usual punching-irons;[1] they all seem to be of low weight but of good metal. The only mints that can be ascertained with any

[1] The coin in Rashleigh sale, lot 631, is perhaps also from a punch-worked die, but has rather the appearance of being engraved in imitation of punched lettering.

certainty are Bristol, Oxford, and Wareham;[1] **CA** is presumably
not Canterbury (see above, p. lxxxvi), possibly Calne.[2] The coins were
most probably all struck between 1139 and 1142; those of Bristol,
which was probably always her chief base, may have been issued at
any time between these dates; perhaps the coins with the inscription
Imperatrix preceded those that have the name *Matildis* in addition
to the title. The Oxford coins were perhaps struck at, or shortly
after, Easter, 1141, when the castle was surrendered to the Empress
by Robert d'Oilly; it seems likely that dies then fell into her hands,
for the reverses of these coins are struck from dies made apparently
from the regular punching-irons, and have all the appearance of the
coinage of Stephen.[3] They might have been struck in June, 1141,
after the flight from London, or in September–December, 1142,
when she was besieged at Oxford by Stephen; but the occasion of
her entry to Oxford in the course of her triumphal progress to
London in March, 1141, seems the more probable date. Wareham,
one of Robert of Gloucester's strongholds, seems to have surrendered
to Stephen in 1138, but was certainly in rebellion in the following
year when Baldwin de Redvers landed there; it was not recovered
by Stephen till June, 1142, when he took it from William of
Gloucester, who was put in charge in his father's absence; it was
retaken by Robert, after a siege of three weeks, in November.
Stephen's attempt to recover it in the following year was
unsuccessful.

Other coins that have been attributed to Matilda are the variety
of Stephen's first issue which bears the inscription PERERIC, &c.
(see above, pp. lxxxii ff.), and two coins of Stephen's second type
(*British Numismatic Journal*, vol. vii, p. 85, and Pl. II, 35, 36),
but these are ill-struck and illegible, and I see no reason for the
attribution.

---

[1] The former attribution of these and other coins (see below, p. cxxxi) to
Warwick was, as Mr. Andrew has pointed out, most improbable.

[2] See below, pp. clxiv f., and *Num. Chron.*, 1915, p. 115.

[3] See *Num. Chron.*, 1915, p. 114.

HENRY OF ANJOU.

Type I.

(*a*) As first issue of Stephen.

Obverse.	Reverse.	Wt.	Provenance, &c.
✠HENRICVS ▨▨ Pl. LXI. 8.	✠WILLEL▨▨ ▨HEREFORD		B. Roth.
]INN:HIOI Pl. LXI. 7.	From same die as preceding.	17·6 pierced	British Museum, no. 275.

The mint on these two coins might possibly read BEDEFORD; both coins are clipped through the mint name.

:✠HENRICV S Pl. LXI. 9.	✠PIC▨RIC:ON HER:	15·9	British Museum, no. 274.
:REX· AN:	✠W[ ]RI:D E:MAL▨▨:		B. Roth.

From its style and fabric this coin seems to belong to this series.

A coin of this type, but of Scottish style, which must be attributed to Earl Henry, son of David, was found at Bute (see above, p. xcviii).

(*b*) As variety III 7 of Stephen (see above, pp. xci ff.).

✠HENRIC:⁘ Pl. LXI. 10.	✠RADEWLF :ONⓞLO	16·7	British Museum, no. 276 (from the Winterslow find).

(*c*) *Obv.* As first issue of Stephen.

Rev. As last issue (type XV) of Henry I.

Obverse.	Reverse.	Wt.	Provenance, &c.
ENRICVS +ON:CAO(or **O**) [ ]: Pl. LXI. 12.		12·4	British Museum, no. 277 (from the Winterslow find).

Two coins similar to preceding, illegible, in P. W. P. Carlyon-Britton and H. M. Reynolds collections.

+ENRICVO Square crown without ornaments: inscription begins to r. of sceptre and is not divided by bust. Pl. LXI. 11.	**+[ ]LEMO N:CRVT**		B. Roth.
]N[Ornament between face and sceptre. Pl. LXI. 13.	**ELFRE[** **A:**]	16·5	British Museum, no. 278 (from Winterslow find).
+ NRICVO REx Broad double diadem in place of crown. Pl. LXI. 14.	Illegible.	16·4 clipped	British Museum, no. 279 (Winterslow find), and W. T. Ready (same dies).

Another similar, illegible, in P. W. P. Carlyon-Britton collection.

Type II.

(*a*) *Obv.* Bust facing, crowned, between two stars.

Rev. Cross botonnée over quadrilateral with pellet at each angle.

| **ENRICV[** Pl. LXI. 15. | **+AREFIN:O NBRI** | 16·6 | British Museum, no. 280. |

Obverse.	Reverse.	Wt.	Provenance, &c.
✠ҺE[ ]ᒐⅤS R[Pl. LXI. 16.	From same die as pre-ceding.		Copenhagen Museum.
]RIᒐⅤ[	From same die as pre-ceding.	15·5	H. M. Reynolds.
✠ҺEⅬRIᒐⅤS :RE: Pl. LXII. 1.	✠OⅬ:SI[ ]Ⅴ RⅬI	16·1	British Museum, no. 281 (Win-terslow find).
✠DIⅬIⅬƆⅤ[ ]Ⅼ Pl. LXII. 3.	✠ⅬDⱯ☒:OⅬⱲ IⅤEᒐOᒐ	16·0	British Museum, no. 282.
✠PⅬOⅤ☒E☷ OI Pl. LXII. 4.	ⅬIⅤOⅤⅬIⅬ ☒OHIⅬ·	14·4	British Museum, no. 283.

The last two coins are perhaps contemporary imitations of the Duke's coins

(b) As preceding issue, but the cross botonnée on the reverse is voided.

Obverse.	Reverse.	Wt.	Provenance, &c.
✠ҺEⅬ[Pl. LXII. 2.	✠ELF[ ]:Ⱥ	7·6 cut half-penny	British Museum, no. 284 (Win-terslow find).
]Ⅼ[	✠[ ]ᒐDEⅤ [ ]ⱭI	15·4	Rashleigh sale, lot 627.
✠E☷☷IIЯEⅹII ⅬIIᒐ: (retrograde) Annulet enclosing pellet above each star. Pl. LXII. 9.	✠ⱲⱯ☒TE☷☷ S:OⅬ:	16·0	P. W. P. Carlyon-Britton.

Mr. Andrew[1] reads the obverse of this coin—not retrograde—
+:ҺVИFREI· DE BVhuN. It seems to me to be a blundered
coin of Henry or possibly William.

'Anno gratiæ MCXLIX, qui est XIIII regni regis Stephani, Henricus
dux Normannorum venit in Angliam cum magno exercitu, et reddita sunt
ei castella multa et munitiones quamplures; et fecit monetam novam,
quam vocabant monetam ducis; et non tantum ipse, sed omnes potentes,
tam episcopi quam comites et barones, suam faciebant monetam. Sed
ex quo dux ille venit, plurimorum monetam cassavit.'[2]

The above passage occurs in Roger of Hoveden's Chronicle under
the year 1149, and seems to be an original statement of his own,
and not, like the great part of his history of this period (1148-69),
taken from the Chronicle of Melrose. In his introduction to Roger
of Hoveden's Chronicle, Stubbs says: 'The notices of the years
1148 to 1169 which are neither taken directly from the Chronicle
of Melrose, nor connected closely with the Becket contest, are very
few, and some of them, I think, of very questionable authenticity.
. . .   Of the striking of money by Henry in 1149 called "the
duke's money", and of the appointment of Henry as justiciar to
Stephen in 1153, it is impossible to say that they are false, but
equally impossible to say that they are in the least degree
probable.'
There were four (or three?) occasions on which Henry came to
England during Stephen's reign:

(1) In late autumn, 1142, then nine years old, he was sent over
to Bristol and lived there four years, returning to Normandy towards
the end of 1146.

[(2) In the spring of 1147, in order to create a diversion on
behalf of Gilbert of Clare, who was attacked in Pevensey by
Stephen, he brought a small band of adventurers and was joined
on landing by Robert of Leicester; he made an attack on Cricklade
and on Bourton (Gloucestershire?); both attacks failed, his men

---

[1] *Num. Circ.*, 1914, p. 632.
[2] Roger of Hoveden (Rolls Series, no. 51), vol. i, p. 211.

began to desert, and at the end of May he returned to Normandy from Wareham. *Perhaps an invention of the* Gesta.[1]]

(3) Early in 1149 he returned, apparently for the purpose of being knighted by David of Scotland; landing probably at Wareham, he was at Devizes on April 13, and thence went to the court of David at Carlisle, where he was knighted on May 22. Of the rest of his movements we know nothing till his return to Normandy in January, 1150.

(4) In January, 1153, at the request of the beleaguered garrison of Wallingford, he arrived with a force said to consist of 150 men-at-arms and 3,000 foot-soldiers. He reduced the keep of Malmesbury, raised the siege of Wallingford, and, after a short time, visited his head-quarters at Bristol, after which he made an armed progress through the midlands, from Winchcombe (?) to Evesham, Warwick, Stamford, and Nottingham; Stamford Castle surrendered to him, but the garrison at Nottingham, by firing the town, caused his retreat. On Aug. 10, 1153, the death of Eustace gave the opportunity for a compromise which culminated in the peace ratified in Council at Winchester on Nov. 6, 1153.

The passage above quoted from Roger of Hoveden is at least confused in chronology—the visit of Henry when he was accompanied by a large force, and received the surrender of several castles, was that of 1153, not of 1149; in the sentence referring to the 'duke's money', if we may believe the statement, the chronicler is evidently similarly inaccurate, and probably relates under the mention of Henry a traditional tale. If the statement that he made a new coinage, and that the bishops and barons did likewise, is correctly placed to his visit of the year 1149, his suppression of this baronial coinage can hardly have occurred during his same stay in England, which lasted not longer than nine months. Apart from its chronological inaccuracy, the statement, which does not in itself sound like a groundless fabrication, finds support in the coins which may with much probability be attributed to the Duke, or rather, the Angevin party in England.

---

[1] See Round, *Feudal England*, pp. 491 ff.

These coins were at one time supposed to belong to the reign of Henry I, but their presence in the Winterslow find,[1] and their absence in the finds of coins of Henry I, show them to have been issued in the reign of Stephen. It is still sometimes suggested that Earl Henry, son of David, may have issued this coinage or part of it; but a comparison of the inscription **✠AREFIИ:OИ BRI** with **✠ARFENI:⬛⬛BRI⬛T** on a coin of Empress Matilda, and **✠PIC⬛RIC:OИ ɦER:** with coins of Stephen, pp. 340-1, nos. 38 and 39, leaves no doubt that, whoever this Henry was, he coined at Bristol and Hereford. The Scottish prince cannot have coined in the West, nor would he have put on his coins the title REX, which is likely to be adopted only by a claimant to the throne.[2] Further, in connexion with these coins must be considered the coins similar to the later issue (described as type II above), but bearing other obverse titles, which seem only explicable as a baronial coinage imitating the coinage of Henry, such as Hoveden tells us was suppressed by the Duke on his arrival.

There is much difficulty in determining when this coinage can have been issued by Henry; the earliest type, presumably, is the direct imitation of the first issue of Stephen, which can hardly have been the type in issue at the royal mints in the late autumn of 1142, when Henry first landed in England.

Matilda had on, or shortly after, her arrival issued a coinage which imitated the first issue of Stephen, the coinage at that time (1139) presumably still in issue, or at least the most frequent type in currency;[3] this type she continued to issue without change until perhaps her flight from Oxford in December, 1142, from which date her claim was practically abandoned, and her

---

[1] See above, p. xxx.

[2] At the same time it must be remembered that a coin is known of the type of Stephen's first issue having on the obverse the name *Henricus* (without title), which must be attributed to Earl Henry, owing to its Scottish style and very close resemblance to coins of David of the same type, and also on account of its Scottish provenance (Bute find) and its probable attribution to Carlisle and the moneyer Erebald (see above, p. xcviii).

[3] See p. lxxv.

party were held together by Robert of Gloucester in the name of
Henry. Henry's confirmation of his mother's charter to Aubrey de
Vere, attributed to July–November, 1142,[1] and indeed the guarantee
given by the Empress in her original charter (not later than June
in the same year), that she would obtain her son's ratification, show
that in this year (1142) she was fighting for the cause of her son as
rightful heir to the throne, and had abandoned her own claim.
It is to this period, c. 1142–3, that I should attribute the substitution of the name of Henry for that of Matilda on the coinage
of the Angevin party in England, the original type being continued for a time.[2] In October, 1147, Robert of Gloucester died,
and the Angevin cause in England practically ceased to exist, the
Empress herself leaving the country in the following February ; it
revived with the third (second?) visit of Henry in 1149. The profile
types I have above assigned to the period immediately following
the change in the Empress's position from claimant in her own
right to claimant in the right of her son, that is to say, c. 1142,
I (c) being presumably somewhat later than I (a) and (b). The later,
or full-face, types, the obverse of which is presumably based on that
of type III of Stephen, must, I think, at least have commenced
their currency before Robert's death in 1147. Of this I find
confirmation in the finds of coins of this reign. In the Awbridge
find the absence of coins of Henry struck before his accession
might possibly be explained by assuming that he recalled his coins
from circulation at the same time as he put down the baronial
issues, though that seems hardly possible if the later type of
his coinage was not brought into circulation before 1153. The
Winterslow find seems more definite. No account exists of this find,
but B. C. Roberts seems to have had a representative selection
from it, and to judge from his coins the hoard contained specimens

---

[1] Round, *Geoffrey de Mandeville*, pp. 184 ff.

[2] See *Num. Chron.*, 1915, p. 118. I was there mistaken in saying that
Mr. Andrew assigned all the profile types of Henry to 1149 ; Hks. 259 he
places in 1142, and with it I understand him to include all those with the
reverse of Stephen's first type (except the coin of Scottish style from the
Bute find ; see *Brit. Num. Journ.*, vol. ix, p. 414), the *remaining* profile coins
(described above as type I (c)) in 1149 and the full-face issues in 1153.

of all the varieties of Henry of Anjou excepting type I (*a*); and of the true coinage of Stephen, types I, II, and III were represented. The later issue of Henry of Anjou was therefore most probably introduced during the issue of the third or fourth type of Stephen, that is to say, probably not many years after 1145.

The mints that can be identified with likelihood are: of type I (*a*) Hereford and Malmesbury, of type I (*b*) Gloucester, of type I (*c*) 'Crst'[1] (Cirencester in Gloucestershire?), the others being uncertain; of type II (*a*) Bristol (the same moneyer, Arefin, seems to have struck coins of the Empress, see above, p. cxviii), Sherborne?, Wiveliscombe?; of type II (*b*) none are certain.

Even if the mints could be interpreted with certainty, it is not likely that a consideration of them in connexion with such evidence as we have of Henry's movements would assist towards dating the coinage; for these issues of Henry represent, I think, rather the coinage of his party than his own private issues. At this time, after 1142, the West of England was Angevin, and at the Angevin strongholds, such as Bristol, Gloucester, Wareham, &c., there was probably a more or less continuous output of coins in the name first of Matilda, and later of Henry, and these coinages are likely to have been the main currency of the West.[2]

Type I (*b*) is of some interest as it varies from the regular type of Stephen, and is identical in type with a variety described above, variety III 7 (see above, pp. xci ff.); that variety was shown to have occurred in finds of late coins of the reign, and not in finds containing coins of the first issue (except one specimen in the Linton find), and therefore was apparently first issued at the end of the period when type I was being minted, and continued in circulation to the beginning of Henry II's reign. Why there should be this curious connexion it is impossible to say; one cannot suppose that Henry issued coins bearing Stephen's name; it may be that they were issued in the same locality, and perhaps the dies made

---

[1] The usual interpretation of CRST as Christchurch seems to me very doubtful. The town was called Twynham. Christchurch was the name of the monastery only. I suggest Cirencester conjecturally.

[2] See *Brit. Num. Journ.*, vol. ix, p. 414.

by the same engravers, though the difference of style is against
this; perhaps the variety of uncertain attribution is the work
of some baron in the West of England, where Henry's coins were
mostly in circulation, but if so, the use of Stephen's title on an
imitation of Henry's coin is not easily explained.

ROBERT (OF GLOUCESTER?).

Type of Stephen's second issue.

Obverse inscriptions: **▓▓BETV** (penny. B. Roth).

]ROBETV[(halfpenny. B. Roth).

Pl. LXII. 5, 6.

Reverse inscriptions quite uncertain; the penny reads
VND:ON: —, the mint-name has some appearance of being
hERE or LERE, or possibly LINC. The attribution is quite
uncertain; the coins may represent a baronial issue, or money of
necessity. One would not expect Robert of Gloucester to issue
coins except in the name of the Empress or Henry.

Another Robert may be the issuer. If LERE is the reading of
the mint-name on the penny (but this is very doubtful), Robert
de Beaumont, the favourite of Stephen, who went over to Henry
on his arrival in 1147 (?), is more probable (see *Brit. Num. Journ.*,
vol. vi, p. 366, and vol. vii, p. 88).

WILLIAM (OF GLOUCESTER?).

Type I.

As type of Henry of Anjou, I (c). See p. cxxii.

Obverse.	Reverse.	Wt.	Provenance, &c.
]LELCO Square crown with ball ornaments; inscription begins to r. of sceptre.	**]LEL[**	14·0	H. M. Reynolds.

i

Type II.

(*a*) As type of Henry of Anjou, II (*a*). See p. cxxii.

Obverse.	Reverse.	Wt.	Provenance, &c.
✠LVILL·EИD V·O· Two rows of pellets take the place of the crown. Pl. LXII. 10.	**✠ẀLLEMON :CRꙆT**	15·0	H. M. Reynolds.

(*b*) As type of Henry of Anjou, II (*b*). See p. cxxiii.

✠ẀILLELꙨ Vᴦᶻ Pl. LXII. 8.	**✠[ ]ΛNDO NDOB**		P. W. P. Carlyon-Britton.
✠ẀILLELꙨ Vꙃ: Pl. LXII. 11, 12.	**✠ROꙄIER :D EẀAR**	15·0 14·5	P. W. P. Carlyon-Britton and H. M. Reynolds (same dies).
✠ẀILLELꙨ Vꙃ: Pl. LXII. 7.	**✠VИ[ ]ON· ẀIꙅ**	15·4 broken	British Museum, no. 285.
From same die as preceding.	**]Λꙅ·OИ:[**	16·0	British Museum, no. 286.

These coins are evidently struck in direct imitation of the issues of Henry, not only of the later but also of the earlier, or profile, class.[1] In one case, type II (*a*), there seems to be an attempt to express some title as well as the name on the obverse; this difficult inscription may perhaps be read WILLEM DVO (for DVX?) or WILLem ᴄoMes DVO(?). Mr. Andrew[2] reads WILLelmus ᴄoMes DVrOtrigum and attributes the coin to William de Mohun, Earl of Dorset and Somerset; but the letter of Brian FitzCount to the Legate, published

[1] I am very doubtful whether this coin, described as type I, should be classed with the other William coins.

[2] *Num. Circ.*, 1914, p. 631.

by Mr. Round in *Eng. Hist. Rev.*, 1910, pp. 297 ff., shows that William de Moyon deserted the Empress before the end of 1143, and there seems no reason to suppose that he returned to her side. The coin certainly belongs to the latter half of the reign.

It is noteworthy that not only the types but also the mint-names (so far as they can be interpreted) are identical with those on coins of Henry or the Empress. The name CRST occurs again (possibly Cirencester? see above, p. cxxviii), also at WAR (doubtless Wareham) the same moneyer, Roger, coined under the Empress; DOB or DOR (Dorchester?) and WIS (Wiveliscombe?) are quite uncertain. The weight of the coinage is low. These considerations and the extent of this coinage, if it may be attributed to one person (which is doubtful), suggest that the magnate who issued it was at some time leader of the Angevin party in England; this position may have fallen to William of Gloucester between his father's death in 1147 and the arrival of Henry in 1149, a period of which historical records are very meagre; but any attribution of the coins must be a matter of considerable doubt. The coin of type II (*b*), with mint-reading WIS, came from the Winterslow find.

BRIAN FITZCOUNT?

Type of Henry of Anjou, II (*a*), and William (of Gloucester?), II (*a*).

   Obv. ✠B·R·C·IT·[

   Rev. ✠BRIIT▨▨▨▨I·TO:

Wt. 15·9 grs.   P. W. P. Carlyon-Britton.   **Pl. LXII. 13.**

Mr. Andrew (*Num. Circ.*, 1914, p. 632) reads these inscriptions: B·R·ComITIS DEVonIæ and BRILTDPI·TO (a blundered copy of an Exeter reverse of the last issue of the reign of Henry I); he thus follows Montagu (*Num. Chron.*, 1890, Proceedings, p. 5) in attributing the coin to Baldwin de Redvers. I am not by any means satisfied that the latter part of the obverse inscription can be read as Mr. Andrew has read it. I prefer to remain content with the proposal of Packe (*Num. Chron.*,

i 2

1896, pp. 63 f.), reading the inscription as *Brianus Comitis Filius*; the reverse inscription seems to me likely to be a copy of that on the obverse. Brian FitzCount declared for Matilda in 1139 and concerted with Robert of Gloucester in plans of campaign; he was blockaded in Wallingford by Stephen, but relieved by Milo in the same year. He was with the Empress at London in June, and at Oxford in July, 1141, and after the siege of Winchester fled with her to Devizes; he was with her at Bristol[1] at the close of 1141, and at Oxford in the spring of 1142; to his castle at Wallingford Matilda fled at Christmas, 1142. He was besieged by Stephen at Wallingford in 1146, and again in 1153, when Henry relieved him on his fourth (third?) arrival in England. Perhaps this coin might be attributed to the siege of Wallingford in 1146.

Baldwin de Redvers was created Earl of Devon by the Empress before June, 1141.[2] He revolted from Stephen in 1136, was besieged, capitulated and fled to the Isle of Wight, and surrendered on hearing of Stephen's approach from Southampton; he was banished and took refuge with Geoffrey of Anjou. In 1139 he landed at Wareham and took Corfe Castle; he joined the Empress and was present at the siege of Winchester in 1141. After that we hear little of him except as a benefactor of religious houses. He died in 1155.

UNCERTAIN BARONIAL COINS.

(1) *Obv.*   ]ᴄoᴍ   Bust in armour r., holding sword.

     Rev. ✠ⱷ[   ]oɴːⱷᴀ   Quadrilateral, fleured at angles, over cross fleury.

     Wt. 15·8grs.(clipped). British Museum, no. 292. **Pl. LXII.14.** From the Winterslow find.

Mr. Andrew[3] attributes this coin to Patrick, Earl of Salisbury.

---

[1] Dugdale, *Monasticon*, vol. vi, p. 137.
[2] Round, *Geoffrey de Mandeville*, pp. 271-2.
[3] *Num. Circ.*, 1914, p. 632.

(2) *Obv.* ✠TⱵ(or ℧?)EFN   Bust facing, crowned, holding sceptre, star to r.

Rev. ✠ⱢⱢFⱤDONTOM: Cross pattée, annulet enclosing pellet in each angle.

Wt. 15·2 grs.   British Museum, no. 293.   **Pl. LXII. 15.**

Perhaps the obverse inscription represents a blundered form of STIEFNE. The resemblance of the reverse type to that of the following piece is noteworthy.

(3) *Obv.*]NEPᴦ:✠   Bust to r., holding sceptre (as on first issue of Stephen).

Rev. ✠WⱢLEMON[Cross pattée, annulet enclosing pellet in each angle.

Wt. 16 grs.   British Museum, no. 294.   **Pl. LXII. 16.**

ORGANIZATION AND CONTROL OF THE MINT.

The only officials of the mints of whose existence we have any literary evidence during the Norman period are the *monetarii*, or moneyers, whose names appear on the coins.[1] An *aurifaber*, or goldsmith, was probably employed for the designs of the coinage and perhaps controlled the engraving of dies; a function which seems to have been hereditary in the family of the goldsmith Otto from the time of Domesday, and apparently developed at a later date into the post of Cuneator or Engraver of the Dies, which was held in definite tenure of the king. Otto the Goldsmith appears in Domesday[2] in possession of lands in Essex and Suffolk; a charter of Henry I directed to Maurice, Bishop of London, who died in 1107, confirmed to William FitzOtto (presumably son of Otto of Domesday) lands held by his father and

---

[1] See below, pp. cxli ff.

[2] II. 97 b, 106 b, 286 b. Other goldsmiths mentioned in Domesday are: Grimbaldus (I. 74), Alwardus (I. 63 b), Leawinus (I. 58 b), Nicholaus (aurifaber comitis Hugonis, II. 279), Rainbaldus (II. 273), Teodricus (I. 36 b, 63, 160 b). A pedigree of the Otho family, with citations from records, is published in *Num. Chron.*, 1893, p. 145.

the craft of the dies; in the sixth year of John, May 16, 1205, a writ
to William FitzOtho ordered him to make dies for the Royal and
Episcopal mints of Chichester, and in the forty-first year of the
following reign an inquiry was held into the conditions of tenure
under which Otto FitzWilliam, then dead, had held the custody
of the king's die in England. From this it appears that the
hereditary office of *Aurifaber* of the time of William I developed
in, or before, the reign of John into an office definitely attached
to the Mint. Of any other officers of the Mint we find no evidence
at all, nor can any conclusion be drawn from an inquiry into the
organization of the Mint in later times. The administration was
not at this early period divided into separate Government depart-
ments; the first sign of breaking away from the old centralization
of financial, judicial, and administrative authority in a single
executive board first appears in the reign of Henry II. Under the
Norman kings, at least, the Mint was no doubt treated as an
inseparable part of the king's treasury or exchequer,[1] and I think
one may assume that the same executive officers controlled the
work of the moneyers at the royal mints throughout the country
as audited the accounts of the king's sheriffs; at the same time
the moneyers were probably more independent than at a later
period.

Some reference has already been made to the means at the
disposal of the king or his officers for controlling the moneyers.
The most obvious method was the engraving of the moneyer's name
and of his mint on his reverse dies; this would seem inadequate
without some periodical trial of the money, and it has been suggested
above[2] that the periodical change of the coin-types was made with
the object of marking a periodical assay which might be the origin
of the Trial of the Pyx; assaying was certainly known and
employed at this time, for payments in Domesday are sometimes
'blanched', *i.e.* assayed and compensated.

---

[1] That a financial department existed at this time and earlier, there seems no
doubt (see Hughes, Crump and Johnson, *Dialogus de Scaccario*, introduction,
p. 13, and references in foot-note).
[2] p. xiii.

Whether the dies for provincial mints were all made in London has long been under dispute; but the evidence of Domesday on the question seems so strong that I think it may be accepted with slight reservation. The Domesday passages which bear on the subject are the following statements of fees paid by moneyers on receipt of dies after the introduction of a new type:[1]

In civitate Wirecestre habebat Rex Edwardus hanc consuetudinem. Quando moneta vertebatur quisque monetarius dabat xx solidos ad Londoniam pro cuneis monetæ accipiendis (I. 172).

Septem monetarii erant ibi (in Hereford). Unus ex his erat monetarius episcopi. Quando moneta renovatur dabat quisque eorum xviii solidos pro cuneis recipiendis: et ex eo die quo redibant usque ad unum mensem dabat quisque eorum regi xx solidos. Et similiter habebat episcopus de suo monetario xx solidos (I. 179).

Tres monetarios habebat ibi (in Sciropesberie) rex. Qui, postquam coemissent cuneos monetæ ut alii monetarii patriæ, xv die dabant regi xx solidos unusquisque. Et hoc fiebat moneta vertente (I. 252).

A certain amount of evidence on this subject may be adduced from the coins themselves, but not sufficient to afford any definite conclusion.

In favour of the engraving of all dies at London, emphasis has always been laid on the very close similarity of coins struck at mints in all parts of the country; the similarity of style is indeed striking, and it is impossible, with the exception of a few coins which are mentioned below, to attribute a coin to its mint by examining the style of the obverse. But this does not take into account the method of engraving dies, which was apparently

---

[1] The payment of fees is also mentioned, but without notice of the receipt of dies, in the following passages: In burgo de Lewes, cum moneta renovatur dat xx solidos unusquisque monetarius (I. 26). Ibi (in burgo Dore Cestre) erant ii monetarii, quisque eorum reddens regi unam markam argenti, et xx solidos quando moneta vertebatur (I. 75). Ibi (in Brideport) erat unus monetarius, reddens regi unam markam argenti et xx solidos quando moneta vertebatur (I. 75). Ibi (in Warham) ii monetarii, quisque reddens unam markam argenti regi, et xx solidos quando moneta vertebatur (I. 75). Ibi (in burgo Sceptesberie) erant iii monetarii, quisque reddebat i markam argenti, et xx solidos quando moneta vertebatur (I. 75).

a system of reproducing a set model with mathematical precision and with the assistance of punching tools and did not leave much scope for individuality. The use of a model or pattern die, or rather, the copying of one die from another, seems to be the only possible explanation of a curious reproduction of errors on Thetford coins of the second type of William I.[1] These are the three coins described below, p. 27, nos. 144–6; they are all struck from different reverse dies, on each of which appears the very rare omission of the initial cross; on each the inscription begins a little to the right of the limb of the voided cross of the design instead of beginning in the usual place exactly above the limb, and the readings are:

ᚦINRIᚦON✠IEOᚦNF
ᚦINRIᚦOND✠IEOᚦNF
ᚦINRIᚦOND✠IEOᚦNF

The first reading contains a very natural punch-worker's error, ✠I for Đ, the use of a straight instead of a crescent-shaped punch; the other two both reproduce this error, but, apparently with the intention of correcting it and on the supposition that the misgraven letter represented H, the letter D is inserted before it. This is a very curious and, I think, quite certain proof of the copying of die from die; for there is no doubt whatever that the coins nos. 145 and 146 are struck from two different reverse dies, though each reproduces the extraordinary mistaken attempt to correct the error of no. 144. The engraving of dies was therefore a matter of copying, the original being presumably made by the chief engraver and supplied to the workmen to copy. This does not decide the question whether the copying of the original die and the recopying of die from die were done at London or locally; it does show, however, that, if the dies were all made at London, either a model was kept by the *cuneator* at London, or a number of dies, and not a single pair, were delivered to the

---

[1] *Num. Chron.*, 1911, pp. 283-4. I there held the view that this proved that dies were engraved locally, but it may equally be explained as the work of engravers at London working from a set model.

moneyer at the introduction of the new issue;[1] for we know from specimens of dies of hammered coinage, though later in date, which still survive, that the dies when returned after use were not in a condition to be copied by the engraver.

A coin which affords some, though rather conjectural, evidence that the dies were made in London, is described on p. 114, no. 608: it is a Chichester coin on the reverse of which the outline of ✖ is visible below the second and third letters (**IⅭ**) of the mint; the coin is in very good condition and there is no trace of overstriking. The letter ✖ was evidently wrongly engraved on the die; if, as seems likely, the engraver began to engrave the mint as Exeter instead of Chichester, the die must have been made at London and not at Chichester for such confusion to arise.[2]

Perhaps the strongest support for a literal interpretation of the passage above quoted from Domesday is to be found in the consideration of the meaning of the reverse inscriptions, and of occasional efforts of the moneyers to make them illegible by tampering with their dies. There can be no doubt that the moneyer's name and that of his mint were placed on the coins of this period for the purpose of identification of the person responsible for any coin that might be found of low weight or base standard. Certain coins have been found, and are described below (pp. cxlix ff.), which were struck, usually of low weight, from reverse dies on which some ingenuity has been spent in changing the names in the legend or in making them illegible;[3] these are clearly attempts on the part of the moneyers to make profit by the usual fraudulent practice of coining at low weight, while minimizing the risk of conviction by tampering with the mark

---

[1] To Bury St. Edmunds one set of dies only was supplied at a time, and that only on return of the old set. But Stephen granted the Abbot as many as three sets (see below, p. clxiv).

[2] Note also, on p. xlv, the possible evidence of the use of identical punches in making the dies of different mints.

[3] See *Num. Chron.*, 1911, pp. 285 ff. I am not now of opinion, as I then was, that these coins are evidence of the moneyers being in possession of official graving punches.

of identification which the coins bear. If the engraving of the dies had been done locally, it would presumably have been done by, or under direction of, the moneyers, who seem to have been important officials responsible for the operations of the mints at which they worked; in this case, the altering of the inscription on reverse dies would be an unnecessary labour, as it would be in the moneyer's power to have his dies originally engraved with a false inscription.

The chief argument to be opposed to the theory that the dies were made at London, is that certain coins of a certain locality, while differing from the coins of the other mints, bear a very close resemblance in style to each other. Most noteworthy of these are the coins of William I which are attributed to the mints of St. Davids and Cardiff (see **Pl. XIX.** 1-3, and **Pl. XXIII.** 13-16); and I think it must be conceded that, even if the evidence of Domesday is right, exception must be made of the Welsh mints,[1] for they, unlike other so-called coarse or barbarous issues, were evidently not made with the usual punches that were used for the rest of the coinage. Other coins of the reign of William I [2] have a peculiarity of style (see *Num. Chron.*, 1911, p. 283); the most important instance is the coins of type IV of Lincoln, Stamford, and York, which are all of very rough work and all closely similar in style. Similar also are some of the Lincoln coins of type II (see **Pl. IV.** 13, 14). The coarseness of these coins seems to be due not to the use of punches of irregular form, but to the careless handling of the punches and clumsy engraving of the dies. This might well be explained by the assumption that the dies were cut locally or at a separate centre for the Yorkshire and Lincoln-shire mints; but this explanation is not a necessary one; it may equally be explained by the assumption that the work was distributed to the engravers at London by localities, and that inexperienced workmen were at this period given the dies

---

[1] Coins of Rhuddlan, however, are not of 'barbarous' work (see **Pl. XXIII.** 8).

[2] I purposely avoid making mention here of coins of Stephen, as peculiarities of that reign might be attributed to baronial work.

to engrave for the northern and north-eastern part of the country.

We may, therefore, conclude that one of the methods by which the authorities controlled the work of the moneyers was the engraving of their dies at London; but this statement requires some modification. Not only does it seem necessary to attribute the engraving of dies of the Welsh mints to local workmen using locally made tools, but it is also necessary to concede that in some circumstances it was allowed, or at least possible, for an obverse die to be borrowed by a moneyer of one mint from a moneyer of another.[1]

The following instances, all of the 'Paxs' type of William I, occur of a die being sent from one mint to another (traces on the coins of rust-marks or cracks on the dies usually furnish evidence at which mint the die was first used):[2]

From Barnstaple (Seword, nos. 498, 499) to Exeter (Semær, no. 668).

From Canterbury (Godric, no. 554) to Hythe (Edred, no. 712).

From Guildford (Seric, nos. 690-2) to Chichester (Bruman, nos. 600-2).

From Marlborough (Cild, no. 827) to Salisbury (Esbern or Osbern, nos. 897-8).

From Salisbury (Esbern, nos. 899, 900) to Marlborough (Cild, no. 828). (These two Marlborough coins are from the same reverse die, no. 828 being the later.)

From Salisbury (Esbern or Osbern, nos. 895-6) to Wilton (Sewine, no. 1062).

From Wilton (Sefaroi and Sewine, nos. 1058-9, 1063) to Salisbury (Osbern, nos. 901-2).

From Cricklade (Ælfwine, no. 625) to Wilton (Ælfwine, no. 1057).

From Shrewsbury (Godesbrand, no. 938) to St. Davids (Turri, no. 883).[3]

From London (Ælfred, nos. 763-4) to Southwark (Osmund, nos. 976-7).

---

[1] The use of an obverse die by two or more moneyers at the same mint is very frequent.

[2] See *Num. Chron.*, 1911, pp. 274 ff. The London and Ipswich die mentioned on p. 278 (*op. cit.*) is omitted, as the coin that purports to be of Ipswich is certainly a forgery (see below, p. 136, no. 722).

[3] The close resemblance of both obverse and reverse of the Shrewsbury coin to the coarse work of St. Davids causes some doubt whether its attribution to Shrewsbury is correct; see below, p. clxxx.

In type II of William I, the same die was used (there is no evidence at which mint it was first used) at :

London (Godwine?, no. 128) and Thetford (Cinric, no. 145); the reverse die of the London coin had been tampered with, see below, p. cl.

Thetford (Cinric, no. 146) and MAINT . . . (Brihtwi, no. 130).

In type III of William I, a die was sent from London (Sibode, no. 201) to Exeter (Ælfwine, no. 184).

It will be noticed that, disregarding the Shrewsbury—St. Davids die (and indeed Shrewsbury was probably the most accessible, if not the nearest, mint to St. Davids), the two mints using the same die are almost invariably in close proximity. The only exceptions are London—Thetford, and London—Exeter; whether the London—Thetford die was used first at London or Thetford is uncertain, but the London—Exeter die is shown with certainty, from rust-marks in the crown, to have been sent from London to Exeter. We have, then, two distinct phenomena: in the first place that of a die being sent from one mint to another in the vicinity, and secondly, a die being sent from London all the way to Exeter, and another either from London to Thetford or from Thetford to London (presumably, by analogy, from London to Thetford). The former case is no doubt simply the borrowing or purchase of a die from a neighbour as an emergency measure; whether it was an authorized measure or illegal, one cannot say. The second case is very different; it seems to be a definite illustration of the theory that dies were delivered from London to the provincial mints, as I think one can only explain the transfer of a die from London to a mint so far distant as Exeter as a stop-gap measure, an old die being sent when the need at Exeter was urgent, in order to save the time of engraving the new die.

The large number of irregular issues in the north of England during the reign of Stephen may perhaps be attributed to a temporary collapse of the direct control from the London mint.

Moneyers.

The position of the moneyer in Anglo-Saxon times is obscure; in the reign of Æthelred II, he had workmen under him for whom he was personally responsible;[1] in the laws of Cnut the moneyers seem themselves to have been under the authority of the reeve, for if they affirmed that they made false coin with his permission the reeve was to undergo the triple ordeal, and, if guilty, to suffer the same penalty as a guilty moneyer.[2] In the laws of Æthelstan, Æthelred II, and Cnut the same penalty—amputation of the hand, and its exposure over the mint—was fixed for false coining.[3] The number of moneyers was reduced by Æthelred II:[4] for every chief town three, for every other town one (to judge by the names appearing on consecutive issues of the coins of this reign, this law was repealed or modified).

In the Winton Domesday (fol. 2) Godwine Socche is described as having been 'master moneyer' in the time of the Confessor.

In Domesday, more information is given on this subject; we have already (p. cxxxv) quoted passages which, show that the moneyers, when the type was changed, purchased their new dies at London and then paid their fees—the king's moneyers to the king, the bishop's to the bishop.

At Oxford, the moneyer Suetman has a free house (*domus*) rated at forty pence. Suetman has two *mansiones muri* and pays three shillings (I. 154).

At Wallingford, a moneyer has a house (*haga*) free[5] so long as he works at the mint (I. 56).

At York, Nigellus de Monneville has one *mansio* of a moneyer (I. 298).

---

[1] Liebermann, *Gesetze*, p. 236 (IV. Æthelred, 9, 1).

[2] *Op. cit.*, p. 314 (II. Cnut, 8, 2).

[3] *Op. cit.*, pp. 158, 234, 314 (II. Æthelstan, 14, 1; IV. Æthelred, 5, 3; II. Cnut, 8, 1).

[4] *Op. cit.*, p. 236 (IV. Æthelred, 9).

[5] Not necessarily, as Ruding translates it, 'rent-free'; the word *liber* may carry further privileges or immunities (cf. Maitland, *Domesday Book and Beyond*, p. 89, &c.)

At Hereford, in the time of the Confessor, when the king came
to the city, the moneyers made for him as many pennies as he
required from the king's silver (*i.e.*, presumably, as opposed to
the bishop's); the seven moneyers had sac and soc; if one of
the king's moneyers died, the king had twenty shillings in relief,
and, if he died intestate, his whole property; if the reeve went
to Wales with an army, they (the moneyers) went with him under
penalty of forty shillings (I. 179).

Under the Confessor, Walter, Bishop of Hereford, had one
moneyer in Hereford (I. 181 b).

At Leicester, the moneyers paid twenty pounds (at the rate of
twenty pennies to the ounce) yearly; of this, Hugh de Grantmesnil
received the *tertius denarius* (I. 230).

At Huntingdon there were, in the time of the Confessor, but not
at the time of the Survey, three moneyers paying forty shillings
between the king and the earl (I. 203).

At Colchester, both in the time of the Confessor and at the time
of the Survey, the moneyers paid four pounds (II. 107).

At Norwich, the bishop, if he wished, had the privilege of one
moneyer (II. 117 b).

The following payments *monetae, de moneta,* &c., are noted:
Pevensey, twenty shillings (I. 20 b); Malmesbury, 100 shillings
(I. 64 b); Gloucester, twenty pounds (I. 162); Colchester and
Maldon, twenty pounds, apparently reduced by William to ten
pounds (II. 107 b);[1] Thetford, forty pounds (II. 119); Hunting-
don—Rex W. geldum monete posuit in burgo—(I. 203); Lincoln
—Geldum regis de monedagio [2]—(I. 336 b).

In the reign of Henry I there is some legislation with regard to
the coinage, and some reference to moneyers, forgers, &c. In his
Coronation Charter (Aug. 5, 1100):[3]

Monetagium commune quod capiebatur per ciuitates et comitatus, quod
non fuit tempore regis Eadwardi, hoc ne amodo sit, omnino defendo (§ 5).

---

[1] The passage seems corrupt; see translation by J. H. Round in *Victoria
County History of Essex.*

[2] See above, pp. lxix-lxx.   [3] Liebermann, vol. i, p. 522.

Si quis captus fuerit, siue monetarius siue alius, cum falsa moneta, iusticia recta inde fiat (§ 5, 1).

The following charter *de moneta falsa et cambiatoribus* is attributed to the date 1100–1 or 1103 : [1]

Henricus rex Anglorum Samsoni episcopo et Ursoni de Abetot et omnibus baronibus, Francis et Anglis, de Wirecestrescira salutem.

Sciatis quod uolo et precipio, ut omnes burgenses et omnes illi qui in burgis morantur, tam Franci quam Angli, iurent tenere et seruare monetam meam in Anglia, ut non consentiant falsitatem monete mee.

Et si quis cum falso denario inuentus fuerit, si warant inde reuocauerit, ad eum ducatur; et si illum inde conprobare poterit, fiat iusticia mea de ipso warant. Si uero non poterit illum probare, de ipso falsonario fiat iusticia mea, scilicet de dextro pugno et testiculis. Si autem nullum warant inde reuocauerit, portet inde iudicium, se nescire nominare uel cognoscere aliquem a quo acceperit.

Praeterea defendo, ne aliquis monetarius denarios mutet nisi in comitatu suo, et hoc coram duobus legittimis testibus de ipso comitatu. Et si in alio comitatu mutando denarios captus fuerit, captus sit ut falsonarius.

Et nullus sit ausus cambire denarios nisi monetarius.

Teste Willelmo cancellario et Roberto comite de Mellent et R[odberto] filio Hamonis et R[icardo] de Retuers. Apud Westmonasterium in natale Domini.

In the Chronicles of Roger of Hoveden, Eadmer, Florence of Worcester, and Symeon of Durham, the following is recorded under the year 1108 : [2]

Monetam quoque corruptam et falsam [3] sub tanta animadversione corrigi statuit, ut quicunque falsos denarios facere deprehensus fuisset, oculos et inferiores corporis partes sine ulla redemptione amitteret; [4] et quoniam saepissime dum denarii eligebantur, flectebantur, rumpebantur,

---

[1] Liebermann, p. 523. Cf. *Num. Chron.*, 1901, p. 475.

[2] The text followed is that of Hoveden (Rolls Series, no. 51, vol. i, p. 165); variants of the other chroniclers are given in the notes.

[3] *Item moneta corrupta et falsa multis modis multos affligebat. Quam rex . . .* Eadmer.

[4] *Ut nullus qui posset deprehendi falsos denarios facere aliqua redemptione quin oculos et inferiores corporis partes perderet iuvari valeret.* Eadmer, Florence of Worcester, Symeon of Durham.

respuebantur, statuit, ut nullus denarius vel obolus, quos et rotundos esse iussit, aut etiam quadrans,[1] [si] integer esset, respueretur.[2] Ex quo facto magnum bonum[3] toti regno provisum[4] est, quia ipse rex[5] hæc in sæcularibus ad relevandas terræ ærumnas[6] agebat.

William of Malmesbury, in his brief epitome of the reign of Henry I, states after a mention of Henry's return from Normandy (Spring, 1107):[7]

Contra trapezetas, quos vulgo monetarios vocant, præcipuam sui diligentiam exhibuit; nullum falsarium, quin pugnum perderet, impune abire permittens, qui fuisset intellectus falsitatis suæ commercio fatuos irrisisse.

In the Anglo-Saxon Chronicle under the years 1124–5 occur the following passages:[8]

1124. That (the high price of food, &c.) was because there was little corn, and the penny was so bad, that the man who had at a market a pound could by no means buy therewith twelve pennyworths.

1125. In this year, before Christmas, King Henry sent from Normandy to England, and commanded that all the moneyers that were in England should be deprived of their members; that was the right hand of each, and their testicles beneath. That was because the man that had a pound could not buy for a penny at a market (*sic*). And the Bishop Roger of Salisbury sent over all England, and commanded them all that they should come to Winchester at Christmas. When they came thither they were taken one by one, and each deprived of the right hand and the testicles beneath. All this was done within the twelve nights; and that was all with great

---

[1] *quos . . . quadrans* omitted by Eadmer. *instituit* for *iussit* Florence, Symeon.

[2] For [*si*] . . . *respueretur* Eadmer, Florence, and Symeon read *integer esset*, which is not intelligible.

[3] Eadmer inserts *ad tempus*.

[4] *creatum* Eadmer, Florence, Symeon.

[5] *quia ipse rex* omitted by Eadmer.

[6] Eadmer inserts *interim rex*.

[7] W. Malm., *G. R.* v. 399 (Rolls Series, no. 90, vol. ii, p. 476).

[8] The translation is that of Thorpe in the Rolls Series (no. 23). Ruding says that the Anglo-Saxon Chronicle mentions the punishment of six forgers in 1124, but there is no reason to suppose that the six men there mentioned were forgers.

justice, because they had fordone all the land with their great quantity of false money which they all bought.

The same event is related by most of the Chroniclers;[1] the Margam Annals place it in the year 1124, and Symeon of Durham in 1126.

In the Margam Annals the number of moneyers is given as ninety-four; according to the Winton Annals all the moneyers of England were mutilated except three of Winchester. The height of food prices in 1125 is attributed in the Margam Annals to rain-storms in the summer, by Florence of Worcester to the reform of the coinage which followed this punishment of moneyers. Wykes adds to the penalty of mutilation that of banishment.

In the Pipe Roll of Henry I (1130) two men at London owe a fine for forfeitures for false coining:

Algarus et Sprachelingus debent x marcas argenti pro forisfacturis falsorum denariorum.

But there is no reason to suppose that these are moneyers; the name Algar occurs on coins of London of this period but not that of Spracheling, unless, as Mr. Andrew suggests, the name Sperling on the coins is identical. Similarly, in the following entry, we have no reason to suppose the debtor to be a moneyer,[2] nor can we conjecture what the offence was:

Godwinus Quachehand debet iiii marcas auri ut haberet pacem de placito Monetæ.

Definite references to moneyers occur:

under Hampshire (Hamtona):

Saietus monetarius debet cclxxviii marcas argenti pro placito ii cuneorum.

---

[1] W. Malm., Roger of Hoveden, Margam Annals, H. Hunt., Waverley Ann., Winton Ann., Cont. Flor. Worc., Sym. Dur., Matt. Paris, Wykes.

[2] A coin of Henry I, type XV (T. Bliss collection) reads **GODPINE GV: ON** - - - . The identification of this reading with Godwine Quachehand of the Pipe Roll (*Num. Chron.*, 1901, p. 283) is possible, but doubtful.

k

under Honor de Arundel:

Brand Monetarius reddit compotum de xx libris ne esset disfactus cum aliis monetariis.

Et idem Vicecomes reddit compotum de i marca argenti de hominibus monetariorum Cicestriæ.

under Norfolk:

Eadstanus debet c solidos de pecunia Ulchetelli monetarii.

under Pembroke:

Gillopatric monetarius reddit compotum de iiii libris pro forisfacturis veteris Monetæ.[1]

In his summary of the character of Henry I, William of Malmesbury (Rolls Series, no. 90, vol. ii, p. 487) says:[2]

Fures et falsarios latentes maxima diligentia perscrutans, inventos puniens: parvarum quoque rerum non negligens.

Cum nummos fractos, licet boni argenti, a venditoribus non recipi audisset, omnes vel frangi vel incidi præcepit.

In the reign of Stephen we have no reference to the coinage and mint officials, except the brief allusions to baronial issues which have been quoted above (p. lxxii).

The information to be obtained with regard to the status of the moneyers is very scanty. At the time of the Domesday Survey, if we may argue from particular cases to the general (which is very doubtful), we find that they were free tenants of the king, having *sake* and *soke*, i.e. presumably the 'lower justice' (Maitland, *op. cit.*, p. 81), or limited jurisdiction over their own men and their property; they were subject (in Hereford at least) to military service; in some cases they held an official residence, *mansio* or *haga*, during their term of office, and the king did not have the *consuetudo* of the moneyer's *haga* at Wallingford. The property of moneyers (at Hereford) was not free from the king's relief at their death, nor from reversion to the king in case of intestacy.

The Pipe Roll of Henry I (Honor de Arundel) shows that the moneyers had workmen under them, and we have already seen

---

[1] See above, p. xxxiii, note 4.   [2] See below, pp. cxlviii f.

that in the reign of Æthelred II the moneyers were personally responsible for their workmen.

They were, therefore, of burgess rank, and that they were men of some property may perhaps be concluded from the amounts of payments made or owed by them in the Pipe Roll; Brand of Chichester, for instance, has the penalty of mutilation commuted to payment of twenty pounds (probably the fine is still owing from the Christmas of 1125, when so many moneyers suffered the penalty). Saiet of Southampton owes the large sum of 278 marks of silver. It is true that these sums are owed and not paid, but it is unlikely that Brand could have had his sentence commuted to a fine unless he could give some security or at least show himself likely to clear the debt within a reasonable time; nor is it probable that Brand or Saiet would be continued in their office of moneyer if they were unlikely ever to clear themselves of their fines. The sums they owe are large; Saiet owes as much as £185 6s. 8d., which at least gives an impression that moneyers were in Norman times men of no small means. We know that in the time of Henry III moneyers were burgesses of good position who not infrequently held the office of sheriff or reeve,[1] and that they were sometimes men of wealth.[2] So early as the reign of Stephen, if (as there seems little doubt) Thomas FitzUlf is correctly identified with the alderman of York mentioned in the Pipe Roll,[3] an alderman is acting as moneyer; that he is coining under a baron and not directly under the king is, for the present purpose, unimportant. There is certainly nothing in Domesday to prove that the moneyers of William I were men of equal status to their successors, but Domesday Book does tell us that they were burgesses with certain privileges, and it hardly justifies us in assuming that their position underwent any material change during the eleventh century.

---

[1] *Num. Chron.*, 1885, pp. 209 ff.

[2] In 1242 Nicholas de Sancto Albano farmed the *cambium* of London and Canterbury (Calendar of Close Rolls). Thomas de Weseham was the king's surgeon (*Brit. Num. Journ.*, vol. ix, p. 159).

[3] See above, p. cxiii.

The passage quoted above (p. cxlvi) from William of Malmesbury's character of Henry I (Rolls Series, no. 90, vol. ii, p. 487—*Cum nummos fractos, licet boni argenti, a venditoribus non recipi audisset, omnes vel frangi vel incidi præcepit*) is of considerable interest, as Mr. Andrew has shown in *Num. Chron.*, 1901, pp. 55, 492;[1] the meaning of the passage is undoubtedly that the king, finding that cracked coins, although of good silver, were not accepted by traders, ordered all coins to be cracked or incised; that is to say, by ordering all coins to be issued from the mint with a crack or incision in their edge the king compelled the acceptance of cracked coins.

This clearly refers, as Mr. Andrew pointed out, to a sharp cut which appears on coins of this reign; the most clear instance is seen on **Pl. XLI. 4**, but on this coin the cut has penetrated much further into the coin than usual; nos. 14 and 15 on the same plate, and 7, 9, 13 on **Pl. XLII**, are perhaps better examples.

This incision occurs on all the coins that I have seen of types VII to XII inclusive,[2] and also on a very few coins of types XIII, XIV, and XV (**Pl. XLIII. 3,**[3] **15; XLVI. 8; XLVII. 13**), but not on any coins of types I to VI. This is an interesting confirmation of the order in which the types of this reign have been placed;[4] types I to VI clearly precede the introduction of this measure, and XIII to XV, of which incised, or snicked, coins are unusual, must have been issued after the withdrawal of the measure. Unfortunately, we are given no date of either its introduction or withdrawal; Mr. Andrew supposes that it was given up when the coinage was reformed after the punishment of moneyers at Christmas, 1125; if he is right, type XII is earlier than 1125 and does not, as I conclude

---

[1] See also *Brit. Num. Journ.*, vol. viii, pp. 132-3, where Mr. Andrew connects the passage with the issue of cut halfpennies and farthings.

[2] I cannot be quite certain of all the coins of type XII; the incision cannot be seen on the coin of Lincoln (no. 82), perhaps because the coin is clipped.

[3] The coin has cracked towards the centre from the end of the incision after the incision was made; the incision can be distinguished from an accidental crack by its regular shape.

[4] Mr. Andrew comments on this, but fails to observe that the incisions are not found on coins of types IV, V, and VI, which in his grouping of the types fall between the types which I have numbered VII and XII.

below (p. cliv), follow the reform; but it is quite possible that the practice continued for a time after 1125, and was later found unnecessary.

Legislation against debasing the currency is severe and continually reiterated, and also against secret coining and all kinds of forgery. Yet at this period, as throughout the mediaeval English coinage, forgery and the fraudulence of moneyers were, or were reputed to be, the cause of much distress in the country. In 1108, and again in 1125, this feature is noted by the Chroniclers, and on the latter occasion it led to the mutilation, and, according to Wykes, the banishment, of an enormous number of moneyers.

The coins give evidence of continual debasement and forgery of this sort; not only are there several coins evidently struck in the regular mints of light weight and base metal, but also some pieces which show attempts to evade the penalties by falsification of the reverse dies.[1]

A series of these coins seems to have been issued by the moneyer Ælfsi, or Æolfsi, of London, during the first three issues of the reign of William I. A coin of type I in Major Carlyon-Britton's collection is struck from a reverse die on which the original inscription **✠ELFSIONLIINDE** has been changed to **✠ELPPIONE✕ELSDE**. The following drawing shows by shaded lines the alterations made in the original inscription:

$$\text{✠ELPSIONEᵻEᵴDE}$$

the weight of this coin is 16·3 grains (PL. II. 6).

Some coins of type II, which are not uncommon, bear an inscription which has been changed, I think, from **✠IELFSON LIINDENI**[2] to **IDEFIONEⲚ▨▨ENI** thus:

$$\text{✠IBEFSONEⲘⲚDENI}$$

Three of these coins, weighing 18·1, 17, and 15·9 grains, are

---

[1] See *Num. Chron.*, 1911, pp. 285 ff. The blocks are reproduced by kind permission of the Council of the Royal Numismatic Society.

[2] For this reading of the moneyer's name cf. Carlyon-Britton sale, 1913, lot 645.

described in this Catalogue, nos. 109–11 (Pl. V. 2), two of which are struck from the same obverse die as a coin reading ✠IEOLF SIONLIINDEN

A coin of type III in Major Carlyon-Britton's collection has the reverse inscription, ✠IELFSIONLIINDENEN, partly defaced by cuts:

✠ℕEℍℝℬ︎IONℂℍℕℍENEN

the coin weighs 17·5 grains.

These coins are evidently forgeries of the same moneyer, Ælfsi or Æolfsi, of whom we know at present no coins later than the third type of William I. The coins are all of appreciably low weight, and the most noteworthy feature is that in each case the alteration on the die is evidently done with the object of obscuring the moneyer's name and that of his mint, the unimportant parts of the inscription—the word ON and the last letters of the mint— being untouched.

Similarly, a coin of William I, type II, in the York Museum, is struck from a reverse die which was altered from ✠IELPI NEONLIINDNE to ✠IDLPINEONLINƆONE (Pl. IV. 16).

A coin of Godwine of London, also of the second type of William I (Catalogue, p. 24, no. 128), is similarly altered:

✠ᴆ︎Oℙ︎ℂℍ ℕEON ℙ︎ℐ︎ℕI

it weighs 16·4 grains. The reverse inscription is more clearly seen on a duplicate coin in Mr. L. E. Bruun's collection (Pl. V. 6). The obverse die was (previously, I think) used at Thetford by the moneyer Cinric.

Another die of this same moneyer and of the same type was used to strike a coin in the York Museum with the inscription changed from ✠ƆODPINEONLⅤ︎ᴆ︎E to ✠IELFPINE ONℂⅤ︎FI.

The coin of type VII of this reign described in this Catalogue, p. 86, no. 462, is another instance of this, but the original inscription of the reverse die cannot be deciphered with certainty;

perhaps it was ✠IELFPINEONLII, the altered inscription beginning half-way through the moneyer's name of the original. Another attempt to obscure the reverse inscription may be found on p. 38, no. 199.[1] That these coins are all of the London mint and of the reign of William I is perhaps a coincidence; I have seen similar coins of Anglo-Saxon and 'Short-cross' (Henry II— Henry III) times.

Perhaps the same Godwine of London, who struck the coins mentioned above with altered reverse dies, forged the reverse die reading ✠IILIPINEONGPINII (see Catalogue, p. 136, no. 722), as the coin struck from this forged die is struck from an obverse die which is used with a genuine reverse, reading ✠GODPINEONLIIND (p. 151, no. 811).

With regard to coins that are struck of low weight or base metal from good dies, it is of course not possible to draw any fixed line, and say that coins below a certain weight were necessarily struck light; the decision must depend on the allowance made for loss of weight, and this is again dependent on the length of time for which a coin was in currency, the extent of corrosion which it has suffered, the amount of cleaning which it has undergone, and other unascertainable data. Further, though we assume the standard weight of the penny during this period to have been $22\frac{1}{2}$ grains, this is not a matter of certain knowledge, nor even that the standard remained the same throughout the period with which we are dealing. In his account of the Beaworth find, Mr. Hawkins gave the average weight of coins of the various types, both of coins in the find and of coins in the British Museum before the discovery; the contrast of these figures is sufficient to condemn any attempt to discover a standard weight by an average of existing coins; nor is the average weight of coins in a find of any practical value, for it will obviously include coins that were fraudulently struck light, and coins that have suffered severely from clipping or wear; and even

---

[1] It need hardly be said that the alteration of a die need not always have been the work of a forger (cf. pp. 193-4, nos. 1043-5, which are quite good coins and of good weight).

in the Beaworth find, which was remarkable for the fine condition
of the coins, there were some forgeries (*e. g.* p. 136, no. 722), and
some coins in worn condition (some of the Lewes coins of type VIII
are instances). The standard weight must be left to conjecture,
which may perhaps best be based upon a table showing the number
of coins of different weights of each type. In the following table the
highest number of coins of each type is printed in heavy fount, in order
to emphasize the extent of variation of weight of the most numerous
set of coins of each type. Types represented by less than twenty
coins in all should be disregarded: they are only inserted here
for the sake of completeness. These numbers omit pierced and
clipped coins, and coins which for any definite reason can be
declared false, such, for example, as the forgeries mentioned above.

The figures in this table are not incompatible with the standard
weight of common tradition, viz. 22·5 grains, if we except the
first five types of William I (those types where no figure is shown
in italics are of course also excepted, because through their scarcity
their evidence is valueless); on the other hand, these first five
types, or at least the first three, render figures which certainly
give an impression that the coins were in the early part of the
reign struck on a lower standard. But the figures of type II are
instructive; it is obvious that, however low the standard weight
is conjectured to be at this period, there must be a long tail of
coins struck very considerably below it. Place the standard as
low as 20 grains, then at least the twenty-three coins which weigh
less than 17 grains must be considered as having been struck light.
The significance of these figures is, I think, that the lower weight
of the early types of William I denotes not a lower standard of
the coinage, but a laxity in the control of the moneyers; perhaps
a slight drop or slight rise in the general weight of coins may,
as a rule, be taken to signify a relaxing or tightening of the
king's authority.

Throughout the whole Norman period there are evidently many
coins which were struck below the standard weight, and this is
most prominent in the second type of William I, and the fourteenth

	12–12.9	13–13.9	14–14.9	15–15.9	16–16.9	17–17.9	18–18.9	19–19.9	20–20.9	21–21.9	22–22.9	over 23
William I, type I	1	3	1	1	1	2	7	22	31	4	—	—
,, ,, II	—	—	2	7	10	12	8	22	20	1	1	—
,, ,, III	—	—	—	—	1	6	4	12	14	3	1	—
,, ,, IV	—	—	—	1	—	1	7	17	29	15	—	—
,, ,, V	—	—	—	—	1	1	5	18	48	25	3	—
,, ,, VI	—	—	—	1	2	2	5	12	13	24	3	2
,, ,, VII	—	—	—	—	—	2	4	4	11	10	7	1
,, ,, VIII	—	—	—	—	—	—	4	11	163	425	1	—
William II, type I	—	—	—	—	1	1	1	3	13	44	—	—
,, ,, II	—	—	—	1	—	—	5	8	32	53	—	—
,, ,, III	—	—	—	—	—	—	—	—	16	36	4	—
,, ,, IV	—	—	5	1	—	—	2	1	8	14	—	—
,, ,, V	—	—	—	—	—	3	1	2	7	11	—	—
Henry I, type I	—	—	—	—	1	—	—	1	2	10	—	—
,, ,, II	—	—	—	—	—	1	3	1	1	1	—	—
,, ,, III	—	—	—	—	1	—	2	1	—	—	—	—
,, ,, IV	—	—	—	—	—	—	—	—	1	1	1	—
,, ,, V	—	—	—	1	2	1	—	2	5	4	4	—
,, ,, VI	—	—	—	—	—	—	3	1	2	—	—	—
,, ,, VII	—	—	—	—	—	—	—	1	5	3	3	1
,, ,, VIII	—	—	—	—	—	—	1	2	3	—	7	—
,, ,, XI	—	—	—	—	2	8	5	8	1	12	1	—
,, ,, X	—	—	—	1	—	1	3	2	6	34	4	3
,, ,, XII	—	—	—	—	—	1	6	1	23	57	23	—
,, ,, XIII	—	—	5	—	2	1	3	1	12	55	33	3
,, ,, XIV	—	—	—	—	—	1	2	2	19	3	5	2
,, ,, XV	—	—	—	—	—	—	2	—	2	—	—	—
Stephen, type I	—	—	—	1	—	—	—	—	—	—	—	—
,, ,, II	—	—	—	—	2	1	—	7	1	—	—	—
,, ,, III	—	—	—	—	—	—	—	—	—	—	—	—
,, ,, IV	—	—	—	—	—	—	—	—	—	—	—	—
,, ,, V	—	—	—	1	—	1	—	—	—	—	1	—
,, ,, VI	—	—	—	—	—	—	—	—	—	—	—	—
,, ,, VII	—	—	—	—	2	1	—	7	11	14	8	2

of Henry I. This latter case is noteworthy; on the assumption that the types were regularly changed at intervals of two or three years, this type would come into issue after 1130—about 1132—some seven years after the great punishment of moneyers at Christmas, 1125; in any case, we can hardly suppose that it was in issue at that time, as we should then leave one type only for the remaining ten years of the reign. There are, in fact, other indications that the type then current, and presumably then put out of issue, was the 'double-inscription' type, the eleventh of the reign. One may reasonably suppose that a punishment of the moneyers on so large a scale was followed by what is commonly known as a reform of the coinage, that is to say, not a change in standard but a general inquiry and reorganization similar to those we hear of in 1180, 1205, and 1247, and we should expect this to be marked by a general improvement in workmanship.[1] I think we may find a gradual decadence in style of the coins of Henry I from the fifth type, continuing to and culminating in the eleventh, or 'double-inscription' type, and this is followed by a marked improvement in the twelfth, or 'smaller profile and cross-and-annulets' type, which shows a much neater and more compact style, with a more definite attempt at portraiture. Thus there is probability in placing the end of the issue of the eleventh type at Christmas, 1125.[2] That so many coins in an issue of some six or seven years after the inquiry of 1125 were struck light—and many, to judge by their appearance, of base metal—shows how soon a warning of this sort was forgotten, and how willing the moneyers were to risk the most severe penalties for the sake of the profit available from debasement of the coinage.

The only other occasion during the Norman period when we

---

[1] Mr. Lawrence gives a diagrammatic explanation of the effect of these 'reforms' on the coinage, in an article shortly to be published in the *British Numismatic Journal*, where he deals with the coinage of 1205.

[2] Mr. Andrew also places this type here, though he calls it the twelfth of the reign, but I cannot agree that the coins at present known are of base metal (see *Num. Chron.*, 1901, pp. 78-9). See also above, p. cxlviii, on the incision of coins of type XII.

have definite evidence of any inquiry into the coinage which would be likely to produce a 'reform' of this sort is that of 1108, which has been quoted above. Applying the above principle of degradation to this occasion, the obvious conclusion is that the fourth type was then in issue and at this period superseded by the fifth; this conclusion allows a period of seventeen years for seven types, nos. V to XI, which is consistent with the average duration of two and a half years for each type (see above, p. lxix). It allows eight years for the first four types, which is also consistent with that figure if we suppose that type IV had not completed its natural period when the inquiry was held.

Similarly, by this reckoning, the last four types of the reign would cover a period of almost exactly ten years, assuming that Stephen's name was placed on the coins immediately after his accession. This assumption is most probable, as Stephen's claim was doubtful, and all possible means of publishing his accession were desirable, whereas Henry II, who seems to have allowed Stephen's last issue to continue till 1156 or 1158, was without any rival claimant to the throne.

The names of the moneyers of this period occur in the English form[1] until the Latin termination is occasionally adopted in the reigns of Henry I and Stephen; this appears first in the sixth type of Henry I, and is afterwards occasional in use, being more frequent than previously in the last two types of his reign and in the first of Stephen.

In the Table of Mints, Moneyers, and Types the forms are mostly retained which occur on the coins, varieties being inserted so far as space will allow; an attempt to restore the true form of the names would in many cases be arbitrary, and is best left to specialists. The names which appear on the coins are frequently varied in many ways, partly owing to late forms being used after the Conquest (Ægel- for Æthel-, -wi for -wig, &c.), partly owing to the clipping of terminations and omission of letters in order

---

[1] A foreign termination sometimes appears, such as Bundi, Sendi.

to abbreviate the inscriptions (Wixie for Wihtsige, Goldhfc for Goldhafuc), and partly owing to carelessness of engraving (Lesis for Lesig or Leising, Gowi for Godwi, Brwode for Brihtword? see p. 99, no. 518; Wægelwine for Ægelwine?); sometimes the identity in form of the letters P and W, and the similarity of A and V, S and G, cause difficulty. The original name is consequently difficult to trace; Ælmær, for example, may represent Ælfmær or Ægel-(Æthel-)mær. The termination -wi appears to represent not only -wig, but also in some cases -wine; at London, for example, Godwine occurs on types II to VI (inclusive) and VIII of William I, and on II and III of William II; Godwi occurs on types III, V, and VII of William I, and is therefore likely to be the same moneyer. At Hamtun, Sæwine occurs on types II–V and VIII of William I, types I, II, V of William II, and type II of Henry I; Sæwi on type IV of William I, and types I and II of William II. At Wilton, Sæwine on II, IV, VII, VIII of William I, and I and II of. William II; Sæwi on V of William I, and III of William II. At London, Eadwine on I–V of William I, type II of William II, and types IX and XI of Henry I; Eadwi on all types from the fifth of William I to the third of William II inclusive. At Malmes-bury, Brihtwi on II and IV, Brihtwine on V, of William I; at Oxford, Ægelwi on type III of William I, and Ægelwine on II and III of William II. In which of these, if any, the termination -wi may represent -wine, it is impossible to say, but this certainly seems likely with Godwi at London, and with Sæwi at both Hamtun and Wilton. Some names are quite obscure, such as Inhuhe (p. 157), Api or Awi (p. 317), Bat (pp. 232, 249).

In the following list, in which notes of interrogation refer not to the existence, but to the classification, of the name, the names of moneyers of William I are roughly classified:

ANGLO-SAXON.

Ægel-, -briht, -mær, -ric, -wi, -wine; Ælf-, -gæt, -geard, -heah, -noth, -red, -ric, -si, -wi, -wine, -word; Æstan;[1] Alhsige (Alcsi);

---

[1] York Powell (Eng. Hist. Rev., 1896, p. 766) classifies Eastan as Scandinavian,

Blacsun ; Briht-, -mær, -noth, -red, -ric, -wi, -wine, -wold, -word; Brun-, -gar,[1] -inc, -man, -stan,[1] -wine; Ceorl; Cild?; Cen-, ric, -stan; Cnihtwine; Cuthbert; Deorman: Duninc; Ead-, -red, -ric, -ward, -wi, -wine, -wold; Eald-, -gar, -red, -ulf; Earnwi?; Folcheard; Forna?; God-, -a, -esbrand?, -inc, -leof, -noth, -red, -ric, -wi, -wine; Gold-, -man, -stan, -wine; Heathewi; Heregod; Howord (Howorth)?; Hwateman; Leisinc?; Leof-, -inc, -red, -ric, -stan, -sun, -wi, -wine, -wold, -word; Mann-, -a, -inc, -wine; Ord-, -ric, -wi; Os-, -mær, -wold; Ræfwine?; Sæ-, -fara?, -grim,[1] -mær, -ric, -wi, -wine; Si-, -bode, -brand, -ferth, -lac, -mær, -ward, -wulf; Side-, -loc, -man; Sunulf; Swet-, -inc, -man; Theodred; Wideman; Wig-, -inc, -mund; Wiht-, -red, -ric, -sige (Wixsi, &c.) ; Winc;[2] Wulf-, -bold, -gæt, -mær, -noth, -red, -ric, -si, -stan, -wi, -wine, -word; Wyn- (Win-), -dæg, -red.

SCANDINAVIAN.

Aleif; Arncetel; Arthulf; Atser or Acer; Autholf; Beorn; Brand; Col-, -bein, -blac, -grim, -inc,[3] -man,[3] -swein; Guthred; Horn?[4]; Osbern or Esbern; Osmund; Oter; Oth-, -bern, -grim, -ulf; Roscetel; Swein; Spraceling; Swart-, -brand, -col, -linc[3]; Thor; Thor-, -bern, -cetel, -stan; Ulf; Ulfcetel; Uspac or Ospac (Unspac).

OTHER FOREIGN NAMES.

Agemund, Anderbode, Baldric, Garvin, Gifel?, Owi[ne] ?

UNCERTAIN.

Inhuhe, Turri, Unnulf (possibly Scandinavian, or variant of Sunulf, see p. 113).

---

but Æthelstan, Æstan, and Eastan, which all occur on Winchester coins of the Confessor, are probably the same name; similarly in Domesday (I. 185) Æthelstan, Bishop of Hereford, is called Æstan.

[1] Scandinavian ?
[2] If Silac-wine at Gloucester is to be treated as two names.
[3] Anglo-Saxon ?
[4] Lifwine Horn at Rochester.

The reign of William II adds—

ANGLO-SAXON.

Ægelword, Ælfgar, Ælfstan, Algod, Barcwit ?, Ealdwine, Gold, Goldhafuc, Goldinc, Herman (= Hereman) ?, Leofnoth, Leofsi, Ordgar, Sewold, Siwate, Smewine, Sperhafuc, Sprot ?, Theodric, Wibern (= Wigbeorn), Wulfgar.

SCANDINAVIAN.

Ascetel (Ascil), Colbern, Hal[f]dene.

OTHER FOREIGN NAMES.

Baldwine, Bat ?, Bundi ?, Coc ?, Hathebrand, Sindi (Sendi) ?, Walcin.

The reign of Henry I adds—

ANGLO-SAXON.

Ail-, -noth, -wald ; Blacman, Derlinc, Ealla, Edmund, Essuwi (= Æscwig ?), Estmund, Folcred, Godhese ?, Herdig ?, Leftein (= Leofthegen ?), Osulf, Saiet (= Sægæt ?), Sawulf, Sigar, Sperling ?, Suneman, Wibert.

SCANDINAVIAN.

Chitel, Odde, Oslac or Aslac, Othen (Owthin), Ravenswart, Sihtric, Stanchil, Thored, Toc ?, Winterlede.

OTHER FOREIGN NAMES.

Acel, Adalbot, Andreu, Api or Awi ?, Boniface, Burchart, Chippig (= Hilping ?), Cristret ?, Dort ?, Durant, Engelram, Erembald, Everard, Gahan, Geffrei, Gosfrei, Germane, Gillebert ?, Gillemor, Gilpatric, Gregori, Hlud, Mor ?, Norman, Paien, Raulf, Ricard, Rodbert, Roger, Rolland, Stefne, Stigant, Sultan, Tovi[1] ?, Walter, Warmund, Willem.

The reign of Stephen adds—

ANGLO-SAXON.

Edgar, Gladwine, Godmer, Hermer (= Heremær ?), Siber (= Sigbeorn ?), Wynstan.

---

[1] Scandinavian (= Tofa) ?

FOREIGN NAMES.

Adam, Adelard, Alisander, Etrei?, Falche, Farman, Fobund, Godard, Gurdan, Hamund, Henri, Hue, Hunfrei, Iun, Martin, Tierri, Tomas.

The English and Scandinavian names of this period are nearly all found on Anglo-Saxon coins; of the foreign names the doubtful Owi is the only one of the reign of William I which has not already appeared in Anglo-Saxon times; to this are added in the reign of William II, Hathebrand, Sindi, Walcin, and the doubtful Bat and Coc. It is in the reign of Henry I, and chiefly toward the end of the reign, that new foreign names appear in any number; these are mostly Frankish, a few Romance and Biblical; more are added in the reign of Stephen, and these again are mostly Frankish in origin.

MONEYS OF ACCOUNT.

The Moneys of Account of Domesday Book, and of the Laws, are thus related to each other and to the penny:

2 *Ferdingi, Quadrantes,* &c. = 1 *Obolus, Maille,* &c.
2 *Oboli,* &c.   = 1 *Denarius.*
12 *Denarii*   = 1 *Solidus.*
20 *Solidi*   = 12 *Orae* or *Unciae Auri* = 1 *Libra.*
6 *Librae*   = 9 *Marcae Argenti*
                            = 1 *Marca Auri.*

Minuta also occurs once in Domesday, and was supposed by Sir Henry Ellis to represent the Northumbrian *Styca.* Perhaps farthing is a more likely interpretation.

In the Laws, the Mercian and West-Saxon shillings of 5 and 4 pence respectively are still found. The *Thrymsa* (= $\frac{1}{6}$ *Ora*?) also occurs.

The Domesday methods of payment [1] are by tale, by tale of pennies of standard weight (20 to the ounce), by weight, by weight

---

[1] Hughes, Crump and Johnson, *Dialogus de Scaccario*, pp. 34 ff.

of silver of approved fineness or (occasionally) blanched, by tale
of pennies of standard weight and fineness. In the first Pipe Roll
(1130), in addition to payments by tale and by weight, *blanch*
payments are in regular use. A method of payment, *ad scalam*,
which seems to occur in the reign of Henry I, but to have fallen
into disuse before 1130, is the addition of 5 per cent. in lieu of
assay.[1]

MINTS.
(See Table of Mints, Moneyers, and Types.)

If we assume as correct our attribution of the coins, we know of
sixty-seven mints in operation in the reign of William I, as against
seventy-three in the reign of the Confessor. The mints of the
Confessor, or Harold II, of which no coins of the Conqueror's reign
are now known, are Axbridge,[2] Aylesbury, Berkeley, Bridgnorth,
Buckingham, Bury St. Edmunds,[3] Horndon, Islip, Langport, Lyd-
ford, Lymne, Newport, Pershore, Petherton, Reading, Richborough;
in the Conqueror's reign are added Bridport, Cardiff, Christchurch
or Twynham, Durham, Launceston, Marlborough, Northampton,
Pevensey, Rhuddlan, St. Davids. The mints of William II number
fifty-seven, no coins of this king being known of Barnstaple,[4]
Bath,[4] Bedwin, Bridport, Cardiff, Christchurch,[4] Durham,[4] Northampton,[4] Rhuddlan, St. Davids, Winchcombe, and only one new
mint, Totnes, being added. In the reign of Henry I the mints
of Carlisle and Pembroke first appear, and of Bury St. Edmunds
the first coins since the reign of the Confessor, and no coins are
known of Cambridge, Cricklade, Guildford, Hertford, Hythe,
Launceston,[5] Maldon, Malmesbury, Marlborough, Pevensey,[5]
Stafford,[5] Steyning, Watchet.[5] Stephen's mints number fifty or

---

[1] R. L. Poole, *The Exchequer in the Twelfth Century*, p. 32.

[2] For many of these attributions see *Brit. Num. Journ.*, vol. vi, pp. 13 ff.

[3] But see below, p. clxiv, for coins attributed to this mint, and for confirmation of the grant of a moneyer by William I.

[4] Coins of Henry I are known of these mints.

[5] Coins of Stephen are known of these mints, but the attribution to Launceston is doubtful.

fifty-one,[1] two, or perhaps three, new mints appearing, namely Castle Rising, the uncertain Bran . . ., and perhaps Rye, and no coins being known of Christchurch, Dorchester, Ilchester, Rochester, Romney, Southampton, Totnes, Wallingford, Wareham.

To determine the number of moneyers employed in each mint at this period is impossible. The largest number of names occurring in any one type will frequently be too high, as the moneyers may not all have been working contemporaneously, some having taken over the dies of others during the issue of that particular type. An estimate of the number of names which overlap in more than one type will probably in most cases be too low, owing to the comparative rarity of the coins at the present day, and the consequent omission of names in types where they ought to appear. But a comparison of the two estimates will provide a standpoint from which the mints may be viewed in relation to each other, and in relation to their own position in the reign of the Confessor. In the reigns of Henry I and Stephen, the great rarity of most of the types prevents any estimate being made of the lowest possible number of moneyers.

In the following notes on the mints, these conjectural estimates of the numbers of moneyers working immediately before and after the Conquest are considered. The estimate of the Confessor's reign is based mainly upon the British Museum collection and the principal public and private cabinets. References to numbers of moneyers in Domesday Book are noted, and also those in the Greatley and subsequent laws; but it must not be concluded that from the time of the Greatley Edict of Æthelstan there was a steady increase of moneyers until the reign of the Confessor, for the enormous output of the reign of Æthelred seems to have necessitated at all the mints a great increase in their number, which is reduced again by the time of the Confessor.

Barnstaple (Domesday: *Barnestaple*). The attribution to this mint of coins previously attributed to Bardney is satisfactorily

---

[1] This does not include coins of 'irregular issues'.

established.[1] The coins of Leofwine (William I, type II) read apparently *Bur* (p. 15, no. 74), *Buri* (W. C. Wells); Major Carlyon-Britton (*Brit. Num. Journ.*, vol. ix, p. 143) assigns them to Bury St. Edmunds. The Godesbrand coins (William I, type VIII), here attributed to Bath, are by Major Carlyon-Britton described under Barnstaple.

Of the Confessor's reign, only one moneyer,.Ælfric, is at present known; the post-Conquest coins also justify an assumption that Barnstaple was one of the boroughs which had one moneyer only. At this mint the increase of moneyers in the reign of Æthelred II is noteworthy; no fewer than three (Ælfsige, Birhsige and Huniga) seem to have been at work at the same time.

Bath (Domesday: *Bade*). In the grant by William Rufus of the city and its customs to Bishop John, which is assigned to the period 1089—January 1091,[2] the mint is specially mentioned, and also in the confirmation of this charter by Henry I;[3] the properties of the mint, therefore, presumably escaped the fire of 1088, or were quickly restored, though at present we know no Bath coins of William II. In Domesday (I. 87) the mint pays 100 shillings. The attribution of coins of Godesbrand to Barnstaple or Bath is quite uncertain.

As the name Osmær occurs on coins of the Confessor and of types I, V, and VIII of the Conqueror, and Brungar on type III of the Conqueror, we may assume that these two moneyers were contemporaneous; in the Confessor's reign also, two at least worked together, namely Æglmær and Wædell (followed by Æthelmær), and, later, Godric (followed by Willewine) and Osmær.

Bedford (Domesday: *Bedeford*). In the reigns of William I and William II, two moneyers at least were working at the same time. In the early part of the reign of the Confessor there seem to have been at least three, perhaps four; in the latter part of his reign also not fewer than three.

---

[1] *Num. Chron.*, 1897, pp. 302 ff.; 1898, pp. 274 ff.; 1911, p. 274.
[2] Davis, *Regesta*, vol. i, no. 326.
[3] Dugdale, *Monasticon*, vol. ii, p. 268.

Bedwin or *Great Bedwin* (Domesday: *Bedvinde*). For an account of this mint see *Num. Chron.*, 1902, pp. 20–5. Coins are preserved only of the reign of the Confessor and of the first type of the Conqueror. Only one moneyer, Cild, is known.

Bran . . . occurs on coins of the last type of Stephen's reign. Their attribution is quite uncertain. Mr. Andrew (*Num. Circ.*, 1914, p. 632) suggests Braines, now Bradninch, in Devonshire, citing a specimen in the Carlyon-Britton collection as ORGAR ON BRAES; but the last two letters of this inscription are uncertain, and seem to me to be better interpreted as ME or NE; another specimen from the same dies, in Copenhagen Museum, misses the same two letters.

Bridport (Domesday: *Brideport*). Domesday (I. 75) says that in the time of the Confessor there was one moneyer here.

Of the last type of William I we have coins of two moneyers, who were presumably not working at the same time; no other coins of his or any other reign are yet known of this mint.

Bristol (Domesday: *Bristou*). In the reigns of the two Williams two is the lowest possible number of moneyers working together, but so few as two are unlikely, and would necessitate a succession of Ceorl—Hwateman—Brihtword—Barcwit, and of Leofwine—Swein[1]—Brunstan[1]—Colblac—Sendi.[2] A larger number is probable. In the 'Paxs' type, five names appear.

In the early part of the Confessor's reign three is the lowest possible number, and five names occur in type (Hildebrand) D; in the latter part of the reign two is possible, and three names occur in type G. Either a reduction of moneyers took place at this mint during the Confessor's reign, or, as seems more probable, the

---

[1] A common obverse die of these two moneyers is more rusted when used by Brunstan, and therefore shows that, unless they were contemporaneous, Brunstan was later than Swein.

[2] The name of this moneyer has been variously read as Sinot, Senwi, &c. A comparison of the coins shows that they are all of the same moneyer and his name seems to be Sendi or Sindi (see Table).

Bristol coinage of the last few years before, and of the period after, the Conquest is poorly represented at the present day.

Coins of 'Irregular Issues' of the reign of Stephen struck at this mint are described above; they are of variety I 'Erased Obverse' (p. lxxvi), variety II, 'Pereric' (p. lxxxii), Empress Matilda (p. cxviii), Henry of Anjou (pp. cxxii f.).

Bury St. Edmunds (Domesday: *Villa ubi quiescit humatus Sanctus Eadmundus*). The grant of one moneyer to the Abbot by the Confessor (Brit. Mus., MS. Addit. 14847, fol. 31) was confirmed by William I and William II (*ibid.*, fol. 36 b and 38), and Henry I (*ibid.* fol. 33 b). One die only was allowed to the Abbot, for Stephen's confirmation charter (*ibid.*, fol. 36) adds a second die, and is followed by another charter granting a third die, implying possibly the addition of a second and a third moneyer. Apart from Major Carlyon-Britton's attribution of the coins of the Conqueror's second type which read LEOFPINE ON BVRI, &c., no coins of either of the two Williams are assigned to this monastic mint. In the reigns of Henry I and Stephen the name of the mint is represented by an abbreviated form of *Sancti Edmundi*, or occasionally of *Edmundi* (*Sancti* being omitted), and as far as we know at present the earliest instance of the form *Bury* (*Beri*) on coins is of the latter part of the reign of Henry III.[1] In charters of the Norman period, as in Domesday, *Villa Sancti Edmundi* seems to be usual, though in the Confessor's charter the form *Seint Edmundesbiri* is used. Confusion with the mint of Sandwich is inevitable, and with coins reading SA, SAN, &c., this Catalogue has mainly followed the principle of assigning to Bury coins of moneyers who can be shown by other coins to have struck at this mint, and the remainder to Sandwich; the attributions are not likely to be correct in every case.

Calne (Domesday: *Cauna, Calne*). Some coins of the Empress Matilda are tentatively attributed to this borough (see above,

[1] Unless a coin of Stephen's last type in Mr. B. Roth's collection, on which the moneyer's name is illegible and the mint is represented by the letters BVR, should be assigned to Bury.

p. cxx). Calne is situated west of Marlborough and midway
between Malmesbury in the north and Devizes in the south; it
therefore lay in a district essentially Angevin, and was presumably
in Angevin possession throughout the Civil War. On her way to
Bristol in 1139, the Empress travelled by way of Calne, and at this
point Waleran of Meulan left her in charge of the Legate.[1]

Cambridge (Domesday: *Grantebrige*). The employment of
only one moneyer after the Conquest is just possible on the
evidence of the coins at present known, but it seems unlikely.
As many as three, or even four, moneyers seem to have been
employed in the reign of the Confessor. No coins are yet known
later than the reign of William II.

Canterbury (Domesday: *Cantuaria*). In the Greatley laws
seven moneyers of Canterbury are mentioned, four of the King,
two of the Archbishop, and one of the Abbot. In the reign of
the Confessor seven moneyers must have been working together,
and after the Conquest six or seven overlap from the end of the
Conqueror's into Rufus's reign, though from the coins at present
known as few as three moneyers may have been employed at the
beginning of the reign of William I. Eight names occur in the
' Paxs' type. The low number of moneyers immediately after
the Conquest is probably due to the chance circumstance of rarity
of the coins at the present day; and there appears to be an
establishment of seven moneyers, as in the reign of Æthelstan, both
in the reign of the Confessor and after the Conquest.

Irregular coinages in the reign of Stephen, bearing the mint-
name of Canterbury, are of varieties I ('Erased Obverse')? and II
('Pereric'). Coins of the Empress have been attributed to this
mint. See above, pp. lxxviii, lxxxii, cxx.

Cardiff. The attribution to Cardiff of a few coins of the last
type of William I is based on their resemblance in style and fabric
to the coins of St. Davids, and on the forms *Cairdi, Cariti*, by

---

[1] Rössler, *Mathilde*, p. 250; William of Malmesbury (Rolls Series, no. 90),
vol. ii, p. 556.

. which the mint is rendered on them. It is supposed that
William I established the castle at Cardiff in 1080 on his return
from the expedition to St. Davids.[1] If correctly attributed, the
coins must have been struck a few years after the building of
the castle.

Carlisle. In 1092 the city was refounded under English
sovereignty and the castle built; but no coins are known of the
mint of Carlisle earlier than the fourteenth type of Henry I, that
is to say, about the time of, or shortly before, the establishment
of the bishopric under the metropolitan of York in 1132. At the
beginning of 1136 Carlisle was seized by David, and in the terms
of the peace it was granted to his son Henry, with the earldom of
Huntingdon. One of the coins described below, p. 337, no. 17,
bears strong resemblance in style to the Scottish coinage of David,
and was perhaps struck after Scottish occupation. Coins seem to
have been struck here by Earl Henry (Burns, *Coinage of Scotland*,
Pl. III. 24 A) and by King David (Burns, op. cit., pp. 27 ff.); those
which copy the first type of Stephen being presumably the earliest,
and struck in, or shortly after, 1136. A coin of David which
bears the type of the last issue of Henry I (L. A. Lawrence
collection) was struck by a moneyer Erebald; if the mint, which is
not clearly legible, is to be read as Carlisle (the name Erembald
occurs also on Edinburgh coins of David I, cf. Rashleigh sale,
lot 1090), the coin was presumably struck rather later than the
issue of Henry I from which it was copied; for the Scottish king
was not, as far as we know, in possession of Carlisle before he
seized it in the year 1136. (See H. W. C. Davis, *England under
the Normans and Angevins*, p. 529.)

Castle Rising[2] (Domesday: *Risinga*). This seems to be the
only possible attribution for coins of the last issue of Stephen, on
which the mint-name appears as *Risinge* (p. 370, no. 189) and
Risinges; the moneyer's name is Iun or Hiun.

---

[1] See Ramsay, *Foundations*, vol. ii, p. 122.
[2] See *Num. Chron.*, 1889, pp. 335 ff.

Coins of types II and VI of the same reign struck by Robert *On Ris* may also with probability be attributed to Castle Rising. Those of Rawulf *On Rie* of Stephen's second type are here also given to this mint, but may perhaps be assigned to Rye,[1] which is sometimes identified with the New Borough of Domesday (I. 17). The coin of Stephen's first type of uncertain moneyer *on Ri* (p. 337, no. 20) is also of doubtful attribution.

Chester (Domesday: *Cestre*). The first appearance of the form *Cestre* on coins is an isolated instance in the last issue of William I (see below, p. 113, no. 598); other coins of the same type, and from the same obverse die (p. 112, nos. 594, 595), retain still the old name *Legecestre* or *Lehecestre*. The difficulty of distinguishing the Chester and Leicester coins, therefore, continues in this period, and, though the main principle of distinction is now clearly explained,[2] the abbreviated readings on the coins are frequently ambiguous, and must be considered in connexion with the moneyers' names; for example, the readings *Legr, Legri, Lehri* on coins of Ægelwine necessitate the attribution to Leicester of the remaining coins of this moneyer, which read *Leg, Legi, Leh*, and might otherwise be equally well assigned to either *Lege-(Lehe-)cestre* or *Legra-(Lehra-)cestre*. The old form continues in the reign of William II (*Leiec, Lecstr*), and even as late as the third type of Henry I, if the Carlyon-Britton coin is correctly read (*Legc*). Later in Henry's reign there are some coins with ambiguous readings, and these are here attributed to Leicester in order to avoid, where possible, the attribution of any but *Cestre* readings to Chester at so late a period.

Not fewer than three moneyers—Lifinc, Lifwine, and Sunulf—appear to be working together at the end of the Conqueror's reign; four names appear in the ' Paxs ' type (five if Sunulf and Unnulf are not identical), and also in the fourteenth type of Henry I; in William I's second type there are six. The coins of the Confessor suggest a larger number, for in his reign eight moneyers can be counted whose issues overlap in two or more types, namely, Ælfsige,

---

[1] *Num. Circ.*, 1914, p. 632.
[2] *Num. Chron.*, 1891, pp. 12 ff.

Alcsige, Brunninc, Colbrand, Huscarl, Leofnod, Leofwine and Sweartcol.

Chichester (Domesday: *Cicestre*). The Greatley Synod mentions Chichester as having one moneyer. In the Norman period there were two at least, for Brunman and Godwine were certainly working together in the reign of William II, and Brand and Godwine in the reign of Henry I; in the 'Paxs' type two names only appear. In the reign of the Confessor the number was apparently not less than three (Ælfwine, Godwine and Wulfric).

Christchurch (Domesday: *Thuinam, Tuinam*). This mint has been identified on coins of William I and Henry I by Major Carlyon-Britton in *Brit. Num. Journ.*, vol. vi, pp. 161 ff. The coins of Henry of Anjou and William (of Gloucester?) which bear a mint-name *Crst* have also been attributed to Christchurch (see p. cxxviii); but in the reign of Stephen Christchurch was still probably the name of the Abbey only, and Twynham the name of the town.

Cirencester is here suggested as the mint of the coins of Henry of Anjou and William (of Gloucester?) above mentioned, which have previously been assigned to Christchurch (see above, pp. cxxviii, cxxxi). Cirencester was probably an important Angevin centre; it was the scene of the council held by the leaders of that party in 1142 (W. Malm.).

Colchester (Domesday: *Colecestra*). No mention is made of this mint in the laws of Æthelstan (in *Num. Chron.*, 1901, p. 161, and *Brit. Num. Journ.*, vol. v, p. 116, following *B. M. Catal., Anglo-Saxon Coins*, vol. ii, p. cix, it seems to have been confused with Rochester). In Domesday (II. 107) the moneyers paid, and had paid in the time of the Confessor, four pounds, but their number is not given; also (II. 107 b) the burgesses of Colchester and Maldon paid twenty pounds, reduced by William I to ten pounds, for their mint.[1] In the reign of the Conqueror, three moneyers at least were contemporaneous, probably four; four

---

[1] See above, p. cxlii, note 1.

occur in the 'Paxs' type; in the reign of Rufus their number seems to have been not less than four, if doubtful coins have been correctly read; in the reign of the Confessor five is the lowest number estimated from the coins now known.

Cricklade (Domesday: *Crichelade*). In the reign of the Confessor two moneyers seem to have been employed at Cricklade; after the Conquest there were probably two, though one will just suffice for the coins at present known, assuming a succession of moneyers, Leofred—Wulstan—Ælfwine—Edouf; two names occur in the fifth, and one in the eighth, type of the Conqueror. No coins of this mint are known later than the reign of William II.

Derby (Domesday: *Derby*). After the Conquest it is not necessary to assume an establishment of more than two moneyers at Derby, and two names occur in the 'Paxs' type; but in the early part of the reign of the Confessor there appear to have been three at the same time (Froma, Swartinc, and Wulfeh).

For irregular coinage (variety IV A (*b*)) of the reign of Stephen see above, p. xcv.

Devizes (Domesday: *Theodulveside*). For a coin of the reign of Stephen attributed to this town see Rashleigh sale, 1909, lot 603 (now in the Fox collection). Also in the same sale, lot 627, a coin of Henry of Anjou. But the form 'Vises' is not used in contemporary documents.

Dorchester (Domesday: *Dorecestre*). In the Greatley laws one moneyer is allowed to Dorchester. In Domesday Book (I. 75) two moneyers are mentioned as paying each a mark of silver, and twenty shillings *quando moneta vertebatur*, in the time of the Confessor. From the coins we may conclude that the two moneyers in the Confessor's reign were Godwine, followed by Hwateman, and Blacaman.[1]

Coins of the Norman period justify the assumption that two moneyers continued to work at this mint after the Conquest. No coins are yet known of the first three types of the Conqueror;

---

[1] The coin described in *B. M. Catal.*, *Anglo-Saxon Coins*, vol. ii, p. 355, no. 194, I should attribute to Warminster (cf. coin of Harold I, *Brit. Num. Journ.*, vol. vi, p. 41).

possibly none were struck at Dorchester so soon after the ravages following the rising in the South-west in 1068.

A coin of William (of Gloucester ?) may possibly be attributed to this mint, see above, p. cxxxi.

Dover (Domesday: *Dovre*). In the reign of the Confessor as many as four moneyers overlap in the last two types, and four also appear to be contemporaneous in the early part of his reign. After the Conquest three run from the reign of William I to that of William II (this calculation omits both Goldwine and Manwine owing to the possibility that each of these names may denote two moneyers striking the earlier and later issues on which the name appears); in the ' Paxs ' type five names occur.

Durham. No coins are known of this mint earlier than the ' Paxs ' type of William I; but no definite evidence can be obtained from this concerning the date of that type, as the charter of William I, which was supposed to confer the right of coinage among other privileges upon the bishops, is certainly spurious (see Davis, *Regesta,* vol. i, no. 148).

Erami ... See *Brit. Num. Journ.*, vol. ix, pp. 138-9, for a coin of the fifth type of William I which is attributed to Great Yarmouth.

Exeter (Domesday: *Execestre, Exonia*). The Greatley Synod mentions Exeter as having two moneyers under Æthelstan.

In the reign of the Confessor there appear to be five moneyers working at the same time, and after the Conquest the same number seems to be required by the coins at 'present known of the earlier part of the Conqueror's reign, or four if we assume that two different moneyers of the name of Lifwine struck in the first and last types of the reign. Only three names occur on coins of the ' Paxs ' type. Perhaps the number was reduced in the middle of the reign of William I. Possibly the ravages of 1068 are reflected in the rarity of Exeter coins of the Conqueror's second type; if so, the mint quickly recovered its former activity.

Gloucester (Domesday: *Glowecestre*). At the time of the Domesday Survey (I. 162) the mint of Gloucester paid twenty pounds to the King. Under the Confessor there appear to be no fewer than six moneyers employed, but perhaps the number was reduced by William I, in whose reign four moneyers only overlap in successive types, and four names only occur on coins of the 'Paxs' type.

For a coin of Henry of Anjou attributed to Gloucester see above, p. cxxi.

Grombes ... A coin of the second type of William I in the York Museum reads ✠ERPIONGROMBES. The moneyer's name (Earnwi?) suggests Shrewsbury, and the confusion of G and S is not uncommon on coins. But Grimsby (Domesday: *Grimesbi*) is not impossible.

Guildford (Domesday: *Gildeford, Geldeford*). From the coins known at the present day one would suppose this mint to have employed one moneyer only after the Conquest, and in the time of the Confessor also this is possible, assuming a succession of moneyers, Ælfwine — Blacaman — Ælfric — Godwine — Leofwold, followed after the Conquest by Seric—Ælfric.

Hastings (Domesday: *Hastinges*). One moneyer was allowed by the laws of Æthelstan. At the end of the Confessor's reign at least three moneyers, Colswegen, Duninc and Theodred, worked together at Hastings, and in the reign of William II the same number was employed, though two names only appear on the last issue of William I.

Hedu ...? A coin of Stephen's last type, which is in the Hunterian collection, reads ✠GERARS:OH:ḰEDV⊟. The identification of the mint is quite uncertain, but Hythe is possible (cf. Domesday *Hede*).

Hereford (Domesday: *Hereford*). Domesday (I. 179) tells us of seven moneyers having been employed at this mint in the reign of the Confessor, one of them being the Bishop's moneyer. From the evidence of the coins at present known, not more than five moneyers can be shown to have worked together in the reign of the Confessor and not more than four after the Conquest; five is the largest number of names appearing in any type of the Confessor, and four occur in the 'Paxs' type of the Conqueror.

For coins of Henry of Anjou struck at Hereford see above, p. cxxi.

Hertford (Domesday: *Herford, Hertforde*). There appear to have been not fewer than three moneyers employed at Hertford in the reign of the Confessor. As many as five names occur in his third type in the British Museum Catalogue (Hildebrand C), but the readings are not all certain. In the reigns of the two Williams two moneyers seem to be at work. No coins are known after the reign of William Rufus.

Huntingdon (Domesday: *Huntedone, Huntedun*). Domesday (I. 203) says that three moneyers were here in the time of the Confessor, but not at the time of the Survey. The coins now known show only two moneyers overlapping in successive types of the Confessor, but as many as four names occur in one of his types (*B. M. Catal.*, xi, Hildebrand G). After the Conquest two moneyers are evidently contemporaneous in the early part of the reign of William I, but one only occurs in the 'Paxs' type. In the reign of William II one only is certain.

Hythe (Domesday: *Hede*). Presumably a borough employing one moneyer only. In the Confessor's reign, though as many as four names occur, there is no reason to suppose that more than one worked at one time. After the Conquest, Edred is the only moneyer at present known. No coins are known after the reign of William II, unless the Hunterian coin of Stephen's last issue (see above, *Hedu* . . .) may be assigned to this mint. The rusty condition of the obverse dies which struck the Conqueror's coins of this mint is noteworthy, and also the use at this mint of dies previously used at Canterbury.

Ilchester (Domesday: *Givelcestre*). Only a few coins of the Confessor's reign are known, but two moneyers at least seem to have been working together. After the Conquest the same number is necessary for the coins at present known. Wægelwine on p. 46, nos. 237, 238, is presumably an engraver's error for Ægelwine.

The bar across one of the limbs of the reverse cross on coins of William. I's sixth type is curious and evidently serves some definite purpose, as the same feature is found on coins of this mint of the Confessor's reign (see *B. M. Catal., Anglo-Saxon Coins*, vol. ii, p. 371, nos. 432–5).

Ipswich (Domesday : *Gipeswic, Gipewiz*). Domesday (II. 290 b) says that in the time of the Confessor the moneyers paid four pounds a year, and at the time of the Survey twenty pounds; in the four years previous to the Survey they paid only twenty-seven pounds. Under the Confessor not fewer than four moneyers appear to have been employed, and in the reign of the Conqueror no fewer than three; in the 'Paxs' type as many as six moneyers' names occur.[1]

Lansa ... Coins of the first type of Stephen with this reading of the mint were tentatively attributed by Rashleigh in his account of the Watford find (*Num. Chron.*, 1850, p. 157) to Lancaster. They are now assigned to Launceston (*Brit. Num. Journ.*, vol. iii, p. 113). For *Lanwa*, in lots 518 and 519 of Rashleigh sale, I should read *Canwa* (Canterbury).

Launceston (Domesday : *Lanscavetone*). The Domesday passage (I. 120 b), *Canonici Sancti Stefani tenent Lanscavetone*, leaves little doubt of the correctness of Major Carlyon-Britton's attribution of coins to the church of St. Stephen at Launceston (*Brit. Num. Journ.*, vol. iii, pp. 107 ff. ; vol. iv, pp. 68 ff.). The earliest coin of this mint at present known (William I, type V) has no moneyer's name, but has a reverse legend which is clearly intended for *Sancti Stefani*; and the Hunterian coin of type VI, which reads **ᏟODᏒIᏟ ON SIИͲSͲFИI** (see Pl. XIV. 15), connects the earlier reading which omits the moneyer's name with the later which omits the

---

[1] Possibly on coins of the 'Paxs' type the moneyer's name should be read as Ulfwine (i. e. Wulfwine) rather than Alfwine, in which case five moneyers only are known of this type.

title *Sancti.* Coins of Stephen, mentioned above, with the reading *Lansa*, may possibly be assigned to Launceston.[1]

The *Lawa* coins of Henry I, type XIV, are probably of Lewes.

Leicester (Domesday: *Ledecestre*). The moneyers of Leicester paid the King at the time of the Survey (I. 230) twenty pounds yearly; their number is not mentioned. Not fewer than four moneyers seem to have worked together in the Confessor's reign, namely Ægelric, Ægelwine, Godric and Leofric, but the attribution of the Ægelric and Leofric coins is doubtful. In the Conqueror's reign only two are apparent on the coins, perhaps even one only might have been employed;[2] but the amount of the moneyers' payment in Domesday suggests a larger number. For attributions to this mint see foot-notes to Table of Mints, Moneyers, and Types and also notes on Chester above (p. clxvii).

Lewes (Domesday: *Lewes*). Two moneyers were allowed to Lewes by Æthelstan. In Domesday (I. 26) moneyers are mentioned as paying twenty shillings *cum moneta renovatur*, but their number is not given. In the reign of the Confessor there were not fewer than four moneyers (Eadward, Eadwine, Godwine and Oswold) overlapping in types (Hildebrand) F and H; the coins known of the two Williams will allow of so low a number as two; but as this necessitates the close sequence Oswold—Ælfric—Brihtmær, and hence the supposition that no new types of these moneyers remain to be found, one may assume that the number was not less than three. Three seem to overlap from the reign of William II to that of Henry I. In the 'Paxs' type three occur.

Lincoln (Domesday: *Lincolia*). Domesday (I. 336 b) says that the mint at Lincoln then paid seventy-five pounds. In the early part of the Confessor's reign not fewer than ten, and towards the end of the reign not fewer than eight, moneyers seem to have been employed. At the beginning of the reign of William I, there seem

---

[1] Perhaps also the coin of type III (Hks. 276) in Cuff (lot 758), Murchison (lot 33), and Simpson Rostron (lot 40) sales, now in Captain Alan Dawnay's collection.

[2] If the coin of Godric of type II is, as seems likely, a misreading.

to be seven moneyers who continue from the reign of the Confessor or Harold II, and seven names occur in his second type; similarly, in his fourth and fifth types, five or six appear to be working together; but in the 'Paxs' type only two names occur. This great decrease in the number of moneyers represented on coins of the end of the Conqueror's reign may possibly be due to a comparative scarcity of coins of the Northern mints in the Beaworth find, and a consequent loss of moneyers' names of these mints; but this is not a probable explanation, for in the Beaworth hoard there were 171 coins of Lincoln representing only two moneyers, whereas of ·Canterbury 285 coins represented as many as eight moneyers, and of Hereford fifty-nine coins served to produce four moneyers' names. In the reign of William II there appear to be two or three moneyers, but the coins are few and some readings uncertain. Probably there was a decrease in the establishment of the mint at Lincoln towards the close of the Conqueror's reign, though Domesday gives no signs of any serious decrease in the prosperity of the city; for, though 240 *mansiones* out of a total of 1,140 had disappeared since the Confessor's day, 166 of these had been demolished in building the castle and only seventy-four had fallen into ruin owing to misfortunes, poverty, and fire.

On the coins of the twelfth and of the last two types of Henry I, and on most of the coins of Stephen's first type, the form *Nicole* is used for the name of the mint.

For irregular coinages (II and IV B (*a*)) of the reign of Stephen see above, pp. lxxxii, xcvi f.

London (Domesday: *Lundonia*). In the reign of Æthelstan London had eight moneyers. Under the Confessor we find from the coins no fewer than twenty-five moneyers working together in the early part of the reign, and in the middle of the reign at least twenty, but at the end of the reign about twelve only seem to be contemporaneous, and in his last type but one (Hildebrand A, *var.* c) only twelve names are known as opposed to thirty-two in his third (?) type (Hildebrand B). Under William I there seem to be not fewer than nine or ten moneyers employed at the begin--

ning of the reign, and in the 'Paxs' type eight names occur. Probably a reduction of the staff of the London mint took place in the Confessor's reign, perhaps concurrently with an increase in the activity of the smaller provincial mints.

Maint . . . The attribution of these coins of the second type of William I is quite uncertain; all that I have seen are from the same dies and from an obverse die which was also used at Thetford. The low weight of the British Museum specimen (I have not ascertained the weight of the Hunterian and York specimens) suggests forgery, but there is no trace of false work, or even of any altering of the die, on the coins.

Maldon (Domesday: *Melduna*). Two moneyers at least were employed in the reign of the Confessor, and also after the Conquest. Three names occur in the 'Paxs' type, but the alteration of the die that was used to strike no. 821 (see below, p. 153, note, and *Num. Chron.*, 1911, p. 285) suggests some confusion between Ælfwine and Ælfword. No coins are known after the reign of William II.

The payment by the burgesses of Maldon for their mint is assessed in Domesday with that of the Colchester burgesses.

Malmesbury (Domesday: *Malmesberie*). This borough is mentioned in Domesday (I. 64 b) as paying 100 shillings for the mint. From the coins now known one moneyer only may have been employed at the mint. Two occur in the 'Paxs' type. No coins of regular issues are known after the reign of William II.

For a coin of Henry of Anjou (?) attributed to Malmesbury see above, p. cxxi.

Marlborough (Domesday: *Merleberge*). In *Num. Chron.*, 1902, pp. 23 ff., Major Carlyon-Britton has shown that the mint and the moneyer, Cild, were probably transferred from Bedwin to Marlborough. Coins of Marlborough are known of this moneyer only, and only of the last six types of William I, and of the first of William II.

Newark. For coins of the variety of Stephen's reign described as IV A (*a*), see above, p. xcv.

Northampton (Domesday: *Northantone, Hantone*). The only coins, earlier than the thirteenth type of Henry I, which can with any certainty be attributed to this mint are those of the second type of William I which bear *Nothant* as the name of the mint. The moneyer is Sæwine. Hence it is possible that other coins of this moneyer on which the form *Hamtune* occurs should be attributed to Northampton rather than Southampton, q. v., p. clxxxii. See *Brit. Num. Journ.*, vol. ix, pp. 140 ff. At the end of the reign of Henry I as many as four moneyers occur at this mint, and not less than two of these must have worked together.

Norwich (Domesday: *Norwic*). From Domesday (II. 117 b) we learn that the bishop could have one moneyer at this mint if he wished.

Not fewer than five moneyers appear to have worked together at Norwich under the Confessor; after the Conquest four is the lowest number available from the coins at present known. As many as eight names appear in the 'Paxs' type; but of these some, such as Godwid and Inhuhe, are uncertain and may perhaps be blundered forms of names already included. As many as twelve names, if the coins are correctly attributed, appear in the first type of Stephen. The reading NON is attributed to Norwich (see below, p. 362, no. 163).

Coins of Stephen's reign struck from erased obverse dies are known of this mint (see above, pp. lxxvi ff.).

Nottingham (Domesday: *Snotingeham, Snotingham*). Domesday (I. 280) mentions two moneyers here in the time of the Confessor. Coins of the Confessor's reign are rare and show no satisfactory sequences, but they confirm the number of moneyers mentioned in Domesday as being, at least, the lowest number possible. The coins of the reign of William I show that there were two moneyers at least after the Conquest, and two names occur in the 'Paxs' type. For varieties of Stephen's reign, I and IV A (c) (Nottingham or Tutbury?), see above, pp. lxxvii, xcvi.

Outchester, where most of the coins of Henry, Earl of Northum-

berland, have been found, is suggested as the possible place of
mintage of the varieties IV C (*a*), (*b*), (*c*).   See above, pp. xcviii ff.

Oxford (Domesday: *Oxeneford*).   In the reign of the Confessor
seven seems to be the lowest number of moneyers that can have
worked together, and seven is the largest number of names occurring
in any one type.   Immediately after the Conquest at least six
seem to be contemporaneous, but in the 'Paxs' type only three
names occur.

For Oxford coins of the Empress Matilda see above, p. cxix.

Pembroke.   Coins of this mint of the fourteenth type of Henry I
have been identified by Major Carlyon-Britton (*Brit. Num. Journ.*,
vol. ii, pp. 54–6) from an entry on the Pipe Roll of 1130, in
which a payment is made by Gillopatric the moneyer.   A coin of
Stephen's first type was recently acquired by the British Museum
(see below, p. 348, no. 88 A) on which the same mint and moneyer
are identified.

P (or *W*?)*ene* ...   A coin of the ninth type of Henry I (Hks. 263)
in Copenhagen Museum reads ✠ALVRED:ON:PENE:
The mint is quite uncertain; possibly Winchester?

Peterborough (Domesday: *Burg*).   In 1067 William I confirmed
in a charter to Peterborough Abbey (Davis, *Regesta*, vol. i, no. 8) the
privileges granted by Edgar and other kings.   The grant of Edgar
(Birch, *Cartularium Saxonicum*, vol. iii, pp. 543 and 582) included
one moneyer in Stamford, but the moneyer is not mentioned in the
charter of William I.   The bull of Eugenius III, published in
Dugdale's *Monasticon*, vol. i, p. 390, grants the Abbey the privileges
it formerly held, and makes specific mention of the coining-die in
Stamford.   If one of the Stamford moneyers, of whom there were
not less than four in the Conqueror's reign, was working for the
Abbot of Peterborough through the Norman period, I do not think
that he can now be identified.

Pevensey (Domesday: *Pevenesel*).   No coins of Pevensey are
known before the Conquest.   In the reigns of the two Williams,

Ælfheh was the Pevensey moneyer, and in Stephen's reign Alwine. Pevensey was presumably one of the boroughs that were allowed one moneyer only.

Reading. In the foundation charter of Henry I (1125) a grant was conferred upon the Abbey of a mint and moneyer at Reading ('donavi Radingiam . . . cum moneta et uno monetario apud Radingiam ').[1] This privilege seems to have been soon exchanged for the use of a moneyer at London, and Roger, Bishop of Salisbury, probably not many years later, at the king's order granted to the Abbot and monks one moneyer in London, namely Edgar.[2] The privilege of one moneyer at London was confirmed by Stephen.[3] We may therefore assume that some, at least, of the London coins bearing the name Ædgar, which are of the last type of Henry's reign, were struck for the Abbot of Reading. We do not at present know any coins of this moneyer of the reign of Stephen ; he may still have been working for the Abbot or have already been replaced by another moneyer.

Rhuddlan (Domesday : *Roelend, Roelent*). There can be no doubt of the attribution of 'Paxs' type coins of William I to Rhuddlan, where Domesday says (I. 269) that Robert de Roelent held 'medietatem . . . monetæ' (see *Brit. Num. Journ.*, vol. ii, pp. 41 ff.). Only one moneyer, Elfwine, is known.

Rhyd y Gors. See p. lxxii.

Rochester (Domesday : *Rovecestre*). In the laws of Æthelstan Rochester had three moneyers, two for the king and one for the bishop. Whether the bishop's privilege continued to the time of the Conquest and after, we have no knowledge. Coins of this mint are not common at any period, but in the reign of the Confessor the coins are sufficient to show that not fewer than three moneyers worked together. After the Conquest two moneyers only are necessary. Two names only occur in the 'Paxs' type, but of

---

[1] Brit. Mus., Harley MS. 1708, fol. 16.

[2] *Ibid.*, fol. 113. Printed in full in Dugdale's *Monasticon*, vol. iv, p. 41, and in *Num. Chron.*, 1901, pp. 373–4.

[3] Brit. Mus., Harley MS. 1708, fol. 28.

this mint only nine 'Paxs' coins were described in the account of the Beaworth hoard. Two moneyers, or perhaps three as in Æthelstan's time, may be assumed to have been employed in Norman times. No coins of this period are yet known later than the first type of Henry I.

Romney (Domesday : *Romenel*). Two moneyers at least were employed by the Confessor (Wulfmær and Brungar—Estin—Leofric). As many as three seem to have been working after the Conquest, though two only occur in the 'Paxs' type ; for Coc appears in the first issue of William II, and both Winedi and Wulfmær continue from the reign of William I to the second type of William II.

Rye. On the proposed attribution of some coins of Stephen to this mint see above, p. clxvi (Castle Rising).

St. Davids. For the attribution of coins reading 'Devitun' to St. Davids, or Dewi-town, see *Brit. Num. Journ.*, vol. ii, pp. 47 ff. The identity of the obverse die of a coin attributed to Shrewsbury (p. 175, no. 938) with that of a St. Davids coin is curious ; but the coarse work of both obverse and reverse of that coin suggests that possibly it should itself also be attributed to the mint of St. Davids.

Salisbury (Domesday : *Sarisberie*). Three moneyers at least seem to have worked here in the reign of the Confessor, and after the Conquest the same number is likely ; for, though two are, from the coins at present known, not impossible in the reign of William I, three moneyers are required by the coins of William II.

Sandwich (Domesday : *Sandwic, Sanwic*). The confusion between this mint and Bury St. Edmunds, both in the Norman period and in the reign of the Confessor, is at present hopeless. In the Confessor's reign some coins of the moneyer Leofwine, reading *Sand* and *Sandw*, are no doubt correctly attributed to Sandwich, but a coin of the same moneyer of type (Hildebrand) G which reads *Sance* (*B. M. Catal.*, no. 1161) might, one would think, be assigned with equal certainty to Bury;[1] in which case there was more than one moneyer allowed to Bury at this period, for Morcere was coining there in this issue, as well as in earlier and later types. In the Conqueror's reign, Ælfheh, Ælfgæt, and Godwine are clearly Sandwich moneyers, and show that at least two moneyers were employed together. Of the later moneyers Ælfgar and Godhese must be of Sandwich, but the remainder are quite uncertain.

Shaftesbury (Domesday: *Sceptesberie*). By the laws of Æthelstan this mint was allowed two moneyers. In the reign of the Confessor there were three moneyers paying each a mark of silver and twenty shillings *quando moneta vertebatur* (Domesday, I. 75). This number agrees with the figure deduced from the coins now known of the Confessor's reign, if we assume that the Ælfward of type (Hildebrand) A was a different moneyer from that of type G; but if the same Ælfward worked continuously through the reign there would appear to be not fewer than four moneyers employed. In the Conqueror's reign also, there appear to have been three moneyers, and three occur on coins of the 'Paxs' type. There is some confusion between this mint and Shrewsbury, as both mints seem to have had a moneyer of the name of Godesbrand in the reign of William I (see *Num. Chron.*, 1911, p. 273).

Sherborne. For a coin of Henry of Anjou attributed to Sherborne see above, p. cxxviii.

Shrewsbury (Domesday: *Sciropesberie*). The city of Shrewsbury had, in the time of the Confessor, three moneyers who paid twenty shillings apiece within fifteen days of the receipt of their dies, *et hoc fiebat moneta vertente* (Domesday, I. 252). From the coins of his reign one would have supposed that as many as four moneyers were working under the Confessor, for Ælfheh, Leofstan, and Wulfmær run from types (Hildebrand) A to F, and Leofwine

---

[1] This lends some colour to Major Carlyon-Britton's attribution to Bury of coins of William I's second type reading *Leofwine on Bur*; see above on Bury St. Edmunds, p. clxiv.

occurs in type E, which certainly precedes F; but it may be that the coins of type E and F were not struck by the same Ælfheh as struck those of type A,[1] as the intervening types (C, B, D) are, I believe, not known of this moneyer. In the reign of William I three moneyers were evidently contemporaneous and three names occur in the 'Paxs' type. The attribution of coins of Hathebrand is uncertain (see below, p. 264).

On the coin described on p. 175, no. 938, see St. Davids, p. clxxx, and on the difficulty of the identification of the Shaftesbury and Shrewsbury mints on coins of Godesbrand see Shaftesbury, p. clxxxi.

Southampton (Domesday: *Hantone, Hantune, Hanitune*). On the confusion between Northampton and Southampton see Northampton, p. clxxvii. Under Æthelstan, 'Hamtune' (=Southampton) had two moneyers. Assuming the present attribution of coins to Southampton to be correct, there seem to have been not fewer than two moneyers at this mint both in the Confessor's reign and after the Conquest. One name only occurs on 'Paxs' coins. It may be noted that, in the *Gesta Regum*, William of Malmesbury always, with one exception only (in the partition of the Anglo-Saxon kingdoms, a part of his work which is probably not original, where the form *Suthamtunensis* is used: *Rolls Series*, no. 90, vol. i, p. 100), uses the forms *Hamtona* or *Hamtuna* for Southampton, and invariably uses *Northantona* or *Northantuna* for Northampton.

For an issue of the reign of Stephen (variety III 7), which may possibly be attributed to this mint, see above, pp. xci ff.

Southwark (Domesday: *Sudwerca, Sudwerche*). The similarity of the abbreviated forms of the names Southwark and Sudbury makes the attribution of the coins difficult. In the Table of Mints, Moneyers, and Types the forms found on coins of these two mints are inserted in foot-notes. In the reign of the Confessor the only moneyer that can be assigned with any certainty to Sudbury is Folcwine; if the doubtful moneyers are all to be attributed to Southwark, there are still only three contemporaneous moneyers

---

[1] Hildebrand, no. 645.

necessitated by the coins now known. After the Conquest also, three must have worked together, and four names occur on 'Paxs' coins.

Stafford (Domesday: *Stadford, Statford*). From the few coins known of the Confessor's reign, there is no reason to assume the existence of more than one moneyer at Stafford, but in the reign of William II the coin of Ælfward of the second type shows this moneyer to have been working with Godric, of whom we have a sequence of coins through the whole reign. In the second and last types of the Conqueror, two moneyers' names occur.

Stamford (Domesday: *Stanford*). The coins at present known show as many as eight moneyers to have been working at Stamford in the early part of the Confessor's reign; in the latter half of the reign there seem to be only five. Immediately after the Conquest there were not fewer than three, or perhaps four, moneyers, and three only are at present known in the Conqueror's last issue. This great reduction in the staff of the Stamford mint is similar to that at the neighbouring mint of Lincoln, but seems to have taken place at an earlier period.

Coins of the first two varieties of Stephen's reign occur of this mint (see above, pp. lxxvii, lxxxiii).

Steyning, Sussex, (Domesday: *Staninges*). One moneyer only seems to have been employed here both before [1] and after the Conquest. Two, however, appear to have been employed by William II. No coins are yet known later than the reign of William II.

Sudbury (Domesday: *Sutberie*). The phrase of Domesday (II. 286 b), 'ibi sunt monetarii', suggests the existence of more than one moneyer at Sudbury, but one only is apparent from the coins both before and after the Conquest. In the Abbey Register of Westminster (Brit. Mus., Cotton MS., Faustina A. 111, fol. 79)

---

[1] The coin of Godwine of the Confessor's last type (*B. M. Catalogue*, no. 1218) I should assign to Stafford.

Henry I confirms the dedication by Wulfric, his moneyer, of the church of St. Bartholomew at Sudbury to the use of the monks of Westminster. This confirms the attribution to Sudbury of the coins struck by Wulfric in the reigns of William I, William II, and Henry I.

On the confusion of Sudbury and Southwark see above, p. clxxxii.

Tamworth (Domesday: *Tameworde*). Two moneyers seem to have been employed at Tamworth in the Confessor's reign and in the reigns of the two Williams.

Taunton (Domesday: *Tantone*). Only one moneyer may have been employed at this mint both in the reign of the Confessor and after the Conquest.

Coins of variety III 7 of Stephen's reign have been attributed to Taunton (see above, p. xcii).

Thetford (Domesday: *Tetford, Tedfort*). At the time of the Domesday Survey (II. 119) Thetford paid 40 pounds a year to the king for the mint. In the Confessor's reign at least five, or perhaps six, moneyers seem to have worked together, and seven is the highest number of moneyers in any one type of the reign; in the reign of William I, six[1] is the lowest number possible of contemporaneous moneyers, and six occur in the 'Paxs' type.

Coins of this mint of varieties I and IV B (*b*), of Stephen's reign, are described above, pp. lxxviii, xcvii.

Totnes (Domesday: *Totenais, Totheneis*). No coins of Totnes are known of the Confessor's reign. The second issue of William II was the only post-Conquest type known of this mint until a coin of the first type of Henry, struck by the same moneyer, Dunic, was recently found in the Old Sarum excavations.

Tutbury. For a variety of Stephen's reign, IV A (*c*), attributed to this mint, see above, p. xcvi.

Twynham. See Christchurch, p. clxviii.

---

[1] Assuming Folcærd, who coined for the Confessor, to have been at work in the early issues of the Conqueror.

Wallingford (Domesday: *Walengeford, Walingeford*). Domesday mentions a moneyer here having a house free (I. 56). Under the Confessor as many as five moneyers seem to have been employed, and in the early part of the Conqueror's reign three; two names only appear in the 'Paxs' type.

A coin of the sixth type of William I, struck by a moneyer Swartbrand, on which the mint is represented by the letter P (for W ?), has been tentatively assigned to Wallingford (see *Brit. Num. Journ.*, vol. iv, pp. 54 and 56).

Wareham (Domesday: *Warham*). In the laws of Æthelstan, Wareham had two moneyers. There were also two moneyers in the time of the Confessor, who paid one mark of silver to the king, and twenty shillings *quando moneta vertebatur* (Domesday, I. 75). The coins of the Confessor confirm the existence of two, at least. In the reign of William I there seem to be not fewer than three employed, and four names are known in the 'Paxs' type.

There is sometimes difficulty in distinguishing coins of Wareham and Warwick; the mint-readings are inserted in the notes of the Table of Mints, Moneyers, and Types.

For Wareham coins of the Empress Matilda and of William (of Gloucester?) see above, pp. cxix, cxxx.

Warwick (Domesday: *Warwic*). Under the Confessor there seem to have been not fewer than three moneyers employed at Warwick; probably the same number were working in the reigns of the two Williams, though two might just suffice for the coins known at present; four names occur in the 'Paxs' type, and three in the first and second types of William II. On the possibility of confusion with Wareham see above.

Watchet (Domesday: *Wacet*). One moneyer only seems to have been employed at Watchet, both in the Confessor's reign and after the Conquest.

Wilton (Domesday: *Wiltone, Wiltune*). In the Pipe Roll of Henry I, Tomas, a moneyer, is mentioned under Wiltshire as having had his fine reduced on account of poverty; perhaps this is the

Tomas of the first type of Stephen, but we do not yet know any coins struck by him in the reign of Henry I. In a grant in Wilton to the church of Salisbury (c. 1200), William of Wilton, the organist, is mentioned as son of William, the moneyer;[1] this moneyer is probably the William who struck coins of the last type of Stephen and of the first issue of Henry II.

There seem to have been not fewer than five moneyers employed at Wilton in the latter half of the reign of the Confessor, and as many as six names occur in one type (Hildebrand H). In the early part of the Conqueror's reign, as many as four, or five (if Ælfwine of William I is identical with the Ælfwine of the Confessor), seem to be contemporaneous; at the end of the reign not more than three are necessary from the coins now known, and three names occur in the 'Paxs' type.

Winchcombe (Domesday: *Wincelcumbe*). For the attribution of coins to the borough of Winchcombe see *Brit. Num. Journ.*, vol. vi, pp. 49 ff. One moneyer seems to have worked here both before and after the Conquest. No coins are yet known later than the reign of William I.

Winchester (Domesday: *Wincestre, Wintonia*). In Æthelstan's laws Winchester was allowed six moneyers. In the Winton Domesday, Alwinus Aitardessone (fol. 1), Godwinus Socche (*magister monetariorum*, fol. 2), Andrebodus (fol. 3), Alwardus filius Etardii (fol. 7), Alestan (fol. 8 b) are mentioned as moneyers of the reign of the Confessor, and Odo (fol. 8), Sanson (foll. 15, 16), Siward (foll. 16, 23 b) as moneyers at the time of the Survey (between 1107 and 1128); and the wife of Wimund the moneyer had a house at the time of the Survey (fol. 2 b). On fol. 4 b occurs the phrase 'Et in mercato fuerunt v monete, que fuerunt diffacte precepto regis' (see *Brit. Num. Journ.*, vol. vi, pp. 164–5). In the reign of the Confessor not less than nine moneyers seem to have worked at the same time; in the Conqueror's reign, though six would suffice for the coins at present known, eight names appear in the 'Paxs' type.

[1] Charters, &c., of Salisbury (Rolls Series, no. 97), no. lxxv.

For a coin of variety II of Stephen's reign, attributed to Winchester, see above, p. lxxxiii.

Wiveliscombe. For coins of Henry of Anjou and William (of Gloucester?) which may have been struck at Wiveliscombe see above, pp. cxxiii, cxxxi.

Worcester (Domesday: *Wirecestre*). Moneyers of Worcester are mentioned in Domesday (I. 172) as having paid, in the time of the Confessor, twenty shillings each at London on receipt of dies *quando moneta vertebatur.* This city seems to have had not fewer than five, or perhaps six, moneyers in the reign of the Confessor; as many as six moneyers appear to overlap from the Confessor's to the Conqueror's reign, but later in the reign of William I and in that of William II not more than four are necessary; four occur in the 'Paxs' type.

Yarmouth. See above, p. clxx, *Erami* ...

York (Domesday: *Eboracum*). In the early part of the Confessor's reign as many as seventeen moneyers seem to have been employed, and in the latter half at least ten appear from the coins to have been contemporaneous. On coins of the second type of William I as many as eleven distinct names occur, all of which are found on coins of the Confessor or Harold, or of the Conqueror's first type; but in the second half of the reign only four moneyers appear, from the coins at present known, to have been working at the same time, and four names only are found on 'Paxs' coins. This great decrease in the staff of the York mint was perhaps the result of the ravages of 1069.

We do not know how many moneyers were allowed to the Archbishops, but in a suit of 1279 the Archbishop, William, pleaded that they had had two dies (which perhaps imply two moneyers) from time immemorial, and also, at one time, a third die which was then in the king's hands; and his claim was allowed.

The form EBO occurs on a coin of the seventh type of Henry I (B. Roth collection).

For irregular coinages of Stephen's reign which were struck at

York see varieties I, IV D, Eustace FitzJohn and Robert de Stuteville (pp. lxxviii, cvi ff.).

The comparative importance of the mints in the second half of the eleventh century may be summarized by the following classification in groups, the number of moneyers being, as previously remarked, only an approximate estimate from the coins now available, and probably in many cases below the actual number employed.[1] The mints which occur in two groups, showing a decrease during the Conqueror's reign, are in italics; and an asterisk marks those which show a reduction during the reign of the Confessor.

6 moneyers and over	5 moneyers	4 moneyers	3 moneyers	2 moneyers	1 moneyer
*London, 9 or 10	*Exeter* (early)	*Chester	Bristol	Bath	Barnstaple
York (early), 11	Norwich	*Colchester	*Exeter* (late)	*Bedford	Bedwin
*Winchester, 7 or 8	*Wilton* (early)	Dover	Hastings	*Cambridge	Bridport
Canterbury, 7		*Gloucester	*Lewes	*Chichester	Bury ?
Lincoln (early), 7		*Hereford ? (see pp. clxxi f.)	*Oxford* (late)	Cricklade	Cardiff
Oxford (early), 6		Ipswich	Romney (or 2 ?)	*Derby	Christchurch
Thetford 6		*Worcester* (late)	Salisbury	Dorchester	Durham
Worcester (early), 6		*York* (late)	Shaftesbury	*Hertford	Guildford
			Shrewsbury	*Huntingdon	Hythe
			Southwark	Ilchester	Launceston
			*Stamford	*Leicester	Malmesbury
			Wallingford (early)	*Lincoln* (late)	Marlborough
			Wareham ? (see p. clxxxv)	Maldon	Northampton
			Warwick	Nottingham	Pevensey
			Wilton (late)	*Rochester	Rhuddlan
				Sandwich	St. Davids
				Southampton	Steyning (see p. clxxxiii)
				Stafford	Sudbury
				Tamworth	Taunton
				Wallingford (late)	Totnes
					Watchet
					Winchcombe

[1] Hereford, where seven moneyers are said in Domesday to have been employed in the time of the Confessor, though only five are apparent from his coins, is a probable instance of too low an estimate. Shrewsbury, where three moneyers are mentioned in Domesday and four appear from the coins to have been working together, shows the possibility of error in the opposite direction, owing probably to one name denoting two moneyers working successively. The classification of one-moneyer mints is likely to be correct in most cases.

ABBREVIATIONS USED, COLLECTIONS QUOTED, ETC.

The numismatic publications which are quoted in this Catalogue have for the most part appeared in either the *Numismatic Chronicle* or the *British Numismatic Journal*, which are quoted as *Num. Chron.* and *Brit. Num. Journ.*[1] Spink's *Numismatic Circular* (referred to as *Num. Circ.*) contains in the issue of 1902 Major Carlyon-Britton's original list of coins of the reigns of William I and William II; as these lists are now in course of revision in the *British Numismatic Journal*, reference has not been made to them except in the Table of Mints, Moneyers, and Types. The ordinary handbooks have been used and are quoted under their authors' names, Hawkins, Grueber, &c.

Historical matter has been introduced only so far as is necessary for the elucidation of the coinage. The operations of the mints seem to have been very little influenced by the political and military history of the period except during the reign of Stephen. The irregular coinages during the period of civil war have necessitated more historical detail, for which purpose Sir William Ramsay's *Foundations of England* and Mr. J. H. Round's *Geoffrey de Mandeville* have been extensively used. References are given in full to such historical works as have been consulted.

In compiling the Catalogue much difficulty has been experienced owing to the large number of collections which contain coins of this period. But the kindness of many owners of collections and curators of museums has enabled me to see a very large number of coins and to obtain impressions of many for comparison, by which means several readings of coins in the British Museum have been verified or ascertained and gaps in this collection supplemented in the tables of the coins; many coins in other collections are also figured in the Plates of the Catalogue, and are there marked with the initials or name of the collection to which they

---

[1] The date which appears on each volume of the *British Numismatic Journal* is that of the Proceedings which are described in it, and not the date of publication.

belong. The following abbreviations have been used for the collections quoted:

A.H.B.	Mr. A. H. Baldwin.
A.M.	Mr. Alexander Mann.
Ashm.	Ashmolean Museum, Oxford.
Bodl.	Bodleian Library, Oxford.
B.R.	The late Mr. Bernard Roth.
Brln.	Kaiser Friedrich Museum, Berlin.
Cpnhn.	National Museum, Copenhagen.
F.A.W.	Mr. F. A. Walters.
F.Mus.	Fitzwilliam Museum, Cambridge.
H.L.F.	Miss Helen Farquhar.
H.M.R.	Mr. H. M. Reynolds.
Hntr.	Hunterian collection, Glasgow.
H.S.	Mr. Henry Symonds.
H.W.M.	Col. H. W. Morrieson.
J.B.M.	Mr. J. B. S. McIlwaine.
J.E.C.	Mr. J. E. Cree.
J.H.D.	Mr. J. H. Daniels.
J.W.P.	Mr. J. W. Parkes.
J.Y.	Mr. J. Young.
L.A.L.	Mr. L. A. Lawrence.
L.E.B.	Mr. L. E. Bruun.
Lewis	Lewis collection, Corpus Christi College, Cambridge.
Mint	Royal Mint, London.
Nott.	Castle Museum, Nottingham.
Old Sarum	Old Sarum excavations.
Paris	Bibliothèque Nationale, Paris.
P.C.B.	Major P. W. P. Carlyon-Britton.
R.C.L.	Mr. R. C. Lockett.
R.T.	The Hon. R. Talbot.
S.M.	Sheriff Mackenzie.
S.M.S.	Mr. S. M. Spink (Messrs. Spink and Son).
Stkm.	Royal Museum, Stockholm.
T.B.	The late Mr. T. Bliss.
T.C.C.	Trinity College, Cambridge.
T.Mus.	Castle Museum, Taunton.
W.C.W.	Mr. W. C. Wells.
W.E.H.	Mr. W. E. Hidden.

W.J.R. . . . Mr. W. J. E. Ryan.
W.S.L. . . . Mr. F. W. Lincoln (Messrs. W. S. Lincoln and Son).
W.S.O. . . . Mr. W. Sharp Ogden.
W.T.R. . . . The late Mr. W. T. Ready.
York . . . . York Museum.

To the owners and curators of the above collections I am greatly indebted for the facilities which they have given me for seeing and for publishing their coins; the difficulty of the subject has been materially lessened by the large number of coins thus put at my disposal. I have obtained much help from Major P. W. P. Carlyon-Britton, F.S.A., not only by free access to his large collection of coins, but also by the use of manuscript notes which he has kindly lent me. To Dr. George Macdonald, F.B.A., Hon. Curator of the Hunterian collection, I owe special obligations for time and trouble most generously given both in showing me the Hunterian coins and in making impressions of several of them for my use. My sincere acknowledgements are due to Mr. H. A. Grueber, F.S.A., formerly Keeper of Coins, who has read proofs of the introduction and also gave me much assistance in the early stages of the work; also to Mr. L. A. Lawrence, F.S.A., and Mr. W. J. Andrew, F.S.A., who have read proofs of the introduction and helped me with many suggestions and corrections; and especially to Mr. G. F. Hill, Keeper of Coins, who has read proofs of the whole work, and whose help and encouragement have done much to lighten the sometimes arduous work of preparing the Catalogue. Nor must I forget to express my indebtedness to the helpful care of the Reader of the Clarendon Press.

TABLE OF FINDS

TABLE

THE numbers in this table include both pennies and cut halfpennies and farthings,
+ implies that one or more coins of the type occurred, but the number is not
This table contains only the regular English issues.   For the irregular issues and

	WILLIAM I								WILLIAM II				
	I	II	III	IV	V	VI	VII	VIII	I	II	III	IV	V
Soberton, 1851	23	..		..	..	..	..	..	..	..	..	..	..
York, 1845	1?	165	..		..	..	..	..	..	..	..		
York, 1882	4	MULE 4	4	..	..	..	..	..	..	..	..	..	
Whitchurch	4	4	+	..	..	..	..	..	..	..	..	..	
St. Mary Hill Church, 1771	+	+	4	MULE 1	+	..	..		..	..	..		
City of London, 1872	1	2		5	..	..	..	..	..	..	..	..	
Malmesbury, 1828	..	1	..	12	..	..	..		..	..	..	..	
York Minster	..	..		..	6	5			..	..	..	..	
Beaworth, 1833		6?	..	..	31	34	11	MULE 6	6457				
Tamworth, 1877	..		..	..	..	..	..	30	97	MULE 3	164	..	..
Shillington, 1871	..	..		..	..	..	..	1	+	+	+	+	..
Bermondsey, 1820	..	..		..	..	..	..	..	..	3	5	..	
Bari, 1891?	..	..		..	..	..		..	..	..	..		
Canterbury, 1901?	..	..		..	..	..	..	..	..	..	..		
Lowestoft, 1905	.			..	..	..	..	..	..	..	..		
Battle, 1860?				..	..	..	..	..	..	..	..		
Watford, 1818					1	..	..	..	..	..	..		
Smaller Watford, 1818		..	..		..	..	..	..	..	..	..		
Nottingham, 1880	..			..	..	..	..	..	..	..	..	..	
Dartford, 1825	.			..	..	..	..	..	..	..	..		
Sheldon, 1867					..		..	..	..	..	..		
Linton, 1883				..	..	..	..	..	..	..	..		
Bute, 1863				..	..	..	..	..	..	..	..		
Winterslow, c. 1804				..	..	..	..	..	..	..	..	..	
Awbridge, 1902?	..	..		..	..	..	..	..	..	..	..		

OF FINDS

each halfpenny and farthing counting as one coin.

known.

other coins represented in the finds, see the detailed description on pp. xvi–xxxii.

| HENRY I | | | | | | | | | | | | | | | STEPHEN | | | |
I	II	III	IV	V	VI	VII	VIII	IX	X	XI	XII	XIII	XIV	XV	I	II	VII	
..	..	..	..	..	..	..	..	..	..	..	..	..	..	..	..	..	..	Soberton, 1851
..	..	..	..	..	..	..	..	..	..	..	..	..	..	..	..	..	..	York, 1845
..	..	..	..	..	..	..	..	..	..	..	..	..	..	..	..	..	..	York, 1882
..	..	..	..	..	..	..	..	..	..	..	..	..	..	..	..	..	..	Whitchurch
..	..	..	..	..	..	..	..	..	..	..	..	..	..	..	..	..	..	St. Mary Hill Church, 1774
..	..	..	..	..	..	..	..	..	..	..	..	..	..	..	..	..	..	City of London, 1872
..	..	..	..	..	..	..	..	..	..	..	..	..	..	..	..	..	..	Malmesbury, 1828
..	..	..	..	..	..	..	..	..	..	..	..	..	..	..	..	..	..	York Minster
..	..	..	..	..	..	..	..	..	..	..	..	..	..	..	..	..	..	Beaworth, 1833
..	..	..	..	..	..	..	..	..	..	..	..	..	..	..	..	..	..	Tamworth, 1877
..	..	..	..	..	..	4 or 5?	..	..	..	..	..	..	..	..	..	..	..	Shillington, 1871
5	..	..	..	..	..	..	..	..	..	..	..	..	..	..	..	..	..	Bermondsey, 1820
..	..	3	24	..	..	..	..	..	..	..	..	..	..	..	..	..	..	Bari, 1891?
..	..	..	..	..	..	..	..	..	3	..	1	MULE 1	353	..	..	..	..	Canterbury, 1901?
..	..	..	..	..	..	..	..	..	..	..	..	..	6	6	..	..	..	Lowestoft, 1905
..	..	..	..	..	..	..	..	..	1	1	..	..	..	10	..	..	..	Battle, 1860?
..	..	..	..	..	..	..	..	..	..	..	..	..	58	419	643	..	..	Watford, 1818
..	..	..	..	..	..	..	..	..	..	..	..	..	+	+	+	..	..	Smaller Watford, 1818
1	..	..	..	..	..	..	..	..	..	1	..	..	..	7	upwards of 150	..	..	Nottingham, 1880
..	..	..	..	..	..	..	..	..	..	..	..	..	..	4	44	..	..	Dartford, 1825
..	..	..	..	..	..	..	..	..	..	..	..	..	..	3	76	MULE 2	2?	Sheldon, 1867
..	..	..	..	..	..	..	..	..	..	..	..	..	..	7	40	39	..	Linton, 1883
..	..	..	..	..	..	..	..	..	..	..	..	..	..	..	3	..	..	Bute, 1863
..	..	..	..	..	..	..	..	..	..	..	..	..	..	..	1	4	..	Winterslow, c. 1804
..	..	..	..	..	..	:	..	..	..	..	..	..	..	..	..	..	31	Awbridge, 1902?

TABLE OF MINTS, MONEYERS,
AND TYPES

The majority of the readings which are included in the following table have been taken from the coins themselves or, in a few cases, from casts or photographs of the coins; the remainder, which are inserted from published or unpublished lists or from free-hand drawings, are in italics (the Stockholm coins in italics are from readings kindly supplied by Major P. W. P. Carlyon-Britton, the remainder from casts sent to me from the Stockholm Museum). Italics are also used in the columns of moneyers' names to denote, in the left-hand column, names which occur on coins of the Confessor or Harold II and, in the right-hand column, those which occur on coins of the first issue ('Tealby' type) of Henry II.

The foot-notes contain readings from various publications, many of which are certainly incorrect; some, which may well be correct, are withheld from the table itself owing to lack of evidence for the existence of the coins. No readings have been inserted on the sole evidence of the Spicer Manuscript (*Num. Chron.*, 1904), because that work has been found to reproduce or originate many errors. Readings were inserted in it from sale catalogues without discrimination; the columns were sometimes confused, as in the mint of Romney where the entries under 239–40 should evidently have been placed under 241–2; and the columns have themselves been misread by later writers—in *Brit. Num. Journ.*, vol. ix, p. 132, for example, the *Eadweard* reading, which is of type VI (243) in Spicer, appears under type VIII. The MS. Catalogue of the B. C. Roberts collection has been the source of many errors, which are here, so far as possible, identified and corrected. Confusion of types, especially of (Hawkins) 243 and 247, and of 238 and 250 (the two 'Two-Stars' types), is not uncommon; in the A. W. Hankin sale catalogue (1900), for example, both coins described in lots 409 and 410 as of (Hawkins) 247 are of 243, being now in the Col. Morrieson collection. Misprints are another obvious source of error, as in *Num. Chron.*, 1880, p. 72, where the *Wulfnod* coin of (Hawkins) 234 is described as 244. The foot-notes do not include all published readings; such obvious mistakes as *Alic* for *Alif* or *Aleif*, *Strop* for *Sprot*, *Lestic* for *Lesinc*, &c., are omitted, and the insertion of many attributions which arise from the confusion of London and Lincoln, Chester and Leicester, and other similar pairs of mints is obviated by a cross reference from one mint to the other.

Other collections are only quoted in the table to supplement gaps, or doubtful readings, in the British Museum collection.

The abbreviations of sale catalogues and other publications, which are used in the table, are as follows:

+ . . . . British Museum Catalogue.
+ (app.) . . . .   „   „   „   (Appendix).
Allen . . . . . W. Allen sale, 1898.
Ast. '06 . . . . Astronomer sale, 1906.
B.N.J. . . . . . British Numismatic Journal.
Bscm . . . . . G. J. Bascom sale, 1914.
Btmn . . . . . W. and T. Bateman sale, 1893.
Circ. '02 . . . . Numismatic Circular, 1902 (*William I and II, their Mints and Moneyers*, by P. W. P. Carlyon-Britton).
Clark . . . . . H. Clark sale, 1898.
Cuff . . . . . J. D. Cuff sale, 1854.
Currer . . . . Miss R. Currer sale, 1862.
Drrnr . . . . . E. Durrner sale, 1853.
F.A.W., lot 61, &c. F. A. Walters sale, 1913, lot 61, &c.
H. H. Allan . . . H. H. Allan sale, 1908.
Knrd . . . . . D. F. Kennard sale, 1892.
L.A.L. 43, &c. . . L. A. Lawrence sale, 1903, lot 43, &c.
Lscbe . . . . . C. W. Loscombe sale, 1855.
M'Ewn . . . . C. McEwen sale, 1854.
Mntgu . . . . . H. Montagu sale, 1896-7.
Mrdch . . . . . J. G. Murdoch sale, 1903.
N.C. '69, &c. . . . Numismatic Chronicle, 1869, &c.
Nlgn . . . . . Rev. Dr. Neligan sale, 1851.
P.C.B. 743, &c. . . P. W. P. Carlyon-Britton sale, 1913, lot 743, &c.
Rash. . . . . . E. W. Rashleigh sale, 1909.
Rstn . . . . . Simpson Rostron sale, 1892.
S. i. '57, 6, &c. . . Sotheby sale, January, 1857, lot 6, &c.
Sntl . . . . . R. Sainthill, *Olla Podrida*.
Stnr . . . . . C. L. Stainer, *Oxford Silver Pennies*.
Tplis . . . . . J. Toplis sale, 1890.
Webb . . . . . H. Webb sale, 1895.
Witte . . . . . J. Witte sale, 1908.

For other abbreviations see list of collections on pp. cxc, cxci

		WILLIAM I							WILLIAM II							
	I	II	III	IV	V	VI	VII	VIII	I	II	III	IV	V	I	II	III
BARN-STAPLE																
Leofwine	..	+?	..		..	..	..	..	..	..	..	..		..	..	
Oter	..	..	..		..	..	..	..	..	..	..	..	..	..	..	
Seword	..	..	..	..	(NC '69 p. 355	+	..	+	..	..	..	..	..	..	..	..

Godsbrand (William I, type VIII). See above, p. clxii.

	I	II	III	IV	V	VI	VII	VIII	I	II	III	IV	V	I	II	III
BATH																
Ægelmæ[r]	..	..		..		..	..	+	..	..	..	..	..	..	..	
Brungar	..	..	P.C.B.	..		..	..		..	..	..	..	..	..	..	
Godesbrand	..	..		..	..	..	..	+	..	..	..	..	..	..	..	
Osmær	Hntr	..		..	+	..	..	+	..	..	..	..	..	..	..	
Winterlede	..	..		..	..	..	..		..	..	..	..	..	..	..	

Osbern (Henry I, type XIV). E. W. Rashleigh sale, 1909, lot 399 = Num.

	I	II	III	IV	V	VI	VII	VIII	I	II	III	IV	V	I	II	III
BEDFORD																
Edric ?	..	..		..		..	..		..	..	..	..	..	..	..	
Godric	..	..		..		..	..		..	+	..	..	..	..	..	
Lifwi	..	..		..		..	..		+	..	..	..	..	..	..	
Sibrand	+	..	Hntr	..		..	..	+	..	..	..	..	..	..	..	
Sigod (Sægod)	..	+	+	+	+	..			(P.C.B. 743	+	+	..	..	..	..	
Uncertain	..	..		..		..	..		..	..	..	..	..	..	..	

Alwine (Stephen, type VII). W. Allen sale, 1898, lot 378 = R. Roth coll. (Pevensey); F. A. Walters
    sale, 1913, lot 71, probably Pevensey.
Lifwine (William II, type II). Num. Chron., 1877, p. 342 = Catalogue, p. 228, no. 82 (Derby).

	I	II	III	IV	V	VI	VII	VIII	I	II	III	IV	V	I	II	III
BEDWIN																
Cild	+	..		..		..	..		..	..	..	..	..	..	..	
BRAN- -																
Orgar	..	..		..		..	..		..	..	..	..	..	..	..	
Willem	..	..		..	..	..	..		..	..	..	..	..	..	..	
BRIDPORT																
Ælfric	..	..		..		..	..	+	..	..	..	..	..	..	..	
Brihtwi	..	..		..		..	..	+	..	..	..	..	..	..	..	

Brihtwine (William II, type I). S. Rostron sale, 1892, lot 17 = Astronomer sale, 1906, lot 216.
    See Bristol.

	HENRY I												STEPHEN			
IV	V	VI	VII	VIII	IX	X	XI	XII	XIII	XIV	XV	I	II	III–VI	VII		
..	..	..	..	..	..	..	..	..	..	..	..	..	..	..			**BARN-STAPLE**
																	Leofwine
..	..	..	..	..	..	..	..	..	+	+?) P.C.B.)	..	..	..	..	.		Oter
..	..	..	..	..	..	..	..	..	..	..	..	..	..	..	.		Seword

IV	V	VI	VII	VIII	IX	X	XI	XII	XIII	XIV	XV	I	II	III–VI	VII		
..	..	..	..	..	..	..	..	..	..	..	..	..	..	..	..		**BATH**
..	..	..	..	..	..	..	..	..	..	..	..	..	..	..	..		Ægelmæ[r]
..	..	..	..	..	..	..	..	..	..	..	..	..	..	..	..		Brungar
..	..	..	..	..	..	..	..	..	..	..	..	..	..	..	..		Godesbrand
..	..	..	..	..	..	..	..	..	+	P.C.B.	..	..	..	..	..		Osmær
																	Winterlede

Chron., 1850, p. 151 and 1901, p. 112 = Catalogue, p. 311, no. 164 (Sandwich).

IV	V	VI	VII	VIII	IX	X	XI	XII	XIII	XIV	XV	I	II	III–VI	VII		
..	..	..	..	..	..	..	..	+	..	..		..	..	..	..		**BEDFORD** Edric!
..	..	..	..	..	..	..	..	..	..	..		..	..	..	..		Godric
..	..	..	..	..	..	..	..	..	..	..		..	..	..	..		Lifwi
..	..	..	..	..	..	..	..	..	..	..		..	..	..	..		Sibrand
..	..	..	..	..	..	..	..	..	..	..		..	..	..	..		Sigod (Sægod)
..	..	..	..	..	..	..	..	..	..	..	+	..	..	..	..		Uncertain

Sigod (William II, type V). Brit. Num. Journ., vol. iv, p. 51 ('type 5' misprint for 'type 4') = Catalogue, p. 243, no. 175.

IV	V	VI	VII	VIII	IX	X	XI	XII	XIII	XIV	XV	I	II	III–VI	VII		
..	..	..	..	..	..	..	..	..	..	..	..	..	..	..	..		**BEDWIN** Cild
																	BRAN - -
..	..	..	..	..	..	..	..	..	..	..	..	..	..	P.C.B.	..		Orgar
..	..	..	..	..	..	..	..	..	..	..	..	..	..	..	+		Willem
																	BRIDPORT
..	..	..	..	..	..	..	..	..	..	..	..	..	..	..	..		Ælfric
..	..	..	..	..	..	..	..	..	..	..	..	..	..	..	..		Brihtwi

Thidræd (William II, type II). Num. Chron., 1904, p. 256. Probably Warwick (cf. Catalogue, p. 241, no. 164).

	WILLIAM I								WILLIAM II					
	I	II	III	IV	V	VI	VII	VIII	I	II			V	I
BRISTOL														
Ailwald (Ailwold)	..	..	..	..	..	..	..	..	..	..	..		..	
Barewit (Barcit)	..	..	..	..	..	..	..	..	..	..	..	H.M.R.	*Stkm*	..
Brihtword (Brwode, &c.)	..	..	..	..	..	(Cuff 712)	(S.1'57 6)	+	+	+	(+ (app.)	..	..	
Brunstan	..	..	..	..	..	..	..	+	..	..	..		..	
Ccorl (Carel, Cerl)	+	..	+	Hntr	+? P.C.B.	..	..	..	..	..	..		..	
Colblac	..	..	..	..	..	..	..	+	+	+	..		..	
Edric (Edricus)	..	..	..	..	..	..	..	..	..	..	..		..	
Far[m]an?	..	..	..	..	..	..	..	..	..	..	..		..	
Gurd[an]?	..	..	..	..	..	..	..	..	..	..	..		..	
Herdig	..	..	..	..	..	..	..	..	..	..	..		..	
Hwateman	..	..	..	..	+	..	..	..	..	..	..		..	
Leofwine (Lifwine, &c.)	(Malgu t. 181)	Hntr	Hntr	+	+	+	..	+	..	..	..		..	
Riccard	..	..	..	..	..	..	..	..	..	..	..		..	
Sendi (Sindi)	..	..	..	..	..	..	..	..	..	..	H.W.M.		+	H.
Swegn (Swein)	..	..	..	..	..	..	..	+	..	..	..		..	
Turchil	..	..	..	..	..	..	..	..	..	..	..		..	

Ailward (Henry I, type XIV). E. W. Rashleigh sale, 1909, lot 400 = Catalogue, p. 300, no. 107 (Ailwald).

Aldred (Stephen, type II). D. F. Kennard sale, 1892, lot 126. Perhaps = S. M. Spink coll. (Hastings).

Brihtwine (William II, type I). Astronomer sale, 1906, lot 216 = S. Rostron sale, 1892, lot 17. Apparently a London coin, see Brit. Num. Journ., vol. v, p. 106 (assigned to Lincoln).

Colnine (William II, type II). Num. Chron., 1877, p. 342 = Catalogue, p. 227, no. 71 (Colblac).

Edwold (William I, type VIII). Brit. Num. Journ., vol. vi, p. 152. Possibly a misreading of a Norwich coin?

Geraud (Henry I, type XIV). Num. Chron., 1901, p. 126, from Withy and Ryall.

	I	II	III	IV	V	VI	VII	VIII	I	II	III	IV	V	I
BURY ST. EDMUNDS														
Ace[1] (Acel[lus]?)	..	..	..	..	..	..	..	..						
Gilebert[2]	..	..	..	..	..	..	..	..						
Godric[3]	..	..	..	..	..	..	..	..						

[1] Type I. **SANT**; II. **S:EDMVND.**   [2] Henry I. **EDMN**;

Stephen, **EDM, SA.**   [3] Type XIII. **S:EDM**; XIV. **SA'E, SAN.**

See also Sandwich.

	I	II	III	IV	V	VI	VII	VIII	I	II	III	IV	V	I
CAMBRIDGE														
Æghun[r] (Ælmær)	..	..	..	P.C.B. 697	+	..	..	..	..	..	..	..	..	
Godric	+	..	..	..	..	..	..	..	..	..	..	..	..	
Odbearn	..	..	..	(Hntr P.C.B.	..	..	..	..	..	..	..	..	..	
Ulfcil (Ulfcitl)	..	..	..	..	Hntr	..	(Drrnr 43)	+	..	..	..	..	..	
Wibern	..	..	..	..	..	..	..	..	+	*Stkm*	Brln	..	..	

Wulfric (Stephen, type II). H. Montagu sale, 1896, lot 322. Prob

HENRY I													STEPHEN				
I	IV	V	VI	VII	VIII	IX	X	XI	XII	XIII	XIV	XV	I	II	III–VI	VII	**BRISTOL**
..	..	..	..	..	..	..	..	..	..	..	+	..	..	..	..	..	Ailwald (Ailwold)
B.R.	..	..	..	..	..	..	..	..	..	..	..	..	..	..	..	..	Barewit (Bareit)
..	..	..	..	..	..	..	..	..	..	..	..	..	..	..	..	..	Brihtword (Brwode, &c.)
..	..	..	..	..	..	..	..	..	..	..	..	..	..	..	..	..	Brunstan
..	..	..	..	..	..	..	..	..	..	..	..	..	..	..	..	..	Ceorl (Carel, Cerl
..	..	..	..	..	..	..	..	..	..	..	..	..	..	..	..	..	Colblac
..	..	..	..	..	..	..	..	..	..	NC '01 Pl.VII.3	+	..	..	..	..	..	Edric (Edricus)
..	..	..	..	..	..	..	..	..	..	..	..	..	B.R.	..	..	..	Far[m]an ?
..	..	..	..	..	..	..	..	..	..	..	..	..	+	..	..	..	Gurd[an] ?
..	..	..	..	..	..	+	..	..	..	..	+	..	..	..	..	..	Herdig
..	..	..	..	..	..	..	..	..	..	..	..	..	..	..	..	..	Hwateman
..	..	..	..	..	..	..	..	..	..	..	..	..	..	..	..	..	Leofwine (Lifwine, &c.)
..	..	..	..	..	..	..	..	..	..	..	..	+	..	..	..	..	Riccard
..	..	..	..	..	..	..	..	..	..	..	..	..	..	..	..	..	Sendi (Sindi)
..	..	..	..	..	..	..	..	..	..	..	..	..	..	..	..	..	Swegn (Swein)
..	..	..	..	..	..	..	..	..	..	..	..	+	..	..	..	..	Turchil

Grim (William I, type VIII). M. W. Peace sale, 1894, lot 59. Probably misreading for Swein.
Lifwine (William II, type V). Num. Circ., 1902, p. 5467 = P. W. P. Carlyon-Britton sale, 1913, lot 782 (probably Derby).
Smiwi (William II, type III). Brit. Num. Journ., vol. vi, p. 153 = H. W. Morrieson coll. (Sendi).
Smiri (William II, type V). E. W. Rashleigh sale, 1909, lot 398   ⎫ = Catalogue,
Sinot   ,,   ,,   Brit. Num. Journ., vol. vi, p. 153   ⎬ p. 261, no. 257
Sinwi   ,,   ,,   P. W. P. Carlyon-Britton sale, 1913, lot 781 ⎭ (Sindi).
Thurcit (William II, type IV). Brit. Num. Journ., vol. vi, p. 153 = Catalogue, Pl. xxxvi. 1 (Barc[w]it).
A coin in A. H. Baldwin coll. of Henry I, type X, reads - -VIG, perhaps *Lavig* or *Levig*.

III	IV	V	VI	VII	VIII	IX	X	XI	XII	XIII	XIV	XV	I	II	III–VI	VII	**BURY ST. EDMUNDS**
..	..	..	..	..	..	..	..	..	..	..	..	..	+ ?	+	..	+ ?	Ace [1] (Acel[lus]?)
..	..	..	..	..	..	..	..	..	..	..	..	+	+	..	..	..	Gilebert [2]
..	..	..	..	..	..	..	..	..	..	R.C.L.	+	..	..	..	..	..	Godric [3]

For coins of William I and William II assigned to this mint see above, p. clxiv.
Aldred (Henry I, type XIV). J. G. Murdoch sale, 1903, lot 226. Probably Shaftesbury.
Odde   ,,   ,,   Num. Chron., 1901, p. 392 = P. W. P. Carlyon-Britton coll. (moneyer's name doubtful).

III	IV	V	VI	VII	VIII	IX	X	XI	XII	XIII	XIV	XV	I	II	III–VI	VII	**CAMBRIDGE**
..	..	..	..	..	..	..	..	..	..	..	..	..	..	..	..	..	Æglmæ[r] (Ælmær)
..	..	..	..	..	..	..	..	..	..	..	..	..	..	..	..	..	Godric
..	..	..	..	..	..	..	..	..	..	..	..	..	..	..	..	..	Odbearn
..	..	..	..	..	..	..	..	..	..	..	..	..	..	..	..	..	Ulfcil (Ulfcitl)
..	..	..	..	..	..	..	..	..	..	..	..	..	..	..	..	..	Wibern

= H. O. O'Hagan sale, 1907, lot 428 = S. M. Spink coll. (Sandwich).

	WILLIAM I								WILLIAM II					
	I	II	III	IV	V	VI	VII	VIII	I	II	III	IV	V	I
CANTER-BURY														
Ædward, see Eadweard	..	..	..	..		..		..		..				..
Ægelric	..	..	..		+	..		..	+					..
Ælfred	..	..	..	Hntr	+	+	..	+		+	+	F.Mus.		
Ælred	..	..	..	..		..		..						
Aghemund (Ahemund, &c.)	..	..		..		..		..				+		F.A.W. lot 61 T.B.
Aldred (Ældred, &c.)	..	..	..	..		..		..			+			..
Algar	..	..	..	..		..		..						..
Algod	..	..	..	..		..		..				+		..
Brihtwold (Brihtwod, &c.)	..	..	..	..		..		+	F.Mus. Mint	P.C.B.	+			
Burnoth	..	..	..	..		..		..						
Eadweard (Ædward, &c.)	+	..	..	..		..		..						
Edwine	..	..	..	..		..		..				T.C.C.	+	T.B.
Godhese	..	..	..	..		..		..						..
Godric	..	..	..	..		..	+	..						..
Gregori	..	..	..	..		..		..						..
Manna (Mann, &c.)	+	+	+	+	+									
Perin	..	..	..	..		..		..						
Rodbert (Rodberd, &c.)	..	..	..	..		..		..						
Rogier	..	..	..	..		..		..						
Simer	..	..	..	..		..		+		Brln T.C.C	..			..
Willem	..	..	..	..		+		..						..
Winedi (Windi, &c.)	..	..	..	..		..		+	+	+	Hntr	+	MULE L.E.B. +	..
Wulbold (Wulbod)	..	..	..	..		..		+		+				
Wulfred	+	..	..	..		..		..						
Wulfric (Wulvric)	..	..	..	+		..		+						+
Wulfwine	..	..	P.C.B.?	..		(Clark 50)								
Wulsi	..	..	..	..		..		..						

Abelin (Stephen, type I). Num. Chron. 1850, p. 155 = Catalogue, p. 355, no. 3 (Bury St. Edmunds, Acc—?).

Ældwien (William II, type V). H. Clark sale, 1898, lot 60 = T. Bliss coll. (Ældred); Num. Chron., 1904, p. 257 (Ældwinen) = same coin?

Ælfræd (William II, type I). W. Allen sale, 1898, lot 363 = Catalogue, p. 248, no. 23 (London).

Ælfword (William II, type III). Rev. H. Christmas sale, 1864, lot 225.

Athebrand   „   „   Num. Circ., 1902, p. 5468. Probably = Catalogue, p. 252, no. 219 (Shrewsbury).

Brihtred (William II, type I). Num. Circ., 1902, p. 5467, from Num. Chron., 1877, p. 342. Probably = Brihtwold.

Brihtwod (William II, type IV). Brit. Num. Journ., vol. vii, p. 9. Not in Fitzwilliam Museum, Cambridge; perhaps = coin of type I?

Eadwine (William I, type IV). Brit. Num. Journ., vol. vii, p. 7 = Evans coll. = Catalogue, Appendix, p. 401, no. 258 A (London).

Edmund (Henry I, type XIII). L. A. Lawrence sale, 1903, lot 107 = B. Roth coll. (Edwine).

Everard (Stephen, type I). J. B. Bergne sale, 1873, lot 333 = H. Webb sale, 1894, lot 36 = T. Bliss coll. (Warwick).

Gefrei (Stephen, type I). Num. Chron., 1850, p. 156. Probably Winchester.

		HENRY I								STEPHEN				
/III	IX	X	XI	XII	XIII	XIV	XV	I	II	III–VI	VII		CAN
..	..	..	..	..	..	..	..	..	..	..	..		Ædwa
..	..	..	..	..	..	..	..	..	..	..	..		Ead
..	..	..	..	..	..	..	..	..	..	..	..		Æglri
..	..	..	..	..	..	..	..	..	..	..	..		Ælfre
..	..	..	..	..	..	P.C.B.	..	..	..	..	..		Ælred
													Agher
..	..	..	Hntr	..	..	..	+	..	..	..	..		(Ah
													&c.)
													Aldre
													dræ
..	..	..	..	..	..	P.C.B.	..	..	..	..	..		Algar
..	..	..	..	..	..	..	..	..	..	..	..		Algod
..	..	..	..	..	..	..	..	..	..	..	..		Briht
													(Bri
													&c.)
..	..	..	..	..	..	..	..	..	..	..	..		Burno
													Eadw
..	..	..	..	..	..	..	..	+	+	..	..		(Æd
													&c.)
..	..	..	..	..	B.R.	..	..	+	..	..	..		Edwi
..	..	..	..	..	..	..	..	..	..	..	..		Godh
..	..	..	+	..	..	..	..	..	..	..	..		Godri
..	..	..	..	..	..	..	..	..	..	..	..		Grego
													Mann
													(Ma
..	..	..	..	..	..	..	..	..	..	..	..		Perin
													Rodb
..	..	..	..	..	..	..	+	+	H.M.R. L.E.B.	P.C.B. (VI)	+		(Rod
													&c.)
..	..	..	..	..	..	..	..	..	+	W.J.R. (VI)	+		*Rogic*
..	..	..	..	..	..	..	..	..	..	..	..		Simœi
..	..	..	..	..	..	+	+	+	..	..	..		Wille
..	..	..	..	..	..	+	+	..	..	..	..		Wine
													(Wi
..	..	..	..	..	..	..	..	..	..	..	..		Wulb
													(Wu
..	..	..	..	..	..	..	..	..	..	..	..		Wulfi
..	Stkm	..	..	..	..	..	..	H.M.R. P.C.B. +?	..	..	..		Wulfi (Wu
..	..	..	..	..	..	..	..	P.C.B.	..	..	..		Wulf
..	..	..	..	..	..	..	..	..	..	..	..		Wulsi

ype I).   G. J. Bascom sale, 1914, lot 85 = Catalogue, p. 348, no. 88 A (Pembroke

type IIl).   J. L. Henderson sale, 1888, lot 34.   Possibly London?

XIV).   Num. Chron., 1901, p. 136, from Withy and Ryall.

  type III).   Num. Circ., 1902, p. 5468 = Roberts MS. Catalogue reading o

ue, p. 244, no. 179 (Wulbold).

)e IV).   Num. Circ., 1902, p. 5467 = Catalogue, p. 259, no. 256 (York).

ype I).   Brit. Num. Journ., vol. vii, p. 8.   Probably misreading of Catalogue

Shrewsbury).

;, type IV).   Akerman, Num. Journ., vol. ii, p. 106.   Probably = Miss Hele

. (London, Ægelwine).

/pe III).   Rev. T. F. Dymock sale, 1858, lot 179 = J. B. Bergne sale, 1873, lot 31

I, type I).   F. A. Walters sale, 1913, lot 61.   Same dies as T. Bliss coi

type IIl).   Archaeologia, vol. iv, p. 356.

II, type IV).   Num. Chron., 1904, p. 258.   Perhaps = Catalogue, p. 257, no. 24

cin), misread in Roberts MS. Catalogue as *Wulfwine on Lu*.

type VI).   Sotheby sale, March 7, 1894, lot 73.

	WILLIAM I								WILLIAM II				
	I	II	III	IV	V	VI	VII	VIII	I	II		IV	V
CARDIFF?													
Ælfsie	..	..	..	..	..	..	..		..	..		..	..
(Ælfsi Turi)	..	..	..	..	..	..	..		..	..		..	..
CARLISLE													
Durant	..	..	..	..	..	..	..		..	..		..	..
Erebald	..	..	..	..	..	..	..		..	..		..	..
Willem	..	..	..	..	..	..	..		..	..		..	..
CASTLE RISING													
Hiun (Iun)	..	..	..	..	..	..	..		..	..		..	..
Rawulf (see above, p. clxvii)	..	..	..	..	..	..	..		..	..		..	..
Rodbert (Rodbret)	..	..	..	..	..	..	..		..	..		..	..
Uncertain (? Ber . . .)	..	..	..	..	..	..	..		..	..		..	..
CHESTER													
Ælfsi [1]	..	..	..						..	..		..	..
Ælfweard [2]	..	..	..						..	..		..	..
Ælfwine [3]	..	..	..							*Silac* P.C.B.		..	..
Ailmar (Ailmer) [4]	..	..	..						..	..		..	..
Airic [5]	..	..	..						..	..		..	..
Alesi [6]	..	..	..						..	..		..	..
Andreu [7]	..	..	..						..	..		..	..
Bruninc [8]	Hur								..	..		..	..
Cristret [9]	..	..	..						..	..		..	..
Frithegist [10]	..	..	..						..	..		..	..
Gillemor [11]	..	..	..						..	..		..	..
Levenod [12]	..	..	..						..	..		..	..
Littine (Litfie, &c.) [13]	..	..	..					*	Mint P.C.B. ? H	..		..	..
Lifnoth [14]	..	..	..						..	? ? P.C.B		..	..
Lifwine [15]		*Rash.* ? 341						*	M.U.L. ? ..	R.C.L. (app.)		..	..
Ravenswert [16]	..	..	..						(app.)	..		..	..
Simonlf [17]	..	P.C.B.							J.Y.	..		..	..
Thurbern [18]	..	..	..						P.C.B.	..		..	..
Unulf [19]	..	..	..						..	..		..	..

[1] *Confessor,* LEICEST, LEICE, LEGECES, LEGEEE; [2] *William I. type II,* LEGECE, LEGECI; VIII. LECESTR, LEHE CE (with the same obv. die). — [2] LEHI   [3] LEIEC, LEIE   [4] CESTR, CES   [5] CESTRE   [6] *Confessor,* LE GECE, LEICEE; *Harold II.* LLEGEC; *William I.* LEGECI   [7] CEST   [8] *Confessor,* LEICE, LEIC, LEGECC, LEC; *William I.* LEG   [9] CES   [10] LEI   [11] CES - - [12] CESTE   [13] *William I.* LEHEC, LCHECST; *William II,* LEICET, LEIECES   [14] LECEC, LEC   [15] *Confessor,* LEGECESR, LEICE, LEI, LEH; *William I.* LECEI, LECE,

	HENRY I													STEPHEN				
III	IV	V	VI	VII	VIII	IX	X	XI	XII	XIII	XIV	XV	I	II	III-VI	VII	
															..			**CARDIFF**
..	..	..	..	..	..	..				..	..	..	..	..	..			Ælfsie
..	..	..	..	..	..	..				..	..	..	..	..	..			? Ælfsi Turi?
																		CARLISLE
..	..	..	..	..	..	..				..	..	+	..	..	..			Durant
..	..	..	..	..	..	..				..	P.C.B.		+	..	..			Erebald
..	..	..	..	..	..	..				..	..	..	+	..	..			Willem
																		CASTLE RISING
..	..	..	..	..	..						..	..	..	..	..		+	Hinn (Iun)
..	..	..	..								..	..	..	+? B.R. H.M.R.	..		..	Rawulf (see above, p. clx)
..	..	..	..								..	..	..	H.M.R.	+(VI)		..	Rodbert (Rodbret)
..	..	..	..								..	..	+	..	..		..	Uncertain (?Ber...)
																		CHESTER
..	..	..	..								..	..	..	..	..		..	Ælfsi [1]
..	..	..	..				..				..	..	..	..	..		..	Ælfweard [2]
..	..	..	..								..	..	..	..	..		..	Ælfwine [3]
..	..	..	..								..	+	+	..	..		..	Ailmar (Ailmær) [4]
..	..	..	..								+	..	..	..	..		..	Airie [5]
..	..	..	..								..	..	..	..	..		..	Alesi [6]
..	..	..	..							..	P.C.B.	..	..	..	..		..	Andreu [7]
..	..	..	..								..	..	..	..	..		..	Bruninc [8]
..	..	..	..				+?				..	+	..	..	..		..	Cristret [9]
..	..	..	..								..	..	..	..	..		..	Frithegist [10]
..	..	..	..								..	+	..	..	..		..	Gillemor [11]
..	..	..	..								..	?	..	..	..		..	Levenod [12]
..	..	..	..								..	..	..	..	..		..	Lifinc (Lifie, &c.) [13]
P.C.B.	..	..	..	..							..	..	..	..	..		..	Lifnoth [14]
..	..	..	..								..	..	..	..	..		..	Lifwine [15]
..	..	..	..								..	+?	+?	..	..		..	Ravenswert [16]
..	..	..	..								..	..	..	..	..		..	Sunoulf [17]
..	..	..	..								..	+	..	..	..		..	Uunulf [18]

LEHCI, LEHC; *William II.* LEICET, LEICT, LEICE [16] CE [17] *William I, type II.* LECEC; VIII, LECES, LECS. LECI, LEHC; *William II, type I.* LECSTR; II. LEIEC [18] CES [19] CESTRE

See also Leicester.

Ælfric (William II, type I). H. O. O'Hagan sale, 1907, lot 415. Perhaps Lewes?

Dunic (William I, type I). J. Loveday sale, 1897, lot 620. Perhaps Hastings?

Lifinc (William I, type III). Brit. Num. Journ., vol. iv, p. 65.

Lifnoth (William II, type IV). Num. Chron., 1904, p. 259. Probably = Capt. Murchison sale, 1864, lot 18 = Catalogue, p. 244, no. 480 (type III).

Winnræd (Henry I, type I). H. Montagu sale, 1896, lot 272 = Col. Durrant sale, 1847, lot 184 (*Winhued*). Probably Lewes, q.v.

	WILLIAM I								WILLIAM II					
	I	II	III	IV	V	VI	VII	VIII	I	II	III	IV	V	I
CHI-CHESTER														
Brand (Brandus)	..	..	..	..	..	..	..	..	..	..	..	..	..	
Brunman (Bruman, &c.)	P.C.B.	..	..	F.Mus.	+	..	P.C.B.	..	+	+	+	P.C.B.	..	
Edwine (= Edwi?)		..	..			..		+	Allen t 304	..	..	..		
Godwine	..		..	..	+				..	+	..	+	P.C.B.	..

Brihtmær (William I, type III). E. H. Evans sale, 1891, lot 27.

Colswegen (William I, type I). G. W. E. Bieber sale, 1889, lot 2 = H. Montagu sale, 1896, lot 181 (Hastings).

Godwine (William II, type III). P. W. P. Carlyon-Britton sale, 1913, lot 765. Mint doubtful, probably London.

	I	II	III	IV	V	VI	VII	VIII	I	II	III	IV	V	I
CHRIST-CHURCH														
Ældred	..	..	..	..	..	..	..	..	..	..	..	..	..	?
Coleman	..	..	..	..	..	+	..	..	..	..	..	..	..	
Tovi	..	..	..	..	..	..	..	..	..	..	..	..	..	
COL-CHESTER														
Ælfric	..	..	..	..	..	..	..	..	..	..	..	..	..	
Ælfsi (Ælfsi, Elsie)	..	..	..	..	..	..	..	..	..	+	..	..	..	
Brihtric	H.W.M.	+	..	..	..	..	..	..	..	+	..	..	..	
Dirman (Dorman, &c.)	..	..	..	..	..	H.W.M.	..	+	..	..	..	..	..	
Edward (Edward?)	..	..	..	..	..	..	..	..	..	..	..	..	..	
Goldhavec (Goldhfe)	..	..	..	..	..	..	..	..	..	..	+	Hntr?	..	
Goldman	P.C.B.	Hntr	..	..	..	..	..	..	..	..	..	..	..	
Goldstan	+	+	..	..	..	..	..	..	..	..	..	..	..	
Siwigen (Swegen, &c.)	..	..	..	..	..	..	..	..	..	+	..	+		
Siword	..	..	..	..	..	..	..	+	..	..	..	..	..	
Wulfric	..	..	..	..	..	..	..	..	..	H.W.M.	..	+	..	
Wulfward (Wulfwod)	..	..	..	..	..	Hntr	P.C.B.	..	..	..	..	..	..	
Wulfwine (Wulwic)	..	..	Hntr	Hntr	P.C.B.	..	Sim	+	+	..	..	..	..	
Uncertain	..	..	..	..	..	..	..	..	..	..	..	..	..	

Ælf[ric] (William II, type IV). Brit. Num. Journ., vol. v, p. 120. Or Ælfsie?

Godwine (William I, type V). Num. Chron., 1904, p. 290.

Goldwine   "   "   Brit. Num. Journ., vol. v, p. 119. Perhaps = preceding?

	I	II	III	IV	V	VI	VII	VIII	I	II	III	IV	V	I
CRICK-LADE														
Ælfwine	..	..	..	..	..	..	..	..	..	..	..	..	..	
Edouf	..	..	..	..	..	..	..	+	..	..	..	..	..	
Leofred (Liofred)	..	..	..	L.E.B.	..	..	..	..	..	T.Mus.	Sim	..	..	
Wulstan	..	+	..	T.C.C.	+	..	..	..	..	..	..	..	..	

Godesbrand (William I, type VIII). Num. Circ., 1902, p. 5469 = Catalogue, p. 173, no. 931 (Shaftesbury).

				HENRY I										STEPHEN				
III	IV	V	VI	VII	VIII	IX	X	XI	XII	XIII	XIV	XV	I	II	III-VI	VII	**CHI-CHESTI**
..	..	..	*NC'01* p.158	P.C.B.?	..	..	+	..	..	+	+	..	..	..	..	..	Brand (Brandu
..	..	..	..	..	..	..	..	..	..	..	..	..	..	..	..	..	Brunman (Brumar &c.)
..	..	..	..	..	..	..	..	..	..	..	..	..	..	..	..	..	Edwine
..	..	..	..	..	..	..	..	P.C.B.	B.R.	+	..	+	..	..	..	..	Godwine

Sprœcline (William I, type VIII). See Catalogue, p. 208, no. 1127 (Winchester), and Num. Chron., 1911, p. 270.
Thursten (William II, type I). Num. Circ., 1902, p. 5469. Perhaps Lincoln?

III	IV	V	VI	VII	VIII	IX	X	XI	XII	XIII	XIV	XV	I	II	III-VI	VII	
																	CHRIS CHUR(
..	..	..	..	..	..	..	..	..	..	..	..	..	..	..	..	..	Ældred
..	..	..	..	..	..	..	..	..	..	..	+	..	..	..	..	..	Coleman
																	Tovi
																	COL-CHEST.
..	..	..	..	..	..	..	..	..	..	..	..	..	..	..	..	..	Ælfric
..	..	..	..	..	..	..	..	..	..	+	..	..	..	..	..	..	Ælfsi (Æf Elsie)
..	..	..	..	..	..	..	..	..	..	..	..	..	..	..	..	..	Brihtric
..	..	..	..	..	..	..	..	..	..	..	..	..	..	..	..	..	Dirman (Dormar &c.)
..	..	..	..	..	..	..	..	..	H.W.M.?	..	..	+	..	..	..	..	Edward (Ædwar
..	..	..	..	..	..	..	..	..	..	P.C.B.	..	..	..	..	..	..	Goldhave((Goldhf(
..	..	..	..	..	..	..	..	..	..	..	..	..	..	..	..	..	Goldman
..	..	..	..	..	..	..	..	..	..	..	..	..	..	..	..	..	Goldstan
+	..	..	..	..	..	..	..	..	..	..	..	..	..	..	..	..	Siwigen (Swegær &c.)
..	..	..	..	..	..	..	..	..	..	..	..	..	..	..	..	..	Siword
..	..	..	..	..	..	..	..	..	..	..	..	..	..	..	..	..	Wulfric
..	..	..	..	..	..	..	..	..	..	..	..	..	..	..	..	..	Wulfward (Wulfw(
..	..	..	..	..	..	..	..	..	..	..	..	..	..	..	..	..	Wulfwine (Wulwi(
..	..	..	..	..	..	..	..	..	..	..	..	..	..	S.M.S.	..	..	Uncertain

Safari (Stephen, type I). E. W. Rashleigh sale, 1909, lot 502 = P. W. P. Carlyon-Britton coll. Mint uncertain.
Wulfwi (Henry I, type XIV). Num. Chron., 1901, p. 167 = Hunterian coll. (Gloucester).

III	IV	V	VI	VII	VIII	IX	X	XI	XII	XIII	XIV	XV	I	II	III-VI	VII	
																	CRICK-LAI
..	..	..	..	..	..	..	..	..	..	..	..	..	..	..	..	..	Ælfwine
..	..	..	..	..	..	..	..	..	..	..	..	..	..	..	..	..	Edouf
..	..	..	..	..	..	..	..	..	..	..	..	..	..	..	..	..	Leofred (Liofred)
..	..	..	..	..	..	..	..	..	..	..	..	..	..	..	..	..	Wulstan

Wulfric (William I, type VIII). A. Durlacher sale, 1899, lot 8.
Wulstane (William I, type VII). P. W. P. Carlyon-Britton sale, 1913, lot 717. Mint uncertain.

	WILLIAM I								WILLIAM II					
	I	II	III	IV	V	VI	VII	VIII	I	II	III	IV	V	I
DERBY														
Brun	..	..		..	..	..	..		..	..	..	..	..	..
Colbein	..	4	P.C.B.?	..	..	..	..		..	..	..	..	..	..
Frona (Froma, Froun)	4	..	..	Hntr	P.C.B.	..	..		..	..	..	..	..	..
Godwine (Gdwine)	..	..	..	..	..	..	..	4	4	4	..	..	..	..
Leofwine (Lifwine)	..	..	..	..	..	..	..	4	4	4	..	..	(P.C.B. 782	..
Uncertain	..	..	..	..	..	..	..		..	..	..	..	..	..

Antholof (William I, type D). Num. Chron., 1904, p. 270. Probably York, Autholf.
Godwine (William I, type VII). E. W. Rashleigh sale, 1909, lot 363. P. W. P. Carlyon-Britton coll. Mint doubtful.

	I	II	III	IV	V	VI	VII	VIII	I	II	III	IV	V	I
DORCHES-TER														
Ælfgæt	..	..	..	..	..	..	..		..	4	..	4 (app.)	..	..
Godwine	..	..	..	H.S.	MULE B.N.J. v. 151	4	H.S.		..	..	..	..	..	..
Litric	..	..	..	..	..	..	..		..	..	..	..	..	..
Osbern	..	..	..	..	..	..	..		..	..	..	..	..	..
Oter	..	..	..	..	..	H.S. Lewis	..		..	..	..	..	..	..
Sween	..	..	..	..	..	..	..		..	..	..	..	..	..
Uncertain	..	..	..	..	..	..	..		..	..	..	..	..	..

Lifwine (William I, type VIII). W. Allen sale, 1898, lot 306. Possibly Lafric?
Oter (William II, type V). Num. Chron., 1904, p. 291. Catalogue, p. 75, no. 163 (William I, type VI).

	I	II	III	IV	V	VI	VII	VIII	I	II	III	IV	V	I
DOVER														
Adam	..	..	..	..	..	..	..		..	..	..	..	..	..
Gustan	..	..	..	..	..	..	..		..	..	..	..	..	..
Edword	..	..	..	..	..	..	..		..	..	..	..	..	..
Godwine	..	..	..	..	..	..	..		..	..	4	..	..	..
Goldwine (Goldwie)	..	..	..	..	..	..	..		..	..	..	..	..	4
Lifwine	..	..	..	..	..	P.C.B.	4		..	..	..	..	..	..
Lulfric (Lufric, &c.)	..	..	..	..	..	..	..		MULE W.33	4	..	..	..	..
Mauwine	4	R.C.L.	..	P.C.B.	Hntr	..	..		..	..	..	4	..	..

Arces (William I, type II). W. Allen sale, 1898, lot 307. Probably York, Arcetl.
Elfwine (William II, mule IxII). Sir R. Abdy sale, 1841, lot 89. Catalogue, p. 229, no. 85 (Lifwine, type II).
Godwine (William I, type V). Num. Chron., 1904, p. 291.

	I	II	III	IV	V	VI	VII	VIII	I	II	III	IV	V	I
DURHAM														
Cuthbrht	..	..	..	..	..	..	..		..	..	..	..	..	..
Henri	..	..	..	..	..	..	..	4	..	..	..	..	..	..
Ordwi	..	..	..	..	..	..	..		..	..	..	..	..	..

Colbran (William I, type II). Num. Chron., 1846, p. 123 = Catalogue, p. 17, no. 84 (Derby).

	HENRY I													STEPHEN				
III	IV	V	VI	VII	VIII	IX	X	XI	XII	XIII	XIV	XV	I	II	III–VI	VII	**DERBY**
..	..	..	..	..	..	..	..	..	..	..	+? } P.C.B.	..	..	..	..	..	Brun
..	..	..	..	..	..	..	..	..	..	..	..	..	..	..	..	..	Colbein
..	..	..	..	..	..	..	..	..	..	..	..	..	..	..	..	..	Frona (Froma, Froam)
..	..	..	..	..	..	..	..	..	..	..	..	..	..	..	..	..	Godwine (Gdwine)
..	..	..	..	..	..	..	..	..	..	..	..	..	..	..	..	..	Leofwine (Lifwine)
..	..	..	..	..	..	..	..	..	..	..	..	..	B.R.	..	..	..	Uncertain

Gudnic (William II, type II). Num. Chron., 1877, p. 342 = Catalogue, p. 228, no. 80 (Godwine).
Lifric (William I, type VIII). Num. Chron., 1904, p. 269. Probably Warwick.
Lifwine (William II, type III). S. Rostron sale, 1892, lot 25 = H. M. Reynolds coll. (Dover).

III	IV	V	VI	VII	VIII	IX	X	XI	XII	XIII	XIV	XV	I	II	III–VI	VII	
																	DORCHESTE
..	..	..	..	..	..	..	..	..	..	..	..	..	..	..	..	..	Ælfgæt
..	..	..	..	..	..	..	..	..	..	..	..	..	..	..	..	..	Godwine
..	..	..	..	..	..	..	..	..	..	..	..	..	..	..	..	..	Lifric
..	..	..	..	..	..	..	..	+	..	P.C.B.	..	..	..	..	..	..	Osbern
..	..	..	..	..	..	..	..	..	..	..	..	..	..	..	..	..	Oter
..	..	..	..	..	..	..	..	..	..	..	+	..	..	..	..	..	Sween
..	..	..	..	..	..	..	..	..	..	+	..	..	..	..	..	..	Uncertain

Walter (Henry I, type XV). E. W. Rashleigh sale, 1909, lot 406 = P. W. P. Carlyon-Britton coll. Mint uncertain.

III	IV	V	VI	VII	VIII	IX	X	XI	XII	XIII	XIV	XV	I	II	III–VI	VII	
																	DOVER
..	..	..	..	..	..	..	..	..	..	..	..	..	..	..	..	+	*Adam*
..	..	..	..	..	..	..	..	..	..	..	..	..	..	..	..	..	Cinstan
..	..	..	..	..	..	..	..	..	..	..	..	..	..	..	..	..	Edword
..	..	..	..	..	..	..	..	..	..	..	..	..	..	..	..	..	Godwine
..	..	..	..	..	..	..	..	..	..	..	..	..	..	..	..	..	Goldwine (Goldwie)
..	..	..	..	..	..	..	..	..	..	..	..	..	..	..	..	..	Lifwine
..	..	..	..	..	..	..	..	..	..	..	..	..	..	..	..	..	Lulfric (Lufric, &c.)
..	..	..	..	..	..	..	..	..	..	..	P.C.B.	..	..	..	..	..	Manwine

Lifstan (William I, type VIII). Archaeologia, vol. xxvi, p. 9 (Beaworth find) = Catalogue, p. 163, no. 873 (Rochester).
Lifwine (William II, mule I × II). Num. Circ., 1902, p. 5470 = J. G. Murdoch sale, 1903, lot 201 (Dover, type I).

III	IV	V	VI	VII	VIII	IX	X	XI	XII	XIII	XIV	XV	I	II	III–VI	VII	
																	DURHAM
..	..	..	..	..	..	..	..	..	..	..	..	..	..	..	..	..	Cutthbrht
..	..	..	..	..	..	..	..	..	..	..	..	..	B.R.	..	..	..	Henri
..	..	..	..	..	..	..	..	..	..	..	+	..	..	..	..	..	Ordwi

Orthbeorn (William II, type III). H. Webb sale, 1894, lot 21. Perhaps a York coin of William I, type V?

o

	WILLIAM I								WILLIAM II				
	I	II	III	IV	V	VI	VII	VIII	I	II	III	IV	V
EXETER													
Ælfwine	..	..	+	S.M.	+	..	..	..	..	..	..	..	..
Ailric	..	..	..		..	..	..	..	..	..	..	..	..
Algar	..	..	..		..	..	..	..		..	..	..	..
Brihtric	P.C.B.	..	..		..	..	..	..		..	..	..	..
Brihtwi (Briedwi, &c.)	..	..	..		..	..	..	..		..	..	..	..
Goda	P.C.B.	..	..		..	..	..	..		..	..	..	..
Hlud		..	..		..	..	..	..		..	..	..	..
Lifwine (Lifwine)	+	..	..		..	..	..	+	.Asbn +309	..	..		H.M.R.?
Livinc	+	..	..		..	..	..	..		..	..	..	..
Semær	..	..	..		..	R.C.L.	..	..		..	..	..	..
Sewine (Sewinc)	..	..	..	..	+	+	S.H no. 153	+	..	..	..	P.C.B. 754?	
Seword (Saward)	..	Asch. +1110	Matgn + 198		..	..	..	..		..	..	..	..
Swottine (Sweotine, &c.)	..		MULE + Hntr	+	..	..	..	..		..	..	..	..
Wulfwine	..		Bodl.	P.C.B.	..	..	..	..		..	..	P.C.B.?	
Uncertain													

Ægebrine (William I, type V). Num. Chron., 1901, p. 264. Probably from Roberts MS. Catalogue reading (Œlwine) of B.M. Catalogue, p. 60, no. 345 (Ælfwine).

Ægei (William I, type II). Sotheby, March 7, 1894, lot 69.

Ælfwine (William I, type VIII). Sotheby, Dec. 19, 1911, lot 224.

Brand (Henry I, type XIV). E. W. Rashleigh sale, 1909, lot 409 = Sainthill, Olla Podrida, ii, p. 154 = Num. Chron., 1850, p. 154, and 1901, p. 185. Catalogue, p. 393, no. 429 (Chichester).

Brihtwine (William II, type III). J. B. Bergne sale, 1873, lot 318, and Sainthill, Olla Podrida, ii, p. 158.

Cotswegen (William I, type I). Sotheby, July 10, 1890, lot 14. Probably Hastings.

Edwine (William II, type IV). P. W. P. Carlyon-Britton sale, 1913, lot 774. Moneyer's name doubtful, perhaps Sewwine?

Elwni (William I, type I). Brit. Num. Journ., vol. v, p. 101. See above, p. cxlix.

	I	II	III	IV	V	VI	VII	VIII	I	II	III	IV	V
GLOU-CESTER													
Alfwine (Alwine)	..	..	..			..	..	..		..	..	..	..
Brihtnoth (Brihtoth, &c.)	..	..	..			..	..	+	MULE Mant	..	..	..	..
Gillebert	..	..	..			..	..	..		..	..	..	..
Godwin (Gowine)	..	..	..			..	..	..		..	..	P.C.B.	..
Liofwine (Lifwine)	..	..	+	..	+	..	..	..		..	..	..	..
Ordric	+	+	..			..	..	..		..	..	..	..
Ralf	..	..	..			..	..	..		..	..	..	..
Rodbert	..	..	..			..	..	..		..	..	..	..
Sawine (Sewine)	..	..	..			..	..	..		..	H.M.R.	..	..
Sawold (Sewold)	..	..	..			..	..	..		P.C.B.	+	..	..
Silac	+?	J.B.M.	..		S.+157 +80	..	..	..		..	..	..	..
Silacwine (Silewine)	..	..	..		P.C.B.	..	..	+		..	..	..	..
Thur	..	..	..			..	..	..		..	..	..	..
Wiberd (Wibert)	..	..	..			..	..	..		..	..	..	..
Wulfget (Ufget, &c.)	..	Hntr P.C.B.	+	..	Stkn	..	..	+		..	..	..	..
Wulfwi (= Wulfwig?)	..	..	..			..	..	..		..	..	..	..

Edwold (William II, type II). Brit. Num. Journ., vol. vi, p. 157. Perhaps Sewold?

,, (William II, type III). W. Allen sale, 1898, lot 353.

	HENRY I														STEPHEN				
II	III	IV	V	VI	VII	VIII	IX	X	XI	XII	XIII	XIV	XV	I	II	III–VI	VII	**EXETE**
..	..	..	..	..	..	..	..	..	..	..	..	..	..	..	..	..		Ælfwine
..	..	..	..	..	..	..	..	..	..	..	..	..	..	+	..	..	..	Ailric (=*Aluric*
..	..	..	..	..	..	..	..	..	..	..	..	..	..	B.R. H.M.R.}	..	..	..	Algar
..	..	..	..	..	..	..	..	..	..	..	..	..	..	..	..	..	..	Brihtric
..	..	..	..	..	..	..	..	..	..	..	..	+	..	+ ?	..	..	..	Brihtwi (Briedwi &c.)
..	..	..	..	..	..	..	..	..	..	..	..	..	..	..	..	..	..	Goda
..	..	..	..	..	..	..	..	..	..	..	..	..	+	..	..	..	..	Hlud
..	..	..	..	..	..	..	..	..	..	..	..	..	..	..	..	..	..	Lifwine (Lfwine)
..	..	..	..	..	..	..	..	..	..	..	..	..	..	..	..	..	..	Livinc
..	..	..	..	..	..	..	..	..	..	..	..	..	..	..	..	..	..	Semær
P.C.B.	..	..	..	..	+ } (app.)	..	..	..	..	..	..	..	..	..	..	..	..	Sæwine (Sewine)
..	..	..	..	..	..	..	..	..	..	..	..	..	..	..	..	..	..	Seword (Sæward
..	..	..	..	..	..	..	..	..	..	..	..	..	..	..	..	..	..	Swottinc (Sweotin &c.)
..	..	..	..	..	..	..	..	..	..	..	..	..	..	..	..	..	..	Wulfwine
..	..	..	..	..	..	..	..	..	..	..	..	+	..	..	..	..	+	Uncertain

Esbern (William I, type V). Num. Chron., 1901, p. 262. Perhaps Salisbury?

Godsbrand (William I, type VII). Brit. Num. Journ., vol. v, p. 102 = Roberts MS. Catalogue reading of B. M. Catalogue, p. 87, no. 473 (Shaftesbury).

Lifwine (William II, type IV). Brit. Num. Journ., vol. v, p. 103 = P. W. P. Carlyon-Britton coll. (Wulfwine?).

Manna (William I, type I). L. A. Lawrence sale, 1903, lot 35 = H. [Montagu sale, 1897, lot 62 = P. W. P. Carlyon-Britton coll. (Canterbury).

Simun (Stephen, type I). J. G. Murdoch sale, 1903, lot 247 = P. W. P. Carlyon-Britton coll. Mint doubtful, possibly Canterbury.

Wulfwine (Henry I, type II). H. Montagu sale, 1896, lot 282 = P. W. P. Carlyon-Britton coll. (Sæwine?).

II	III	IV	V	VI	VII	VIII	IX	X	XI	XII	XIII	XIV	XV	I	II	III–VI	VII	
..	..	..	..	..	..	..	..	..	..	..	..	*NC'01 p. 202)*	+	B.R. S.M.S.}	..	..	..	**GLOU-CESTE** Alfwine (Alwine)
..	..	..	..	..	..	..	..	..	..	..	..	..	..	..	..	..	..	Brihtnoth (Brihtot &c.)
..	..	..	..	..	..	..	..	..	..	..	..	..	..	B.R. P.C.B.}	..	..	..	Gillebert
..	..	+	..	..	..	..	..	..	..	..	..	..	..	..	..	..	..	Godwin (Gowine
..	..	..	..	..	..	..	..	..	..	..	..	..	..	..	..	..	..	Liofwine (Lifwine
..	..	..	..	..	..	..	..	..	..	..	..	..	..	..	..	..	..	Ordric
..	..	..	..	..	..	..	..	..	..	..	..	..	..	..	..	..	+	Ralf (=*Radu*
..	..	..	..	..	..	..	..	..	..	..	..	+	..	..	..	..	..	Rodbert
..	..	..	..	..	..	..	..	..	..	..	..	+	..	..	..	..	..	Sawine (Sewine)
..	..	..	..	..	..	..	MULE Hntr	..	..	..	..	..	..	..	..	..	..	Sawold (Sewold)
..	..	..	..	..	..	..	..	..	..	..	..	..	..	..	..	..	..	Silac
..	..	..	..	..	..	..	..	..	..	..	..	..	..	..	..	..	..	Silacwine (Silewine
..	..	..	..	..	..	..	..	..	..	..	..	..	T.B.	..	..	..	..	Thur
..	..	..	..	..	..	..	..	..	..	..	..	+	..	+	..	..	..	Wiberd (Wibert)
..	..	..	..	..	..	..	..	..	..	..	..	..	..	..	..	..	..	Wulfgæt (Ufgæt &
..	..	..	..	..	..	..	..	..	..	..	..	+	P.C.B.?	..	..	..	..	Wulfwi

Elfwine (Henry I, mule IX×X). Num. Chron., 1901, p. 202 = Hunterian coll. (Sawold).

Segrim (William II, type II). Num. Chron., 1877, p. 343 = Catalogue, p. 236, no. 136 (Shrewsbury).

	WILLIAM I								WILLIAM II								
	I	II	III	IV	V	VI	VII	VIII	I	II	III	IV	V		I	II	II
GUILD-FORD																	
Ælfric	..	..	..			..	..		..	..			+		..	..	..
Seric	..	..		P.C.B.		..	..	+	..	..	+				..	..	..

Ælfric (William II, type III). W. Allen sale, 1898, lot 352. Perhaps Ipswich?

	I	II	III	IV	V	VI	VII	VIII	I	II	III	IV	V		I	II	II
HAS-TINGS																	
Aldred	..	..							..						..		
Boniface	..	..						..							..		
Cipinic	..	..					+								..		
Colswegen	+						..								..		
Dirman (Dorman, &c.)	..								T.C.C.	+		+ (app.)	+		..		
Dunninc (Dunic, &c.)	+	P.C.B.					+		..	+					..		
Godric	..							A.M.	+			+			..		+
Rodbert	..	..													..		
Sawine	..														..		
Sperline (Spirlic, &c.)	..														..		
Thiodred	+														..		
Wenst[an?]	..														..		

Barhuit (Henry I, type II). Num. Chron., 1901, p. 369 — Catalogue, p. 270, no. 18 (Bristol, Barcuit).
Godsa (William I, type VIII). Sotheby, March 7, 1894, lot 71.

	I	II	III	IV	V	VI	VII	VIII	I	II	III	IV	V		I	II	II
HERE-FORD																	
Adebrant															..		
Ægelric	+														..		
Ægelwine (Ægelwi)	..		(S. m '75 49)	MITE P.C.B.				+		+	(Ægel n. 7 354)				..		
Ælfwi (= Ælfwig?)							+	+							..		
Æstan	..	..													..		
Brihtric	..	..		+											..		
Edric	..														..		
Edwine (Edwi)	..	W.S.O.													..		
Godric	..	..							+						..		
Hethewi	..								+						..		
Lifstan (Lifsan, &c.)	..						+		+						..		
Ordwi	..						+		..	+	L.E.B. Hntr. 785	P.C.B.			..		
Revenswert	..						..		..						..		
Sarie (Særie)	..														..		
Siber	..														..		
Witric (Wieric, &c.)	..														..		
Wulfwine	..		P.C.B.												..		

Ægelric (William I, type III). Brit. Num. Journ., vol. vi, p. 173. False? See Brit. Num. Journ., vol. iii, p. 285, no. 39.
    ,, (William I, type VIII). Num. Circ., 1902, p. 5472 = Roberts MS. Catalogue reading of B. M. Catalogue, p. 191, no. 1032 (Wareham).
Ælwi (William I, type IV). Num. Chron., 1840, p. 45.
Eadri   ,,   ,,   Akerman, Num. Journ., vol. ii, p. 106.

IV	V	VI	VII	VIII	IX	X	XI	XII	XIII	XIV	XV	I	II	III-VI	VII	GUILD FO
HENRY I												STEPHEN				
..	..	..	..	..	..	..	..	..	..	..	..	..	..	..	..	Ælfric
..	..	..	..	..	..	..	..	..	..	..	..	..	..	..	..	Seric

Eric (William II, type III). H. Montagu sale, 1896, lot 266. Probably Seric.

IV	V	VI	VII	VIII	IX	X	XI	XII	XIII	XIV	XV	I	II	III-VI	VII	HAS-TIN
..	..	..	..	..	..	..	..	..	..	..	..	..	S.M.S.	S.M.S. (VI)	..	Aldred
..	..	..	..	..	..	*Mntgu* 281	..	..	..	+? P.C.B.	..	..	..	..	..	Boniface
..	..	..	..	..	..	..	..	..	..	..	..	..	..	..	..	Cipinec
..	..	..	..	..	..	..	..	..	..	..	..	..	..	..	..	Colswegen
..	..	..	..	..	..	..	..	..	..	..	..	..	..	..	..	Dirman (Dorman &c.)
..	..	..	P.C.B.	..	..	+	+	..	..	..	..	..	..	..	..	Dunninc (Dunic,
..	..	..	..	..	..	..	..	..	..	..	..	..	..	..	..	Godric
..	..	..	..	..	..	..	..	..	..	..	..	F.Mus. H.M.R.	B.R.	..	L.E.B.	Rodbert
..	..	..	..	..	..	..	..	..	..	..	..	+	..	..	..	Sawine
..	..	..	+	..	..	..	..	..	..	..	..	..	..	..	..	Sperlinc (Spirlic, &c.)
..	..	..	..	..	..	..	..	..	..	..	..	..	..	..	..	Thiodred
..	..	..	..	..	..	..	..	..	..	..	..	L.A.L.	..	..	..	Wenstfan

Sefwie (William II, type II). Num. Circ., 1902, p. 5472 = Roberts MS. Catalogue reading of B.M. Catalogue, p. 241, no. 166 (Wilton, Sefare).

IV	V	VI	VII	VIII	IX	X	XI	XII	XIII	XIV	XV	I	II	III-VI	VII	HERE FO
..	..	F.Mus.	..	..	..	..	..	..	..	..	..	..	..	..	..	Adebrant
..	..	..	..	..	..	..	..	..	..	..	..	..	..	..	..	Ægelric
..	..	..	..	..	..	..	..	..	..	..	..	..	..	..	..	Ægelwine (Ægelw
..	..	..	..	..	..	..	..	..	..	..	..	..	..	..	..	Ælfwi
..	..	..	..	..	..	..	..	..	..	..	..	..	..	..	..	Æstan
..	..	..	..	..	..	..	..	..	..	..	..	..	..	..	..	Brihtric
..	..	..	..	..	..	..	..	..	..	..	A.M.	+	..	..	..	Edric
..	..	..	..	..	..	..	..	..	..	..	+	..	..	..	..	Edwine(E
..	..	..	..	..	..	..	..	..	..	..	..	..	..	..	..	Godric
..	..	..	..	..	..	..	..	..	..	..	..	..	..	..	..	Hethewi
..	..	..	..	..	..	..	..	..	..	..	..	..	..	..	..	Lifstan (Lifsan,
..	..	..	..	..	..	..	..	..	..	..	..	..	..	..	..	Ordwi
..	..	..	..	..	..	..	..	..	..	P.C.B.	..	..	..	..	..	Ravensw
..	..	..	..	..	..	P.C.B.	..	..	..	+	*Rash* 412	..	..	..	..	Saric (Sæ
..	..	..	..	..	..	..	..	..	..	..	..	P.C.B. S.M.S.	..	..	..	Siber
..	..	..	..	..	..	..	..	..	..	..	..	+	..	..	..	Witric (Wicric &c.)
..	..	..	..	..	..	..	..	..	..	..	..	..	..	..	..	Wulfwine

Godard (William II, type III). S. Rostron sale, 1892, lot 27 = G. Deakin sale, 1905, lot 5 (false). Cf. Brit. Num. Journ., vol. iii, p. 283, no. 37.

Hericus (Henry I, type XIV). E. W. Rashleigh sale, 1909, lot 413 = Num. Chron., 1901, p. 218. Probably Saricus.

Lifwine (William II, type V). W. A. Cotton sale, 1889, lot 60, and J. J. Nunn sale, 1896, lot 214. Probably = H. M. Reynolds coll. (Exeter).

Wulfric (Stephen, type I). W. Allen sale, 1898, lot 381. Perhaps Wihtric?

	WILLIAM I								WILLIAM II				
	I	II	III	IV	V	VI	VII	VIII	I	II	III	IV	V
HERTFORD													
Ælgar	..	..	..	..	..	..		..	..	P.C.B.	Hntr	..	..
Sæman (Seman)	P.C.B.	..	..	..	..	..		+	..	..	P.C.B.	..	..
Thidric (Thedric)	..	..	..	..	..	..		+	(+ app.)	+	(+ app.)	..	..

Ælfric (William I, type V). T. B. Kirby sale, 1888, lot 44 = W. A. Cotton sale, 1889, lot 55. Perhaps

	I	II	III	IV	V	VI	VII	VIII	I	II	III	IV	V
HUNTING-													
DON													
Ælfwine	..	..	..	..	..	..		+	..	..	..	..	..
Derlig	..	..	..	..	..	..		..	..	..	..	..	..
Godmer	..	..	..	..	..	..		..	..	..	..	..	..
Godric	+	MULE +	4	..	4	..		..	..	..	..	..	..
Godwine	..	..	..	..	W.E.H.	H.W.M. P.C.B.		..	..	..	..	.	..
Siwate (Siwat)	..	York	..	..	..	..		..	..	+	+	F.Mus.	..

Æglwine (William I, type VIII). Brit. Num. Journ., vol. vii. p. 4.
Ælfric   „   „   Num. Chron., 1904, p. 264.
Ælfwine (William II, type III). H. Clark sale, 1898, lot 62. Perhaps London?
Godric (William II, type II). Num. Chron., 1904, p. 264 = Roberts MS. Catalogue reading of B. M.
        Catalogue, p. 239, no. 91 (Hastings).
Godwine (William II, type IV). Sotheby, Jan. 25, 1899, lot 110. Perhaps mistake for William I,
        type VI?
    „   (Stephen, type VII). H. Montagu sale, 1895, lot 397 = Catalogue, p. 371, no. 191 (Godmer?).

	I	II	III	IV	V	VI	VII	VIII	I	II	III	IV	V
HYTHE													
Edred (Edræd)	..	..	..	..	..	..		+	Mpe 577	4	+	..	..

Arthulf (William I, type IV). Num. Chron., 1904, p. 264 = Roberts MS. Catalogue reading of B. M.
        Catalogue, p. 55, no. 291 (York).

	I	II	III	IV	V	VI	VII	VIII	I	II	III	IV	V
ILCHESTER													
Ægelwine (Wægelwine, &c.)	Circ. '02 5571	..	..	+	+	P.C.B. 711	..	p. 135, no. 717, note	..	..	..	..	..
Ælword (Æhlfward, &c.)	..	..	..	..	..	+	Stkn?	+	+	..	P.C.B. 768	..	..
Elwi	..	..	..	..	..	..	..	..	..	..	..	..	..
Lifwine	..	..	..	..	..	..	..	..	..	+	Hntr	..	..
Wægelwine, *see* Ægelwine	..	..	..	..	..	..	..	..	..	..	..	..	..
Wixie (Wichxsi, &c.)	+	York	+	..	..	..	..	..	..	..	..	..	..

Baldwine (William II, type III). Num. Chron., 1904, p. 265. Roberts MS. Catalogue reading of
        B. M. Catalogue, p. 251, no. 217 (Shaftesbury).

	HENRY I															STEPHEN			
II	III	IV	V	VI	VII	VIII	IX	X	XI	XII	XIII	XIV	XV		I	II	III-VI	VII	
..	..	..	..	..	..	..	..	..	..	..	..	..	..		..	..	..	..	Ælgar
..	..	..	..	..	..	..	..	..	..	..	..	..	..		..	..	..	..	Sæman (Sema
..	..	..	..	..	..	..	..	..	..	..	..	..	..		..	..	..	..	Thidric (Thed

HERTFO:

Thetford, Cinric?

II	III	IV	V	VI	VII	VIII	IX	X	XI	XII	XIII	XIV	XV		I	II	III-VI	VII	
..	..	..	..	..	..	..	..	..	..	..	..	+	..		..	..	..	..	Ælfwine
..	..	..	..	..	..	..	..	..	..	..	..	..	..		..	..	..	..	Derlig
..	..	..	..	..	..	..	..	..	..	..	..	..	..		..	..	..	+	Godmer
..	..	..	..	..	..	..	..	..	..	..	..	..	..		..	..	..	..	Godric
..	..	..	..	..	..	..	..	..	..	..	..	..	..		..	..	..	..	Godwine
..	..	..	..	..	..	..	..	..	..	..	..	..	..		..	..	..	..	Siwate (Siwat

HUNTIN(
D(

Gypat (William II, type II). Rev. H. Christmas sale, 1864, lot 209; W. Allen sale, 1898, lot 314 =
Catalogue, p. 231, no. 97 (Siwat).
Sæwi, Sæwine (William I, type IV). Num. Circ., 1902, p. 5571. Probably Southampton.
   „   „   (William II, type I). Sotheby, May 28, 1891, lot 17; J. J. Nunn sale, 1896, lot 209.
Probably Southampton.
Sefwine (Henry I, type II). Num. Chron., 1901, p. 227 = Hunterian coll. Reading doubtful,
probably Southampton (perhaps an altered die).
Sweatlinc (William I, type IV). Col. Durrant sale, 1847, lot 136 = Catalogue, p. 54, no. 281
(Wallingford).

II	III	IV	V	VI	VII	VII	IX	X	XI	XII	XIII	XIV	XV		I	II	III-VI	VII	
..	..	..	..	..	..	..	..	..	..	..	..	..	..		..	..	..	..	Edred (Edræd

HYTHE

Didman (William II, type III). Num. Circ., 1902, p. 5571 = Catalogue, p. 246, nos. 187-8 (Hastings,
Dirman).
Godric (William II, type II). Num. Chron., 1904, p. 264 = Roberts MS. Catalogue alternative
attribution of B.M. Catalogue, p. 230, no. 91 (Hastings).

II	III	IV	V	VI	VII	VIII	IX	X	XI	XII	XIII	XIV	XV		I	II	III-VI	VII	
																		°	ILCHESTI
																			Ægelwine
																			(Wægelwine
..	..	..	..	..	..	..	..	..	..	..	..	..	..		..	..	..	..	&c.)
																			Ælword
..	..	..	..	..	..	..	..	..	..	..	..	..	..		..	..	..	..	(Æhlfward, 8
..	..	..	..	..	..	..	..	+	..	..	..	..	..		..	..	..	..	Elwi
..	..	..	..	..	..	..	..	..	..	..	..	..	..		..	..	..	..	Lifwine
..	..	..	..	..	..	..	..	..	..	..	..	..	..		..	..	..	..	Wægelwine, s
																			Ægelwine
..	..	..	..	..	..	..	..	..	..	..	..	..	..		..	..	..	..	Wixie (Wichx
																			&c.)

Brihtnoth (William II, mule I×II and type II). Num. Chron., 1877, p. 343 (? = Num. Chron., 1904,
p. 265) = Catalogue, p. 225, no. 67 (Gloucester).
Goldwine (William II, type III). Num. Chron., 1904, p. 265.

	WILLIAM I								WILLIAM II						
	I	II	III	IV	V	VI	VII	VIII	I	II	III	IV	V	I	I
IPSWICH															
Ædgar															
Ægelbriht		+		+	MULE (B.N.J. vol. p.151)										
Ægelwine								+							
Ælfric								+			R.C.L.		+		
Ælfwine (Alfwine)		+					+	+							
Edmund															
Germane															
Gilleber															
Lifstan (Leofstan)		MULE +			+										
Lifwine (Leofwine, &c.)														P.C.B.	
Osbern (Osebern)															
Paien															
Rodland (Rolland)															
Swegen (Swegn)								+							
Wulfwine														··	

Ægelwine. See also Bebester.
Ægtric (William I, type VI). Sir R. Aldy sale, 1841, lot 96. Catalogue, p. 97, no. 357 (Norwich).
Alfwine (Stephen, type b). E. W. Rashleigh sale, 1909, lot 515. B. Roth coll. (Gloucester, same dies as coin in S. M. Spink coll.)
Brunic (William II, type III). Num. Chron., 1901, p. 265.
Godwine   ,,   ,,   Sotheby, June 16, 1915, lot 33.
Lifstan (William I, type VII). Num. Chron., 1901, p. 265.

	I	II	III	IV	V	VI	VII	VIII	I	II	III	IV	V	I	II
LAUN-CESTON															
Ægelm?her									Allen + 1887						
Godric						Hntr Bodl	+								
Willem															
"Sæsgti"															
"Stefanii"					+										

Ædzer (William II, type I). Brit. Num. Journ., vol. ix. p. 72. Perhaps from Num. Chron., 1871, p. 228 (Declirt, see below.

	I	II	III	IV	V	VI	VII	VIII	I	II	III	IV	V	I	II
LEI-CESTER															
Ægelwine [1]			+	+	+		+								
Chitel [2]															
Fulcred [3]															
Godric [4]		(B.N.J. no. 25)					+		MULE + 4 4						
Lieric [5] (= Lifric)		+							(app.)						
Owthin [6]															
Samar [7]															Par
Sewine [8]															
Walter [9]													Hntr		
Warmund [10]															
Wulfwine [11]															··
Uncertain [12]														(Hn (P.C.	

[1-12] See notes on pages ccxviii, ccxix.

	HENRY I													STEPHEN				
III	IV	V	VI	VII	VIII	IX	X	XI	XII	XIII	XIV	XV	I	II	III–VI	VII		IPSWI
Ast. '06 219? }	..	..	..	..	..	..	..	..	..	..	..		P.C.B.	..		..		Ædgar
..																..		Ægelbriht
..	..	..	..	..	..	..	..	..					..	..	..	..		Ægelwine
..	..	..	..	..	..	..	..	..							..	..		Ælfric
..	..	..	..	..	..	..	..			..	..		..			..		Ælfwine (Alfwine
..	..	..	..	..	..	..	..				P.C.B.	..	NC'50 p.157}	+	..	..		Edmund
..	..	..	..	..	..	..	..				+		..	+?	..	..		Germane
..	..	..	..	..	..	..	..				..		..	+	..	..		Gilleber
..	..	..	..	..	..	..							..	..				Lifstan (Liofstan
P.C.B.	..	..	..	..	..								..	..		..		Lifwine (L wine, &c.
..	..	..	..	..	..					..	..	+	+	P.C.B.	..	..		Osbern (Osebern)
..	..	..	..	..	..						..	..	P.C.B.	..	..	..		Paien
..	..	..	..	..	..	..	..		M'Eur) 103}	+	..		..	..	..	..		Rodland (Rolland)
..	..	..	..	..		..				..	..		..	..	..	..		Swegen (Swegn)
..	..	..	..	..	..					..	..		..	..	..	..		Wulfwine

Liofstan (William I, type II). Num. Chron., 1901, p. 265. Perhaps = Catalogue, p. 33, no. 180 (mule I×II)?

Oswold (Henry I, type XIV). E. W. Rashleigh sale, 1909, lot 415 = Num. Chron., 1850, p. 151, and 1901, p. 238 = Catalogue, p. 306, no. 135 (Lewes).

Wægelwine (William I, type IV). W. Boyne sale, 1896, lot 1169. Probably Ilchester.

Wulfwine (William I, type II). Num. Circ., 1902, p. 5372.

III	IV	V	VI	VII	VIII	IX	X	XI	XII	XIII	XIV	XV	I	II	III–VI	VII		LAUN-CESTO
..	..	..	..	..	..		..	..	..	..	..		..	..	..	..		Ægl[m]ær
..	..	..	..	..	..		..	..					+?	..	..	..		Godric
..	..	..	..	..	..		..	..						..	..	..		Willem
..	..	..	..	..	..		..	..			..		..	..	..	..		'Sasgti Stefanii'

Declr (William II, type II). Num. Chron. 1871, p. 228. Probably Æglær.

Willem (Stephen, type III). Brit. Num. Journ., vol. iii, p. 113. Now in Capt. Alan Dawnay coll.

III	IV	V	VI	VII	VIII	IX	X	XI	XII	XIII	XIV	XV	I	II	III–VI	VII		LEI-CEST
..	..	..	..	..	..	..	+?	..	..	..	P.C.B.	..	..	..	..	..		Ægelwine
..	..	..	..	..	..	..	..	..	..	..	..		..	..	..	..		Chitel[2]
..	..	..	..	+	..	..	..	..		..	..		..	..	..	..		Fulcred[3]
..	..	..	..	..	..	..	..	..		..	..		..	..	..	..		Godric[4]
..	..	..	..	..	..	..	..	..		..	..		..	..	..	..		Licric[5]
..	..	..	..	..	..	..	..	..		..	..		..	..	..	..		Owthin[6]
..	..	..	..	..	..	..	..	..		..	..	+	..	..	+?) (V)}	..		Samar[7]
..	..	..	..	..	..	..	..	..		..	+?		B.R.	..	..	..		Sewine[8] Walter[9]
..	..	..	..	..	..	..	..	..		..	J.Y.} P.C.B.}		..	..	..	..		Warmund
..	..	..	..	..	..	..	..	..		..	..		..	..	..	..		Wulfwine
..	..	..	..	..	..	..	R.T.	..		..	..		..	..	..	..		Uncertain

LEICESTER *(continued).*

[1] *Confessor,* **LECR** ; *Harold,* **LEHRI** ; *William I, type* III. **LEC** ; IV.
LECRI ; V. **LECI** ; VII. **LEII**   [2] **LEICES, LEIC**
[3] **LE**   [4] **LEHRE, LEHRE, LEHRI**   [5] *Confessor,*
LEHREC ; *William I.* **LERECE**   [6] **LEESTR**   [7] **LE**
REC, LERE   [8] **LEHR**   *Henry I.* **LECE** ; *Stephen,* **LEC**
STR ? [10] **LEIC** ?, **LE**   [11] **LEI**   [12] **LEREC**

	WILLIAM I								WILLIAM II						
	I	II	III	IV	V	VI	VII	VIII	I	II	III	IV	V	I	
LEWES															
Ælfric									P.C.B. B.C.B.						
Ælfwine (Elwine)													Hstr	+	
Almar															
Brihtmær (Brihmar, &c.)									P.C.B.	T.B.			+	+? T.B.	
Edmund															
Herrev?															
Hunfre?															
Osebern															
Oswold		Boll													
Willem															
Winfred (Winered, &c.)	..	..	Hstr						..	P.C.B			Mstg? ??	A.B	

Brihtred (William II, type II and III). Num. Chron. 1864, p. 296. Probably Brihtmær.
Lefrald (William I, Harold mule). William I, type VII. William II, type III. Various sale catalogue, &c. Fals. cf. Brit. Num. Journ. vol. III, pb. 284.)

	I	II	III	IV	V	VI	VII	VIII	I	II	III	IV	V	I	II
LINCOLN															
Acil (Ascil)															
Ælfnot													Boll?		
Ælmer (Elmar, &c.)		Mull P.C.B.									P.C.B.?				
Agemund (the muna, &c.)		Mull H.M.R													
Arnwi?															
Aslac (Oslac)															
Folcard															
Garrin	Qtohn York											Boll?		..	
Gifei (Gircl)														..	
Gladewin														..	
Godric														..	
Hue															B.I
Lefric				..										..	
Osbert														..	
Oslac, &c. Aslac				..						Stbn?				..	
Outhgrim	..			..										..	
Paen	..			..										..	
Seffarth (Sihtfeorth, &c.)	..	+		+	Boll									..	
Segwiward (Siguuerith)	Bbun 35?	+	Bash ???	+										..	

See also Chester.

Ægelwine (William I, type VIII). Brit. Num. Journ., vol. vii, p. 25, = Num. Circ., 1902, p. 5573, whence it appears to be a misreading of a British Museum coin.

Edmund (Henry I, type XII). L. A. Lawrence sale, 1903, lot 106 = P. W. P. Carlyon-Britton coll. (see Lewes).

Gifric (William I, type II). Num. Chron., 1904, p. 266. Probably Lieric.

Godard (William II, type III). Sotheby, May 3, 1844, lot 355. False? Cf. Brit. Num. Journ., vol. iii, p. 283, no. 37.

Godric (William II, type IV). Num. Chron., 1904, p. 266.

Lifwin (William II, mule I×II and type III). Various sale catalogues, &c. False, cf. Brit. Num. Journ., vol. iii, p. 283, nos. 33, 34.

	HENRY I														STEPHEN				
III	IV	V	VI	VII	VIII	IX	X	XI	XII	XIII	XIV	XV	I	II	III·VI	VII		**LEWES**
..	..	..	..	..	..	..	..	..	..	..	..	..	..	..	..	..		Ælfric
..	..	..	..	..	..	..	..	..	..	..	..	..	..	..	..	..		Ælfwine (Ælwine)
..	..	..	..	..	..	..	..	..	..	..	..	..	..	J.H.D.) T.B. ∫	..	..		Almar
..	..	..	..	..	..	..	..	..	..	..	..	..	..	..	..	..		Brihtmær (Brihmar, &c.)
..	..	..	..	..	..	..	..	..	P.C.B.	..	P.C.B.?	..	..	..	..	..		Edmund
..	..	..	..	..	..	..	..	..	..	..	..	..	Rash.) 523,525∫	..:	..	..		Herrevi
..	..	..	..	..	..	..	..	..	..	..	..	..	..	..	H.M.R.?) (VI) ∫	+? B.R.?∫		Hunfrei
..	..	..	..	..	..	..	..	..	..	..	..	..	+?	+	..	..		Oseborn
..	..	..	..	..	..	..	..	..	..	..	+	..	..	..	..	..		Oswold
..	..	..	..	..	..	..	..	..	..	..	..	..	+? (app.) B.R.	..	..	..		Willem
..	..	..	..	..	..	..	..	..	..	..	..	..	..	..	..	..		Winred (Wi ered, &c.)

Oswold (William I, type III). Num. Chron., 1904, p. 266.

[*Wul*]*mær* (Stephen, type II). Sotheby, July 25, 1910, lot 95. Probably Almar.

III	IV	V	VI	VII	VIII	IX	X	XI	XII	XIII	XIV	XV	I	II	III-VI	VII		**LINCOLN**
..	..	..	..	..	..	..	..	..	..	..	..	..	..	..	..	..		Acil (Ascil)
..	..	..	..	..	..	..	..	..	..	..	..	..	..	..	..	..		Ælfnot
..	..	..	..	..	..	..	..	..	..	..	..	S.M.?	..	..	..	..		Ælmer (Ælmar, &c
..	..	..	..	..	..	..	..	..	..	..	..	..	..	..	..	..		Agemund (Al mund, &c.)
..	..	..	..	..	..	..	..	..	..	..	..	P.C.B.	..	..	..	..		Arnwi?
..	..	..	..	..	..	...	..	..	..	..	..	+	P.C.B.) S.M.S.∫	..	..	..		Aslac (Oslac)
..	..	..	..	..	..	..	..	..	..	..	..	..	..	..	..	..		Folcærd
..	..	..	..	..	..	..	..	..	..	..	..	..	..	..	..	..		Garvin
..	..	..	..	..	..	..	..	..	..	..	..	..	..	..	..	..		Gifel (Givel)
..	..	..	..	..	..	..	..	..	..	..	..	..	+	..	..	..		Gladowin
..	..	..	..	..	..	..	..	..	+	..	+	NC°01) 271 ∫	..	..	B.R.?) (IV)∫	..		Godric
..	..	..	..	..	..	..	..	..	..	..	..	..	..	..	..	B.R.		Hue
..	..	..	..	..	..	..	..	..	..	..	..	P.C.B.	..	..	..	..		Lefric
..	..	..	..	..	..	..	..	..	..	..	..	..	..	..	..	..		Osbert
..	..	..	..	..	..	..	..	..	..	..	..	..	..	..	..	..		Oslac, see Aslac
..	..	..	..	..	..	..	..	..	..	..	..	..	..	..	..	..		Outhgrim
..	..	..	..	..	..	..	..	..	..	..	..	..	..	..	H.M.R.) (IV) ∫	Clark 66		Paen
..	..	..	..	..	..	..	..	..	..	..	..	..	..	..	..	..		Seffarth (Sih feorth, &c.)
..	..	..	..	..	..	..	..	..	..	..	..	..	..	..	..	..		Segwaward (Siguærith)

	WILLIAM I								WILLIAM II						
	I	II	III	IV	V	VI	VII	VIII	I	II	III	IV	V	I	II
LINCOLN (cont.)															
Siword	..	..	..	..	+	T plis 37?	..	.					..		..
Thorstan (Thurestan, &c.)	..	..	..	F.Mus.	+ Hntr	..	..	..	L.A.L. P.C.B.	Mint P.C.B.	F.Mus.	..	..		..
Ulf	..	..	..	+	..	..	..	+	+	P.C.B.	..	..			..
Unce	..	..	..	..	..	..	..	..	..	..	..	..	L.E.B.		..
Unspac	..	..	..	+	+	+	..	..	..	..	..	..	..		..
Wihtric	..	..	..	..	..	..	..	..	..	..	..	..	..		..
Wulfwine	..	..	..	..	..	..	..	..	Stkm	..	..	..	..		..
Wulsi	..	+	..	..	..	..	..	..	..	..	..	..	..		..
Wulstan	..	..	..	+	..	..	..	..	..	..	..	..	..		..
Uncertain	..	..	..	..	..	..	..	..	..	..	..	..	..		..

See also London.

Ælvri (Henry I, type XV). Num. Chron., 1901, p. 239. Royal Mint and Sheriff Mackenzie colls. Readings uncertain.

Ahgemund (Henry I, type I). .. .. .. T. Bliss coll. (Canterbury, same dies as F. A. Walters sale, 1913, lot 60).

Ahithmund (Henry I, type I). H. Montagu sale, 1897, lot 91. T. Bliss coll. (Canterbury, Ahgemund; see preceding).

Brumata (Henry I, type I). Rev. B. Christmas sale, 1864, lot 226.

Brunuan (Henry I, type XV). Num. Chron., 1901, p. 279. Catalogue, p. 333, no. 304 (mint uncertain).

Deodrid (Stephen, type IV). J. G. Murdoch sale, 1903, lot 237. R. Roth coll. (Godric?).

Edmund (Henry I, type XV). Num. Chron., 1901, p. 279, from Withy and Ryall.

Godreus (Henry I, type XI). .. .. p. 271. Catalogue, p. 291, no. 75 (moneyer uncertain).

Hermer (Stephen, type II). D. F. Kennard sale, 1882, lot 134. Perhaps Norwich?

Idlwine (William I, type II). Brit. Num. Journ., vol. viii, p. 43. York Museum. See above, p. cl. Die altered from London, Ælwine.

Lefwine (William II, type II). Sotheby, Jan. 25, 1860, lot 111.

Liford (William I, mule VII < VIII). Various sale catalogues, &c. False, cf. Brit. Num. Journ., vol. iii, p. 282, no. 39.

Liofwod (William I, type VIII). Num. Chron., 1901, p. 267. Cf. Liofwold below.

	I	II	III	IV	V	VI	VII	VIII	I	II	III	IV	V	I	II
LONDON															
Adam	..	..	..	..	..	..	..	..	..	..	..	..	..	..	..
Adelard	..	..	..	..	..	..	..	..	..	..	..	..	..	..	..
Ædgar (Eadgar)	..	..	..	..	..	..	..	..	..	..	..	..	..	..	..
Ædwine, see Eadwine	..	..	..	..	..	..	..	..	..	..	..	..	..		
Ægelric	..	York	+	..	..	..	..	..	..	..	..	..	..		
Ægelwine	..	+ ? (York?)	..	H.L.F.	..	..	..	..	..	..	..	..	..		
Æglword	..	..	..	..	..	..	..	..	..	..	..	+	+		
Ælgar	..	..	..	..	..	..	..	..	..	..	..	+	..		
Ælfred, (Alfred, &c.)	..	..	..	..	..	..	..	+	+	..	..	..	..		
Ælfsi, (Æolfsi, &c.)	+	+	..	..	..	..	..	..	..	..	..	..	..		
Ælfwine (Ælfwine, &c.)	+ (app.)	+	..	+	..	..	+	See Æwi	..	+	+	+	+	+	+
Æwi (= Ælfwine?)	..	..	..	..	..	..	..	+	..	..	..	..	..	..	..
Aldgar, Algar, &c., see Eadgar	..	..	..	..	..	..	..	..	..	..	..	..	..		
Alfric	..	..	..	..	..	..	..	..	..	..	..	..	..		
Alfwine, &c., see Ælfwine	..	..	..	..	..	..	..	..	..	..	..	..	..		

HENRY I												STEPHEN				
IV	V	VI	VII	VIII	IX	X	XI	XII	XIII	XIV	XV	I	II	III–VI	VII	**LINCOLN** (*cont.*)
..	..	..	..	..	..	..	..	..	..	..	..	..	..	..	..	Siword
..	..	..	..	..	..	..	..	..	..	..	..	..	..	..	..	Thorstan (Thurestan, &c.)
..	..	..	..	..	..	..	..	..	..	..	..	..	..	..	..	Ulf
..	..	..	..	..	..	..	..	..	..	..	..	..	..	..	..	Unce
..	..	..	..	..	..	..	..	..	..	..	..	..	..	..	..	Unspac
..	..	..	..	..	..	..	..	..	..	..	..	..	..	..	..	Wihtric
..	..	..	..	..	..	..	..	..	..	..	..	..	..	..	..	Wulfwine
..	..	..	..	..	..	..	..	..	..	..	..	..	..	..	..	Wulsi
..	..	..	..	..	..	..	..	..	..	..	..	..	..	..	..	Wulstan
..	..	..	..	..	*Mrdch 233*	P.C.B.	+	..	..	..	..	..	..	..	..	Uncertain

Lifwold (William I, type VIII). Num. Chron., 1904, p. 267. Probably Winchester.

Liofwold (William I, type VII). H. Montagu sale, 1897, lot 77 = Catalogue, p. 89, no. 485 (Winchester).

Lonoregen (William I, type IV). Num. Circ., 1902, p. 5574 = Roberts MS. Catalogue reading of B.M. Catalogue, p. 49, no. 255 (London, Colswegen).

Nuherd (Henry I, type IV). Num. Chron., 1901, p. 271 = Num. Chron., 1892, p. 84 (mint uncertain).

    ,,   (Henry I, type XI).   ,,   1901, p. 272 = Catalogue, Appendix, p. 407, no. 78 A (reading uncertain).

Osbert (Henry I, type XV).   ,,   ,,   ,,   Possibly London, Osbern?

Ricard (Henry I, type I).   ,,   ,,   from Withy and Ryall.

Sihworth (William I, type IV). P. W. P. Carlyon-Britton sale, 1913, lot 699 (Sihforth?).

Swet (Henry I, type XIV). Num. Chron., 1901, p. 272. Moneyers' names on the coins and in the sale catalogues quoted are doubtful.

Thearstan (William II, mule I×II). M. K. Peace sale, 1894, lot 61. Perhaps 245 a misprint for 246 (type II)?

Toc, Tom (Henry I, type X). Col. Lowlsley sale, 1899, lot 194 = H. W. Morrieson coll. (mint uncertain, coin tooled).

Unce (William II, mule I×II and types II and III). Num. Chron., 1904, p. 268.

Wihtric, Wintric (William I, type IV). Num. Chron., 1904, p. 268. Possibly type V is intended?

Wilfred (William I, type VIII). J. Toplis sale, 1890, lot 34. Perhaps London, Ælfred?

Winwi (William II, type IV). Sotheby, April 29, 1904, lot 242. Perhaps Canterbury, Winedi?

IV	V	VI	VII	VIII	IX	X	XI	XII	XIII	XIV	XV	I	II	III–VI	VII	
																LONDON
..	..	..	..	..	..	..	..	..	..	..	..	..	..	..	H.M.R.	Adam
..	..	..	..	..	..	..	..	..	..	..	..	+	..	..	..	Adelard
..	..	..	..	..	..	..	..	..	..	..	+	..	..	..	..	Ædgar (Eadgar)
..	..	..	..	..	..	..	..	..	..	..	..	..	..	..	..	Ædwine, *see* Eadwine
..	..	..	..	..	..	..	..	..	..	..	..	..	..	..	..	Ægelric
..	..	..	..	..	..	..	..	..	..	..	..	..	..	..	..	Ægelwine
..	..	..	..	..	..	..	..	..	..	..	..	..	..	..	..	Æglword
..	..	..	..	..	..	..	..	..	..	..	..	..	..	..	..	Ælfgar
..	..	..	..	..	..	..	..	..	..	P.C.B.	..	+	..	..	..	Ælfred (Alfred, &c. Ælfsi (Ælolfsi &c.)
..	..	..	..	..	..	..	..	..	..	..	..	..	..	..	..	Ælfwine (= *Alwine*?
Cpnhn	+	P.C.B.	*NC'01 p. 288*	..	+?	..	+	..	+	+	..	..	..	..	..	Æwi (= Ælfwine?)
..	..	..	..	..	..	..	..	..	..	..	..	..	..	..	..	Aldgar, Alga &c., *see* Ealdgar
..	..	..	..	..	..	..	..	..	..	+	..	..	..	..	..	Alfric
..	..	..	..	..	..	..	..	..	..	..	..	..	..	..	..	Alfwine, &c., *see* Ælfwin

	WILLIAM I								WILLIAM II							
	I	II	III	IV	V	VI	VII	VIII	I	II	III	IV	V	I	II	III
LONDON (cont.)																
Algar Man	..	..	..	..										..	..	
Alisander (Alisandre)	..	..		..										..	..	
Baldewin	..	..	..	..										..	..	
Bat	..	..	..	..							+			..	..	..
Beriteri?		..		..										..	..	..
Blacaman (Blacman, &c.)				..										+	NC of (p. 298	..
Blaesunu (Blagsun, &c.)		+ ? York?		+												
Brihtmær (Bricmar, &c.)		..		..	+ ? B.R.					Hntr		..				
Brihtric		..	+		+											
Brihtwine (Brihtri, &c.)		..		..			+	..						NC of p. 295	..	
Brunie	..		..		..							+		Hntr	..	..
Colswegen			..											..	..	..
Dereman (Derman, &c.)		..		..										..		
Dereman R., Ri.																
E——, see also Æ——																
Eadric (Edric)		..	..													
Eadwine (Edwi, &c.)	+	MCff H.H. Allan 56	+	+	+	+	+	+								
Ealdgar (Aldgar, &c.)		+	+	Hntr									+ (app.)	..	Ruil P.C.B.	I
Edward														Rush 122		
Estmær		..				..						I A.W	Rush 122		..	
Estmund		..													..	
Geffrei (Gefrei)		..													..	
Godard															..	
Godric	+	+	+	+ ?	+			+	T.B.						..	
Godwine (Godwi, &c.)		+	+	H.W.M.	+	+	Rush 305				+	Witt 122				
Hamund																
Lefwine		..													..	
Lifred (Lefred)		..													..	
Lifsi (Lifsei)		..													..	
Manic		..													..	
Ordgar (Odgar, &c.)											+	+	+		..	
Osebern															..	
Ranlt (Radulus, &c.)				..											NC of (p. 305	
Ricard (Ricad)																
Rodbert														..	..	
Rogier (Rogir)														..	..	
Sibode			+											..	..	
Sigar (Sighar)														..	..	
Smæwine (Smeawine, &c.)														..	..	J.E.C.
Sperling (Sperlig, &c.)										+ (app.)	+	+	+			
Sultan														Tptis 391	..	
Sieetman	+	..												..	..	R.
Theodric (Thidric, &c.)										B.N.J. vii. 81	+			..	..	

	HENRY I											STEPHEN				LONDON
V	VI	VII	VIII	IX	X	XI	XII	XIII	XIV	XV	I	II	III–VI	VII		*(cont.)*
..	..	..	..	..	..	..	..	..	..	..	P.C.B.	..	..	..	Algar Man
..	..	..	..	..	..	..	..	..	..	..	H.M.R. P.C.B.	..	..	+	Alisander (Alisandr
..	..	..	..	..	..	..	..	..	..	+	+	..	..	..	Baldewin
..	..	..	..	..	..	..	..	..	..	..	..	..	..	..	Bat
..	..	..	..	..	..	..	..	..	..	..	..	..	..	..	Beriteri?
..	..	+	P.C.B.	..	+	P.C.B.	..	(Blacman.	..	+	..	..	..	..	Blacaman (Blacman. &c.)
..	..	..	..	..	..	..	..	..	..	..	..	..	..	..	Blacsunu (Blagsun, &c.)
..	..	..	..	..	..	..	..	..	..	+	+	..	..	..	Brihtmær (Bricmar, &c.)
..	..	..	..	..	..	..	..	..	..	..	..	..	..	..	Brihtric
..	..	..	..	..	..	..	..	..	..	..	..	..	..	..	Brihtwine (Brihtwi, &c.)
..	..	..	..	..	..	..	..	..	..	..	..	..	..	..	Brunic
..	..	..	..	..	..	..	..	..	..	..	..	..	..	..	Colswegen
..	..	..	..	..	..	..	..	..	..	+	+	..	..	+	Dereman (Derman, &c.)
..	..	..	..	..	..	..	..	..	..	+	..	..	..	..	Dereman R Ri.
..	..	..	..	..	..	..	..	..	..	..	..	..	..	..	E——, see a Æ——
..	..	..	..	..	..	..	..	..	..	..	..	..	..	..	Eadric (Edi
..	..	..	..	Stkm	..	P.C.B.	..	..	..	..	..	..	..	..	Eadwine (Edwi, &c
NC'92 p. 84	..	+ (app.)	..	..	NC'01 p. 292	..	..	Bodl H.M.R.	+	..	..	..	..	..	Ealdgar (Aldgar, 8
..	..	..	..	..	..	..	..	..	..	..	..	+	..	..	Edward
..	..	..	..	..	..	..	..	..	..	..	..	..	..	..	Estmær
..	..	..	..	..	..	..	..	..	..	+	+	..	..	..	Estmund
..	.	..	..	..	..	..	..	..	..	..	..	+? F.A.W.? (lot 73)	..	+	Geffrei (Gefrei)
..	..	..	..	..	..	..	..	..	..	..	..	B.R. H.M.R.	..	..	Godard
..	..	..	..	..	..	..	..	..	..	+	+	..	..	..	Godric
..	..	..	..	..	..	..	..	..	+	..	..	..	..	..	Godwine (Godwi, &
..	..	..	..	..	..	..	..	..	..	..	..	+? B.R.	..	..	Hamund
..	..	..	..	..	..	+?	..	..	..	+	..	..	..	..	Lefwine
..	..	..	..	..	..	..	..	..	..	+	+	..	..	..	Lifred (Lefr
..	..	..	..	..	..	..	..	..	..	..	..	..	..	..	Lifsi (Lifsei
..	..	..	..	..	..	..	..	..	..	..	..	..	..	..	Manic
..	..	..	..	..	..	..	..	N.'01 p. 304	+	+	..	..	..	..	Ordgar (Odgar, &
..	..	..	..	..	..	..	..	..	..	+	..	..	..	..	Osebern
NC'92 p. 84	..	..	..	..	..	..	..	+	+	..	..	..	..	+	Raulf (Radt lus, &c.)
..	..	..	..	..	..	..	..	..	..	..	..	..	S.M.S. (VI)	P.C.B. +? P.C.B.	Ricard(Ric Rodbert
..	..	..	..	..	..	..	..	..	..	+	NC'50 p. 158?	..	..	..	Rogier (Ro;
..	..	..	..	..	..	..	..	..	..	..	..	..	..	..	Sibode
NC'92 p. 84	+	+	..	+	+	..	B.R.	+	+	..	..	..	..	..	Sigar (Sigh
..	..	..	..	..	..	..	..	..	..	+	+	..	..	+	Smæwine (Smeawin &c.)
..	..	P.C.B.	..	..	+	..	..	+	..	..	..	..	..	..	Sperling (Sperlig, 8
..	..	..	..	..	..	..	..	..	..	..	..	..	..	..	Sultan
..	..	..	..	..	..	..	..	..	..	..	..	..	..	..	Swetman
NC'92 p. 84?	..	P.C.B.?	..	..	..	..	..	..	..	..	..	..	..	..	Theodric (Thidric,8

	WILLIAM I								WILLIAM II								
	I	II	III	IV	V	VI	VII	VIII	I	II	III	IV	V	I	II	III	I
LONDON *(cont.)*																	
Thured (Thored, &c.)	..	..	..	..	..	..	..	..	..	..	..	..	..	..	..	R.C.L.	
Tierrri D	..	..	..	..	..	..	..	..	..	..	..	..	..	..	..	..	
Tomas	..	..	..	..	..	..	..	..	..	..	..	..	..	..	..	..	
Tovi	..	..	..	..	..	..	..	..	..	..	..	..	..	..	..	..	
Uhtred (= *Wihtred?*)	..	..	+	..	..	..	..	..	..	..	..	..	..	..	..	..	
U - - raven	..	..	..	..	..	..	..	..	..	..	..	..	..	..	..	..	
Walcin	..	..	..	..	..	..	..	..	..	..	..	+	..	..	..	..	
Wulfgar (*Wulgar,* &c.)											+						(*NC* { *p.*
Wulfnoth (Wulfnod, &c.)	..	..	..	..	..	..	..	..	..	..	+	..	..	..	..	..	
Wulfric	..	..	..	+													
Wulfwine (*Wulfwie,* &c.)	+	+	+	+ ?			+	..	..	..	..	..	P.C.B. ?	..	..		
Wulfword (*Wulfward,* &c.)	..	..	..	..	+ ?	..	..		..	..	+	{ L.A.L. { York		+ ?	..	..	

See also Lincoln.

Ædgar (William I, type IV). Num. Chron., 1904, p. 268.

Ægelric (William I, type V). E. W. Rashleigh sale, 1909, lot 364 — S. M. Spink coll. (mint uncertain).
    ,,   (William II, type II). W. Allen sale, 1898, lot 324.

Ælfhen (William II, type I). Num. Circ., 1902, p. 5649. Probably Sandwich.

Ælfred (William II, type II).   ,,   ,,   ,,   Roberts MS. Catalogue reading of Catalogue, p. 231, no. 102 (Lewes, Elfric).

Ælfric (William I, type VIII). Num. Chron., 1877, p. 343. Probably Lewes.
    ,,   (William II, type I). Num. Chron., 1904, p. 268.

Ælfrind (William II, type I). J. D. Cuff sale, 1854, lot 721 — Catalogue, p. 218, no. 21 (Ælfrued).

Ælfwine (William I, type V). C. Cove-Jones sale, 1911, lot 310 (type IV, 238 mis-print for 237).

Ælwine (William I, type VI). Sotheby, July 7, 1870, lot 83.

Æolfstan (William I, type II). W. and T. Bateman sale, 1893, lot 336.

Aldred (Stephen, type VI). H. Webb sale, 1895, lot 67 = H. O. O'Hagan sale, 1907, lot 422 = S. M. Spink coll. (Hastings).

Aldwine (William II, type III). W. Allen sale, 1898, lot 358.

Alfgar (Henry I, type IV). L. A. Lawrence sale, 1903, lot 101 — W. Allen sale, 1898, lot 367 (Algar). see Ealdgar.

Algar (Henry I, type XI). E. W. Rashleigh sale, 1909, lot 425 (Alwine?).

Alwold (Stephen, type I).   ,,   ,,   lot 541. Probably Winchester.

Athlbold (William II, type V). Sotheby, June 16, 1885, lot 44, and H. Montagu sale, 1896, lot 262.

Brant (Henry I, type VII). Num. Chron., 1901, p. 295 — P. W. P. Carlyon-Britton coll. (mint uncertain, perhaps Chichester).

Brihtric (William I, type VIII). C. Warne sale, 1889, lot 199. Perhaps Brihtwi?
    ,,   (William II, type III). Num. Chron., 1904, p. 269.

Brunic (William I, type V).   ,,   ,,   ,,   ,,

Cudberht (Stephen, type I). E. Burns sale, 1869, lot 59. Probably Rodbert.

Eadward (William I, type I). Num. Chron., 1840, p. 45. Probably Canterbury.

Edmund (Henry I, type XII). Visct. Dillon sale, 1892, lot 5 = L. A. Lawrence sale, 1903, lot 106 = P. W. P. Carlyon-Britton coll. (Lewes?).

Gileberd (Henry I, type XV). E. W. Rashleigh sale, 1909, lot 439 = Num. Chron., 1850, p. 146, and 1901, p. 298. Probably Bury St. Edmunds.

Godesbrand (William I, type VIII). H. Webb sale, 1894, lot 16.

Godine (William I, type IV). Num. Chron., 1904, p. 269. Perhaps Godric?

Godwine (William I, type I).   ,,   ,,   p. 270.
    ,,   (Henry I, type I). Num. Chron., 1901, p. 300, from Withy and Ryall. Probably Winchester (cf. Catalogue, Pl. XXXVIII. 16).
    ,,   (Henry I, type XV). E. W. Rashleigh sale, 1909, lot 435 = A. H. Baldwine coll. (Godric?)

Godwine Gu ,,   ,,   Num. Chron., 1901, p. 300 = T. Bliss coll. (mint uncertain; see above, p. cxlv, note 2).

| | HENRY I | | | | | | | | | | | STEPHEN | | | | LONDON |
V	VI	VII	VIII	IX	X	XI	XII	XIII	XIV	XV	I	II	III-VI	VII	*(cont.)*
B.R.	..	..	..	Hntr	..	..	..	..	..	..	..	..	..	..	Thured (Thored, &c.)
..	..	..	..	..	..	..	..	..	..	..	..	+	..	..	Tierrri D
..	..	..	..	..	..	..	..	..	..	*Sotheby 16. vi. '75 54*	..	..	..	Bodl. P.C.B.	Tomas
..	..	..	..	..	..	..	..	..	..	+	+? Cpnhn	..	..	..	Tovi
..	..	..	..	..	..	..	..	..	..	..	..	..	..	..	Uhtred
..	..	..	..	..	..	..	..	..	..	T.B.	..	..	..	..	U - - raven
..	..	..	..	..	..	..	..	..	..	..	..	..	..	..	Walein
+	..	..	..	Stkm	+	..	..	+	+	..	..	..	..	..	Wulfgar (Wulgar, &c.)
..	..	..	..	..	..	..	..	..	..	..	..	..	..	..	Wulfnoth (Wulfnod &c.)
..	..	..	..	..	..	..	..	..	..	..	..	..	..	..	Wulfric Wulfwine
NC'92 p. 84	J.Y. Stkm	..	..	+? P.C.B.	..	..	..	..	..	+	..	..	..	S.M.S.?	(Wulfwic &c.) Wulfword
..	..	..	..	+? P.C.B.	..	..	..	..	+	..	..	..	..	..	(Wulfwar &c.)

Idefs, Iden (William I, type II). Num. Circ., 1902, p. 5617, and Num. Chron., 1901, p. 270 (= 1846, p. 124) = Catalogue, p. 21, nos. 109–111.

Iohan (Stephen, type I and type II or VII?). J. Hall sale, 1849, lots 50 and 54 (lot 50 = Col. Durrant sale, 1847, lot 200).

Leofric (William I, type III). Archaeologia, vol. iv, p. 356.

Leofwold (William I, type IV). J. Dudman sale, 1913, lot 277 (Winchester).

Lepritwold (William II, type I). H. Webb sale, 1894, lot 13 = T. Bliss coll. (Canterbury, Brihtwold).

Lific (William I, type III). Brit. Num. Journ., vol. viii, p. 73.

Lifwine (William II, type II). H. Montagu sale, 1897, lot 85 = Rollin and Feuardent coll. (Edwine, same obverse die as Catalogue, p. 232, no. 110).

Orgar (William I, type VI). Num. Chron., 1904, p. 270. Possibly William II, type IV?

Rawulf (Henry I, type XII). Num. Chron., 1901, p. 305 = P. W. P. Carlyon-Britton coll. (Winchester, Sawulf).

Roberd (Henry I, type XV). „ „ p. 307. Perhaps Canterbury?

Snotr (Henry I, type XII). Sotheby, Dec. 9, 1891, lot 394. Probably = Catalogue, Pl. XLII. 13 (Sigar).

Swir - - e (William II, type IV). E. W. Rashleigh sale, 1909, lot 398 = P. W. P. Carlyon-Britton coll. (Hastings).

Swirtic (Henry I, type X). Num. Chron., 1873, p. 175. Probably Sperlig.

Tierrei (Stephen, type VII). Num. Chron., 1905, p. 355 = Catalogue, p. 372, no. 200 (Geffrei).

Willem, Willelmus (Henry I, type XV). D. F. Kennard sale, 1892, lot 124, and E. W. Rashleigh sale, 1909, lot 433; Num. Chron., 1901, p. 312. Probably Canterbury.

Winfræd, Winræd (William II, type II). W. Allen sale, 1898, lot 321. (? = Num. Circ., 1902, p. 5649) = Catalogue, p. 232, no. 104 (Lewes).

Wulfmær (Henry I, type XV). Sotheby, July 29, 1915, lot 53.

Wulfric (William II, type II). Num. Chron., 1877, p. 344 = Catalogue, p. 239, no. 150 (Sudbury).

Wulfwi (William II, type III). Brit. Num. Journ., vol. viii, p. 81.

Wulfwine (William II, type II). Num. Chron., 1877, p. 344 = Catalogue, p. 234, no. 120 (Maldon).

    „ (William II, type IV). Num. Circ., 1902, p. 5649 = Roberts MS. Catalogue reading of B. M. Catalogue, p. 257, no. 216 (Walein).

    „ (Henry I, mule IV × V). Num. Chron., 1901, p. 314 = Sheriff Mackenzie coll. (contemporary forgery of type V).

    „ (Henry I, type XI). J. D. Cuff sale, 1854, lot 737 = Hon. R. Marsham sale, 1888, lot 252 = S. Rostron sale, 1892, lot 33 = H. Montagu sale, 1896, lot 289 = J. G. Murdoch sale, 1903, lot 216 = H. M. Reynolds coll. (Alfwine?).

Wulfwold (William II, type III). A. B. Richardson sale, 1895, lot 68 = H. Clark sale, 1898, lot 61. Probably Wulfword.

Wulfword (William I, type IV). Brit. Num. Journ., vol. viii, p. 74.

    „ (William II, type II). „ „ p. 79 = Catalogue, p. 238, no. 148 (Stamford?).

Wulst (Henry I, type II). Sotheby, July 14, 1899, lot 141. Probably Canterbury.

Wunric (William II, type II). Num. Chron., 1877, p. 344 = Catalogue, p. 232, no. 107 (Brunine).

		WILLIAM I							WILLIAM II							
	I	II	III	IV	V	VI	VII	VIII	I	II	III	IV	V	I	II	II
MALDON																
Ælfwine	..	..	..	..	..	..	..	+	..	..	..	..	..			
Ælford (Alfwod?)	..	..	..	..	..	..	..	+	..	..	(P.C.B. { 770	..	..			
Lifosun (Liofesunu, &c.)	..	..	*Slkn*	..	..	..	..	MULE + +	+	..	..	..	..			
Wulfwine	..	..	..	..	..	..	..		..	+	..	..	..			

Outhgrim (William I, type IV). H. O. O'Hagan sale, 19(

	I	II	III	IV	V	VI	VII	VIII	I	II	III	IV	V	I	II	II
MALMES-BURY																
Brihtwine (Brihtwc)	..	+	..	+	+	..	..		..	..	..	..				
Godsbrand	..	..	..	..	..	..	MULE +	+	..	..	..	..				
Seword	..	..	..	..	..	..	..	+	+	+	..	..				

Seword (William II, type III). Various sale catalogues, &

	I	II	III	IV	V	VI	VII	VIII	I	II	III	IV	V	I	II	II
MARL-BOROUGH																
Cild	..	..	+	+	+	+	Hntr	+	Allon 325	..	..	..	..			

Seword (William II, type III). Hon. R. Marsham sale, 1888, lot 243

	I	II	III	IV	V	VI	VII	VIII	I	II	III	IV	V	I	II	II
NORTH-AMPTON																
Geffrei	..	..	..	..	..	..	..		..	..	..	..				
Ghahan	..	..	..	..	..	..	..		..	..	..	..				
Gosfrei	..	..	..	..	..	..	..		..	..	..	..				
Paien	..	..	..	..	..	..	..		..	..	..	..				
Sæwine	..	P.C.B. W.C.W.	..	..	..	..	..		..	..	..	..				
Stefne (Stifne, &c.)	..	..	..	..	..	..	..		..	..	..	..				
Wu[ln?]od	..	..	..	..	..	..	..		..	..	..	..				

Stefne, Stiefne, Stephan (William I, type II). M. H. Bobart sale, 1894, lot 5. Probably Sæwine.

	HENRY I												STEPHEN				
IV	V	VI	VII	VIII	IX	X	XI	XII	XIII	XIV	XV	I	II	III-VI	VII		**MALDON**
..	..	..	..	..	..	..	..	..	..	..	..	..	..	..	..	Ælfwine
..	..	..	..	..	..	..	..	..	..	..	..	..	..	..	..	Ælford (Alfw
..	..	..	..	..	..	..	..	..	..	..	..	..	..	..	..	Lifesun (Liofesunu,
												..	..	..	..	Wulfwine

lot 409. Probably York (IVFE; cf. Catalogue, p. 56, no. 294).

IV	V	VI	VII	VIII	IX	X	XI	XII	XIII	XIV	XV	I	II	III-VI	VII		**MALMES- BU**
..	..	..	..	..	..	..	..	..	..	..	..	..	..	..	..	Brihtwine (Brihtwi)
..	..	..	..	..	..	..	..	..	..	..	..	..	..	..	..	Godsbrand
..	..	..	..	..	..	..	..	..	..	..	..	..	..	..	..	Seword

Probably false, cf. Brit. Num. Journ., vol. iii, p. 283, nos. 35, 36.

IV	V	VI	VII	VIII	IX	X	XI	XII	XIII	XIV	XV	I	II	III-VI	VII		**MARL- BOROU(**
..	..	..	..	..	..	..	..	..	..	..	..	..	..	..	..	Cild

H. Montagu sale, 1896, lot 269 (Malmesbury; probably false; see above).

IV	V	VI	VII	VIII	IX	X	XI	XII	XIII	XIV	XV	I	II	III-VI	VII		**NORTH- AMPT**
..	..	..	..	..	..	..	..	..	..	+		..	..	..	..	Geffrei
..	..	..	..	..	..	..	..	..	..	..	W.C.W.	..	..	..	..	Ghahan
..	..	..	..	..	..	..	..	..	..	+		..	..	..	..	Gosfrei
..	..	..	..	..	..	..	..	..	+	+ ? P.C.B.?)	+	S.M.S. ?) W.C.W.?)	..	B.R.) (III))	+ ?	Paien
..	..	..	..	..	..	..	..	..	..	..		..	..	..	..	Sæwine
..	..	..	..	..	..	..	..	..	T.B.	P.C.B.) W.C.W.)	..	..	..	..	..	Stefne (Stifne &c.)
..	..	..	..	..	..	..	..	..	..	+ ?	W.C.W.)	..	..	..	..	Wu[ln ?]od

Stefne, Stiefne, Stephan (Henry I, type XV). E. W. Rashleigh sale, 1909, lots 441 and 443, both in W. C. Wells coll. (mints illegible); J. G. Murdoch sale, 1903, lot 212 = W. C. Wells coll. (Ghahan; same dies as another coin in same collection).

	WILLIAM I								WILLIAM II								
	I	II	III	IV	V	VI	VII	VIII	I	II	III	IV	V	I	II	III	IV
NOR-WICH																	
Ædstan (Etstan, &c.)	..	..	..	..	..	..			..	..	..	..	..	..	..		(8.x) 7
Ædwine, see Eadwine		..	..	..	..				..	..		..		..			..
Ægelric	..	..	..	..	4		..		4	4	..		..	..			..
Ailwi	..	..	..	..			..		..	..				..			..
Alfri (Ælfric(?). &c.)	..	..	..	..					..	4				..			..
Alfward (Ailward)		..	..											..			.
Baldwine?	..	..												..			.
Chitel (Chetel)	..	..	..							..				..			..
Eadwine (.*Ædwine*, &c.)	4	4															
Ed-tan, see Ædstan																	
Edwold	..	..	..		4		..	4	(A. 22 (p.211))								
Etrel	..	..	..						..								
Et-tan, see Ædstan																	
Eustace	..	..	..						..								
Godric (Godruc)	..	..	..	4	4?	8the	4	4									
Godric Brd	..	..						4									
Godwid	..	..	..														
Godwine	..	..	..	.	R.C.L.	P.C.B.		4									
Hermer	..	..							..								
Hilde---	..	..							..								
Howorth (Howord, &c.)	..	..					4				T.C.C. P.C.B. 48	(hd?)	T.B.	P.C.B.	4 (app.)		
Inhuhe(?)	..							4	..								
Liofwold		York P.C.B	..	..													
Oter	..	..	..	..					P.C.B.							4	
Oterche	..	..	..														
Raulf																	
Sihtric (Shitric)	..	..	..														
Stanchil	..	..															
Suneman	..	..							..								
Swetman	..	..							..								
Thor	..	..							..								
Thuregrim, &c.		York	Bodl.	P.C.B.													
Ulfchitel (Ulfetl, &c.)	.	..	..					4									.
Waltier		..	..						..								.
Willem		..	..						..								.

Ælfric (William II, type V). Hon. R. Marsham sale, 1888, lot 242   H. Montagu sale, 1896, lot 259 = Catalogue, p. 262, no. 263 (Guildford).

Ælfwine (William II, type III). Rev. H. Christmas sale, 1864, lot 221.

Aldena (Henry I, type VII). Num. Chron., 1901, p. 331 = Catalogue, p. 280, no. 45 (Nottingham).

Briesel (William II, type V). Sotheby, Jan. 12, 1818, lot 55, and June 4, 1855, lot 31; J. Hall sale, 1849, lot 45.

Coe, Col (Henry I, type XV). W. Boyne sale, 1896, lot 1185; Num. Chron., 1901, p. 334. Probably York (cf. Catalogue, p. 353, nos. 301, 302).

Eadweard (William I, type VI). J. J. Nunn sale, 1896, lot 206.

	HENRY I											STEPHEN				
V	VI	VII	VIII	IX	X	XI	XII	XIII	XIV	XV	I	II	III-VI	VII	NOR-W]
W.C.W.	..	Cpnhn	..	..	+	NC '01 p. 336	..	..	P.C.B.	NC '01 p. 336	+	+	.	..	Ædstan (Etstan, &c.)
..	..	..	..	..	..	..	..	..	..	..	..	..	..	..	Ædwine, Eadwine
..	..	..	..	..	..	..	..	..	..	..	..	..	..	..	Ægelric
..	..	..	..	..	..	..	..	..	..	.:	+	..	..	..	Allwi
..	..	..	..	..	..	..	..	..	..	..	..	Nott.?	..	+ S.M.S.	Alfri (Ælfric (&c.)
..	..	..	..	..	..	..	..	..	..	..	Nott. P.C.B.	B.R.?	..	..	Alfward (Ailwar
..	..	..	..	..	..	..	..	..	..	+	..	..	..	..	Baldwine
..	..	..	..	..	..	..	..	..	.:	..	..	..	..	..	Chitel (Ch
..	..	..	..	..	..	..	..	..	..	+	..	..	..	..	Eadwine (Ædwin &c.)
..	..	..	..	..	..	..	..	..	..	..	..	..	..	..	Edstan, se Ædstan
..	..	..	..	..	..	..	..	..	..	..	..	..	..	..	Edwold
..	..	..	..	..	..	..	..	..	..	..	+	..	..	..	Etrei
..	..	..	..	..	..	..	..	..	..	..	..	..	..	..	Etstan, se Ædstan
..	..	..	..	..	..	..	..	..	..	L.A.L.?	Mint	..	..	..	Eustace
..	..	..	..	..	..	..	..	..	..	..	..	..	..	..	Godric (Godruc
..	..	..	..	..	..	..	..	..	..	..	..	..	..	..	Godric Br
..	..	..	..	..	..	..	..	..	..	..	..	..	..	..	Godwid
..	..	..	..	..	..	..	..	..	..	+	..	..	..	..	Godwine
..	..	..	..	..	..	..	..	..	..	..	+ B.R.	..	..	..	Godwine
..	..	..	..	..	..	..	..	..	..	..	..	+	..	+	Hermer
..	..	..	..	..	..	..	..	..	..	..	..	..	..	..	Hilde - - -
..	..	..	..	..	..	..	..	..	..	..	..	..	..	..	Howorth (Howor &c.)
..	..	..	..	..	..	..	..	..	..	..	..	..	..	..	Inhuhe (?)
..	..	..	..	..	..	..	..	..	..	..	..	..	..	..	Liofwold
..	..	..	..	Stkm?	..	..	..	..	..	+	..	..	..	..	Oter
..	..	..	..	..	..	..	..	..	..	..	+	..	..	..	Oterche
..	..	..	..	..	..	..	..	..	..	..	..	Knrd 132	..	Hntr	Raulf
..	..	..	..	..	..	..	..	..	..	Hntr	P.C.B. S.M.S.	..	..	..	Sihtric (Shitric)
..	..	..	..	..	..	..	..	..	P.C.B.?	..	..	+	..	..	Stanchil
..	..	..	..	..	..	..	..	..	..	+?	+ (app.) P.C.B. S.M.S.	..	..	..	Suneman
..	..	..	..	..	..	..	..	..	..	..	..	..	..	..	Swetman
..	..	..	..	..	..	..	..	..	..	..	..	..	B.R. (VI)	+	Thor (= Thor
..	..	..	..	..	..	..	..	..	..	..	..	..	..	..	Thuregri &c.
..	..	..	..	..	..	..	T.C.C.	P.C.B.	..	..	..	..	..	..	Ulfchitel (Ulfctl,
..	..	..	..	..	..	..	..	..	..	..	Nott.	+?	..	.. B.R.	Waltier
..	..	..	..	..	..	..	..	..	..	..	+	..	+ (III)	B.R. R.C.L.	Willem

Eadweard (William I, type VIII). Brit. Num. Journ.. vol. ix, p. 132. Misreading of Num. Chron., 1904, p. 271 = preceding.

Freline (Henry I, type II). H. Durden sale, 1892, lot 38 = L. A. Lawrence sale, 1903, lot 92 = P. W. P. Carlyon-Britton coll. (mint uncertain).

Osbern (Henry I, type VII). Num. Chron., 1901, p. 338 = P. W. P. Carlyon-Britton coll. (reading uncertain).

Toc (Henry I, type XV). Num. Chron., 1901, p. 335 = F. A. Walters sale, 1913, lot 68 = Catalogue, p. 333, no. 302 (York).

Ulfri (William II, type III). Num. Chron., 1904, p. 272. Probably Alfri.

Wilhemar (Henry I, type VII). Num. Chron., 1901, p. 339.

	WILLIAM I								WILLIAM II					
	I	II	III	IV	V	VI	VII	VIII	I	II	III	IV	V	I
NOTTING-HAM														
Ætser (Atsere, &c.)	..	..	..	..	..	..	..	+	..	+	..	..	..	..
Aldene, *see* Haldene	..	..	..	..	..	..	..	..	..	..	..	..	..	..
Forna (Forn)	*(Tpbs 28)*	+	+	+	..	..	..	..	..	..	..	..	..	..
Haldene (Aldene, &c.)	..	..	..	..	..	..	..	..	..	..	..	T.B.	*(8, u 55, 36)*	..
Manna (Mana, &c.)	..	..	+	+	..	..	MULE +	+	..	..	..	..	..	..
Swein (Svein)	..	..	..	..	..	..	..	..	..	..	..	..	..	..
Wulfric	..	..	..	..	..	..	..	..	+	..	..	..	..	..
Uncertain	..	..	..	..	..	..	..	..	..	..	..	..	..	..

Alaric (Henry I, type XIII). Num. Chron., 1901, p. 350 = Catalogue, p. 297, no. 90 (Haldene ?).
Cetelgrim (William I, type IV). Rev. Neville Rolfe sale, 1882, lot 13.
Elfsi (William I, type II). Num. Chron., 1846, p. 124.
Godbrand (William I, type VI). J. W. Shaw sale, 1894, lot 392. Perhaps Shaftesbury ?
Haldin   ,,   ,,   J. Toplis sale, 1890, lot 37. Perhaps William II, type IV ?
Lifwine (William II, type III). Sotheby, April 16, 1874, lot 10.

	I	II	III	IV	V	VI	VII	VIII	I	II	III	IV	V	I
OXFORD														
Æginoth (Ailnot)	..	..	..	..	..	..	..	..	..	..	..	..	Hatr	+
Ægelwine, &c.	..	..	+	..	..	..	..	..	..	P.C.B?	Hatr P.C.B.	..	..	..
Ælfrig (Elfwi ?)	..	+	..	Hatr	+	..	..	..	..	..	..	..	..	..
Brihtræd (Brihtred, &c.)	..	Stur Pl.XL.3	Ast'05 211	..	..	P.C.B.	Rosb. P.C.B.	+	..	+	..	..	..	..
Elfwi, *see* Ælfwig	..	..	..	..	..	..	..	..	..	..	..	..	..	..
Gahan	..	..	..	..	..	..	..	..	..	..	..	..	..	..
Godwine	T.B.	Hatr	B.R.	+	P.C.B.	..	..	..	..	..	..	..	..	..
Harygod (Heregod, &c.)	Ashm	..	..	+	..	..	+	..	..	..	..	..	..	..
Man	..	York	..	..	..	..	..	..	..	..	..	..	..	..
Rawulf (Raulf)	..	..	..	..	..	..	..	..	..	..	..	..	..	..
Sagrim	..	..	..	..	..	..	..	..	..	..	..	..	..	..
Sawi	..	..	..	..	..	..	..	..	..	..	..	..	..	..
Swetig	..	..	..	..	..	..	..	..	..	..	..	..	..	..
Swetman	..	..	..	..	..	..	..	+	MULE Mint	Mint	+	..	..	..
Wulfwi	..	+	+	+	..	+	Ashm Hatr	+	Ashm	..	..	..	..	..
Uncertain	..	..	..	..	..	..	..	..	..	..	..	..	..	..

Æglnoth (William II, type III). Brit. Num. Journ., vol. x, p. 41 = Catalogue, p. 405, no. 209A
    (Norwich, moneyer uncertain).
Brihtric (William II, type II). W. Allen sale, 1898, lot 327 = Catalogue, p. 235, no. 125 (Brihtræd).
Brunstan (William I, type VI). Num. Chron., 1904, p. 273.
    (William I, type I). Num. Circ., 1902, p. 5652, probably mis-reading of preceding.
Ealfwine (William II, type II). Brit. Num. Journ., vol. x, p. 40 = P. W. P. Carlyon-Britton coll.
    (Ægelwine ?).
Godali (William I, type V). Num. Circ., 1902, p. 5652 = Roberts MS. Catalogue reading of B. M.
    Catalogue, p. 67, no. 360 (Norwich, Godruei).

	HENRY I												STEPHEN				
III	IV	V	VI	VII	VIII	IX	X	XI	XII	XIII	XIV	XV	I	II	III-VI	VII	NOTTI H
..	..	..	..	..	..	..	..	..	..	..	..	..	..	..	..	..	Ætser (At &c.)
..	..	..	..	..	..	..	..	..	..	..	..	..	..	..	..	..	Aldene, s Haldene
..	..	..	..	..	..	..	..	..	..	..	..	..	..	..	..	..	Forna (Fc
..	..	..	..	+	..	..	+	..	..	+	+	..	..	..	..	..	Haldene (Aldene Manna
..	..	..	..	..	..	..	..	..	..	..	..	..	..	..	..	..	(Mana,
..	..	..	..	..	..	..	..	..	..	..	..	..	+	..	..	P.C.B.	Swein (Sv
..	..	..	..	..	..	..	..	..	..	..	..	..	..	..	..	..	Wulfric
..	..	..	..	..	..	..	..	..	..	..	..	..	..	..	+ (iv)	..	Uncertai

Retelgrim (William I, type IV). J. L. Henderson sale, 1888, lot 36; J. Toplis sale, 1890, lot 30.
Ricard (Stephen, type I). Num. Chron., 1883, p. 115.
Wulfric (William I, type VIII). Sotheby, June 16, 1915, lot 52. Perhaps Sudbury ?
    ,,   (Henry I, type IV). Num. Chron., 1901, p. 350 = Catalogue, p. 275, no. 32 (Shrewsbury).
Wulfwine (William II, type IV). H. Clark sale, 1898, lot 59 = T. Bliss coll. (Haldin).
Wulfword   ,,   ,,   See Sandwich. Catalogue, p. 258, no. 249.

III	IV	V	VI	VII	VIII	IX	X	XI	XII	XIII	XIV	XV	I	II	III VI	VII	OXFO
..	..	..	..	..	..	..	..	..	..	..	+?	..	..	..	..	..	Æglnoth (Ailnot
..	..	..	..	..	..	..	..	..	..	..	..	..	..	..	..	..	Æglwine
..	..	..	..	..	..	..	..	..	..	..	..	..	..	..	..	..	Ælfwig (Elfwi) Brihtræd (Brihtr &c.)
..	..	..	..	..	..	..	..	..	..	..	..	..	..	..	..	..	Elfwi, se Ælfwig
..	..	..	..	..	..	..	..	..	..	..	..	..	B.R. S.M.S.	+? p.)	..	..	Gahan
..	..	..	..	..	..	..	..	..	..	..	..	..	..	..	..	..	Godwine Hargod (Herege &c.)
..	..	..	..	..	..	..	..	..	..	..	..	..	..	..	..	..	Man
..	..	..	..	..	..	..	..	..	..	..	..	+	S.M.S.?	..	..	..	Rawulf(I
..	..	..	..	..	..	..	..	..	..	..	..	+	..	..	..	..	Sagrim
..	..	..	..	..	..	..	..	..	..	..	P.C.B.	..	..	..	..	..	Sawi
..	..	..	..	..	..	..	..	..	..	..	..	..	+	..	..	..	Swetig
..	..	..	..	..	..	..	..	..	..	..	..	..	..	..	..	..	Swetmar
..	..	..	..	..	..	..	..	..	..	..	..	..	..	..	..	..	Wulfwi
..	..	..	..	..	..	..	Brln	..	..	..	..	..	..	..	..	..	Uncertai

Godwine (William II, type III). Brit. Num. Journ., vol. x, p. 41 = P. W. P. Carlyon-Brittou sale,
    1913, lot 771 (mint doubtful, probably Salisbury).
Hærgod (William I, type III). F. G. Lawrence sale, 1900, lot 24 = H. W. Morrieson coll. (type VII;
    236 misprint for 239).
Heregod (William I, type II). Num. Chron., 1904, p. 273.
Lifwine (William I, type VIII). W. A. Cotton sale, 1889, lot 64. Perhaps Exeter ?
Walter (Stephen, type VII). Num. Chron., 1903, p. 118 = Catalogue, p. 371, no. 193 (Gloucester, Ralf).
Wulmær (William II, types II and III). W. A. Cotton sale, 1889, lot 61, and Num. Chron., 1904,
    p. 273.

	WILLIAM I								WILLIAM II							
	I	II	III	IV	V	VI	VII	VIII	I	II	III	IV	V	I	II	II
PEM-BROKE																
Gillepatrie	..	..	..	..	..	..	..	..	..	..	..	..	..	..	..	..
PEVEN-SEY																
Ælfheh (Ælfhe, &c.)	..	..	..	..	+?	..	..	+	Alhu 329	..	(app.) +?	..	..	..	..	..
Alwine	..	..	..	..	..	..	..	..	..	..	..	..	..	..	..	..
RHUDD-LAN																
Ælfwine	..	..	..	..	..	..	..	+	..	..	..	..	..	..	..	..
ROCHES-TER																
Ælfstan (Ælstan)	..	..	..	..	..	..	..	..	..	Hntr	+	..	..	B.R.	..	..
Guthræd (Guthred)	..	..	..	..	..	..	..	..	+	+	+	..	..	..	..	..
Lifstan (*Liftan*)	..	York	..	P.C.B.	..	..	..	..	..	..	..	..	..	..	..	..
Lifwine Horn	..	..	..	..	..	..	..	..	..	..	..	..	..	..	..	..
Wulfwine	..	..	..	..	..	..	..	..	..	..	..	..	+	..	..	..

Egelwine (William I, type VIII). Sotheby, May 18, 1855, lot 186.
Godfred (William I, type IV, and William II, type II). Num. Chron., 1904, p. 274.
Guthgara (William II, type II). Num. Chron., 1877, p. 344 : Catalogue, p. 235, no. 427 (Guthræd).

	I	II	III	IV	V	VI	VII	VIII	I	II	III	IV	V	I	II	III
ROMNEY																
Ælmer	..	..	..	..	+	+	..	..	..	..	..	..	..	..	..	..
Coc	..	..	..	..	..	..	..	..	P.C.B.	..	..	..	..	..	..	..
Godricus	..	..	..	..	..	..	..	..	..	..	..	..	..	..	..	..
Gold	..	..	..	..	..	..	..	..	..	..	..	..	..	..	..	..
Windei (Winedi,&c.)	..	..	..	..	..	..	..	+	..	P.C.B.	Hntr	..	B.R.	..	..	..
Wulfmær	+	..	..	..	..	..	..	+	+? {J.W.P.	P.C.B.	+	..	..	..	..	..
Wulfred	..	..	..	..	..	..	..	..	..	..	..	..	..	..	..	..

Brihtmar (William I, type I). Sotheby, Feb. 1, 1900, lot 185. Probably Wulmær.
Citarad (William II, type II). Sotheby, May 27, 1850, lot 31.
Gondine (William I, type II). Sotheby, July 18, 1888, lot 2.

	I	II	III	IV	V	VI	VII	VIII	I	II	III	IV	V	I	II	III
ST. DAVIDS																
Turri	..	..	..	..	..	..	..	+	..	..	..	..	..	..	..	..
SALIS-BURY																
Aldwine	..	..	..	..	..	..	..	..	..	..	..	..	..	..	..	..
Ealla	..	..	..	..	..	..	..	..	..	..	..	..	..	..	..	..
Edword	..	..	..	..	..	..	..	..	+ (app.)	+	..	..	..	..	..	..
Esbern (Osbern,&c.)	..	..	..	..	..	..	..	+	Brln P.C.B.	+	..	..	P.C.B.	..	Hntr	{? {L.A. cast
Godric	Cpnhn {H.W.M.	..	..	..	+	..	+	..	..	..	..	..	..	..	..	..

				HENRY I										STEPHEN				
IV	V	VI	VII	VIII	IX	X	XI	XII	XIII	XIV	XV	I	II	III-VI	VII			
..	..	..	..	..	..	..	..	..	..	P.C.B.	..	+	..	..	..	**PEM-BRO** Gillepatric
..	..	..	..	..	..	..	..	..	..	..	..	..	..	..	..	**PEVEN** **S** Ælfheh (Ælfhe, &
..	..	..	..	..	..	..	..	..	..	..	..	..	+	..	B.R. F.A.W. (lot 71)	Alwine
..	..	..	..	..	..	..	..	..	..	..	..	..	..	..	..	**RHUDI** **L** Ælfwine
..	..	..	..	..	..	..	..	..	..	..	..	..	..	..	..	**ROCHE** **T** Ælfstan (Æl-stan)
..	..	..	..	..	..	..	..	..	..	..	..	..	..	..	..	Guthred (Guthred)
..	..	..	..	..	..	..	..	..	..	..	..	..	..	..	..	Lifstan (Liftan)
..	..	..	..	..	..	..	..	..	..	..	..	..	..	..	..	Lifwine He Wulfwine

Lifstan (William II, type III). Num. Circ., 1902, p. 5633. Perhaps Ælstan?
Wulfmær (William I, type I). Sotheby, Aug. 5, 1815, lot 44. Probably Romney.
Wulfwine (William I, type III). Num. Chron., 1904, p. 274. See Hereford.

IV	V	VI	VII	VIII	IX	X	XI	XII	XIII	XIV	XV	I	II	III-VI	VII	
..	..	..		..	..	..	..	..	..	..	..	..	..	..	..	**ROMNI** Ælmær
..	..	..	..	..	..	..	..	..	..	..	..	..	..	..	..	Coc
..	..	..	..	..	..	..	..	..	MULE P.C.B.	P.C.B.	..	..	..	..	..	Godricus
..	..	..	..	..	..	..	..	..	..	..	..	..	..	..	..	Gold Windei (Winedi,&
..	..	..	..	..	..	..	..	..	..	..	..	..	..	..	..	Wulfmær
..	..	..	..	..	..	+	..	..	..	+	..	..	..	..	..	Wulfred

Lifwine (William II, type V). Num. Chron., 1904, p. 274.
Windei (William I, type VII). ,, ,, ,, Probably type VIII.
Wulfmær ,, ,, ,, ,, p. 275. ,, ,,

IV	V	VI	VII	VIII	IX	X	XI	XII	XIII	XIV	XV	I	II	III-VI	VII	
..	..	..	..	..	..	..	..	..	..	..	..	..	..	..	..	**ST.** **DAVI** Turri
..	..	..	..	..	..	..	..	..	..	+	..	..	..	..	..	**SALIS-** **BUR** Aldwine
..	..	..	..	..	..	..	..	..	..	P.C.B.	..	..	..	..	..	Ealla
..	..	..	..	..	..	..	..	..	..	..	..	..	..	..	..	Edword
..	..	..	..	..	..	..	..	..	..	..	..	..	..	..	..	Esbern (Osbern, &
..	..	..	..	..	..	..	..	..	..	..	..	..	..	..	..	Godric

	WILLIAM I								WILLIAM II						
	I	II	III	IV	V	VI	VII	VIII	I	II	III	IV	V	I	II
SALIS-BURY (cont.)															
Godheue (Godwine)	MULE E.M.		..	..	..	..	..	+	+	+	A.M.?	..	..	..	..
Osbern, see Esbern	..	..	..	..	..	..	..	..	..	..	..	..	..	..	..
Safara	P.C.B.	..	..	..	..	..	..	..	..	..	..	..	..	..	..
Stanning	..	..	..	..	..	..	..	..	..	..	..	..	..	..	..

> *Ærncwi* (William II, type II). Num. Chron., 1877, p. 344. Catalogue, p. 296, no. 133 (Shrewsbury).
> *Cihtwine* (William I, type VII). H. Clark sale, 1898, lot 44. Probably Shaftesbury.
> *Eadwold* (William II, type III). H. Montagu sale, 1897, lot 93. Probably Eadword.
> *Esbern* (William I, type VII). Num. Chron., 1904, p. 275. Probably type VIII.
>   ,, (William II, type III). Num. Circ., 1902, p. 5651. P. W. P. Carlyon-Britton coll. (moneyer doubtful, probably Edword).
> *Godric* (Henry I, type I). Num. Chron., 1904, p. 401. W. Rusher Davies sale, 1883, lot 59. E. H. Evans sale, 1894, lot 30.

	I	II	III	IV	V	VI	VII	VIII	I	II	III	IV	V	I	II
SAND-WICH															
Adalbot [1]	..	..	..	..	..	..	..	..	..	..	..	..	..	..	..
Ælfgæt [2] (Ælfgete, &c.)	..	..	..	P.S.J. Syn. 22	Hntr	S. 70 95 143	..	+	Ghe gat	..	..	..	..	..	..
Ælfheh [3] (Ælfeh, &c.)	..	..	..	..	..	..	+	..	..	..	..	..	..	..	..
Alfgær [4] (Alfgar)	..	..	..	..	..	..	..	..	..	..	Hntr	+	..	..	..
Gothese [5]	..	..	..	..	..	..	..	..	..	..	..	..	..	..	..
Godwine [6]	..	..	..	..	..	Stan	..	..	..	..	..	..	..	..	..
Osbern [7]	..	..	..	..	..	..	..	..	..	..	..	..	..	..	..
Wulfric [8]	..	..	..	..	..	..	..	..	..	..	..	..	..	..	..
Wulfwart [9] (Wulfwor)	..	..	..	..	..	..	..	..	..	..	..	+	+	..	..

[1] SAN   [2] SAND, SAID   [3] SANDP.
SAND   [4] SAID, SAN   [5] SANDP, SAND,
SAN   [6] SAND, SAN   [7] *Henry I.* SAD;
Stephen, SANPI   [8] SAN   [9] SAN

	I	II	III	IV	V	VI	VII	VIII	I	II	III	IV	V	I	II
SHAFTES-BURY															
Ælnoth (Alnoth)	..	..	..	..	+	H.S.	+	+	..	..	..	..	..	..	..
Aldred	..	..	..	..	..	..	..	..	..	..	P.C.B.?	..	..	..	..
Aldwine	..	..	..	..	..	..	..	..	..	..	..	..	..	..	..
Baldwine	..	..	..	..	..	..	..	..	..	..	+	..	..	..	..
Cnihtwine (Citwine, &c.)	..	..	..	..	+	Hntr B.C.L.	+	+	..	..	..	..	..	..	..
Godesbrand (Godsbrand)	..	..	..	..	..	+	+	+	..	..	..	..	..	..	..
Osmund	..	..	..	..	..	..	..	..	..	..	..	..	P.C.B.?	..	..
Ricard	..	..	..	..	..	..	..	..	..	..	..	..	..	..	..
Sagrim	..	..	..	..	..	..	..	..	..	..	..	..	..	..	..
Saric	..	..	..	..	..	..	..	..	..	..	..	..	..	..	..
Wulfgad	..	..	..	..	..	..	..	..	..	+	P.C.B.	..	..	..	..

> *Eseword* (William II, type III). Brit. Num. Journ., vol. v, p. 110. Perhaps Salisbury, Edword.
> *Cnihtwin*   ,,   ,,   Num. Circ., 1902, p. 5653.

	HENRY I											STEPHEN				
IV	V	VI	VII	VIII	IX	X	XI	XII	XIII	XIV	XV	I	II	III-VI	VII	**SALIS-BURY** (cont.)
..	..	..	..	..	..	..	..	..	..	..	..	..	..	..	..	Godwine (Godwinne)
..	..	..	..	..	..	..	..	..	..	..	..	..	..	..	..	Osbern, see Esbern
..	..	..	..	..	..	..	..	..	..	..	..	..	..	..	..	Safara
..	..	..	..	..	..	..	..	..	..	..	..	..	..	..	+	Stanning

Godwine (William I, type VII). Num. Chron., 1904, p. 275. Probably type VIII.
   ,, (Henry I, type XIV). J. G. Murdoch sale, 1903, lot 227. Perhaps Aldwine?
Lifword (William II, type II). Num. Chron., 1877, p. 344 = Catalogue, p. 237, no. 139 (Southwark).
   ,, (Henry I, type I). J. B. Bergne sale, 1873, lot 320.
Segrim (William II, types I and II). Num. Chron., 1877, p. 344. Type II = Catalogue, p. 236, no. 135 (Shrewsbury).
Wulfric (William II, type IV). Sotheby, July 4, 1891, lot 280. Probably Sudbury.

IV	V	VI	VII	VIII	IX	X	XI	XII	XIII	XIV	XV	I	II	III-VI	VII	**SAND-WICH**
..	..	..	H.M.R.	..	..	..	..	..	..	..	..	..	..	..	..	Adalbot [1]
..	..	..	..	..	..	..	..	..	..	..	..	..	..	..	..	Ælfgæt [2] (Ælfgte, &c.)
..	..	..	..	..	..	..	..	..	..	..	..	..	..	..	..	Ælfheh [3] (Ælfeh, &c.)
..	..	..	..		..	..	..	..	..	..	..	..	..	..	..	Alfgær [4] (Alfgar)
..	..	..	..	..	..	..	..	..	P.C.B.?	+	..	..	..	..	..	Godhese [5]
..	..	..	..	..	..	..	..	..	..	+	..	..	..	..	+	Godwine [6]
..	..	..	..	..	..	..	..	..	..	+	..	..	..	..	+	Osbern [7]
..	..	..	..	..	..	..	..	..	..	..	..	..	+	..	S.M.S.	Wulfric [8]
..	..	..	..	..	W.C.W.	..	..	..	..	..	..	..	..	..	..	Wulfwart [9] (Wulfwor)

Ældræd (William II, type III). Brit. Num. Journ., vol. vii, p. 23. Perhaps Shaftesbury?
Alfgad (William II, type IV).   ,,   ,,   ,, = Catalogue, p. 258, no. 248 (Alfgar).
Ricard (Stephen, type I). Num. Chron., 1883, p. 115 = H. Montagu sale, 1896, lot 323 = H. O. O'Hagan sale, 1907, lot 423 = S. M. Spink coll. (Shaftesbury?).
Robert (Stephen, type I). Sotheby, June 16, 1915, lot 55. Probably Canterbury.
Sagr.   ,,   ,, Num. Chron., 1850, p. 159 = E. W. Rashleigh sale, 1909, lot 557 = Catalogue, p. 348, no. 91 (Shaftesbury?).
Ulfgin (William II, type IV). Num. Circ., 1902, p. 5654 = Catalogue, p. 258, no. 248 (Alfgar).
Wulfred (Stephen, type II). D. F. Kennard sale, 1892, lot 151. Probably Wulfric.
Wulfwold (Stephen, type I). Num. Chron., 1850, p. 159.

IV	V	VI	VII	VIII	IX	X	XI	XII	XIII	XIV	XV	I	II	III-VI	VII	**SHAFTES-BURY**
..	..	..	..	..	..	..	..	..	..	..	..	..	..	..	..	Ælnoth (Alnoth)
..	..	..	..	..	..	..	..	..	+	..	..	..	..	..	..	Aldred
..	..	..	..	..	..	..	..	P.C.B.	..	..	..	..	..	..	..	Aldwine
..	..	..	..	..	..	..	..	..	..	..	..	..	..	..	..	Baldwine
..	..	..	..	..	..	..	..	..	..	..	..	..	..	..	..	Cnihtwine (Citwine, &c.)
..	..	..	..	..	..	..	..	..	..	..	..	..	..	..	..	Godesbrand (Godsbrand)
..	..	..	..	..	..	..	..	..	..	..	..	..	..	..	..	Osmund
..	..	..	..	..	..	..	..	..	..	+	..	..	..	..	..	Ricard
..	..	..	..	..	..	..	..	..	+	+?	..	..	..	..	..	Sagrim
..	..	..	..	..	..	..	..	..	+	..	..	..	..	..	..	Saric
..	..	..	..	..	..	..	..	..	..	..	..	..	..	..	..	Wulfgæd

Shelic (William II, type III). Num. Chron., 1904, p. 276. Probably = Catalogue, p. 246, no. 190 (Hastings, Spirlic).
Swgen (William II, type II). Sotheby, Feb. 18, 1881, lot 328.

	WILLIAM I								WILLIAM II					
	I	II	III	IV	V	VI	VII	VIII	I	II	III	IV	V	I
SHREWS-BURY														
Ernwi (*Earnwi, &c.*)	..	P.C.B.	..	+	+	+	..	+	F.A.W.	+	..	+	..	..
Egfric	..	+	..	..	..	..	..	..	..	..	..	..	..	..
Godesbrand	..	..	..	..	..	..	..	..	..	..	..	..	..	..
Hathebrand	..	..	..	..	..	..	..	..	..	..	+	+	+?	..
Revensart	..	..	..	..	..	..	..	..	..	..	..	..	..	..
Rodbert	..	..	..	..	..	..	..	..	..	..	..	..	..	..
Segrim	..	..	..	..	*Nnctr c1*	..	..	..	+	+	..	..	..	..
Wulfmer Wulfric (Wulfie)	..	..	..	+	Hntr	..	..	..	..	..	..	T.C.C.	..	..

Segrim, Segrim (William I, type II). Num. Chron., 1901, p. 276.
"   " (William I, type VII). Num. Circ., 1912, p. 5655 (not in Brit. Mus.; perhaps inserted from William II, type II, where same reading occurs).

	WILLIAM I								WILLIAM II					
	I	II	III	IV	V	VI	VII	VIII	I	II	III	IV	V	I
SOUTH-AMPTON														
Dort?	..	..	..	..	..	..	..	..	..	..	..	..	..	..
Godwine	..	..	..	..	..	..	..	..	..	+	..	..	..	..
Sawine (*Sewi, &c.*)	..	(York.) +P.C.B.	Hntr T.B.	..	..	..	..	..	..	..	..	..	Hntr	1
Swetman	..	..	..	..	..	..	..	..	..	..	..	..	..	..
Uli	..	..	..	..	..	..	..	..	..	..	..	..	..	..
Wulwi	..	..	L.A.L.	..	..	..	..	..	..	..	..	..	..	..

Dÿnan (William II, type IIb). Capt. Murchison sale, 1864, lot 17. Catalogue, p. 216, no. 187 (Hastings, Dirman).
Godric (William I, type II). Num. Chron., 1895, p. 123. Probably Huntingdon.

	WILLIAM I								WILLIAM II					
	I	II	III	IV	V	VI	VII	VIII	I	II	III	IV	V	I
SOUTH-WARK														
Eldoulf [1] (Aldolf, &c.)	..	..	..	..	..	..	..	..	..	..	..	..	..	..
Alfwine [2]	..	..	..	..	..	..	..	..	..	..	..	..	..	..
Algar [3]	..	..	..	..	..	..	..	..	..	..	..	..	..	..
Edward [4]	..	..	..	..	..	..	..	..	..	..	..	..	..	..
Godric [5]	..	..	..	..	..	..	+	..	..	..	..	..	..	..
Godwine (g) [6]	..	..	..	..	..	..	+	..	..	..	+	..	..	..
Leofwine [7] (Lifwine, &c.)	..	+	..	..	+	..	+	..	..	..	..	..	..	P.C.B.?
Lifword [8]	..	..	..	..	..	..	..	..	J.Y. P.C.B.	..	*dessing* 5656	..	..	Nc 91 p. 302
Osmund [9]	..	..	..	..	..	..	P.C.B.	..	..	P.C.B.	..	..	..	..
Sigar [10]	..	..	..	..	..	..	..	..	..	..	..	..	+	..
Sprot [11]	..	..	..	..	..	..	..	..	..	..	..	..	+	..
Turchil [12]	..	..	..	..	..	..	..	..	..	..	..	+	+	..
Wulfwold [13]	..	..	..	..	..	..	..	..	..	..	..	..	..	..
Wulgar [14]	..	..	..	..	..	..	..	..	..	..	..	+	+	..

[1] SVꝹ IE, SVꝹ E, SVꝹ I, SVꝹ EP, SIꝹ   [2] SVꝹ
[3] *William II.* SVꝹ EP, SVꝹ *Henry I.* SVꝹ PER, SVꝹ PE,
SVTWE, SVTW [4] SVꝹ [5] *Confessor.* SVꝹ P; *William I.*

For remaining notes see pages ccxxxviii, ccxxxix.

				HENRY I										STEPHEN			
III	IV	V	VI	VII	VIII	IX	X	XI	XII	XIII	XIV	XV	I	II	III-VI	VII	**SHREW BUR**
..	..	..	..	..	..	..	..	..	..	..	..	..	..	..	..	..	Ærnwi (Earnwi, &
..	..	..	..	..	..	..	..	..	..	..	..	..	..	..	..	..	Eglric
..	..	..	..	..	..	..	..	..	..	..	..	..	..	..	..	..	Godesbrand
..	..	..	..	..	..	..	..	..	..	..	..	..	..	..	..	..	Hathebrand
..	..	..	..	..	..	..	..	..	..	..	..	..	B.R.) S.M.S.)	..	..	..	Revensart
..	..	..	..	..	..	..	..	..	..	..	..	..	+	..	..	..	Rodbert
..	..	..	..	..	..	..	..	..	..	..	..	..	..	..	..	..	Segrim
..	..	..	..	..	..	..	..	..	..	..	..	..	..	..	..	..	Wulfmær
..	+	..	..	..	..	..	..	..	..	..	..	..	..	..	..	..	Wulfric (Wulfie)

Sagrim, Segrim (Henry I, type XIV). E. W. Rashleigh sale, 1909, lot 460. Probably Shaftesbury.
Wilmær (William I, type II). Lake Price sale, 1880, lot 48.

III	IV	V	VI	VII	VIII	IX	X	XI	XII	XIII	XIV	XV	I	II	III-VI	VII	**SOUTH- AMPTO**
..	..	..	..	+	..	..	..	..	..	..	..	..	..	..	..	..	Dort?
..	..	..	..	..	..	..	..	..	..	..	..	..	..	..	..	..	Godwine
..	..	..	..	..	..	..	..	..	..	..	..	..	..	..	..	..	Sæwine (Sæwi, &c.
..	..	..	..	..	..	..	+	..	..	..	..	..	..	..	..	..	Swetman
..	..	..	..	..	..	..	..	..	..	..	..	..	..	..	..	..	Ulf
..	..	..	..	..	..	..	..	..	..	..	..	..	..	..	..	..	Wulwi

Sperlig (Henry I, type VII). Hon. R. Marsham sale, 1888, lot 247 = S. Rostron sale, 1892, lot 29 = H. Clark sale, 1898, lot 63 = J. Dudman sale, 1913, lot 291 = Catalogue, p. 279, no. 40 (Hastings).

III	IV	V	VI	VII	VIII	IX	X	XI	XII	XIII	XIV	XV	I	II	III-VI	VII	**SOUTH- WAR**
..	..	..	..	..	..	..	..	..	..	..	..	..	+	..	..	..	Ældoulf[1] (Aldolf, &c
..	..	..	..	..	..	..	..	..	..	..	..	..	+	..	..	..	Alfwine[2]
..	..	+	..	..	..	..	Mut(at) 299 }	..	..	+	..	..	..	..	..	..	Algar[3]
..	..	..	..	..	..	..	..	..	..	..	..	..	..	..	..	P.C.B.	Edward[4]
..	..	..	..	..	..	..	..	..	..	..	..	..	..	..	..	..	Godric[5]
..	..	..	P.C.B.	..	..	..	..	..	..	..	..	..	..	..	..	..	Godwine?[6]
..	Hntr	..	+	..	+	..	H.M.R.	Hntr	+	..	+	..	..	..	..	..	Leofwine[7] (Lifwine,&
..	..	..	..	..	..	..	..	..	..	..	..	..	..	..	..	..	Lifword[8]
..	..	..	..	..	..	..	..	..	..	..	..	..	..	..	..	..	Osmund[9]
..	..	..	..	..	..	..	..	..	..	..	..	..	H.M.R.	..	..	..	Sigar[10]
..	..	..	..	..	..	..	..	..	..	..	..	..	..	..	..	..	Sprot[11]
..	..	..	..	..	..	..	..	..	..	..	..	..	B.R. R.C.L.)	..	..	..	Turchil[12]
..	..	..	..	..	..	..	..	..	..	..	..	..	+	..	..	..	Wulfwold[13]
..	..	..	..	..	..	..	..	..	..	..	..	..	..	..	..	..	Wulgar[14]

SVÐEPI, SVÐEP, SVÐEI   6 SVDPE   7 Confessor.

SVÐ; William I, SVÐI, SID, SVÐE; William II, SVÐ, SV;

Henry I, type II, SVÐE; IV, SVD; VI, SVT; VIII, SVT; X,

SOUTHWARK (*continued*).

SVTP; XI. SVTPVR; XII. SVD; XIV. SVDPER, SV
DPE, SVDPV, SVD, SVTW   8 SV·DEP, SV
·DEI, SV·DE, SV·DI, SV·D, SVI   9 *Confessor.* SV·DG,
SV·DIE, SV·DE, SI·DI; *Harold II.* SV·DEP; *William I.* S·DPEI,
S·DEP, SV·DE, SV·DI, SV·D; *William II.* SV·DE, SV·D
10 SVT   11 SV·DEI, SV·DEPR, SV·DEPI   12 SVD,
SV   13 SV, S   14 SV·DI, SV·D

	WILLIAM I								WILLIAM II					
	I	II	III	IV	V	VI	VII	VIII	I	II	III	IV	V	I
STAF-FORD														
Ælfnoth											Stka	J.W.P.	H.W.M.	
Godric (Gdric)													
Godwine	P.C.B.	4											
Wulfnoth		York P.C.B.											

Ælfnoth (William II, type I). Num. Chron., 1901, p. 277.

	I	II	III	IV	V	VI	VII	VIII	I	II	III	IV	V	I
STAM-FORD														
Arcil (Arnil)													7	
Brunstan														
Brunwine (*Bunwine*)	+													
Diric		York												
Elfuwine														
Godelef														
Godric						4								
Heirman				7							Nº 69 (p. 355)			4
Lefsi (Levsi)														
Leftein														
Liofric		York	Mon 30											
Liofwine (*Leofwine*, &c.)	4	MULL +	Rstn 5	4	P.C.B.	L.E.B.								
Mor (Morus)														
Siward														
Wulfword						W.C.W.		4	Stka?	+ ? W.C.W.				

Aschetic (Henry I, type XIII). Num. Chron., 1869, p. 357 = Catalogue, p. 268, no. 100 (Thetford).
Driv (Stephen, type VII).   ,,   ,,   ,,   p. 374, no. 214 (Thetford).
Dunic (William I, type VIII).   ,,   ,, p. 354, and 1880, p. 229. Probably Hastings.
Edlgærd (William II, type II). Num. Chron., 1877, p. 345.
Godric (William II, type V). J. E. Moon sale, 1901, lot 42 = H. W. Morrieson coll. (Stafford).
   ,, (Henry I, type III). Num. Chron., 1901, p. 370 = P. W. P. Carlyon-Britton coll. (Thetford?).
Lifsi (William II, type III). Num. Circ., 1902, p. 5657 = Catalogue, p. 253, no. 224 (Steyning).
Liofwine (William I, type II). Num. Chron., 1904, p. 278.

See also Sudbury.
Ælfric (William II, type IV). E. H. Evans sale, 1894, lot 28.
Ælword (William II, type III). W. Allen sale, 1898, lot 360.
Aldwine (William I, type VIII). Num. Chron., 1904, p. 276.
Algar (William II, type II). Num. Chron., 1904, p. 277.
Godric (Henry I, type XIV). Num. Chron., 1901, p. 299.
Godwine (William II, type I). Archd. Pownall sale, 1887, lot 69.
   „   (William II, type II). Num. Chron., 1904, p. 277.
Grot (William II, type IV). H. Clark sale, 1898, lot 57. Probably Sprot.
Leofwine (William I, type VII). Num. Chron., 1904, p. 277.
Sewine (William II, type II).   „   „   „
Siward (Stephen, type I). C. E. Simpson sale, 1903, lot 5 = Stamford.
Sprot (William II, type II). Num. Chron., 1904, p. 277.

	HENRY I													STEPHEN				
III	IV	V	VI	VII	VIII	IX	X	XI	XII	XIII	XIV	XV	I	II	III-VI	VII		STAF-FO[RD]
..	..	..	..	..	..	..	..	..	..	..	..	..	+	..	..	..		Ælfnoth
..	..	..	..	..	..	..	..	..	..	..	..	..	..	..	..	..		Godric (Gd)
..	..	..	..	..	..	..	..	..	..	..	..	..	..	..	..	..		Godwine
..	..	..	..	..	..	..	..	..	..	..	..	..	..	..	..	..		Wulfnoth

Wulfnod (William II, type I). Num. Chron., 1880, p. 72 = William I, type II (244 misprint for 231).

III	IV	V	VI	VII	VIII	IX	X	XI	XII	XIII	XIV	XV	I	II	III-VI	VII		STAM-FO[RD]
+	..	..	..	..	..	..	..	..	..	..	..	..	..	..	..	..		Arcil (Arnt
..	..	..	..	..	..	..	..	..	..	..	..	..	..	..	..	..		Brunstan
..	..	..	..	..	..	..	..	..	..	..	..	..	..	..	..	..		Brunwine (Bunwine
..	..	..	..	..	..	..	..	..	..	..	..	..	..	..	..	..		Diric
..	..	..	..	..	..	..	..	..	..	..	..	..	..	..	..	..		Elfnwine
..	..	..	..	..	..	..	..	..	..	..	..	..	..	..	..	..		Godelef
..	..	..	..	..	..	..	..	..	W.C.W.	..	+	..	..	..	..	..		Godric
..	..	..	..	..	..	..	..	..	..	..	..	..	..	..	..	..		Heirman
..	..	..	..	..	..	..	..	..	..	..	..	NC'01 p. 370	+	..	..	..		Lefsi (Levs
..	..	..	..	..	..	..	..	..	..	P.C.B.	..	..	..	..	..	..		Leftein
..	..	..	..	..	..	..	..	..	..	..	..	..	..	..	..	..		Liofric
..	..	..	..	..	..	..	..	..	..	..	..	..	..	..	..	..		Liofwine (Leofwine &c.)
..	..	..	..	..	..	..	..	..	+	..	P.C.B. W.C.W.	..	..	..	..	..		Mor (Morus
..	..	..	..	..	..	..	..	..	..	..	..	B.R. H.M.R.	..	..	..	..		Siward
..	..	..	..	..	..	..	..	..	..	..	..	..	..	..	..	..		Wulfword

Liofword (William I, type III). Rev. H. Christmas sale, 1864, lot 215. Perhaps Liofwine?
Ravensart (Stephen, type I). Num. Chron., 1851, p. 188, and 1869, p. 357. See Shrewsbury.
Sudward   „   „   E. W. Rashleigh sale, 1909, lot 566 = B. Roth coll. (Siward; from same dies as other coins).
Thurben (William I, type VIII). Num. Chron., 1869, p. 355 = Steyning.
A halfpenny of this mint in H. Montagu sale, 1896, lot 327, described as Stephen, type II, is of type I = Catalogue, p. 350, no. 103.

	WILLIAM I								WILLIAM II						
	I	II	III	IV	V	VI	VII	VIII	I	II	III	IV	V	I	I
STEY-NING															
Derman (Drman)	..	+	..	..	Bod?	H.W.M.									
Lifsi	..										..	..			
Thurbern *(Thurben, &c.)*	..								..	..			H.W.M.	..	

Drman (William II, type IV). A. W. Hankin sale, 1900, lot 160. H. W. Morrieson coll. (William I, type VI).
Durben (William I, type II). Num. Chron., 1904, p. 278.

	I	II	III	IV	V	VI	VII	VIII	I	II	III	IV	V	I	II
SUDBURY															
Folcwine[1]	..	P.C.B.													
God····[2]	..														
Osbern[3]															
Walfric[4]				..							.F.Mus.; P.C.B.	+?			
····ebert[5]															

[1] *Confessor,* SVPBVG; *William I,* SVD; [2] SVDB; [3] SVTB; [4] *William I.* SV, SVDBI, SVD, SVBR; *William II,* SVDBI, SVD, SVI; *Henry I,* SVB, SVTB; [5] SVB · ·

	I	II	III	IV	V	VI	VII	VIII	I	II	III	IV	V	I	II
TAM-WORTH															
Alfred															
Brunine (Brunic)	..					+									
Coline (Colic, &c.)	..	+													
Hermer	..														
Lefwine	..														

Eldred (Henry I, type II). Num. Chron., 1904, p. 429. See Christchurch.
Elfwine (William I, type VI). C. Plumley sale, 1886, lot 456; W. J. Davis sale, 1901, lot 460. H. W. Morrieson coll. (Taunton).

	I	II	III	IV	V	VI	VII	VIII	I	II	III	IV	V	I	II
TAUNTON															
Elfwine (Elwine)	..	..	..	..	+	M.LE	+	SBm	P.C.R.	..	..				
Alfred									R.C.L.						
Brihtric (Brihtric)	M.LE R.C.L.	..	+	+	..	..	..								
Elfric		..	..												

Elfwine (William II, type II). H. Montag

	HENRY I												STEPHEN				
III	IV	V	VI	VII	VIII	IX	X	XI	XII	XIII	XIV	XV	I	II	III-VI	VII	
..	..	..	..	..	..	..	..	..	..	..	..	..	..	..	..	..	**STEY-NI** Dermon (Drman)
..	..	..	..	..	..	..	..	..	..	..	..	..	..	..	..	..	Lifsi Thurbern (Thurben &c.)

Godric (Henry I, type III). H. Montagu sale, 1896, lot 278 = P. W. P. Carlyon-Britton coll. (mint uncertain).

Osbern (William I, type VIII). Num. Chron., 1904, p. 278.

III	IV	V	VI	VII	VIII	IX	X	XI	XII	XIII	XIV	XV	I	II	III-VI	VII	
..	..	..	..	..	..	..	..	..	..	..	..	..	+	..	..	..	**SUDBU** Folcwine [1]
..	..	..	..	..	..	..	..	..	..	..	..	..	..	..	..	..	God - - -[2]
..	..	..	..	..	..	..	..	..	..	Allen 373	P.C.B.	..	..	..	..	..	Osbern [3]
+	..	+	..	..	..	..	..	..	..	..	..	..	..	..	..	..	Wulfric [4]
..	..	..	..	..	..	..	..	..	..	..	..	..	..	..	..	+	- - - ebert [5]

See also Southwark.

Citwine (William I, type VI). F. W. Longbottom sale, 1892, lot 8. Probably Shaftesbury.

Hathbrand (William II, type V). See Shrewsbury.

III	IV	V	VI	VII	VIII	IX	X	XI	XII	XIII	XIV	XV	I	II	III-VI	VII	
..	..	..	..	..	..	..	..	..	..	..	..	..	..	..	..	+	**TAM-WOR** Alfred
..	..	..	..	..	..	..	..	..	..	..	..	..	..	..	..	..	Brunine (Brunic)
..	..	..	..	..	..	..	..	..	..	..	..	..	..	..	..	..	Coline (Coli &c.)
..	..	..	..	..	..	..	..	..	..	..	+	..	..	..	..	..	Hermer
..	..	..	..	..	..	..	..	..	..	Hatr	..	..	..	..	..	..	Lefwine

Brichmær (Henry I, type XIV). Num. Chron., 1901, p. 429. Probably = P. W. P. Carlyon-Britton coll. (Hermer).

Erun (William I, type II). Num. Chron., 1846, p. 124 = Catalogue, p. 27, no. 142 (Brunine).

III	IV	V	VI	VII	VIII	IX	X	XI	XII	XIII	XIV	XV	I	II	III-VI	VII	
..	..	..	..	..	..	..	..	..	..	..	..	..	..	..	..	..	**TAUNT** Ælfwine (Ælwine)
..	..	..	..	..	..	..	..	..	..	..	..	..	+	..	..	..	Alfred
..	..	..	..	..	..	..	..	..	..	..	..	..	..	..	..	..	Brihtric (Brfhtric)
..	..	..	..	..	..	..	..	..	..	..	P.C.B.	..	..	..	..	..	Elfric

sale, 1896, lot 254 = Catalogue, p. 240, no. 159 (Wallingford).

	WILLIAM I								WILLIAM II							
	I	II	III	IV	V	VI	VII	VIII	I	II	III	IV	V	I	II	II
THET-FORD																
Acus	..	..	..	..	..	..	+	+	..	..	..	..	..	..	..	.
Ælfwine	..	..	..	..	..	+	..	..	..	..	..	..	..	..	..	.
Ailnot	..	..	..	..	..	..	..	..	..	..	..	..	..	..	..	.
Alfward	..	..	..	..	..	..	..	..	..	..	..	..	..	..	..	.
Aschetil	..	..	..	..	..	..	..	..	..	..	..	..	..	..	..	.
Baldewin (Baldwine)	..	..	..	..	..	..	..	..	..	..	..	..	..	..	..	.
Brhtoth	..	..	..	..	..	..	..	..	..	..	..	..	..	..	+	.
Bundi (Bundud, &c.)	..	..	..	..	..	..	..	..	..	+	..	..	+	L.A.L.	P.C.B.	.
Burchart (Burhrd)	..	..	..	..	..	..	..	..	..	..	..	..(app.)	..	..	..	P.C
Cinric (Cenric)	P.C.B.	+	..	+	+	..	..	..	..	..	..	..	..	..	..	.
Driv	..	..	..	..	..	..	..	..	..	..	..	..	..	..	..	.
Esbearn (Osbearn, &c.)	..	+	+	+	+	..	..	..	..	..	..	..	..	..	..	.
Folcerd (Folckred, &c.)	..	..	..	..	+	+	MTD +	..	Mint	+	L.N.J. G.J38.	+	..	..	..	.
Gefrei (Geffrei)	..	..	..	..	..	..	..	..	..	..	..	..	..	..	..	.
God	+ (app.)	+	P.C.B.	..	..	..	..	..	..	..	..	..	..	..	..	.
Goddel (Godlef, &c.)	..	..	..	..	..	..	..	..	..	..	..	..	..	..	..	P.C
Godine	..	..	..	..	..	..	..	..	..	..	+	..	..	..	..	.
Godrard (Giodred)	..	..	..	..	+	Rash 283	P.C.B.	+	P.C.B.	..	..	..	..	..	..	.
Godric	P.C.B.	+	Hmr P.C.B.	+	..	..	..	..	..	..	..	..	..	Rash 466	P.C
Godwine	? B.R.	+	+	..	..	..	..	..	..	..	..	..	..	..	..	.
Neigel (Negelus)	..	..	..	..	..	..	..	..	..	..	..	..	..	..	..	.
Norman	..	..	..	..	..	..	..	..	..	..	..	..	..	..	..	.
Odde (Ode)	..	..	..	..	..	..	..	..	..	..	..	..	..	..	..	.
Osbearn (Otbearn), *see* Esbearn	..	..	..	..	..	..	..	..	..	..	..	..	..	..	..	.
Stan --	..	..	..	..	..	..	..	..	..	..	..	..	..	..	..	.
Thurtan	..	..	..	..	..	..	..	..	..	..	..	..	..	..	..	P.C

Aberrond (Henry I, type VI). Num. Chron., 1901, p. 426. See Hereford.
Alfwine (Henry I, type XIII). G. Marshall sale, 1852, lot 73.
Alrond (Henry I, type XIV). E. W. Rashleigh sale, 1900, lot 467. Perhaps Alfward?
Baldric (William II, type I). Num. Chron., 1901, p. 279.
Bunwad (William II, type II). H. Montagu sale, 1897, lot 87. Probably = Catalogue, p. 239, no. 154 (Bundud).
Beund (Henry I, type II). Rev. H. Christmas sale, 1861, lot 228. Probably Bundi.
Blacsunu. See London.
Bunon (William II, mule I-II). Num. Chron., 1901, p. 279. Probably = Bundud, type II (cf. Catalogue, p. 239, no. 154).
Cinric (William I, type VII). Sotheby, Jan. 25, 1860, lot 110.
Dunic (William II, type II). Num. Chron., 1901, p. 279.

	I	II	III	IV	V	VI	VII	VIII	I	II	III	IV	V	I	II	I
TOTNES																
Dunic	..	..	..	..	..	..	..	..	..	+	..	..	..	Old Sarum	..	
TWYN-HAM, *see* **CHRIST-CHURCH**																

HENRY I												STEPHEN				
IV	V	VI	VII	VIII	IX	X	XI	XII	XIII	XIV	XV	I		III–VI	VII	THET-FO
..	..	..	+	..	..	..	..	..	..	P.C.B.	..	..	..	..	..	Acus
..	..	..	..	..	..	..	..	..	..	..	..	..	..	..	..	Ælfwine
..	..	..	..	..	..	..	..	..	..	+	..	..	..	..	..	Ailnot
..	..	..	..	..	..	..	..	Brin	..	+	..	..	..	..	..	Alfward
..	..	..	..	..	..	+	..	..	+	P.C.B.?	..	..	..	..	..	Aschetil
..	..	..	..	..	..	..	..	..	..	..	..	+	+? F.A.W. lot 73	..	..	Baldewin (Baldwir
..	..	..	..	..	..	..	..	..	..	..	..	..	..	..	..	Brhtoth Bundi (Bundnd &c.)
..	..	..	..	..	..	..	..	..	..	..	..	..	..	..	..	Burchart (Burhrd)
..	..	..	..	..	..	P.C.B.	M'LE Hntr	..	..	..	..	..	..	..	..	Cinric (Cenric)
..	..	..	..	..	..	..	..	..	..	..	..	..	..	..	+	Driv
..	..	..	..	..	..	..	..	..	..	..	..	..	..	..	..	Esbearn (Osbearn &c.)
..	..	..	..	..	..	..	..	..	..	P.C.B.?	..	..	..	..	..	Folcærd (Folchred &c.)
..	..	..	..	..	..	..	..	..	..	..	..	+	..	..	+	Gefrei (Geffrei)
..	..	..	..	..	..	..	..	..	..	..	..	..	..	..	..	God
..	..	..	..	..	..	..	..	..	..	..	..	..	..	..	..	Godelef (Godlef, &)
..	..	..	..	..	..	..	..	..	..	..	..	..	..	..	..	Godine
..	..	..	..	..	..	..	..	..	..	..	..	..	..	..	..	Godræd (Godred)
..	..	..	..	..	..	..	..	..	..	..	..	..	..	..	..	Godric
..	+? (app.)	..	..	..	..	..	..	..	..	+	..	..	..	..	..	Godwine
..	Hntr?	..	..	..	..	..	..	..	..	..	..	..	..	..	..	Neigel (Negelus)
..	..	..	..	..	..	..	..	..	P.C.B.	..	..	..	..	..	..	Norman
..	..	..	..	..	..	..	..	..	..	..	+ P.C.B.)	+	..	..	..	Odde (Ode)
..	..	..	..	..	..	..	..	..	..	..	..	..	..	..	..	Osbearn (Otbearn) see Esbea
..	..	..	..	+	..	..	..	..	..	..	..	..	..	..	..	Stan - - -
..	..	..	..	..	..	..	..	..	..	..	..	..	..	..	..	Thurtan (= Tursta

Elfwi (William I, type II). C. E. Simpson sale, 1903, lot 1. Perhaps Oxford?
Engelram (Henry I, type XII). Num. Chron., 1901, p. 428 = Catalogue, Appendix, p. 407, no. 85 A (Winchester).
Folerd (William I, type IV). Num. Chron., 1904, p. 279. Perhaps William I, type VI?
Gipat (William II, type II). C. McEwen sale, 1854, lot 102. Probably Huntingdon, Siwat.
Godræd (William II, type I). Num. Chron., 1904, p. 280.
Godwine (Henry I, type II). Num. Chron., 1901, p. 428 = Catalogue, Appendix, p. 406, no. 23 A (Winchester).
Halun (Stephen, type II). Sotheby, Jan. 25, 1860, lot 127, and E. Burns sale, 1869, lot 49.
Lifnoth (Henry I, type III). Num. Chron., 1901, p. 429 = P. W. P. Carlyon-Britton coll. (Chester).
Necoll (William II, type I). H. Montagu sale, 1897, lot 83 = B. Roth coll. (Neigel).
Swirtine (William I, type VII). Num. Chron., 1904, p. 280.

IV	V	VI	VII	VIII	IX	X	XI	XII	XIII	XIV	XV	I	II	III–VI	VII	
..	..	..	..	..	..	..	..	..	..	..	..	..	..	..	..	**TOTNES** Dunic
																TWYN-HAM, so CHRIST- CHURCH

	WILLIAM I								WILLIAM II						
	I	II	III	IV	V	VI	VII	VIII	I	II	III	IV	V	I	II
WALLING-FORD															
Ægelwine (Æglwine)	..	..	..			..	..	+	..	..	..	..	..	..	..
Ælfwine									+	+	..	..	..	..	..
Brand	+	+	+	+	+				..	..	..	..	..	+	..
Brihtic (= Brihtric?)	..	..	..			..	..		..	..	..	..	..	..	..
Brihtmær (Brihtmar)	+	+	+	Mntgu ,919		..	..		..	+	P.C.B.	..	..	..	..
Colbern												+			
Edword	..	..	..			..	..		..	..	..	..	..	..	..
Godwine	..	..	..			..	..		..	..	..	..	..	..	..
Osulf	..	..	..			..	..		..	..	..	..	..	..	..
Rodberd	..	..	..			..	..		..	..	..	..	..	..	..
Sweartine (Swertic, &c.)	+ (app.)	+	+	+	+	+	+		..	..	..	..	..	..	..
Swetlind	+	..				..	..		..	..	..	..	..	..	..
Wideman	..	..				..	..		..	..	..	..	..	..	..

Anderbode (William I, type I). Col. Durrant sale, 1847, lot 402. Probably Winchester.
Leofwold (William I, type IV). Num. Chron., 1904, p. 280. Probably Winchester.

	I	II	III	IV	V	VI	VII	VIII	I	II	III	IV	V	I	II
WARE-HAM															
Ægelric[1] (Æglric)	+	..	..	P.C.B.		+	P.C.B.	+	..	..	..	..	..	..	..
Bern[2] (Brarn)	..	..	..		Radl. H.W.M.	..	H.S		..	..	..	..	..	..	..
Derline[3] (Derlig)	..	..	..			..	..		..	..	..	..	..	..	..
Godwine[4]	..	..	..		Hntr P.C.B. ,714	..	..		..	..	..	..	..	..	..
Sideloc[5] (Sidloc)	..	..	..			..	+		..	..	T.B.	..	..	..	..
Sideman[6]	+	..	+	+		..	..		..	..	..	..	..	..	..
Turchil[7]	..	..	..			..	..		..	..	..	..	..	..	..

[1] Type I, **PERHA**; IV. **PERHI**; VI. **PERHEI, PERHE**; VII. **PERH**; VIII. **PEREI, PERE, PER, PRE**   [2] *Confessor.* **PERHAM**; *William I,* type V. **PERHEI, PERA**; VIII. **PERHM**   [3] Type V. **PARbA**; VI. **PARA**; XIV. **PARbA**   [4] Type V, **PER**; VI. **PERH**; VIII. **PERE, PERI**   [5] *William I,* **PERHE, PERE**; *William II.* **PERH**   [6] *Confessor.* **PERHAM, PERHA**

	I	II	III	IV	V	VI	VII	VIII	I	II	III	IV	V	I	II
WAR-WICK															
Ælric[1]	..	..	..	..	..	..	..	+	..	..	..	..	..	..	..
Edred[2] (Edredus)	..	..	..	..	..	..	..	..	..	..	..	..	..	..	..
Essuwi[3]	..	..	..	..	..	..	..	..	..	..	..	..	..	..	..
Everard[4]	..	..	..	..	..	..	..	..	..	..	..	..	..	..	..
Forna[5]	..	..	..	..	..	..	..	..	..	..	..	..	..	..	..
Godwine[6]	..	..	..	..	..	..	..	..	..	..	..	..	..	..	..
Goldinc[7]	..	..	..	..	..	..	..	..	+	+	P.C.B.	..	..	..	..
Lifric[8] (Lefric, &c.)	..	..	..	..	..	..	..	+	..	..	..	..	..	..	..

1-8 For notes see pp. ccxlvi, ccxlvii.

	HENRY I												STEPHEN				
IV	V	VI	VII	VIII	IX	X	XI	XII	XIII	XIV	XV	I	II	III–VI	VII		**WALLIN FO.**
..	..	..	..	..	..	..	..	..	..	..	..	..	..	..	..		Ægelwine (Æglwine)
..	..	..	..	..	..	..	..	..	..	..	..	..	..	..	..		Ælfwine
..	..	..	..	..	..	..	..	..	..	..	..	..	..	..	..		Brand
..	..	..	..	..	..	..	..	..	..	..	..	..	..	..	..		Brihtic
..	..	..	..	..	..	..	..	..	..	..	..	..	..	..	..		Brihtmær (Brihtmar)
..	..	..	..	..	..	..	..	..	..	..	..	..	..	..	..		Colbern
..	*NC '92, p. 85*	..	..	..	..	..	..	..	..	..	..	..	..	..	..		Edword
..		..	..	..	..	..	..	..	..	P.C.B.?	..	..	..	..	..		Godwine
..	..	..	..	..	..	..	..	+	+	..	..	..	..	..	..		Osulf
..	..	..	..	..	..	..	..	..	..	+	..	..	..	..	..		Rodberd
..	..	..	..	..	..	..	..	..	..	..	..	..	..	..	..		Sweartline (Swertic, &)
..	..	..	..	..	..	..	..	..	..	..	..	..	..	..	..		Swetlind
..	..	..	..	..	..	..	..	..	..	..	..	..	..	..	..		Wideman

Wulfwine (William I, type VII). Rev. H. Christmas sale, 1864, lot 207.

IV	V	VI	VII	VIII	IX	X	XI	XII	XIII	XIV	XV	I	II	III–VI	VII		**WARE-H.**
..	..	..	..	..	..	..	..	..	..	..	..	..	..	..	..		Ægelric[1] (Æglric)
..	..	..	..	..	..	..	..	..	..	..	..	..	..	..	..		Bern[2] (Brun...
..	*NC '92, p. 85*	+	..	..	..	..	..	..	..	P.C.B.	..	..	..	..	..		Derline[3] (Derlig)
..	..	..	..	..	..	..	..	..	..	..	..	..	..	..	..		Godwine[4]
..	..	..	..	..	..	..	..	..	..	..	..	..	..	..	..		Sideloc[5] (Sidloc)
..	..	..	..	..	..	..	..	..	..	..	..	..	..	..	..		Sideman[6]
..	..	..	..	..	..	..	..	..	..	+? (app.) P.C.B.?	..	..	..	..	..		Turchil[7]

PERI, PER, PARN; *Harold,* PERH; *William I,* PERH, PE RHA 7 PARL, PIRE

See also Warwick.

Godwine (William I, type VII). Brit. Num. Journ., vol. v, p. 112.
   (William II, types III and V). Num. Chron., 1904, p. 281.
Leofwold (William I, type IV). Col. Durrant sale, 1847, lot 135. Probably Winchester.
Lifwine (William I, type III). Brit. Num. Journ., vol. v, p. 111.
Osmær (Henry I, type III). C. Warne sale, 1889, lot 157.
Seoif-man (William I, type IV). L. A. Lawrence sale, 1903, lot 52 = P. W. P. Carlyon-Britton sale, 1913, lot 702 (a double-struck coin, possibly Sideman?).

IV	V	VI	VII	VIII	IX	X	XI	XII	XIII	XIV	XV	I	II	III–VI	VII		**WAR-WIC**
..	..	..	..	..	..	..	..	..	..	..	..	..	..	..	..		Ælric[1]
..	..	..	..	..	..	..	..	..	..	+	..	+	..	..	..		Edred[2] (Edredus)
..	..	..	..	..	..	..	..	..	..	P.C.B.	..	..	..	..	..		Essuwi[3]
..	..	..	..	..	..	..	..	..	..	..	..	+ P.C.B.	..	..	..		Everard[4]
..	..	..	..	..	..	..	..	..	..	..	..	..	..	..	..		Forna[5]
..	..	..	..	..	..	..	..	..	P.C.B.	+	..	..	..	..	..		Godwine[6]
..	..	..	..	..	..	..	..	..	..	..	..	Nott. P.C.B.	..	..	..		Goldinc[7]
..	..	..	..	..	..	..	..	..	..	..	..	..	..	..	..		Lifric[8] (Lefric, &c)

	WILLIAM I								WILLIAM II							
	I	II	III	IV	V	VI	VII	VIII	I	II	III	IV	V	I	II	I.
WAR-WICK (cont.)																
Lufine [9] (Lufic, &c.)	..	..	..	P.C.B.	..	..	..	+	..	..	..	..	..	+	..	.
Sperhafuc [10] (Sperhavoc)	..	..	..	..	..	..	..	..	..	+	..	..	..	+	..	.
Thidred [11] (Thidred)	..	..	..	..	..	..	..	..	+	+	..	..	..	..	..	.
Thurcil [12] (Threil)	P.C.B.	..	..	..	..	+	..	..	+	..	..	..	..	..	..	.

[1] PERPIE [2] PARP, PARPI [3] WAR
[4] PAR [5] PARPI [6] Type XIII, PARPIC; XIV, PARPI
[7] PERP, PERI [8] Confessor, PER'; William I, PERPIE, PERPI,
PEREP; William II, PRPICE; Stephen, WAR [9] Confessor, PÆ
RIN; Harold II, PEARP; William I, type IV, PÆRI; VIII, PERPIC,
PERIC, PERI [10] William II, PRP; Henry I, type I, PR: Mule V×VI.

	I	II	III	IV	V	VI	VII	VIII	I	II	III	IV	V	I		II
WAT-CHET																
Fo --- ?	..	..	..	..	..	..	..	..	..	..	..	..	..	..		
H --- ?	..	..	..	..	..	..	..	..	..	..	..	..	..	..		
Sigolf (Siwolf, &c.)	..	..	..	..	..	+	..	+	..	..	+	..	..	..		
WILTON																
Ægelward (Ailward)	..	..	..	..	..	..	..	..	..	..	..	..	..	..		H.X
Ælfwine	..	..	..	..	+	..	+	+	+	+	..	..	..	..		
Brunig	..	..	..	..	..	..	..	..	..	..	..	..	..	..		
Falche (Falci)	..	..	..	..	..	..	..	..	..	..	..	..	..	..		
Godric	..	..	P.C.B.	+	..	..	..	..	..	..	..	..	..	..		
Owi	+	P.C.B.	..	P.C.B.	..	..	..	..	..	..	..	..	..	..		
Ricard	..	..	..	..	..	..	..	..	..	..	..	..	..	..		
Sefara (Sefar, &c.)	..	+	+	P.C.B.	..	..	..	+	..	+	..	..	..	..		
Sewine (Sæwi)	(S. ιπι ('45,46	H.W.M.	(Witte 116	+	+	..	Sthm	+	P.C.B.	+	+	..	..	..		
Tomas	..	..	..	..	..	..	..	..	..	..	..	..	..	..		
Turchil	..	..	..	..	..	..	..	..	..	..	..	..	..	..		
Willem	..	..	..	..	..	..	..	..	..	..	..	..	..	..		

Brihtmær (William I, type III). M. H. Bobart sale, 1894, lot 5. Probably Wallingford.
Dill[ma]n (Stephen, type VII). Sotheby, Dec. 20, 1911, lot 230. Probably Willem.
Goldwine (William I, type V). Removed to Winchcombe; see Errata.

	I	II	III	IV	V	VI	VII	VIII	I	II	III	IV	V	I	II	II
WINCH-COMBE																
Goldwine [1]	..	..	..	..	+	..	..	+	..	..	..	..	..	..	..	..

[1] Confessor, PINCELE, PINCEL, PIN, PI; Harold II, PINCEL.

		HENRY I										STEPHEN				
VI	VII	VIII	IX	X	XI	XII	XIII	XIV	XV		I	II	III–VI	VII		WAR-W (cont
..	..	..	..	..	..	..	..	..	..		..	..	..	..		Lufinc[9] (Lufic, &
	..	..	..	+	..	..	..	..	..		..	..	..	..		Sperhafuc (Sperha
																Thidræd[1] (Thidred
..	..	..	..	..	..	..	..	..	..		..	..	..	..		
..	..	..	..	..	..	..	..	..	..		..	..	..	..		Thurcil[12] (Threil)

; type X, **PA**   [11] **PRPILE, PRIP**   [12] Type I, **PIERI**
PERIL; VIII, **PERPIL, PERPI**

Tareham.
Villiam I, type IV). W. A. Cotton sale, 1889, lot 53. Probably York.
Villiam I, type VIII). Num. Chron., 1904, p. 281.
William I, type VIII). W. A. Cotton sale, 1889, lot 63. Probably Winchester.

VI	VII	VIII	IX	X	XI	XII	XIII	XIV	XV		I	II	III–VI	VII		WAT-CH
..	..	..	..	..	..	..	..	..		+	..	..			Fo---?	
..	..	..	..	..	..	..	..	..		..	..	..	P.C.B.		H---?	
..	..	..	..	..	..	..	..		..	..	..	..			Sigolf (Si &c.)	
															WILT Ægelward (Ailward	
..	..	..	..	..	..	..	..	+	..	..	..	..			Ælfwine	
..	..	..	..	..	..	..	..	..		..	..	..			Brunig	
..	..	..	..	..	..	..	..	..		+	..	..			Falche (Fa	
..	..	..	..	..	..	..	..	..		..	..	..			Godric	
..	..	..	..	..	..	..	..	..		..	..	..			Owi	
..	..	..	..	..	..	..	+	..		..	..	..			Ricard	
..	..	..	..	..	..	..	..	..		..	..	..			Sefara (Se &c.)	
..	..	..	..	..	..	..	..	..		..	..	..			Sewine (S	
..	..	..	..	..	..	..	..	..		P.C.B. S.M.S.	..	..			Tomas	
..	..	..	..	..	..	..	..	..		+	..	..			Turchil	
..	..	..	..	..	..	..	..	..		..	..	..	+		*Willem*	

(William I, type IV). H. Montagu sale, 1896, lot 208. Probably Winchester.
Villiam I, type VII). Num. Chron., 1904, p. 282. Probably Winchester.

VI	VII	VIII	IX	X	XI	XII	XIII	XIV	XV		I	II	III–VI	VII		WINC COM
..	..	..	..	..	..	..	..	..	..		..	..	..	..		Goldwine

V, **PILL, PINL, PIN, PIL**; VIII, **PINLL, PINL**

	WILLIAM I								WILLIAM II						
	I	II	III	IV	V	VI	VII	VIII	I	II	III	IV	V	I	I
WIN-CHESTER															
Ælfwine (Ailwine, &c.)	+	(L.A.L. 43)	..	..	..	..	..	..	..	..	..	..	..	..	
Æstan (Æstan, &c.)	..	..	..	..	..	+	+	MULE +	+	(B.N.J. vi. 170)	Mint	..	..	..	
Ailward	..	..	..	..	..	..	..	..	..	..	..	..	..	..	
Aldwine	..	..	..	..	..	..	..	..	..	..	Hntr	..	..	..	
Alfric	..	..	..	..	..	..	..	..	..	..	..	..	..	..	
Alwold	..	..	..	..	..	..	..	..	..	..	..	..	..	..	
Anderbode (Andrbod, &c.)	+	(H.H. Allan 37)	+ (app.)	+	+	+	..	..	..	..	..	..	..	..	
Brunic	..	..	..	..	..	..	+	+	..	..	..	..	..	..	
Ckippig, see Kippig															
Edwine	..	..	..	..	..	..	..	..	+	P.C.B.?	+	..	..	..	
Engelram (Hengelram)	..	..	..	..	..	..	..	..	..	..	..	..	..	..	
Gefrei	..	..	..	..	..	..	..	..	..	..	..	..	..	..	
Godnoth	..	+	+	..	..	..	..	..	..	..	..	..	..	..	
Godwine (Gowine, &c.)	..	..	B.N.J. vi. 167	+	+	+	..	+	+	MULE H.M.R. +	P.C.B.	+	S.M.S.	R.C.L.	
Goldine	..	..	+	..	..	..	..	..	..	..	..	..	..	..	
Hengelram, see Engelram															
Hue	..	..	..	..	..	..	..	..	..	..	..	..	..	..	
Kippig (Ckippig)	..	..	..	..	..	..	..	..	..	..	..	..	..	(S.cii'09 114)	
Lefwine	..	..	..	..	..	..	..	..	..	..	..	..	..	..	
Leofwold (Lifwold, &c.)	+	+	+	+	(H.L.F. P.C.B.) +	+	MULE +	+	+	..	..	..	..	..	
Lifine (Livine, &c.)	+	+	+	+	+	+	+	+	..	..	..	+	..	..	
Rogier (Rogir, &c.)	..	..	..	..	..	..	..	..	..	..	..	..	..	..	
Saiet (Saied)	..	..	..	..	..	..	..	..	..	..	..	..	..	..	
Sawulf	..	..	..	..	..	..	..	..	..	..	..	..	..	..	
Siword (Siward, &c.)	..	W.S.O.	+	+	+	+	+	..	..	..	..	..	..	..	
Spræcline (Spraeline)	..	..	..	..	..	..	+	Sthm	Bodl.?	..	..	..	..		
Stigant	..	..	..	..	..	..	..	..	..	..	..	..	..	..	
[T]ovi?	..	..	..	..	..	..	..	..	..	..	..	..	..	..	
Wimund	..	..	..	..	..	..	+	(N.C.'77 p.346?)	..	..	P.C.B.	..	P.C.B.		

Ægelwine (William I, type VIII). C. Simpson sale, 1903, lot 2. Perhaps Wallingford?

Ælfgærd (William I, type VIII). Num. Chron., 1877, p. 346, and J. D. Cuff sale, 1854, lot 709; probably Worcester.

    „ (William II, type II). Num. Chron., 1877, p. 346 = Catalogue, p. 242, nos. 170, 171 (Worcester).

Ælfwine (William II, type III). W. Allen sale, 1898, lot 364.

Ainulf (Henry I, type VII). Num. Chron., 1901, p. 465.

Brihtmær (William I, type I). Col. Tobin Bush sale, 1902, lot 7. Probably Wallingford.

Colbern (William II, type II). H. Montagu sale, 1896, lot 256 = B. Roth coll. (Wallingford).

Colbrac   „   „   Num. Chron., 1877, p. 346; probably Bristol. Colblac.

Edric (William II, type I).   „   „   „   „ = Catalogue, p. 219, no. 29 (London).

Edwine (William I, type I). Num. Chron., 1904, p. 283.

    „ (William II, type IV). Num. Chron., 1904, p. 283 = Roberts MS. Catalogue reading of B. M. Catalogue, p. 259, no. 254 (Godwine).

Godard (William I, type V). Num. Chron., 1904, p. 283; presumably a mistake for William II, type III, see below.

    „ (William II, type III). Various sale catalogues, &c. False, cf. Brit. Num. Journ., vol. iii. p. 283, no. 37.

Godricus (Henry I, type XIV). J. G. Murdoch sale, 1903, lot 232; probably London.

Godwine (Henry I, type III). Num. Chron., 1901, p. 467 = Catalogue, Appendix, p. 406, no. 30 A (Wallingford).

				HENRY I										STEPHEN			WIN-CHEST...
III	IV	V	VI	VII	VIII	IX	X	XI	XII	XIII	XIV	XV	I	II	III-VI	VII	
..	..	..	..	..	..	L.A.L.	..	+? (app.)	..	..	..	..	..	..	..	..	Ælfwine (Ailwine &c.)
..	..	..	..	..	..	..	..	..	..	..	..	..	..	..	..	..	Æstan (Ægstan &c.)
..	..	..	..	..	..	..	..	..	..	..	..	Rash 470	..	..	..	..	Ailward
..	..	..	..	..	..	..	..	..	..	..	..	..	..	..	..	..	Aldwine
..	..	..	..	..	..	..	..	..	..	..	NC'01 p. 465	+	..	..	..	..	Alfric
..	..	..	..	..	..	..	..	..	..	..	..	+	+	..	..	..	Alwold
..	..	..	..	..	..	..	..	..	..	..	..	..	..	..	..	..	Anderbod (Andrbo &c.)
..	..	..	..	..	..	..	..	..	..	..	..	..	..	..	..	..	Brunie
..	..	..	..	..	..	..	..	..	..	..	..	..	..	..	..	..	Ckippig, see Kippig
..	..	..	..	..	..	..	..	..	..	..	..	..	..	..	..	..	Edwine
..	..	..	..	..	..	..	P.C.B.	..	+ (app.)	B.R.	+? P.C.B.	..	..	..	..	..	Engelram (Hengel...)
..	..	..	..	..	..	..	..	..	..	..	..	..	..	+	..	..	Gefrei
..	..	..	..	..	..	..	..	..	..	..	..	..	..	..	..	..	Godnoth
..	Hntr	P.C.B.	..	P.C.B.	..	..	..	..	..	..	+	..	..	..	..	..	Godwine (Gowine &c.)
..	..	..	..	..	..	..	..	..	..	..	..	..	..	..	..	..	Goldine
..	..	..	..	..	..	..	..	..	..	..	..	..	..	..	..	..	Hengelram see Engelra.
..	..	..	..	..	..	..	..	..	..	..	..	..	..	..	..	+	Hue
..	..	..	..	..	..	..	..	..	..	..	+	..	+	..	..	..	Kippig (Ckippig...)
..	..	..	..	..	..	..	P.C.B.	..	..	Bscm 83	+	..	..	..	..	..	Lefwine
..	..	..	..	..	..	..	..	..	..	..	..	..	..	..	..	..	Leofwold (Lifwold &c.)
..	..	..	..	..	..	..	..	..	..	..	..	..	..	..	..	..	Lifine (Li... &c.)
..	..	..	..	..	..	..	..	..	..	..	..	..	+	..	..	..	Rogier (R... &c.)
..	..	..	..	+ (app.)	..	NC'01 p. 469	..	..	..	..	+	+	+	..	..	..	Saiet (Saie...)
..	..	..	..	..	..	..	..	..	P.C.B.	P.C.B.?	..	..	..	..	..	..	Sawulf
..	..	..	..	..	..	..	..	..	..	..	..	..	..	..	+	..	Siword (Siward,...)
..	..	..	..	..	..	..	..	..	..	..	..	..	..	+	..	..	Spræcline (Spracli...)
..	..	..	..	..	..	..	..	..	..	..	+	..	..	..	..	..	Stigant
..	..	..	..	..	..	..	..	..	..	..	..	+	..	..	..	..	[T]ovi ?
..	..	+? (app.)	..	..	+	..	..	..	..	..	..	..	..	..	..	..	Winmund

Harold (Stephen, type I). J. K. Ford sale, 1884, lot 258; perhaps Alwold?

Hilpig „ „ E. W. Rashleigh sale, 1909, lot 578 = Catalogue, p. 353, no. 120 (Kippig).

Leofwine (William I, type VIII). Num. Chron., 1904, p. 284.

Lifword (William I, mule VII × VIII). G. Wakeford sale, 1879, lot 6 = P. W. P. Carlyon-Britton sale, 1913, lot 721 (Lefwold).

Lufric (William I, type I). Sotheby, Jan. 25, 1860, lot 105; probably Lufine.

Siword (William I, mule VII × VIII). Various sale catalogues, &c. False, cf. Brit. Num. Journ., vol. iii, p. 283, no. 31.

Spracline (William I, type IV). Num. Chron., 1904, p. 284.

Swartline (William I, type I). Num. Chron., 1904, p. 284; probably Wallingford.

Sweatline (William I, type IV). Rev. E. J. Shepherd sale, 1885, lot 117 = H. Montagu sale, 1896, lot 211 = J. G. Murdoch sale, 1903, lot 186; probably Wallingford.

Swirtine (William I, type VI). Sotheby, June 4, 1855, lot 26, and S. Rostron sale, 1892, lot 13; probably Wallingford.

Thurstan (William II, type I). F. G. Lawrence sale, 1900, lot 32; probably Lincoln.

Willem (Stephen, type VII). Num. Chron., 1905, p. 355 = Catalogue, p. 375, nos. 217-9 (Wilton).

Wimunt (Henry I, type XV). Num. Chron., 1901, p. 471 = Catalogue, p. 332, no. 296 (Kippig).

Wulfwine (William II, type II). Num. Chron., 1904, p. 284.

Wulword (William I, type V). „ „ „ „

	WILLIAM I								WILLIAM II						
	I	II	III	IV	V	VI	VII	VIII	I	II	III	IV	V	I	II
WORCESTER															
Ælfgærd (Ælfgæt, &c.)	..	..	..	+	..	+	+	+	..	+	..	+	+	..	..
Api or Awi?	..	..	..	..	..	..	..	..	..	..	..	..	..	..	..
Baldric	..	..	..	H.L.F.	..	..	..	+	Mint	P.C.B.	P.C.B.	..	..	..	..
Eastmær (Estmær, &c.)	..	+	+	..	..	(+ app.)	..	+	+	+	..	..	..	..	..
Edwine	..	Cpnhn	..	..	..	..	..	..	..	..	..	..	..	..	..
Garulf	..	+	..	..	L.E.B.	..	..	..	..	..	..	..	..	..	..
Godric	..	..	..	..	..	..	..	..	..	..	..	..	..	..	..
Heathewulf	..	..	..	Hntr	..	..	..	..	..	..	..	..	..	..	..
Liofric	+	..	..	..	..	..	..	..	..	..	..	..	..	..	..
Refwine	..	+	..	..	..	..	..	..	..	..	..	..	..	..	..
Sewine	..	..	..	..	..	..	..	+	..	(NC 77 p.346?)	..	..	..	..	..
Wigine	P.C.B.	..	..	..	..	..	..	..	..	..	..	..	..	..	..
Wulfric	..	..	..	..	..	..	..	..	..	..	..	..	..	..	..

Baldric (William I, type VI). Num. Chron., 1904, p. 285.
Brihtric (William I, type IV). Sotheby, Jan. 25, 1890, lot 107.

	I	II	III	IV	V	VI	VII	VIII	I	II	III	IV	V	I	II
YORK															
Aleif	..	+	..	+	..	..	..	I +	+	+	..	..	..	..	..
Althur (= Althurolf?)	..	..	..	..	York	..	..	..	..	..	..	..	..	..	..
Althurolf	..	..	..	..	+	..	..	..	..	..	..	..	..	..	..
Arcetel	..	+	..	..	..	..	..	..	..	..	..	..	..	..	..
Arthult, see Harthoulf	..	..	..	..	..	..	..	..	..	..	..	..	..	..	..
Autgrim, see Onthgrim	..	..	..	..	..	..	..	..	..	..	..	..	..	..	..
Autholf, see Outholf	..	..	..	..	..	..	..	..	..	..	..	..	..	..	..
Coc, Toc	..	..	..	..	..	..	..	..	..	..	..	..	..	..	..
Forn	..	..	..	..	..	..	..	..	..	..	..	..	..	..	..
Harthoulf (Arthulf, &c.)	York	+	..	+	York	+	..	..	..	..	..	..	..	..	..
Læsing (Leigsine, &c.)	..	+	..	..	..	..	+	..	..	..	P.C.B.	+	..	..	..
Martin	..	..	..	..	..	..	..	..	..	..	..	..	..	..	..
Outhbeorn (Uuthbern, &c.)	..	+	..	(L.E.B. P.C.B.)	Hntr	..	..	+	..	..	..	P.C.B.	..	..	..
Outhgrim (Autgrim, &c.)	+	+	Stkm	+	..	..	..	..	..	..	..	..	..	..	..
Outholf (Autholf)	+	+	..	..	..	..	..	..	..	..	..	..	..	..	..
Ra---?	..	..	..	..	..	..	..	..	..	..	..	..	..	..	..
Roscetel	..	+	..	..	..	..	..	..	..	..	..	..	..	..	..
Sweartcol	..	+	..	..	..	..	..	..	..	..	..	..	..	..	..
Thorr (Thour)	..	+	..	..	..	+	..	+	..	..	..	..	..	..	..
Turstan	..	..	..	..	..	..	..	..	..	..	..	..	..	..	..
Ulf	..	..	..	..	..	..	..	..	..	..	..	..	..	..	..
Ulfcetel (Ulfketel)	York	+	..	..	..	..	..	..	..	..	..	..	..	..	..
Uncertain	..	..	..	..	..	..	..	..	..	..	..	..	..	..	..

Aleif (William I, type I). Num. Chron., 1904, p. 285.
Autholf (William I, type IV). Num. Chron., 1904, p. 286.
Brihtnoth, Brihtred (Henry I, type I). Sotheby, April 16, 1874, lot 42, and T. W. U. Robinson sale, 1891, lot 49. Probably = S. M. Spink coll. (Lewes, Brihtmr).
Brirnrth (Henry I, type III). Num. Chron., 1901, p. 489 = P. W.;P. Carlyon-Britton coll. (Thetford, Burbrd).
Godrewi (William II, type III). Num. Chron., 1904, p. 286 = Roberts MS. Catalogue reading, probably of B. M. Catalogue, p. 253, no. 225 (Thetford, Godric).

		HENRY I										STEPHEN				
IV	V	VI	VII	VIII	IX	X	XI	XII	XIII	XIV	XV	I	II	III-VI	VII	**WORCES-TER**
..	..	..	..	..	..	..	..	..	..	..	..	..	..	..	..	Ælfgærd (Ælfgæt, &c.)
..	..	..	..	..	..	..	..	..	..	+	..	..	..	..	..	Api or Awi?
..	..	..	..	..	..	..	..	..	..	..	..	..	..	..	..	Baldric
																Eastmær
..	..	..	..	..	..	..	..	..	..	..	..	..	..	..	..	(Estmær, &c.)
..	..	..	..	..	..	..	..	..	..	..	..	..	..	..	..	Edwine
..	..	..	..	..	..	..	..	..	..	..	..	..	..	..	..	Garulf
..	..	..	..	..	..	..	..	+	..	..	..	B.R.?	..	..	..	Godric
..	..	..	..	..	..	..	..	..	..	..	..	..	..	..	..	Heathewulf
..	..	..	..	..	..	..	..	..	..	..	..	..	..	..	..	Liofric
..	..	..	..	..	..	..	..	..	..	..	..	..	..	..	..	Refwine
..	..	..	..	..	..	..	..	..	..	..	..	..	..	..	..	Sewine
..	..	..	..	..	..	..	..	..	..	..	..	..	..	..	..	Wigine
..	..	..	..	..	..	..	+	..	..	..	NC'01, p. 478	..	+	..	..	*Wulfric*

Godwine (William II, type II). Num. Chron., 1877, p. 346 = Catalogue, p. 211, no. 169 (Winchester).
Leofwine ,, ,, ,, Archd. Pownall sale, 1887, lot 65.

IV	V	VI	VII	VIII	IX	X	XI	XII	XIII	XIV	XV	I	II	III-VI	VII	**YORK**
..	..	..	..	..	..	..	..	..	..	..	..	..	..	..	..	Aleif
..	..	..	..	..	..	..	..	..	..	..	..	..	..	..	..	Althur (= Althurolf?)
..	..	..	..	..	..	..	..	..	..	..	..	..	..	..	..	Althurolf
..	..	..	..	..	..	..	..	..	..	..	..	..	..	..	..	Arcetel
..	..	..	..	..	..	..	..	..	..	..	..	..	..	..	..	Arthulf, see Harthoulf
..	..	..	..	..	..	..	..	..	..	..	..	..	..	..	..	Autgrim, see Outhgrim
..	..	..	..	..	..	..	..	..	..	..	..	..	..	..	..	Autholf, see Outholf
..	..	..	..	..	..	..	..	..	..	+	..	..	..	..	..	Coc, Toc
..	..	..	..	..	..	..	..	..	P.C.B.	..	..	..	..	..	..	Forn
..	..	..	..	..	..	..	..	..	..	..	..	..	..	..	..	Harthoulf (Arthulf, &c.)
..	..	..	..	..	..	..	..	..	..	+	..	..	..	..	..	Læsing (Leigsine, &c.)
..	..	..	..	..	..	..	..	..	..	..	..	+	..	..	..	Martin
..	..	..	..	..	..	..	..	..	..	..	..	..	..	..	..	Outhbeorn (Uwthbern, &c.)
..	..	..	..	..	..	..	..	..	..	..	..	B.R.	..	..	..	Outhgrim (Autgrim, &c.)
..	..	..	..	..	..	..	..	..	..	..	..	..	..	..	..	Outholf (Autholf)
..	..	..	B.R.	..	..	..	..	..	..	..	..	..	..	..	..	Ra - - -?
..	..	..	..	..	..	..	..	..	..	..	..	..	..	..	..	Roscetel
..	..	..	..	..	..	..	..	..	..	..	..	..	..	..	..	Sweartcol
..	..	..	..	..	..	..	..	..	..	..	P.C.B.	+	..	..	..	Thorr (Thour)
..	..	..	..	..	..	..	..	..	..	T.B.?	Mint?	+	..	..	..	Turstan
..	..	..	..	..	..	..	..	..	..	..	..	..	..	..	..	Ulf
..	..	..	..	..	..	..	..	..	..	..	..	..	..	..	..	Ulfcetel (Ulfketel)
..	..	..	..	..	..	..	H.M.R.	..	..	..	..	..	+	..	+	Uncertain

Godwine (William I, type II). J. D. Cuff sale, 1854, lot 663; probably = J. B. Bergne sale, 1873, lot 291 (Stafford).
Leofwine (William I, type III). Archaeologia, vol. iv, p. 289.
Lifwine (William II, type II). Num. Chron., 1877, p. 346, probably Dover. J. D. Cuff sale, 1854, lot 723 = Catalogue, p. 229, no. 86 (Dover). W. C. Hazlitt sale, 1909, lot 1048 = R. C. Lockett coll. (Dover).
Outhbeorn (William I, type I). Num. Chron., 1904, p. 286.
Sibern (Stephen, type I). Num. Chron., 1850, p. 161; probably Hereford.

TABLE

FOR

CONVERTING ENGLISH INCHES INTO MILLIMETRES

AND THE

MEASURES OF MIONNET'S SCALE

ENGLISH INCHES	MIONNET'S SCALE	FRENCH MILLIMETRES
4·		100
		95
3·5		90
		85
3·	19	80
	18	75
2·5	17	70
	16	65
	15	60
2·	14	55
	13	50
	12	45
1·5	11	40
	10	35
	9	
	8	30
1·	7	25
·9	6	
·8	5	20
·7	4	
·6	3	15
·5	2	
·4	1	10
·3		
·2		5
·1		

TABLE

OF

THE RELATIVE WEIGHTS OF ENGLISH GRAINS AND FRENCH GRAMMES

Grains.	Grammes.	Grains.	Grammes.	Grains.	Grammes.	Grains.	Grammes.
1	·064	41	2·656	81	5·248	121	7·840
2	·129	42	2·720	82	5·312	122	7·905
3	·194	43	2·785	83	5·378	123	7·970
4	·259	44	2·850	84	5·442	124	8·035
5	·324	45	2·915	85	5·508	125	8·100
6	·388	46	2·980	86	5·572	126	8·164
7	·453	47	3·045	87	5·637	127	8·229
8	·518	48	3·110	88	5·702	128	8·294
9	·583	49	3·175	89	5·767	129	8·359
10	·648	50	3·240	90	5·832	130	8·424
11	·712	51	3·304	91	5·896	131	8·488
12	·777	52	3·368	92	5·961	132	8·553
13	·842	53	3·434	93	6·026	133	8·618
14	·907	54	3·498	94	6·091	134	8·682
15	·972	55	3·564	95	6·156	135	8·747
16	1·036	56	3·628	96	6·220	136	8·812
17	1·101	57	3·693	97	6·285	137	8·877
18	1·166	58	3·758	98	6·350	138	8·942
19	1·231	59	3·823	99	6·415	139	9·007
20	1·296	60	3·888	100	6·480	140	9·072
21	1·360	61	3·952	101	6·544	141	9·136
22	1·425	62	4·017	102	6·609	142	9·200
23	1·490	63	4·082	103	6·674	143	9·265
24	1·555	64	4·146	104	6·739	144	9·330
25	1·620	65	4·211	105	6·804	145	9·395
26	1·684	66	4·276	106	6·868	146	9·460
27	1·749	67	4·341	107	6·933	147	9·525
28	1·814	68	4·406	108	6·998	148	9·590
29	1·879	69	4·471	109	7·063	149	9·655
30	1·944	70	4·536	110	7·128	150	9·720
31	2·008	71	4·600	111	7·192	151	9·784
32	2·073	72	4·665	112	7·257	152	9·848
33	2·138	73	4·729	113	7·322	153	9·914
34	2·202	74	4·794	114	7·387	154	9·978
35	2·267	75	4·859	115	7·452	155	10·044
36	2·332	76	4·924	116	7·516	156	10·108
37	2·397	77	4·989	117	7·581	157	10·173
38	2·462	78	5·054	118	7·646	158	10·238
39	2·527	79	5·119	119	7·711	159	10·303
40	2·592	80	5·184	120	7·776	160	10·368

TABLE

OF

THE RELATIVE WEIGHTS OF ENGLISH GRAINS AND FRENCH GRAMMES

Grains.	Grammes.	Grains.	Grammes.	Grains.	Grammes.	Grains.	Grammes.
161	10·432	201	13·024	241	15·616	290	18·79
162	10·497	202	13·089	242	15·680	300	19·44
163	10·562	203	13·154	243	15·745	310	20·08
164	10·626	204	13·219	244	15·810	320	20·73
165	10·691	205	13·284	245	15·875	330	21·38
166	10·756	206	13·348	246	15·940	340	22·02
167	10·821	207	13·413	247	16·005	350	22·67
168	10·886	208	13·478	248	16·070	360	23·32
169	10·951	209	13·543	249	16·135	370	23·97
170	11·016	210	13·608	250	16·200	380	24·62
171	11·080	211	13·672	251	16·264	390	25·27
172	11·145	212	13·737	252	16·328	400	25·92
173	11·209	213	13·802	253	16·394	410	26·56
174	11·274	214	13·867	254	16·458	420	27·20
175	11·339	215	13·932	255	16·524	430	27·85
176	11·404	216	13·996	256	16·588	440	28·50
177	11·469	217	14·061	257	16·653	450	29·15
178	11·534	218	14·126	258	16·718	460	29·80
179	11·599	219	14·191	259	16·783	470	30·45
180	11·664	220	14·256	260	16·848	480	31·10
181	11·728	221	14·320	261	16·912	490	31·75
182	11·792	222	14·385	262	16·977	500	32·40
183	11·858	223	14·450	263	17·042	510	33·04
184	11·922	224	14·515	264	17·106	520	33·68
185	11·988	225	14·580	265	17·171	530	34·34
186	12·052	226	14·644	266	17·236	540	34·98
187	12·117	227	14·709	267	17·301	550	35·64
188	12·182	228	14·774	268	17·366	560	36·28
189	12·247	229	14·839	269	17·431	570	36·93
190	12·312	230	14·904	270	17·496	580	37·58
191	12·376	231	14·968	271	17·560	590	38·23
192	12·441	232	15·033	272	17·625	600	38·88
193	12·506	233	15·098	273	17·689	700	45·36
194	12·571	234	15·162	274	17·754	800	51·84
195	12·636	235	15·227	275	17·819	900	58·32
196	12·700	236	15·292	276	17·884	1000	64·80
197	12·765	237	15·357	277	17·949	2000	129·60
198	12·830	238	15·422	278	18·014	3000	194·40
199	12·895	239	15·487	279	18·079	4000	259·20
200	12·960	240	15·552	280	18·144	5000	324·00

...RIE		SERI
...LLIA ...pes II		HENRY I Types XIV, XV
		A
		B
		C
		D
		E
		F
		G
		h
		I
		K
		L
		M
		N
		O
		P
		R
		S
		T
		V
		P
		X
		T
		Æ
		+

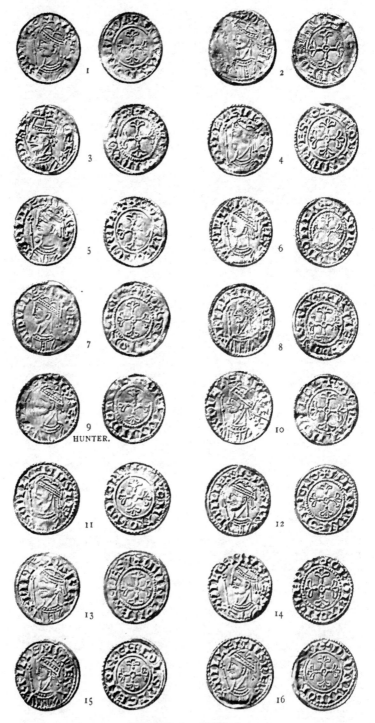

HUNTER.

WILLIAM I.   TYPE I.

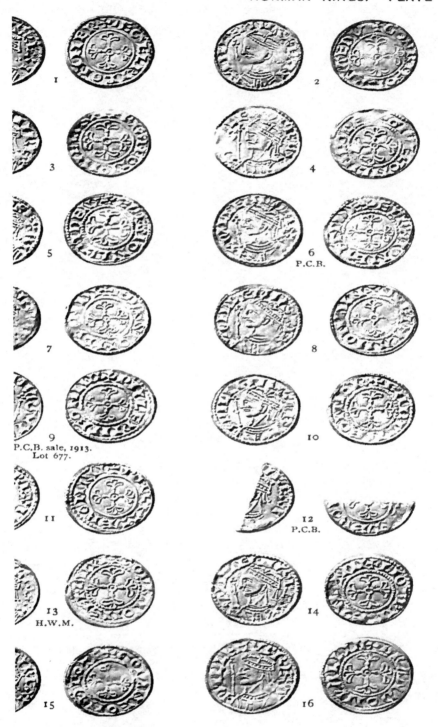

1

2

3

4

5

6
P.C.B.

7

8

9
P.C.B. sale, 1913.
Lot 677.

10

11

12
P.C.B.

13
H.W.M.

14

15

16

WILLIAM I. TYPE I.

1

2

3

4

5

6

7

8

9

10

11

12
YORK.

13

14
P.C.B.

15
R.C.L.

WILLIAM I. TYPE I; MULES: CONFESSOR × II, I × II.

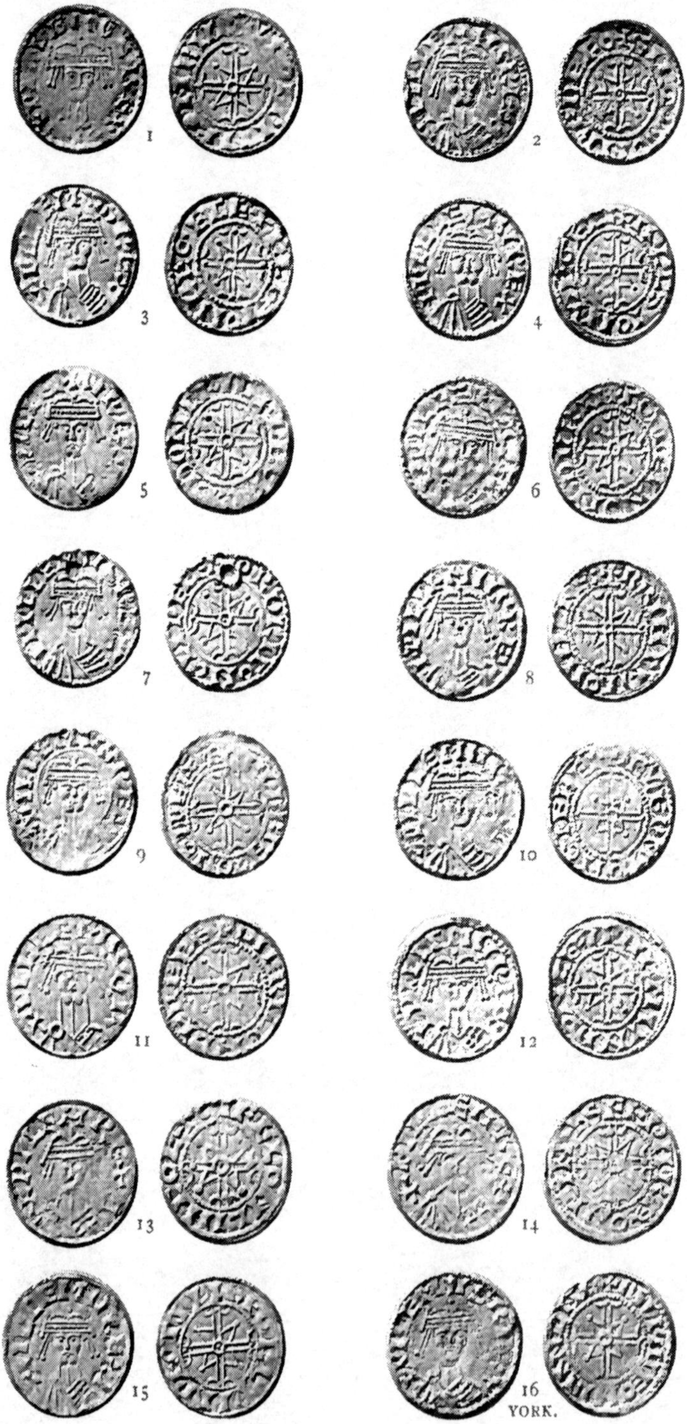
1
2
3
4
5
6
7
8
9
10
11
12
13
14
15
16
YORK.

WILLIAM I. TYPE II.

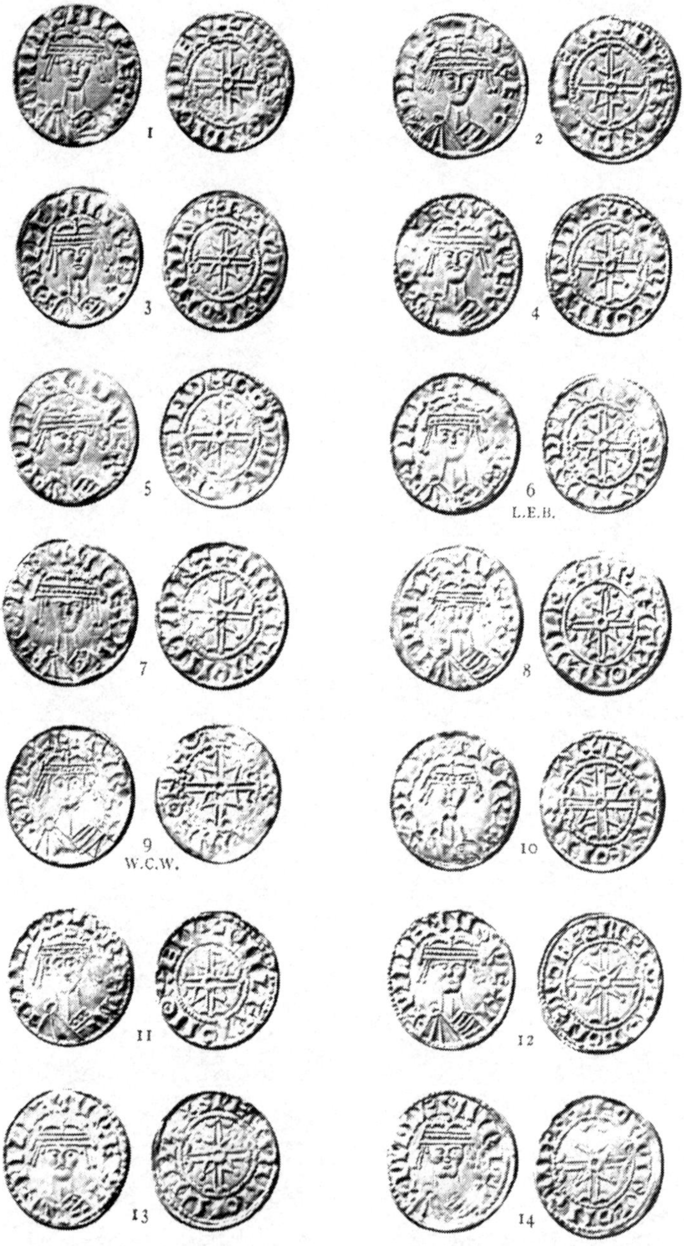
1
2
3
4
5
6
L.E.B.
7
8
9
W.C.W.
10
11
12
13
14
15
16

WILLIAM I. TYPE II.

WILLIAM I. TYPE II; MULE II x III.

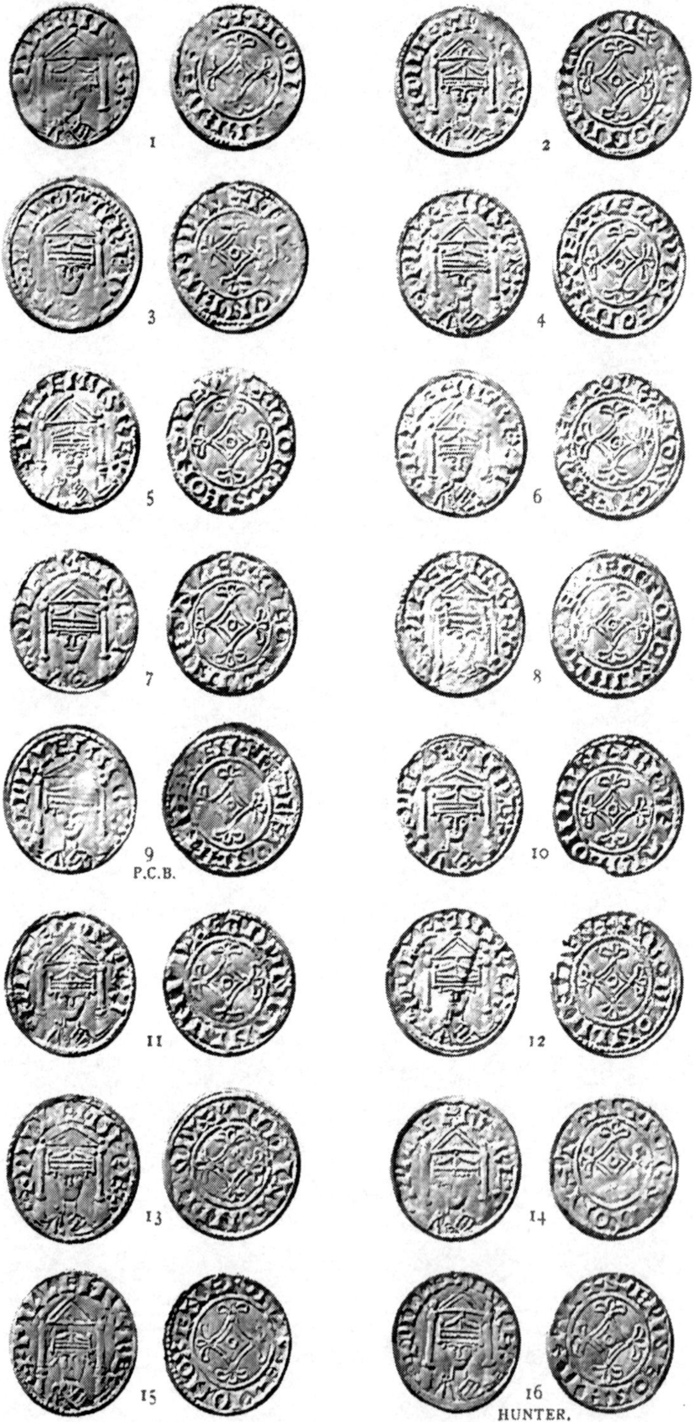
1
2
3
4
5
6
7
8
9
P.C.B.
10
11
12
13
14
15
16
HUNTER.

WILLIAM I. TYPE III.

WILLIAM I.   TYPE III; MULE III × IV; TYPE IV.

WILLIAM I. TYPE IV.

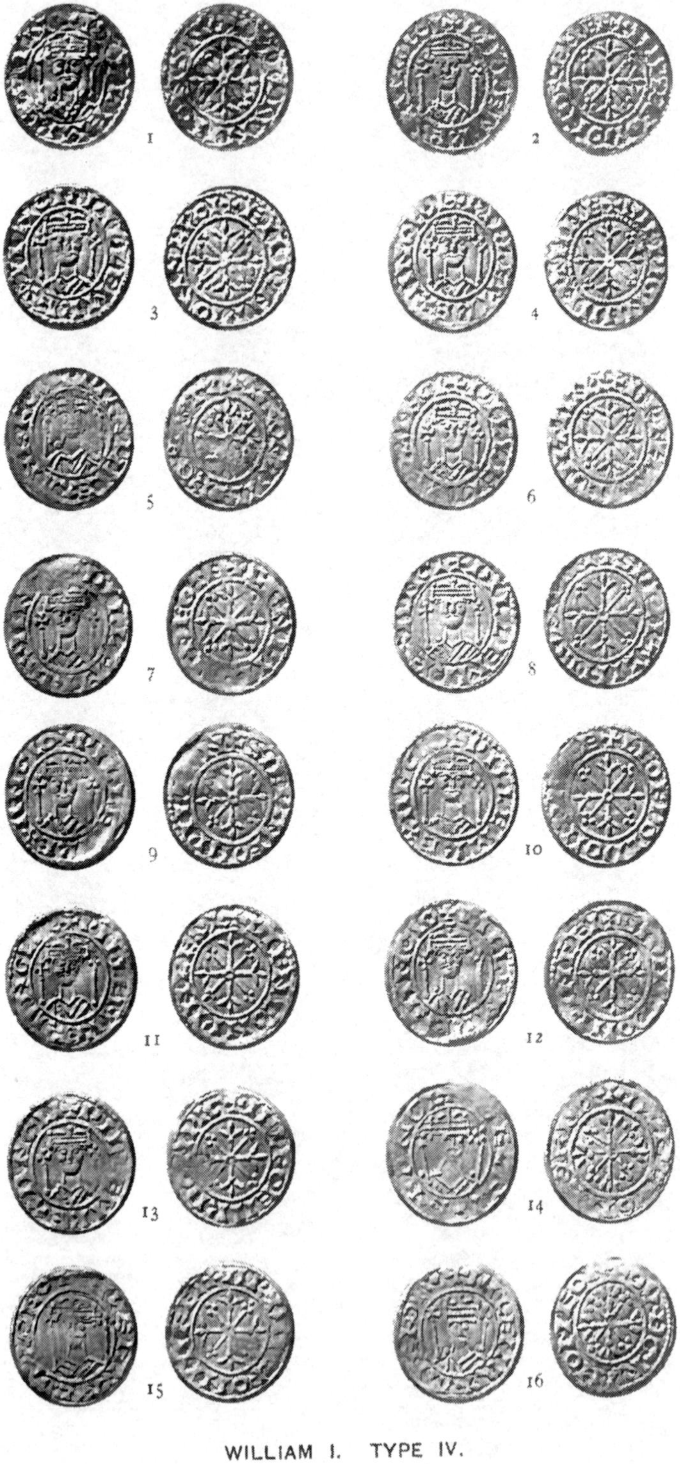
1
2
3
4
5
6
7
8
9
10
11
12
13
14
15
16

WILLIAM I. TYPE IV.

WILLIAM I.   MULE IV x V;   TYPE V.

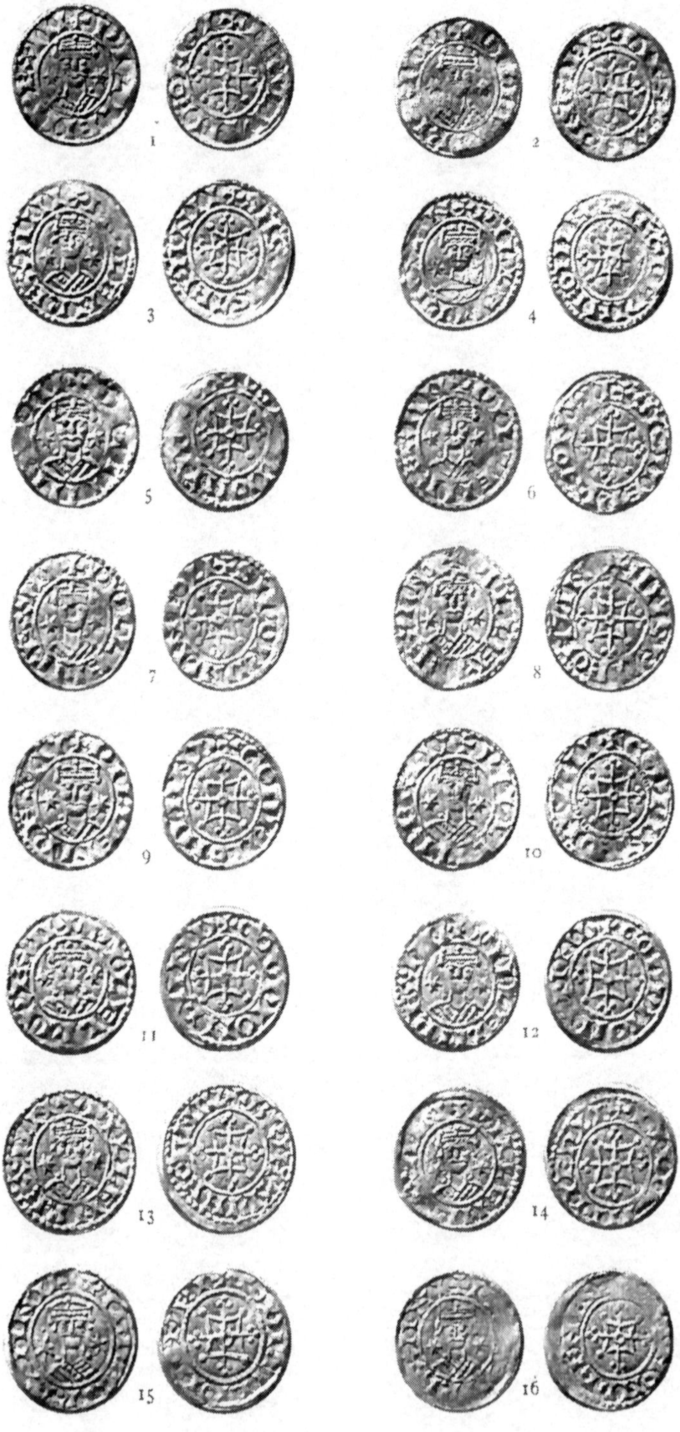
1
2
3
4
5
6
7
8
9
10
11
12
13
14
15
16

WILLIAM I. TYPE V.

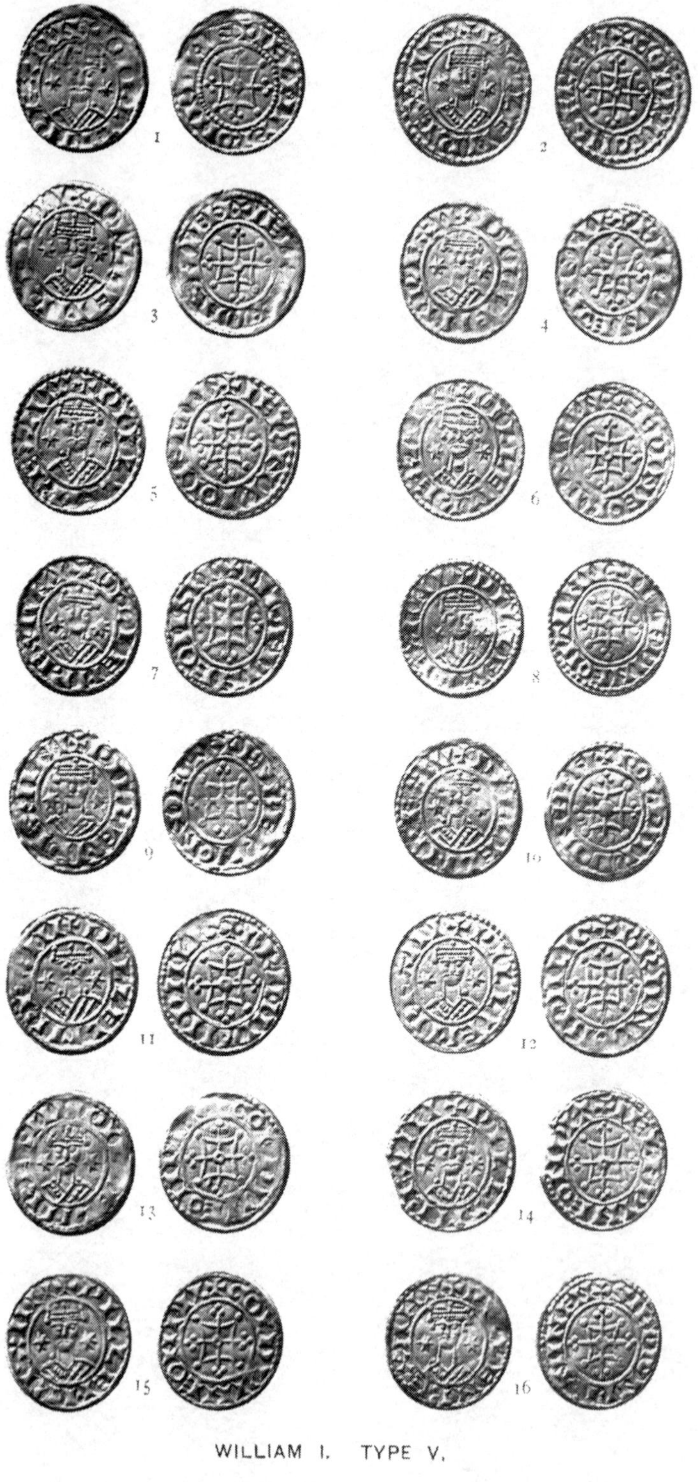

WILLIAM I. TYPE V.

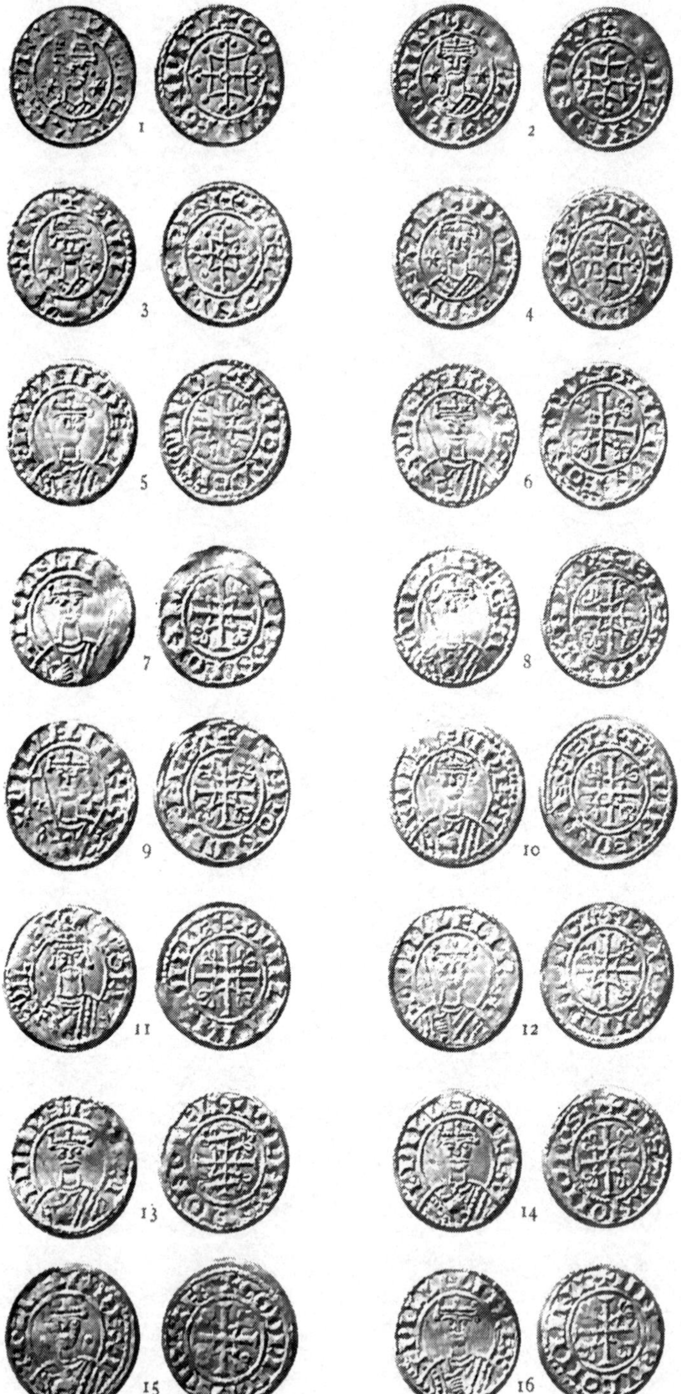
1
2
3
4
5
6
7
8
9
10
11
12
13
14
15
HUNTER.
16

WILLIAM I. TYPES V AND VI.

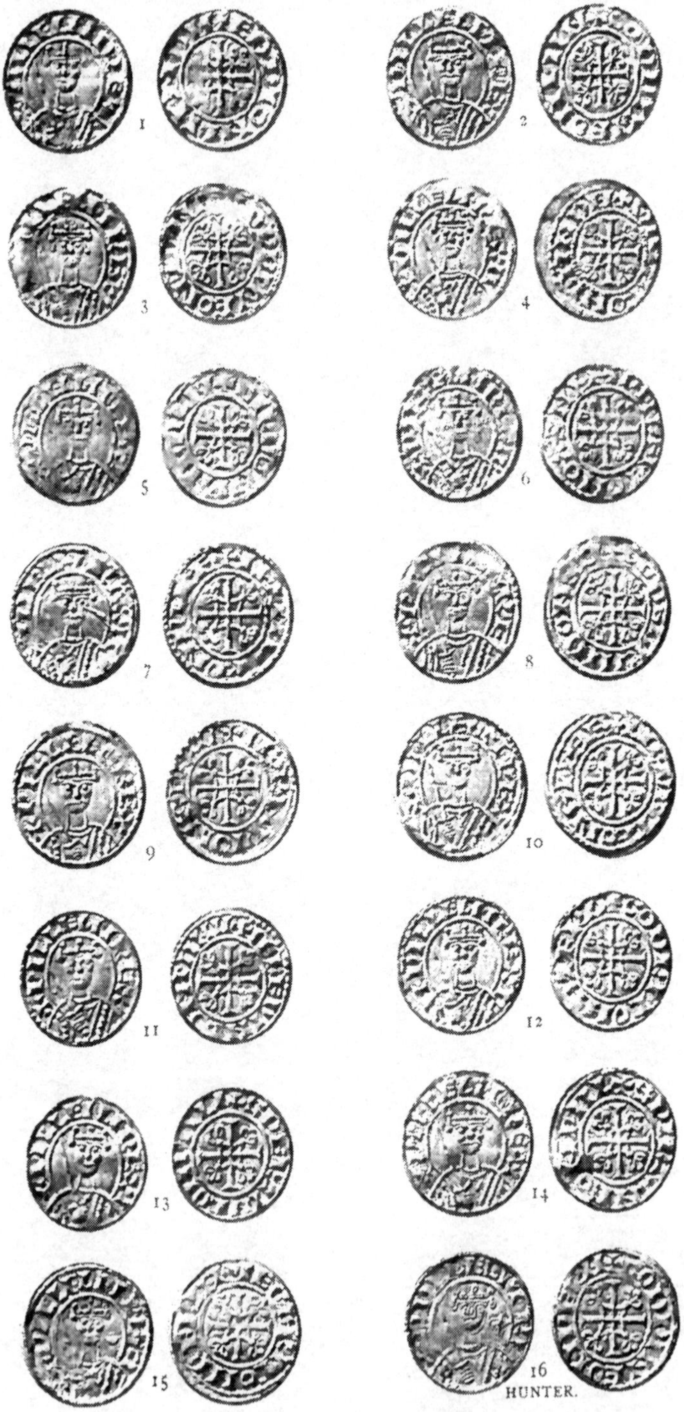
1
2
3
4
5
6
7
8
9
10
11
12
13
14
15
16
HUNTER.

WILLIAM I. TYPE VI.

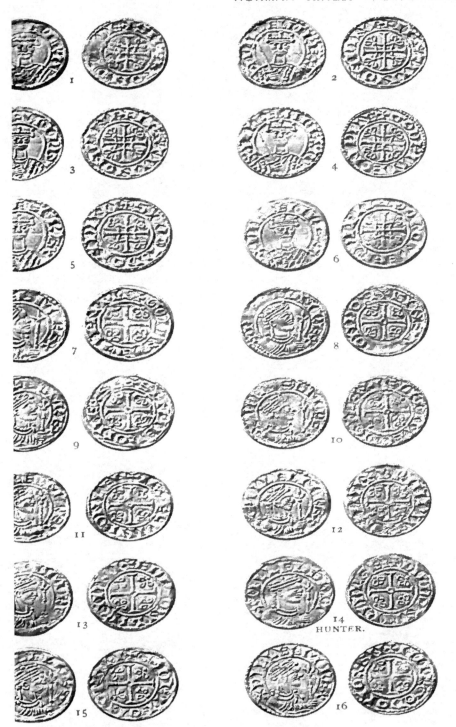

14
HUNTER.

WILLIAM I.   TYPES VI AND VII.

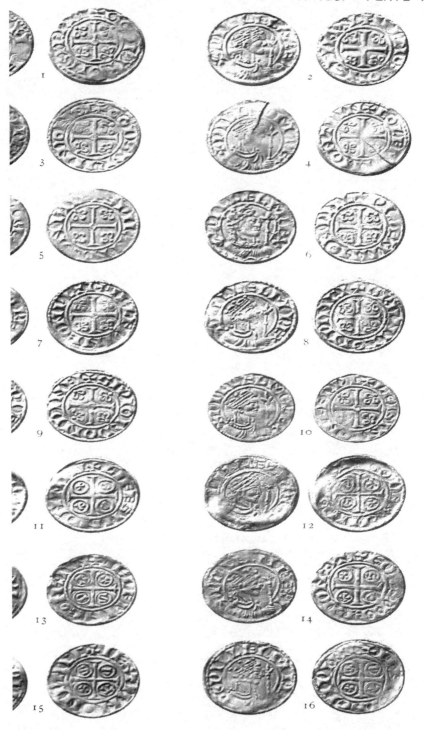

WILLIAM I.   TYPE VII.   MULE VII x VIII.

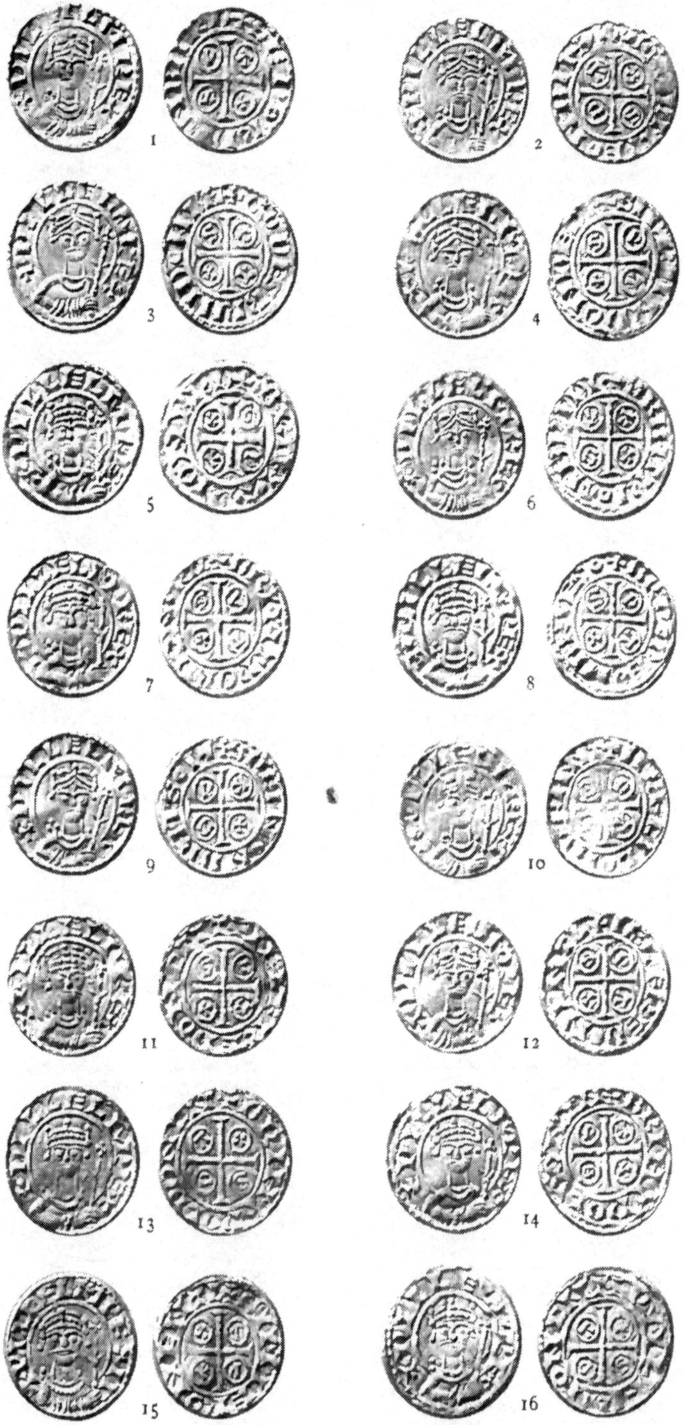
1
2
3
4
5
6
7
8
9
10
11
12
13
14
15
16

WILLIAM I. TYPE VIII.

WILLIAM I.   TYPE VIII.

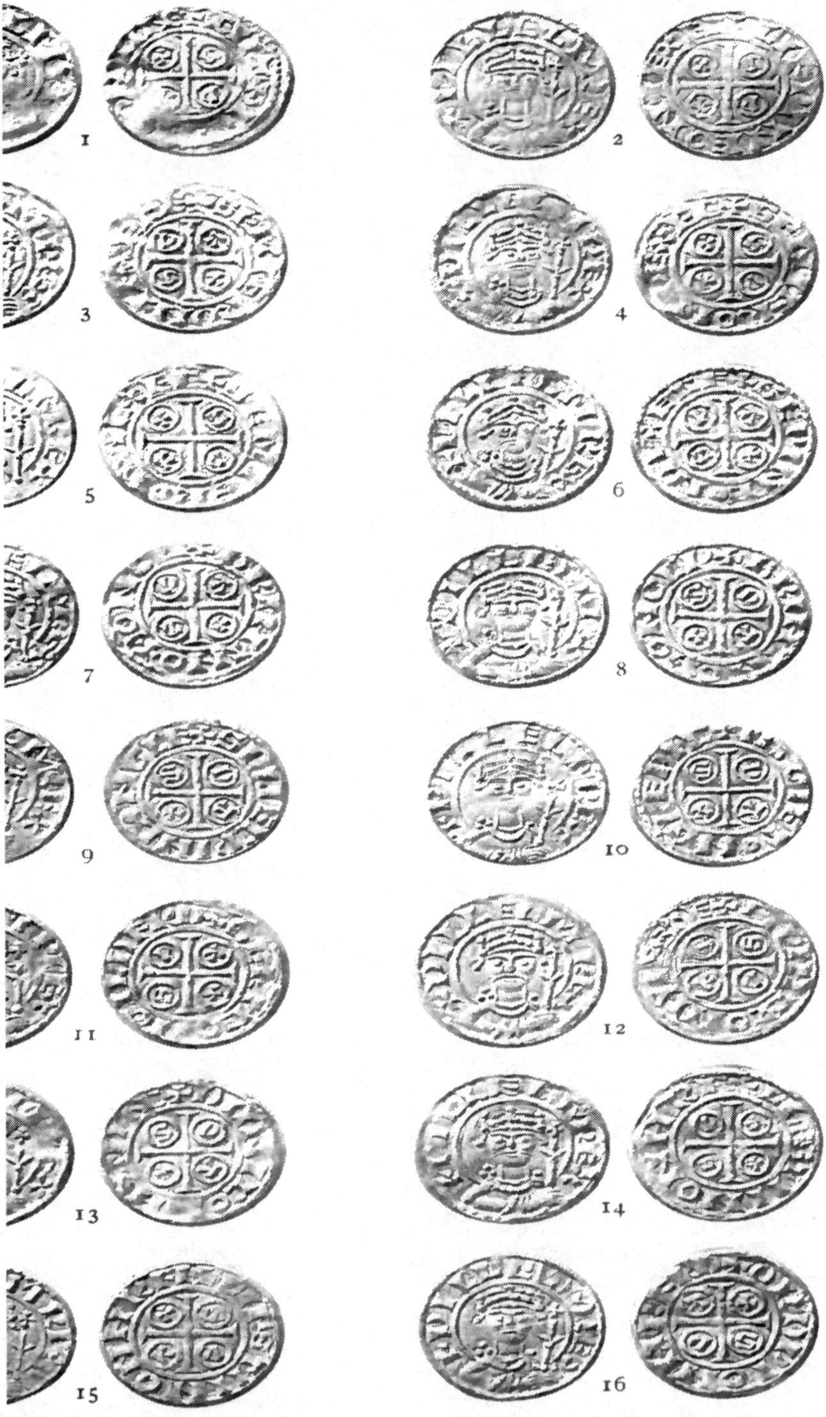

WILLIAM I. TYPE VIII.

WILLIAM I.   TYPE VIII.

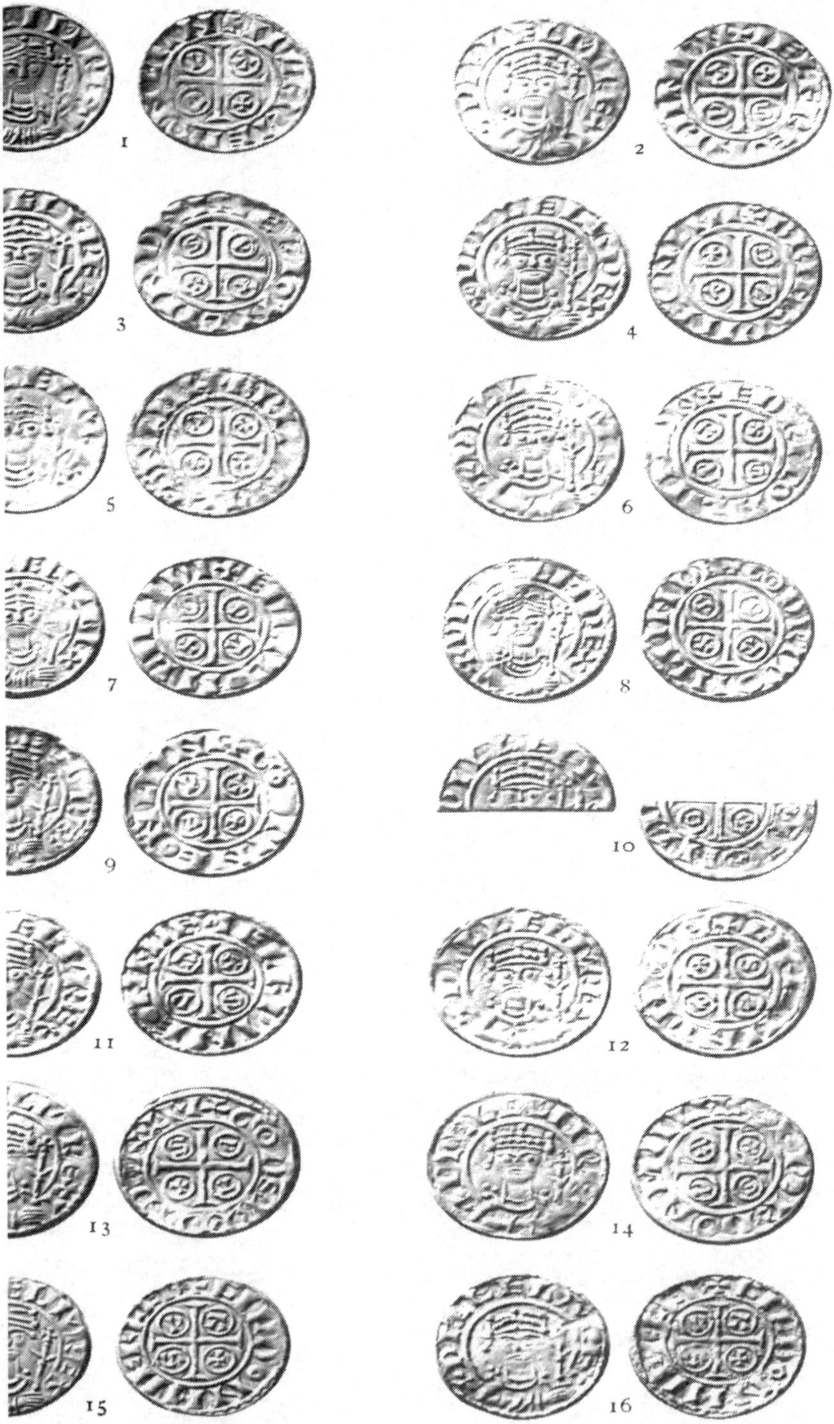
1
2
3
4
5
6
7
8
9
10
11
12
13
14
15
16

WILLIAM I. TYPE VIII.

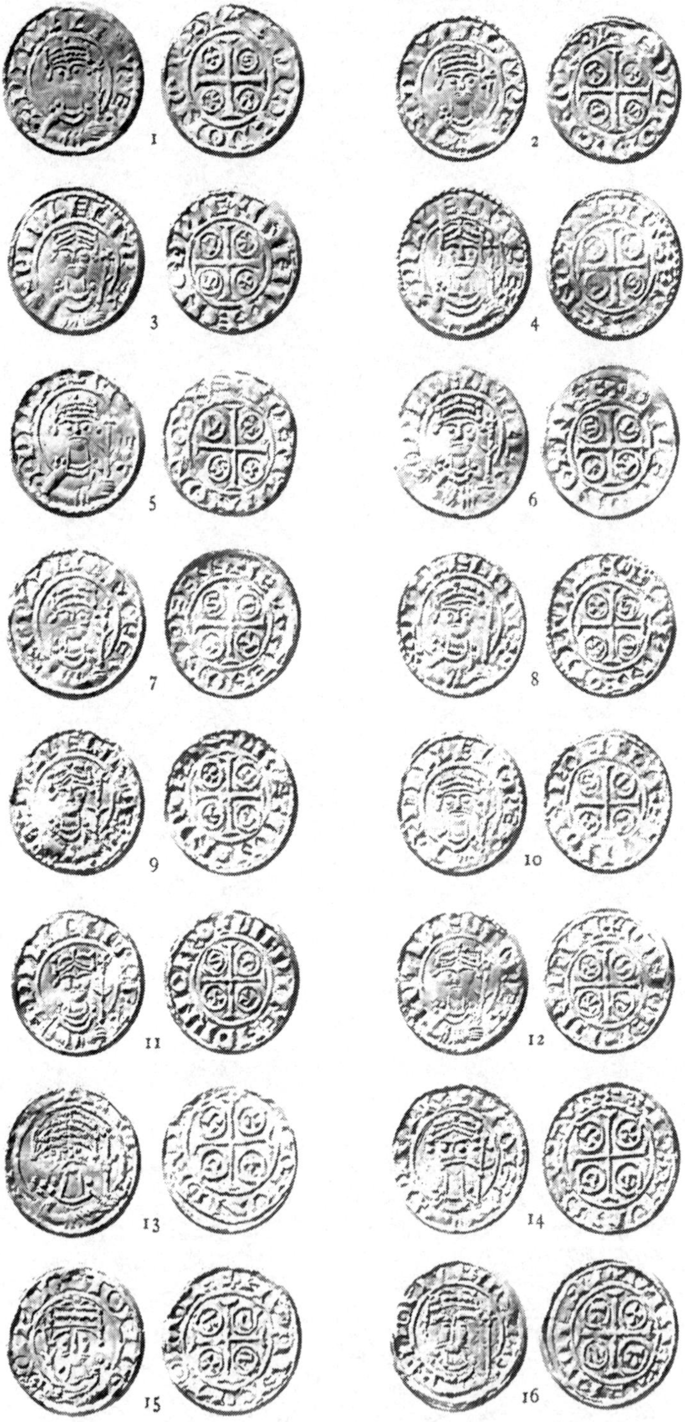
1
2
3
4
5
6
7
8
9
10
11
12
13
14
15
16

WILLIAM I. TYPE VIII.

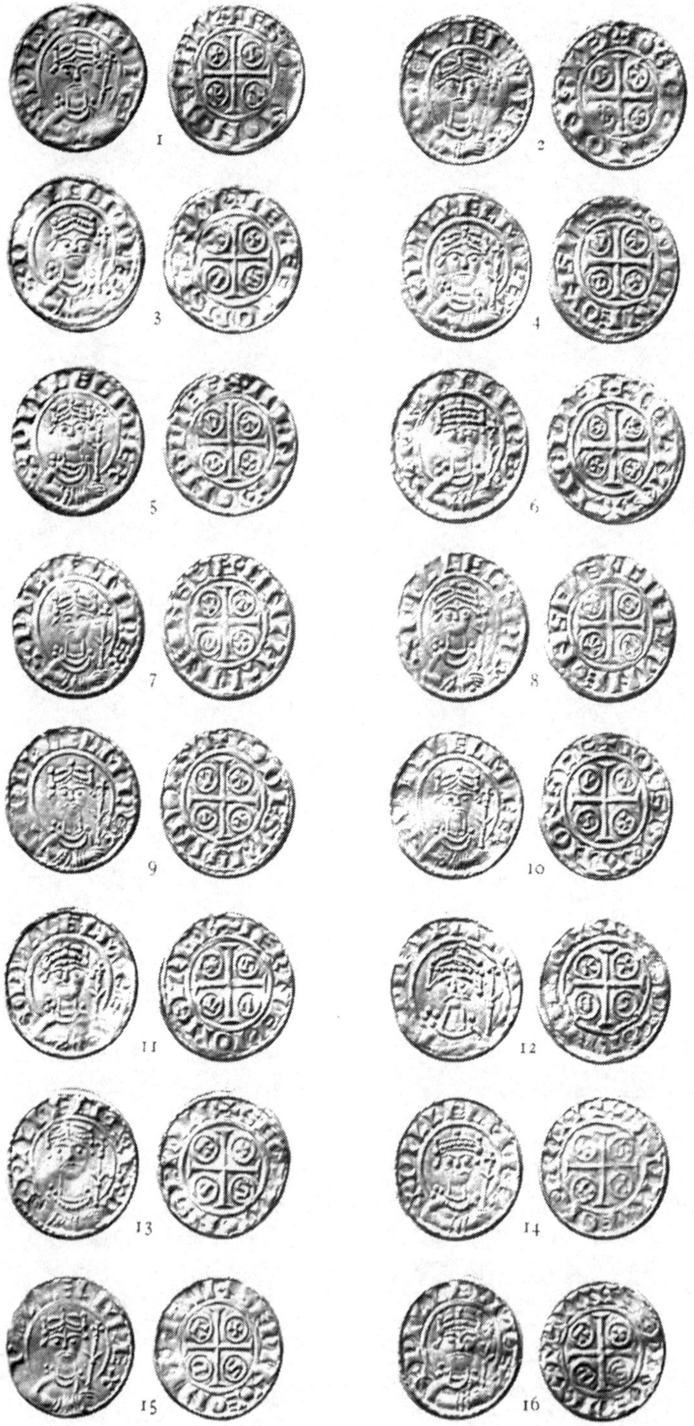
1
2
3
4
5
6
7
8
9
10
11
12
13
14
15
16

WILLIAM I. TYPE VIII.

WILLIAM I. TYPE VIII.

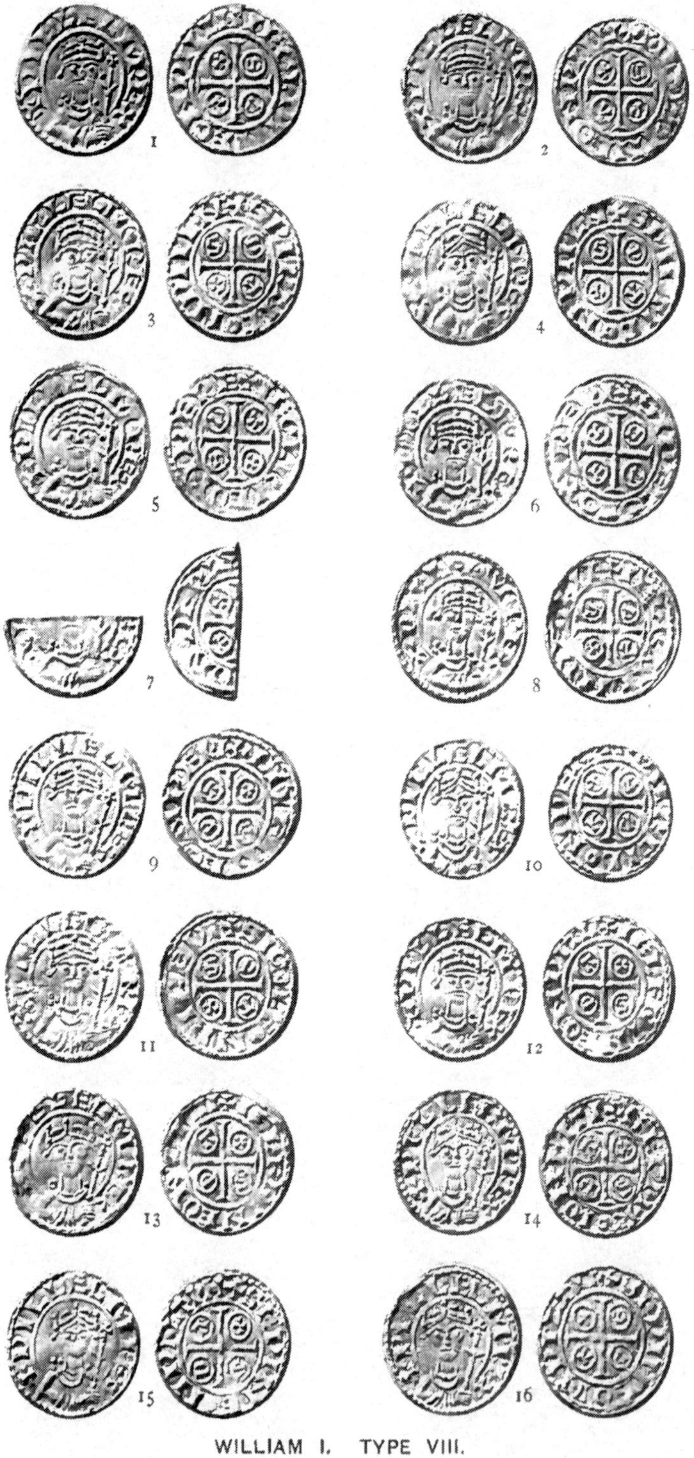

WILLIAM I. TYPE VIII.

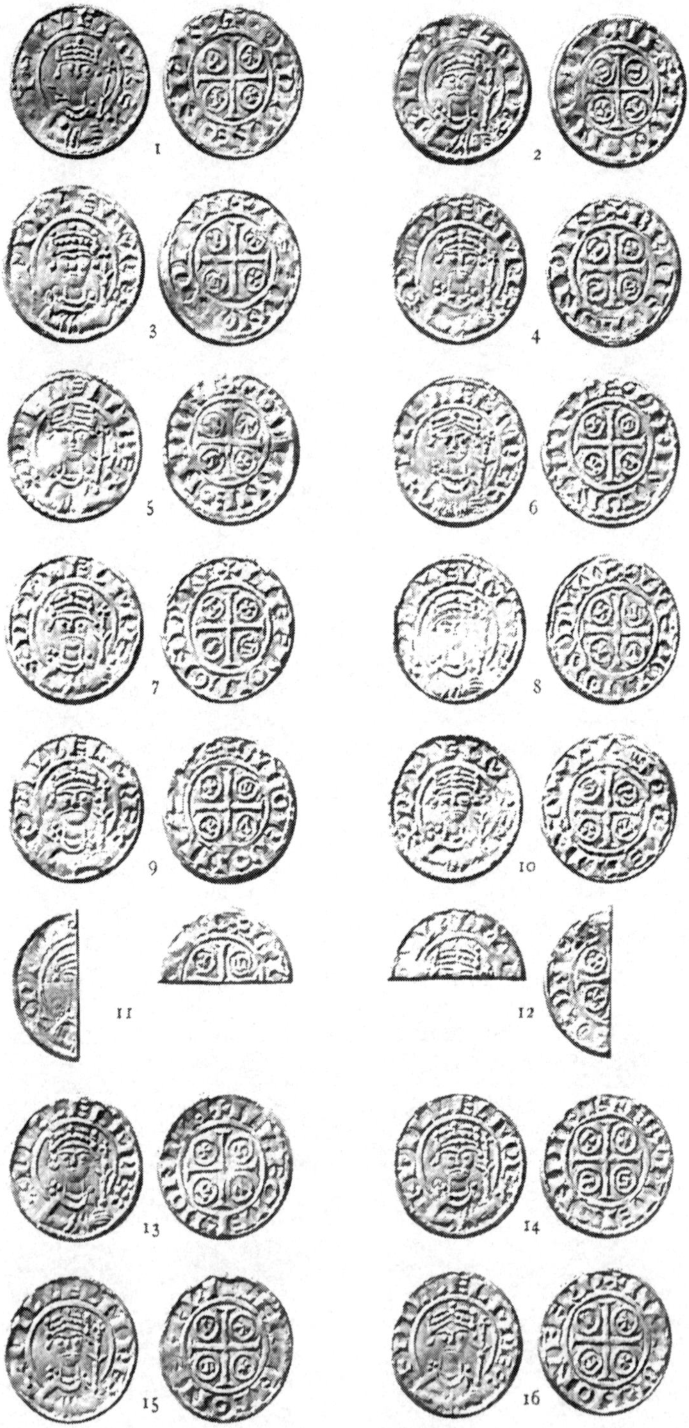
1
2
3
4
5
6
7
8
9
10
11
12
13
14
15
16

WILLIAM I. TYPE VIII.

NORMAN KINGS. PLATE XXVIII.

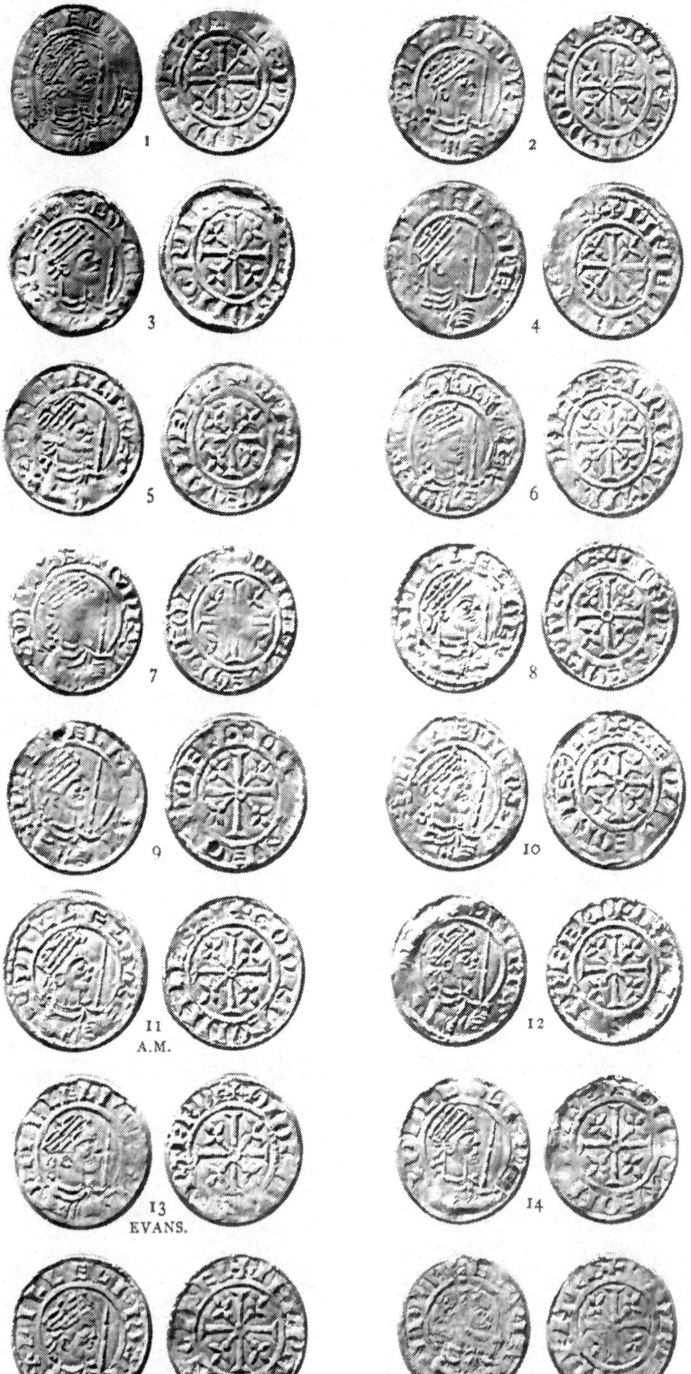
1
2
3
4
5
6
7
8
9
10
11
A.M.
12
13
EVANS.
14
15
16

WILLIAM II. TYPE I.

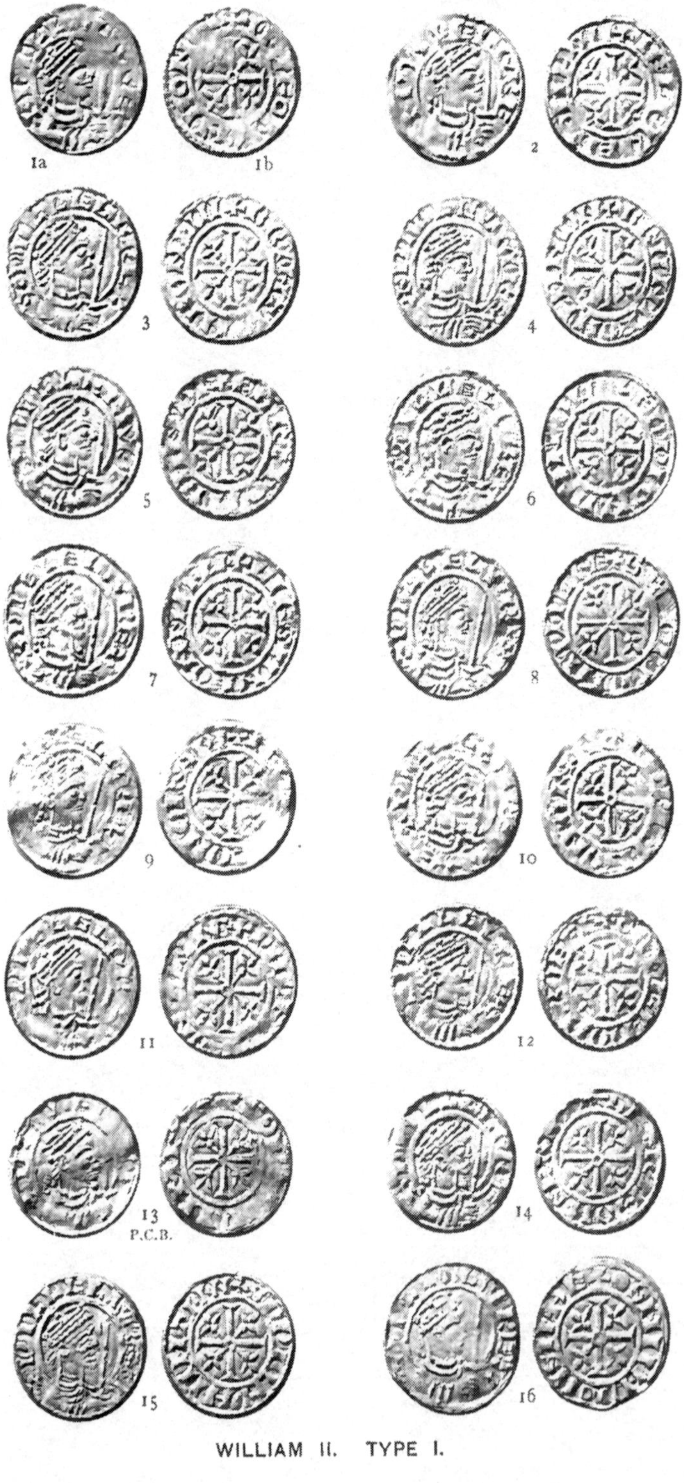

WILLIAM II. TYPE I.

13

EVANS.

WILLIAM II. TYPE I; MULE I × II.

WILLIAM II. TYPE II.

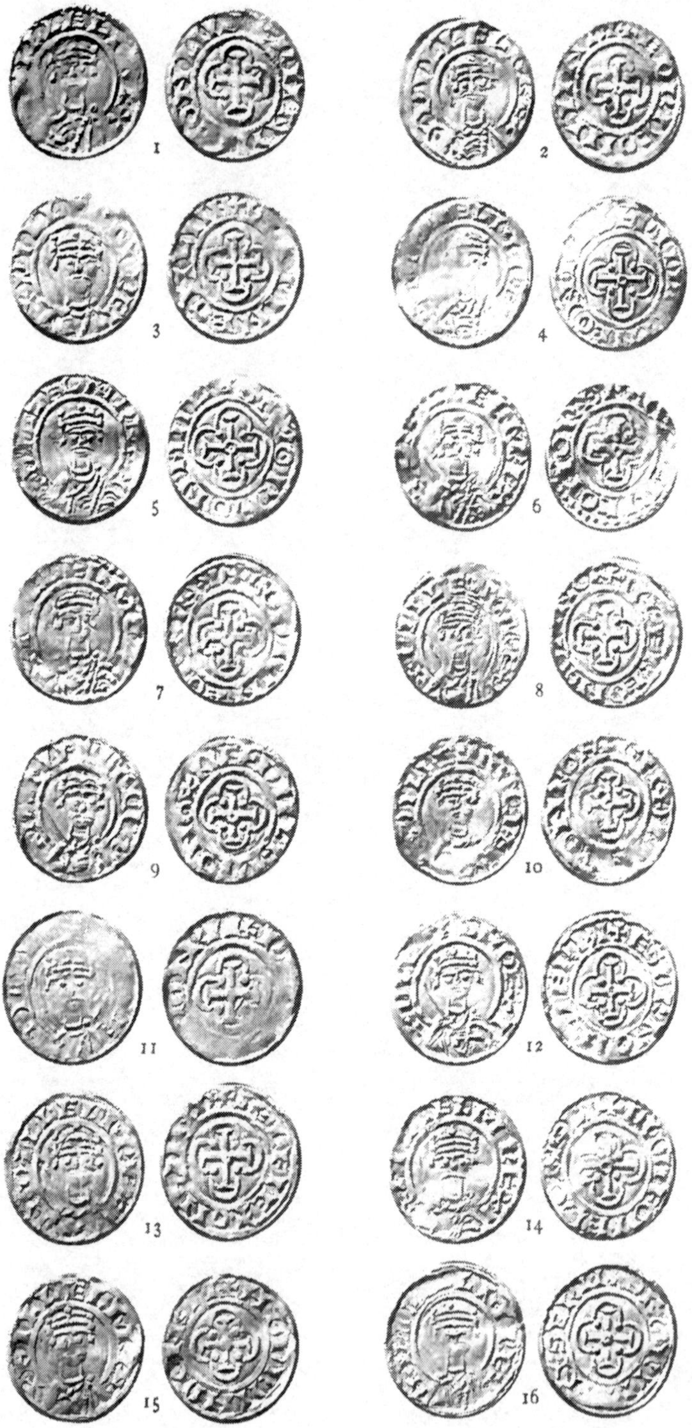

WILLIAM II. TYPE II.

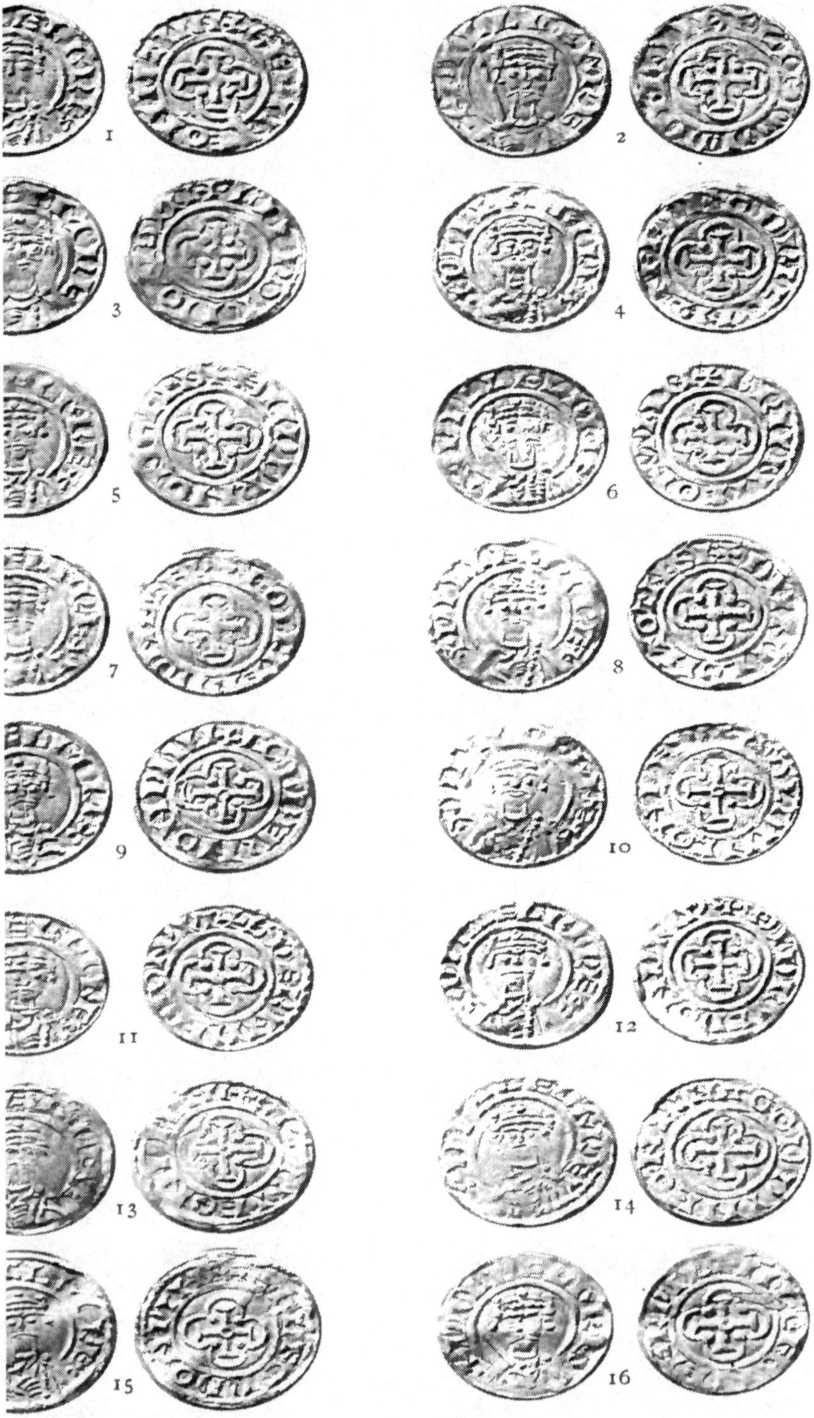

WILLIAM II. TYPE II.

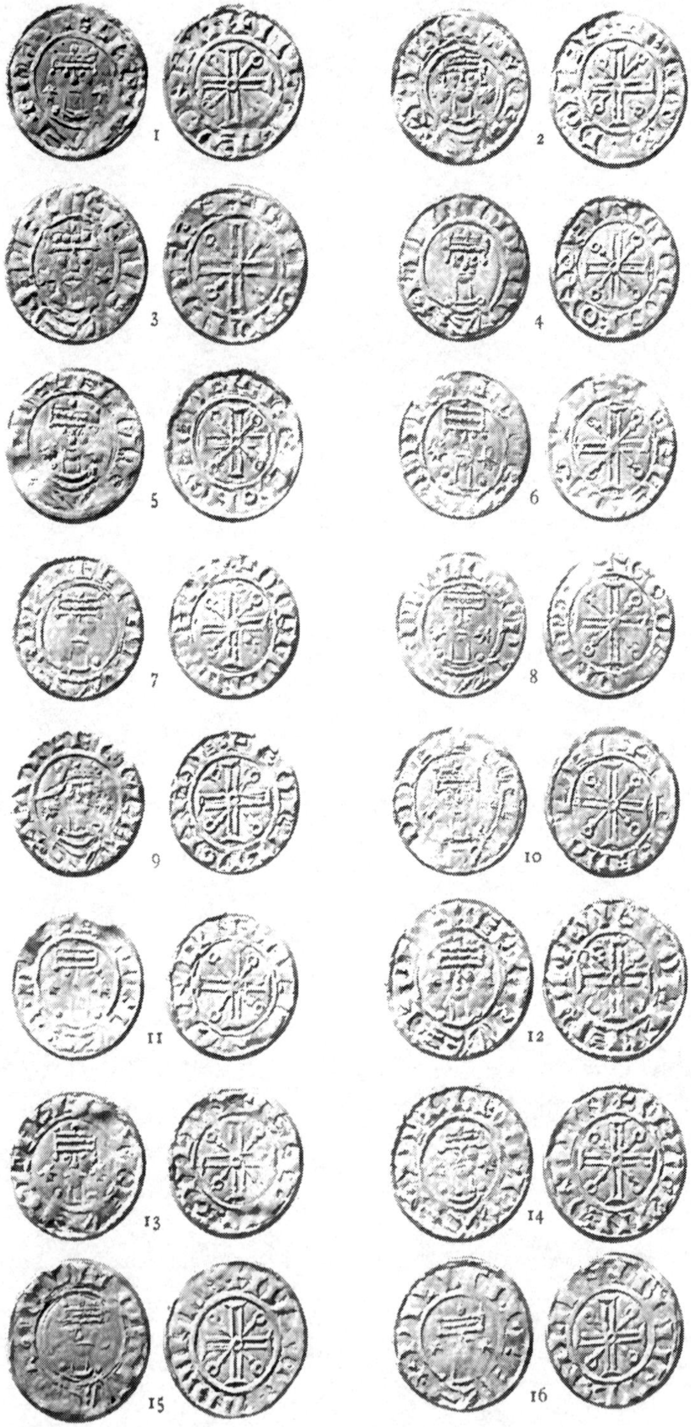

WILLIAM II. TYPE III.

16
COPENHAGEN.

WILLIAM II.   TYPE III.

1
H.M.R.

2

3

4

5

6

7

8

9

10

11

12

13

14

15
L.E.B.

WILLIAM II.   TYPE IV;   MULE IV x V.

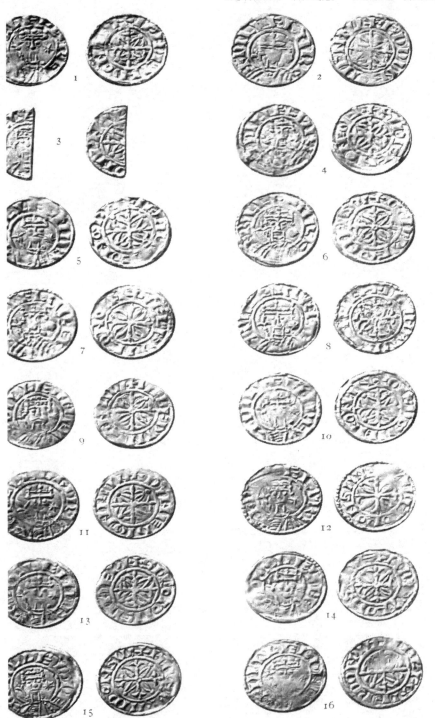

WILLIAM II.   TYPE V.

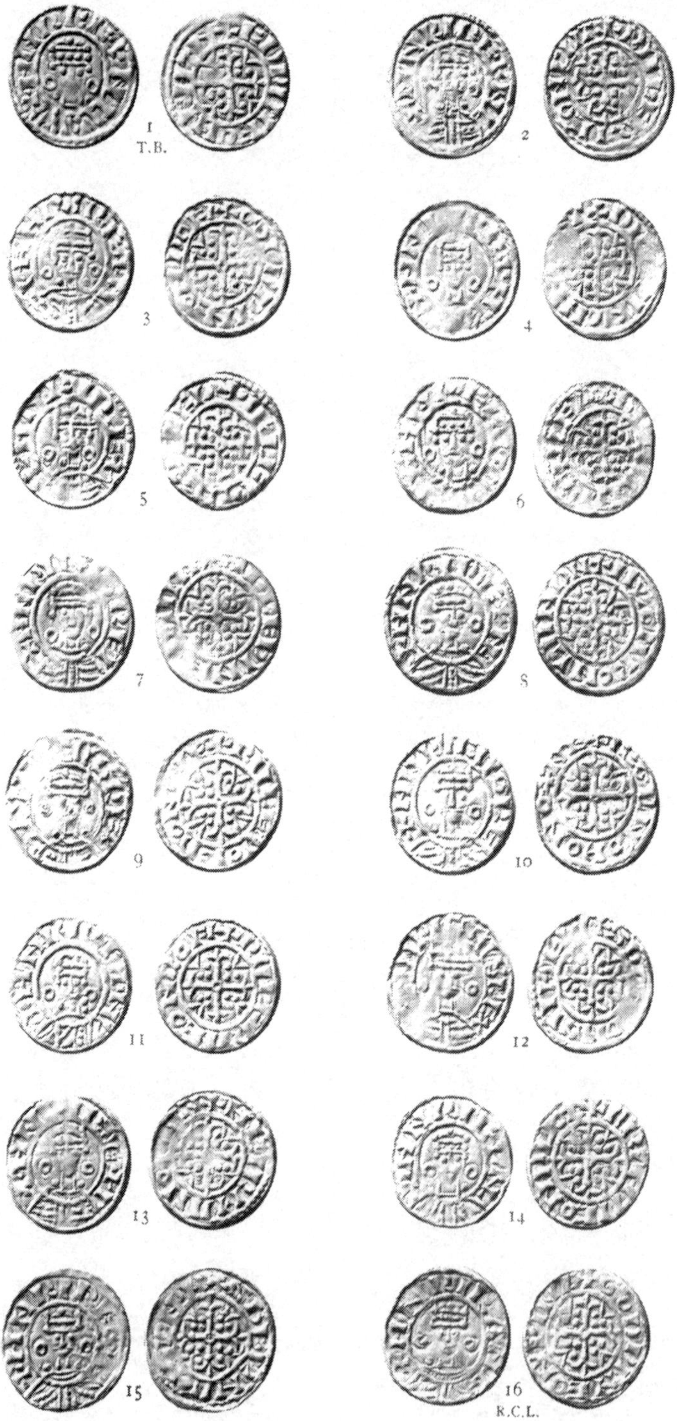
1
T.B.
2
3
4
5
6
7
8
9
10
11
12
13
14
15
16
R.C.L.

HENRY I. TYPE I.

1

2
B.R.

3

4

5

6

7

8

9

10
R.C.L.

11

12

13

14
R.C.L.

15

16
HUNTER.

HENRY I. TYPES II, III, IV.

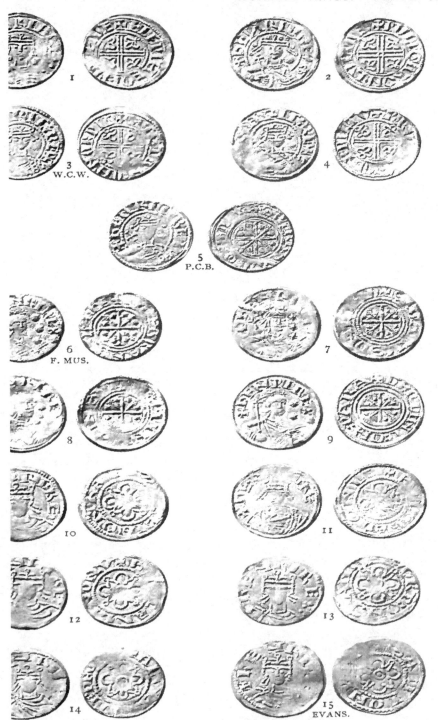

HENRY I. TYPE V; MULE V × VI; TYPES VI, VII.

HENRY I.   TYPES VIII, IX;   MULE IX × X;   TYPE X.

HENRY I.   TYPE X;   MULE XI × X;   TYPES XI, XII.

15
P.C.B.

HENRY I.   TYPE XIII;   MULE XIII × XIV.

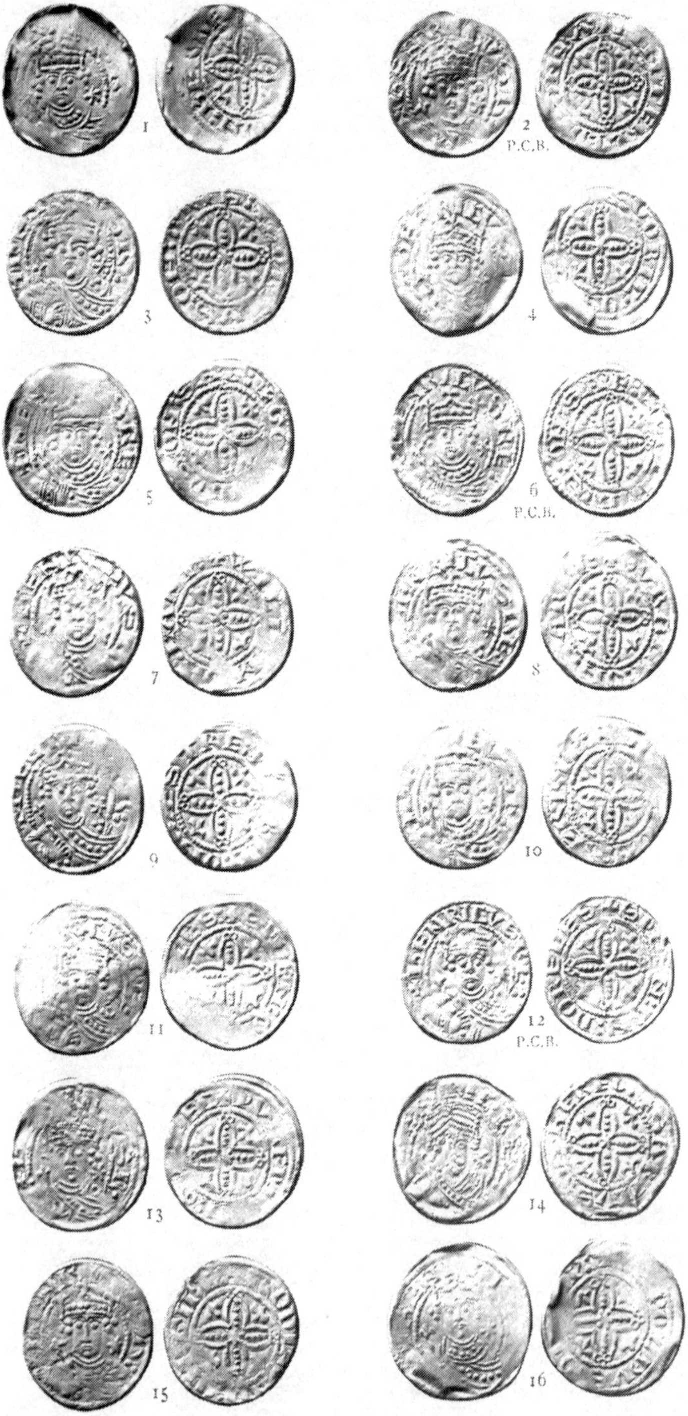
1
2
P.C.B.
3
4
5
6
P.C.B.
7
8
9
10
11
12
P.C.B.
13
14
15
16

HENRY I. TYPE XIV.

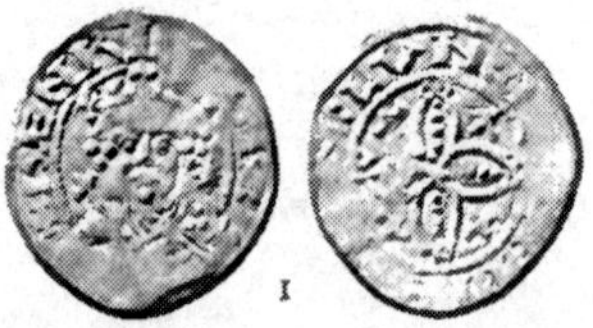
1

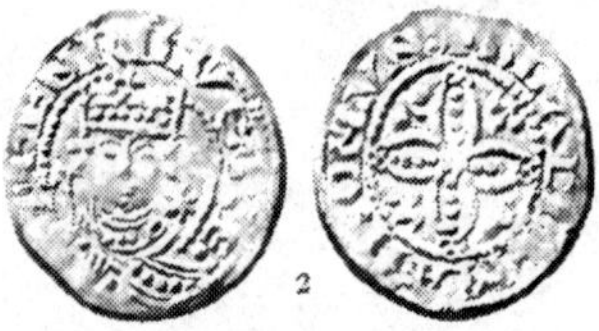
2

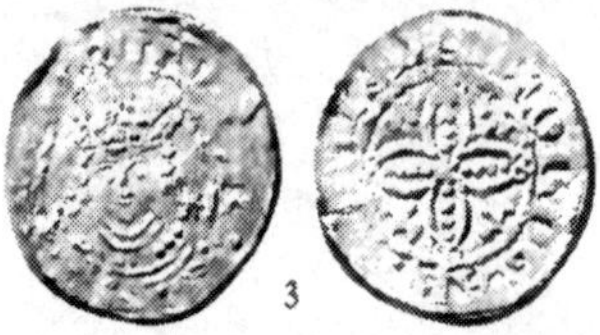
3

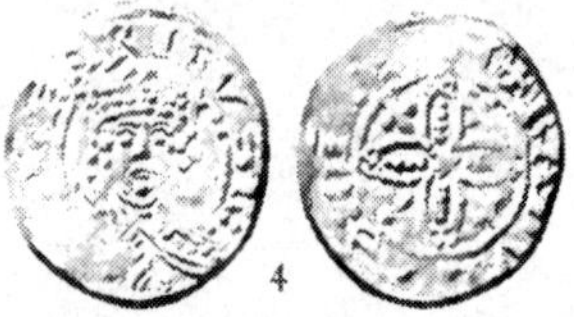
4

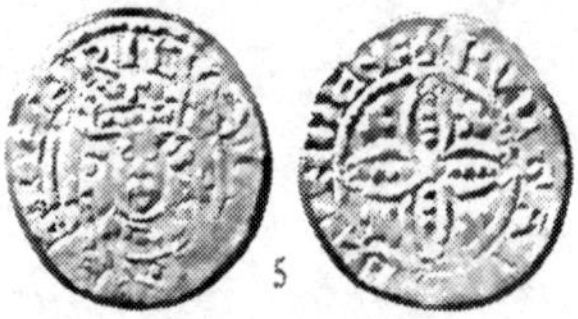
5

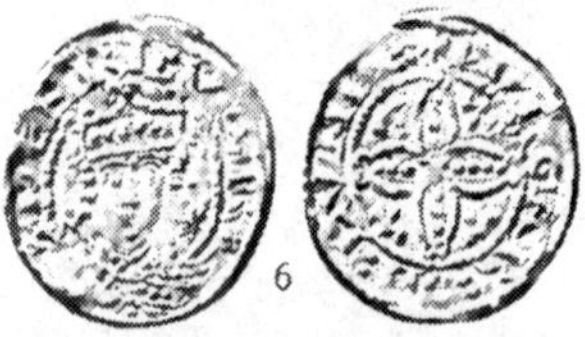
6

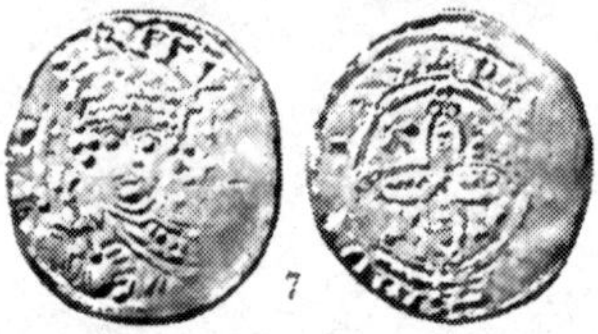
7

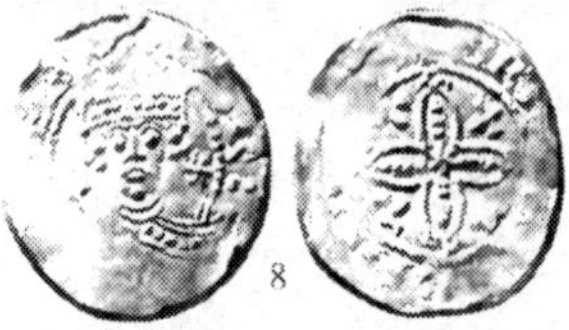
8

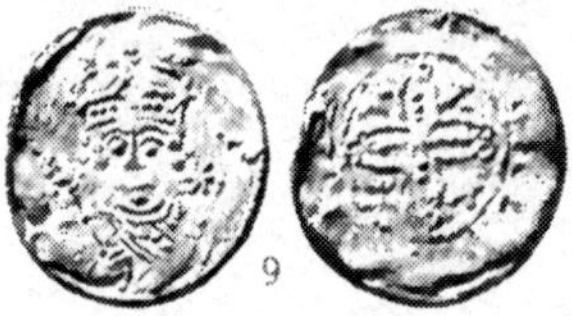
9

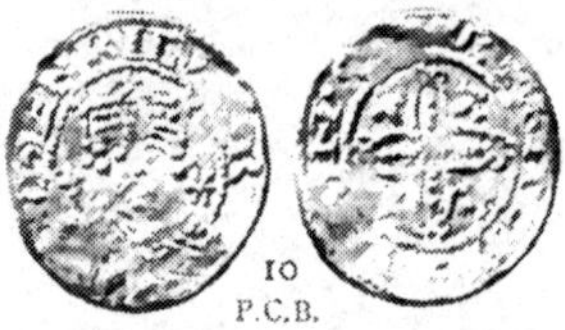
10
P.C.B.

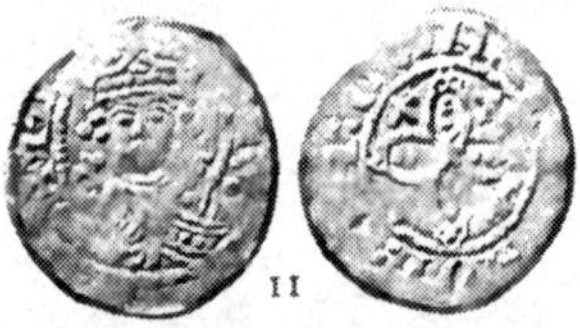
11

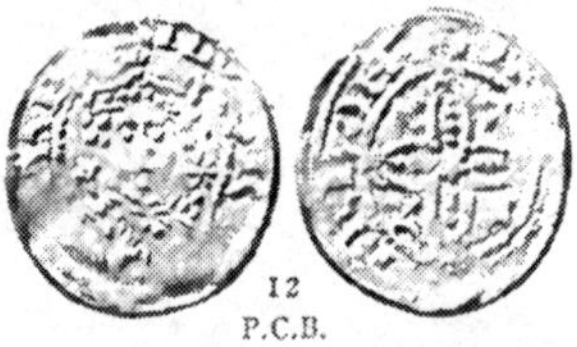
12
P.C.B.

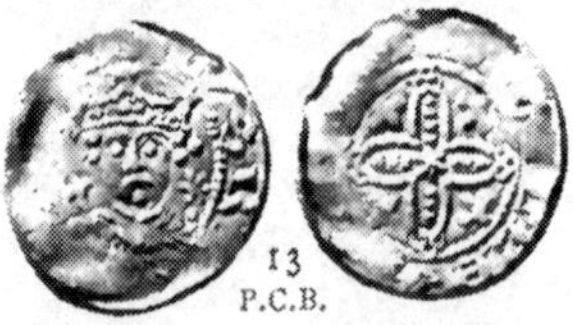
13
P.C.B.

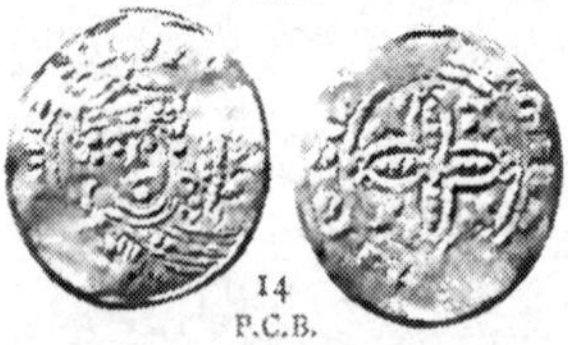
14
P.C.B.

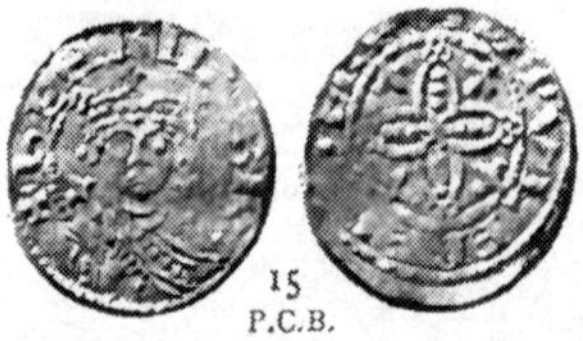
15
P.C.B.

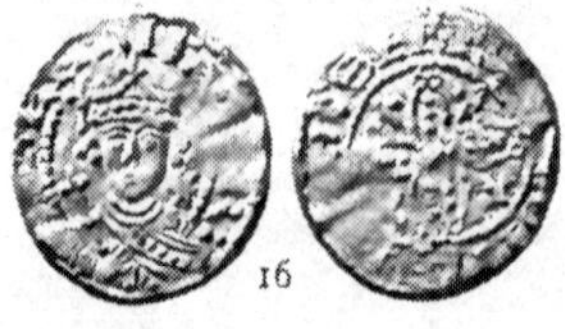
16

HENRY I. TYPE XIV.

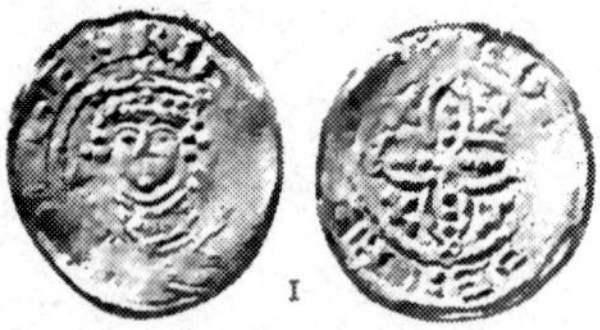
1

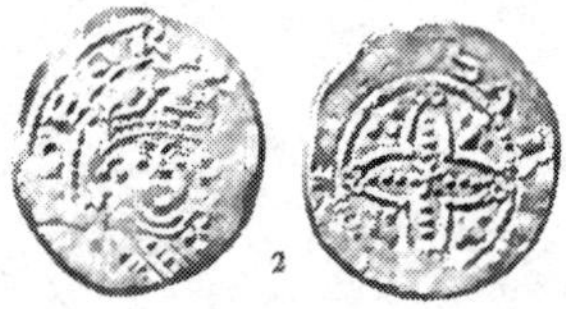
2

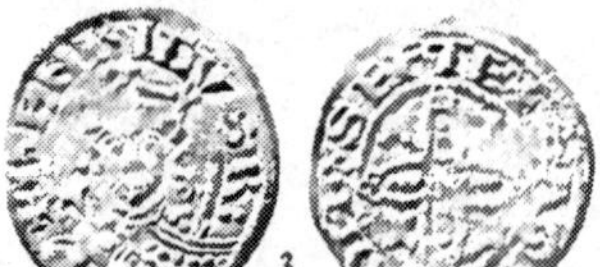
3
P.C.B.

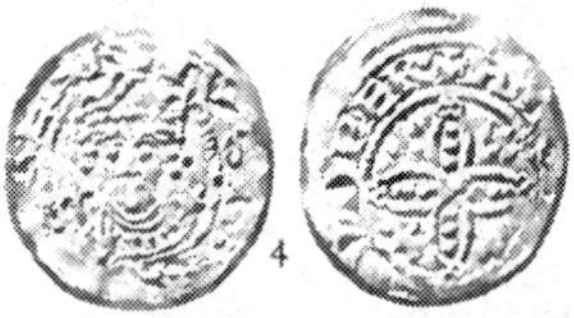
4

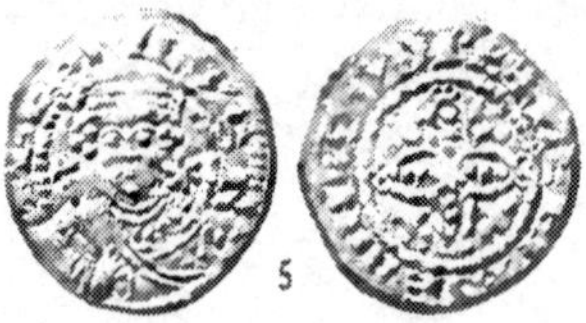
5

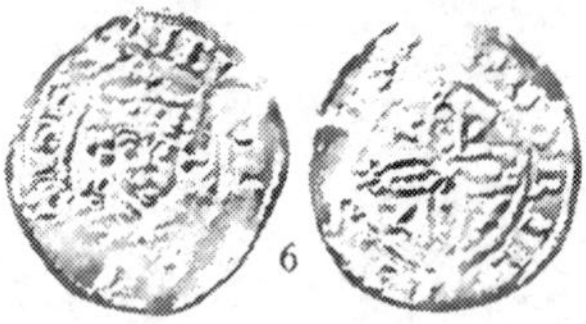
6

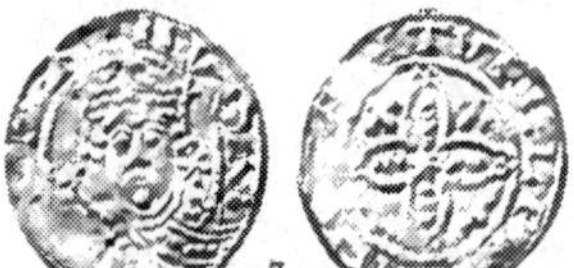
7
P.C.B.

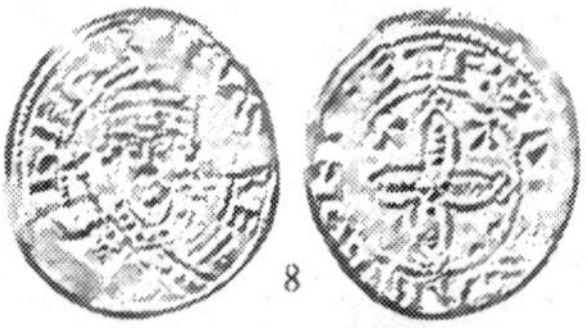
8

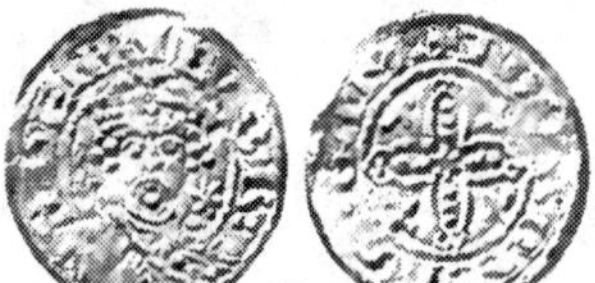
9
P.C.B.

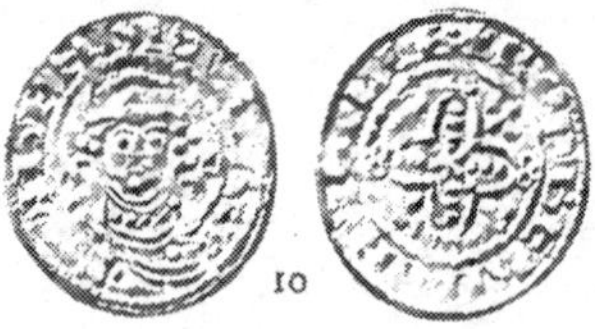
10

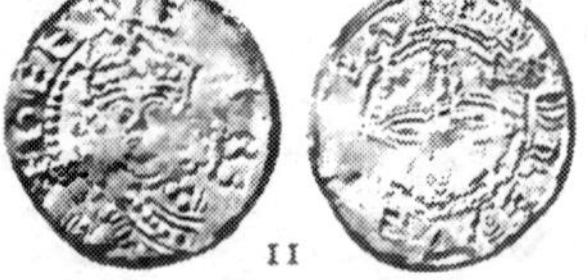
11

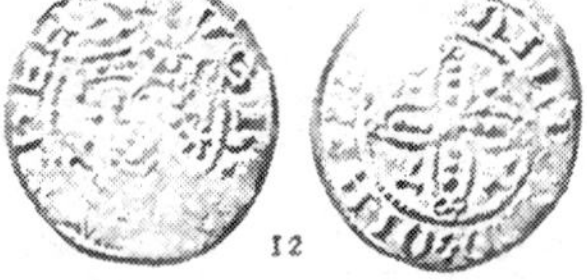
12

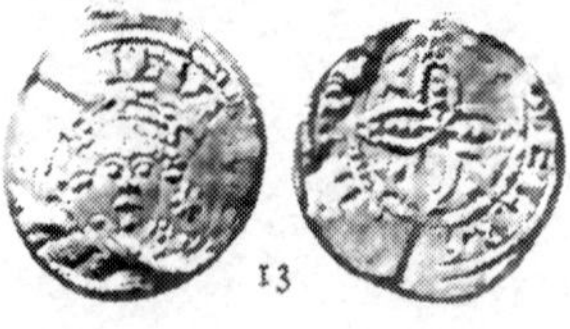
13

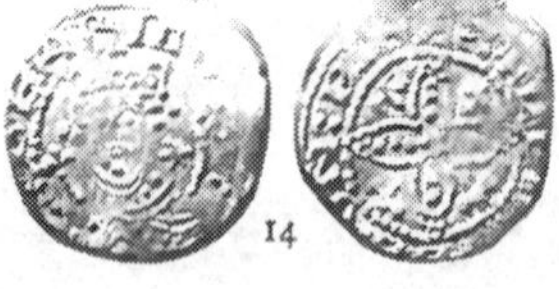
14

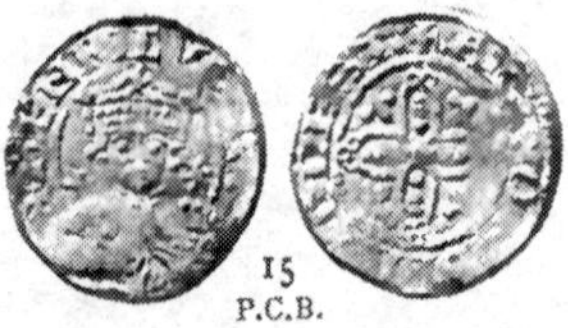
15
P.C.B.

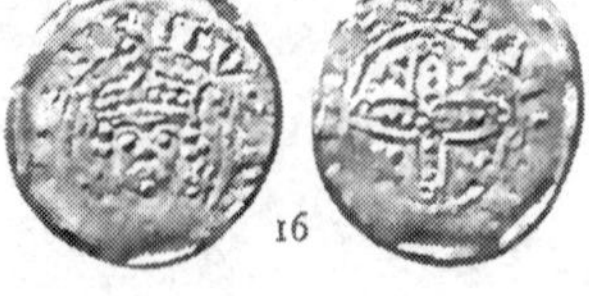
16

HENRY I. TYPE XIV.

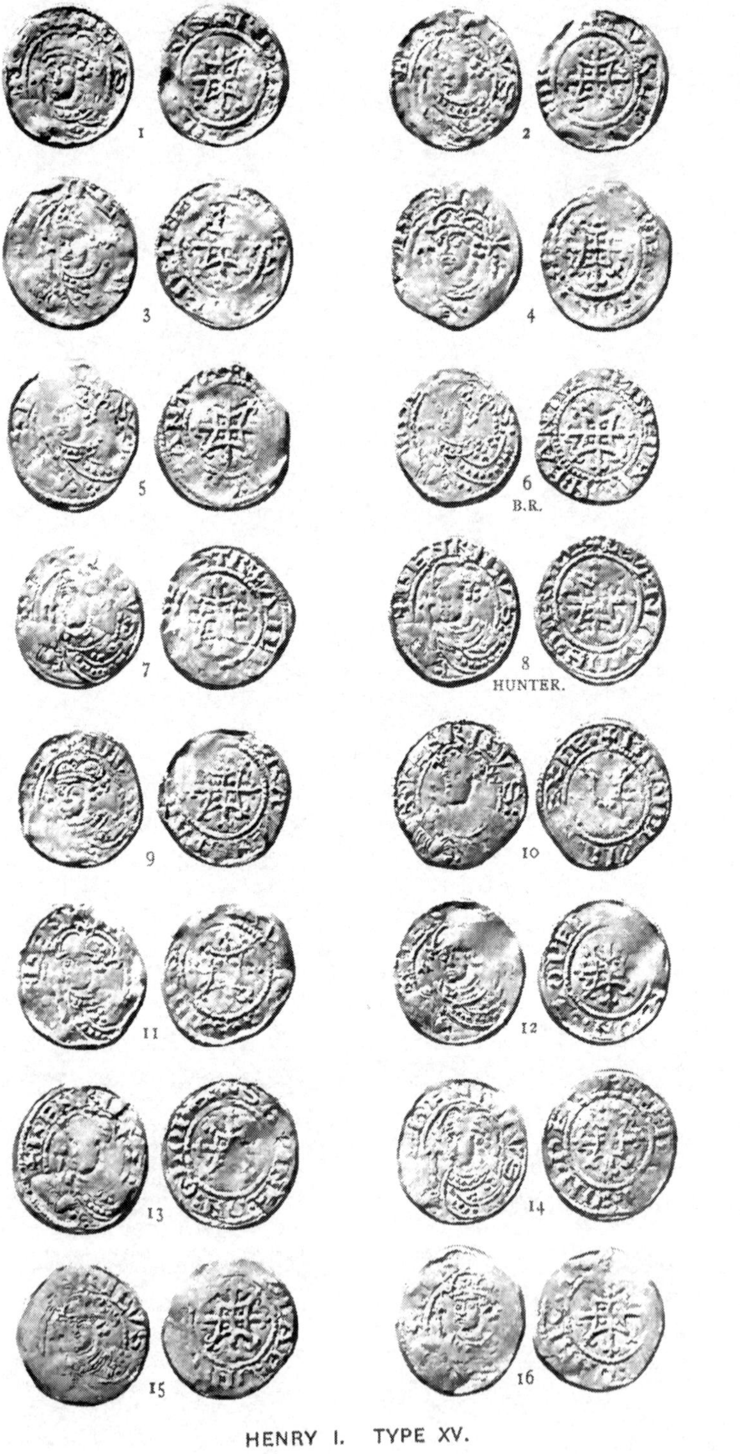
1
2
3
4
5
6
B.R.
7
8
HUNTER.
9
10
11
12
13
14
15
16

HENRY I. TYPE XV.

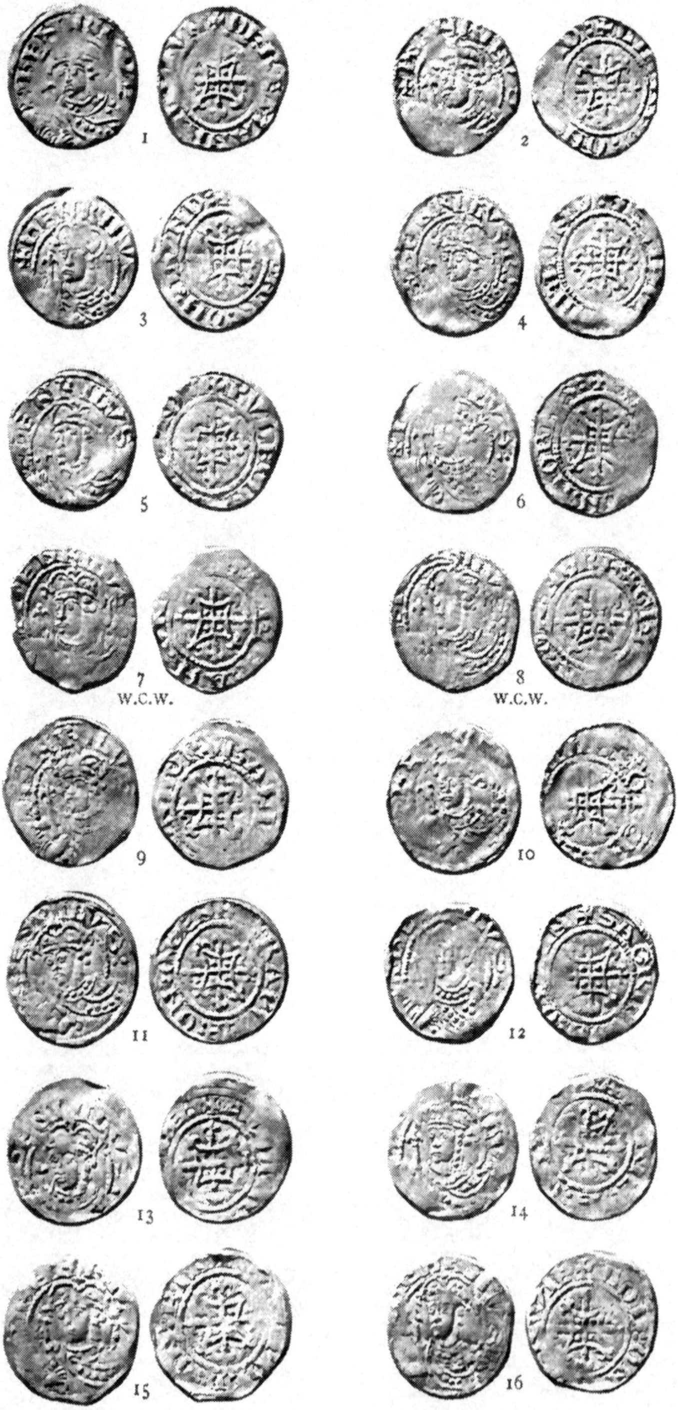
1
2
3
4
5
6
7
W.C.W.
8
W.C.W.
9
10
11
12
13
14
15
16

HENRY I. TYPE XV.

NORMAN KINGS. PLATE XLIX.

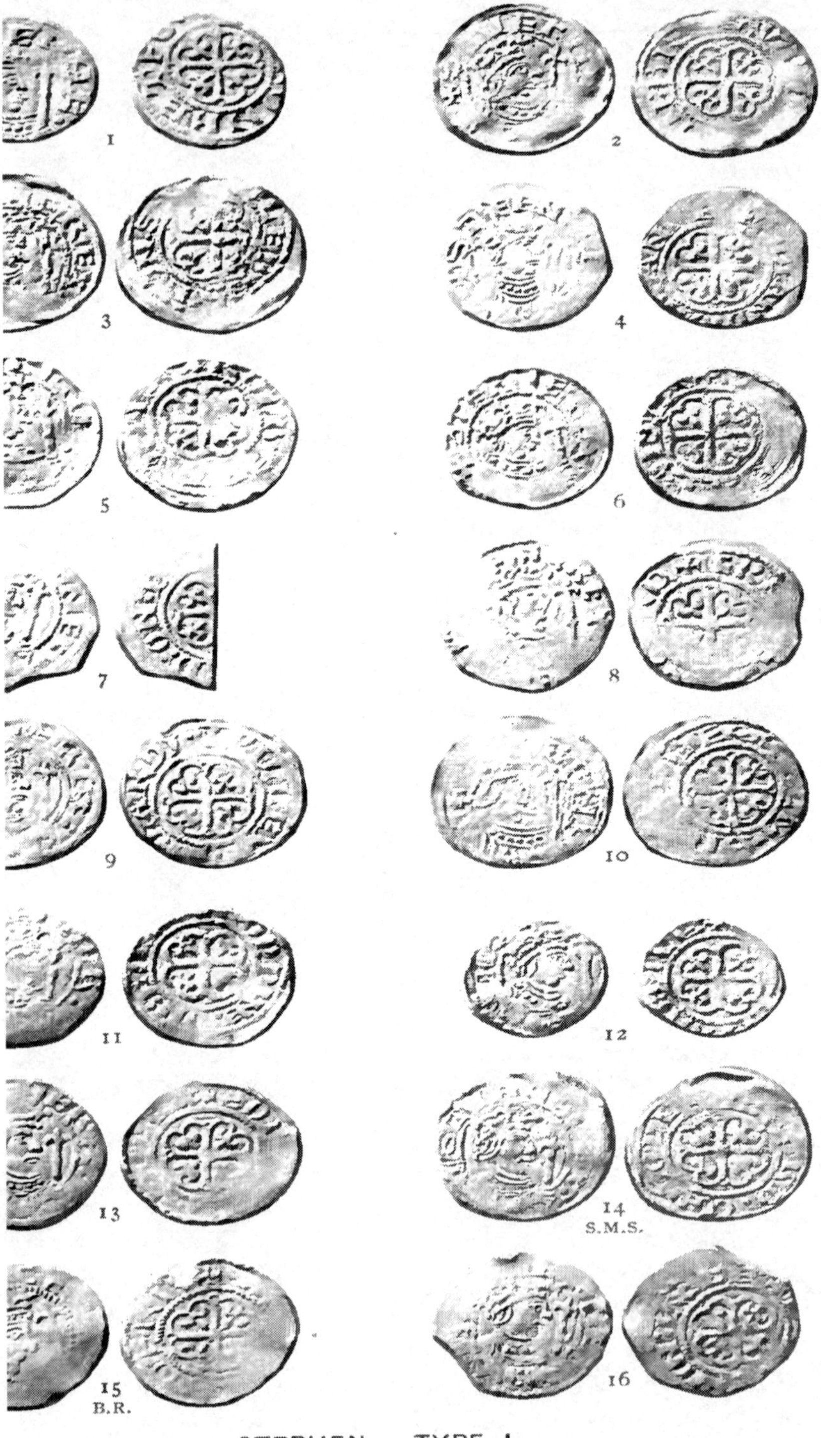

1
2
3
4
5
6
7
8
9
10
11
12
13
14
S.M.S.
15
B.R.
16

STEPHEN. TYPE I.

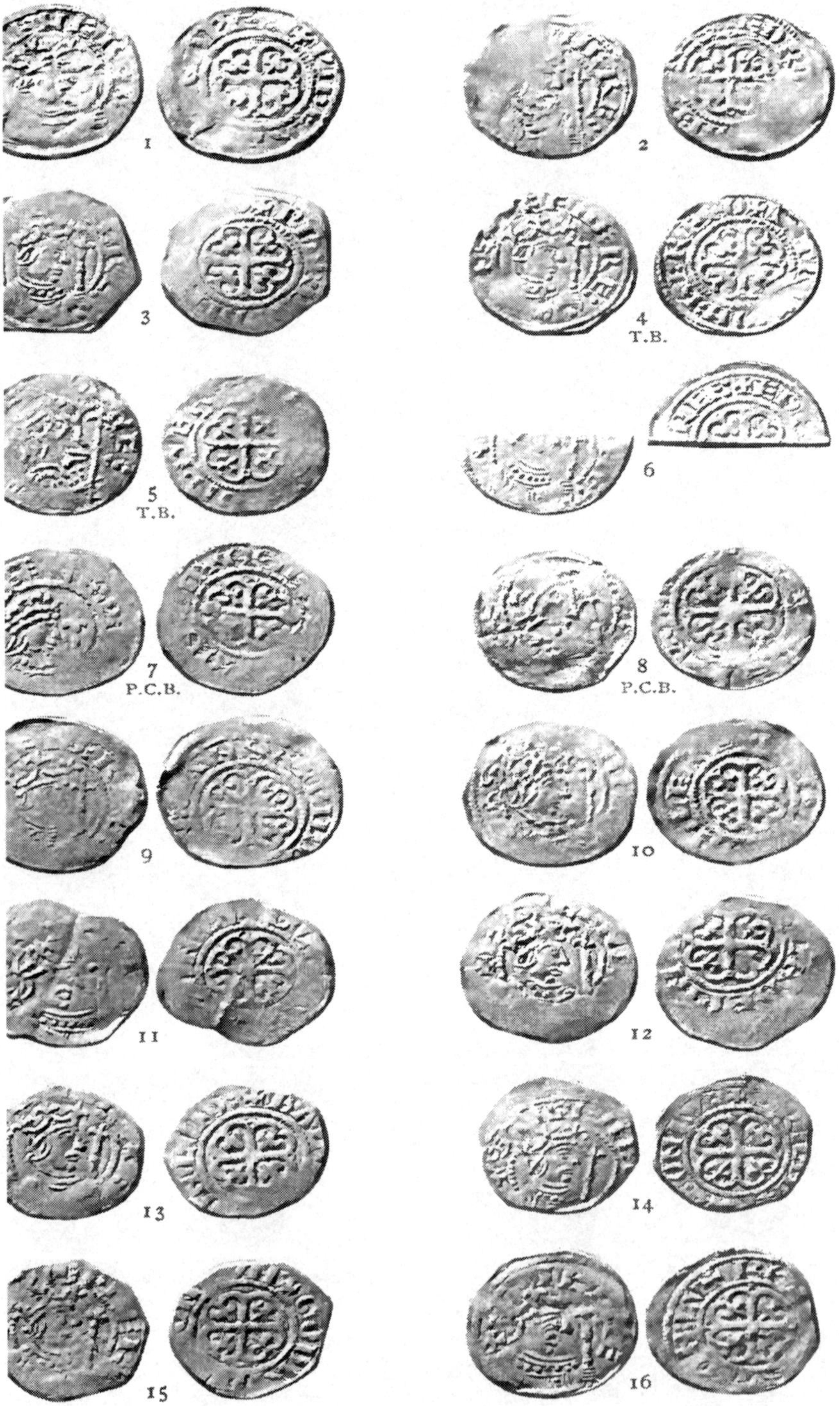

STEPHEN. TYPE I.

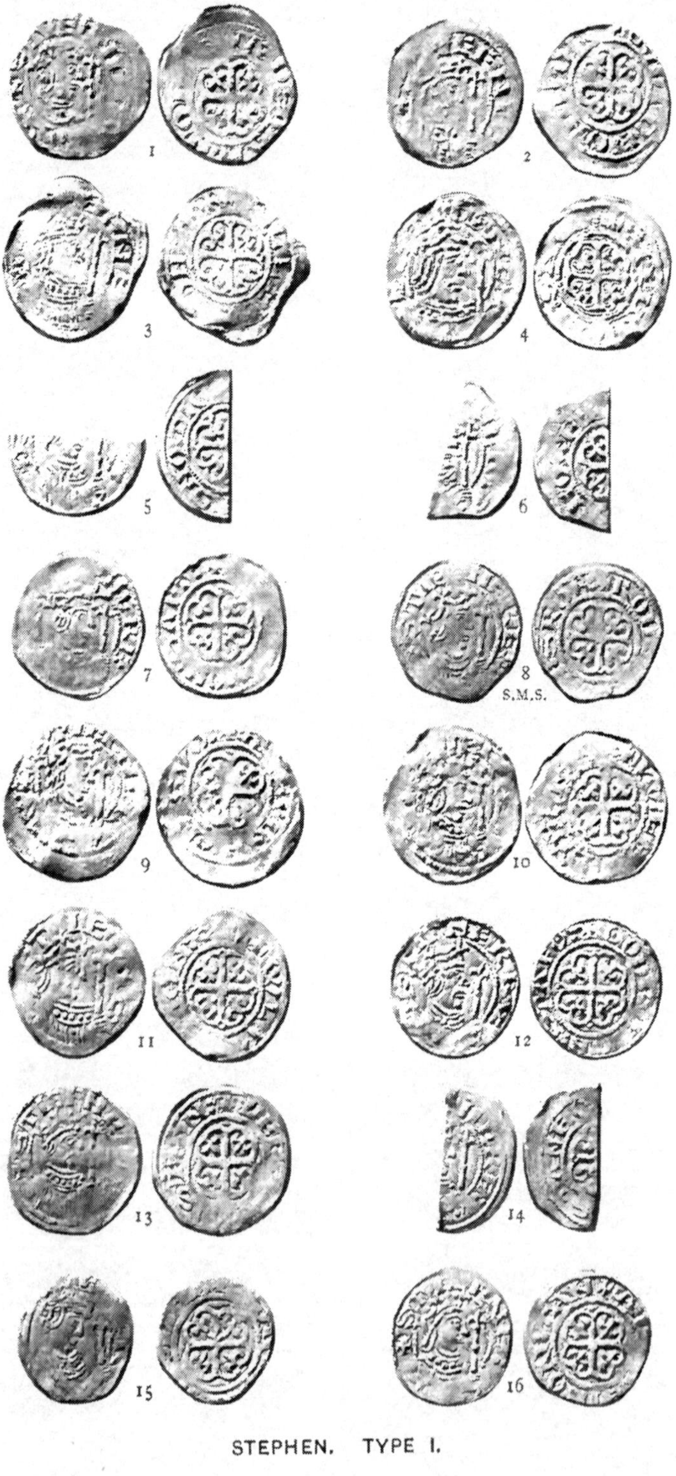

STEPHEN. TYPE I.

W.C.W.

STEPHEN. TYPE I.

SHELDON FIND.

STEPHEN. MULE I x II, TYPE II.

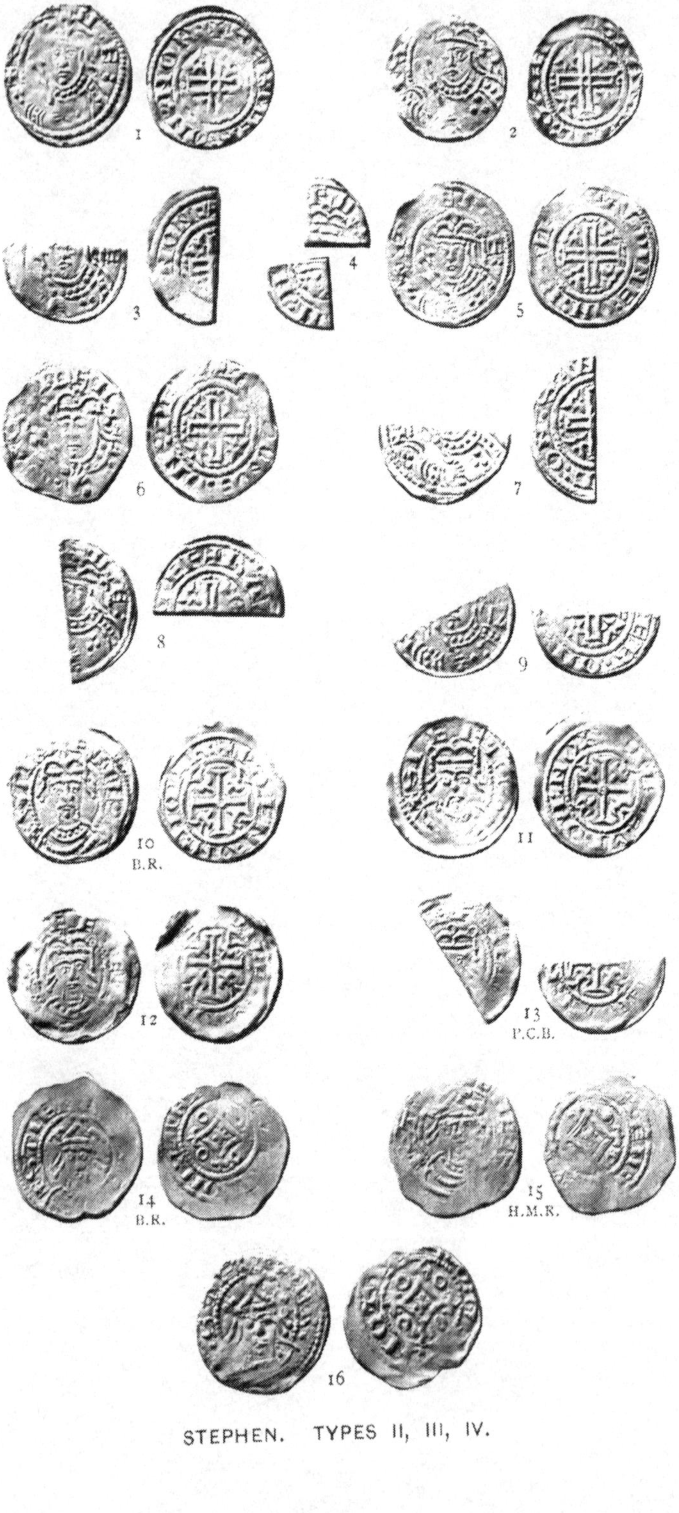
1
2
3
4
5
6
7
8
9
10
B.R.
11
12
13
P.C.B.
14
B.R.
15
H.M.R.
16

STEPHEN. TYPES II, III, IV.

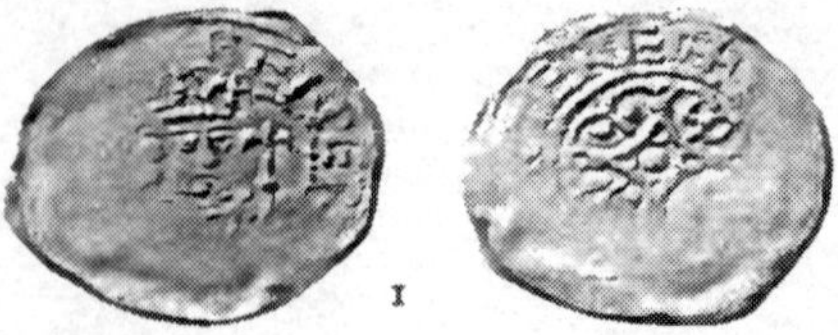

1

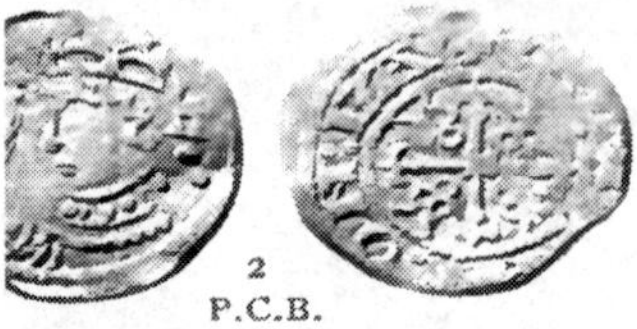

2
P.C.B.

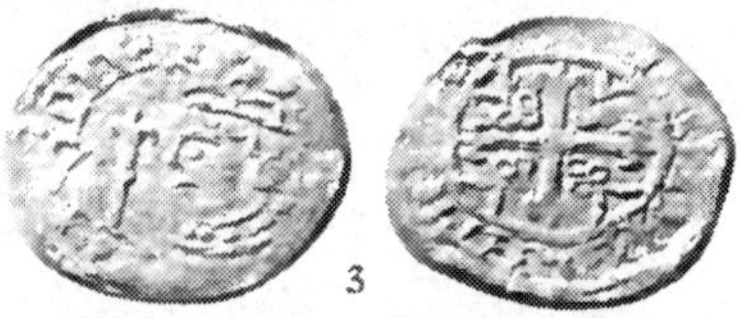

3

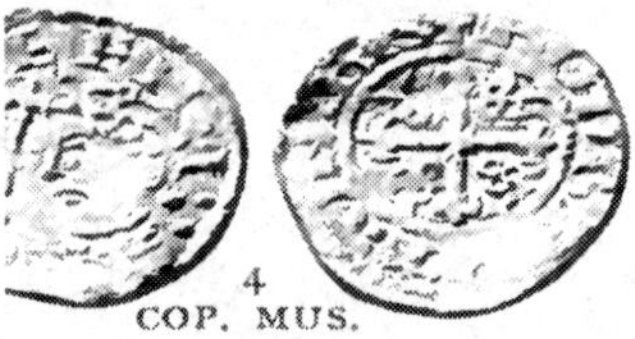

4
COP. MUS.

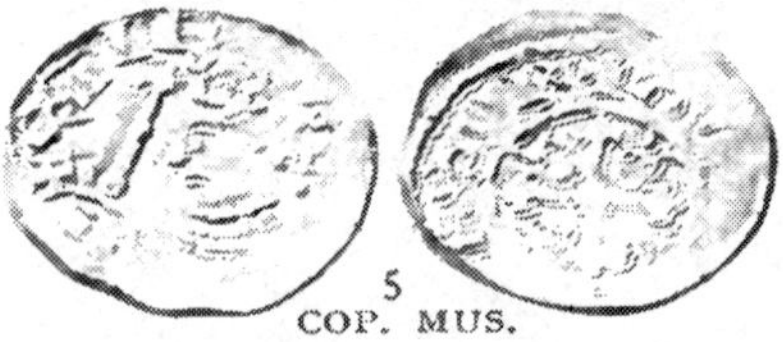

5
COP. MUS.

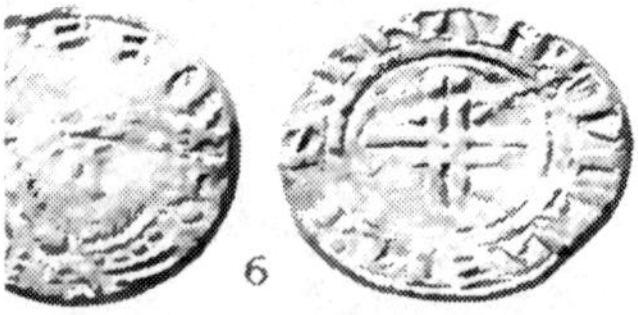

6

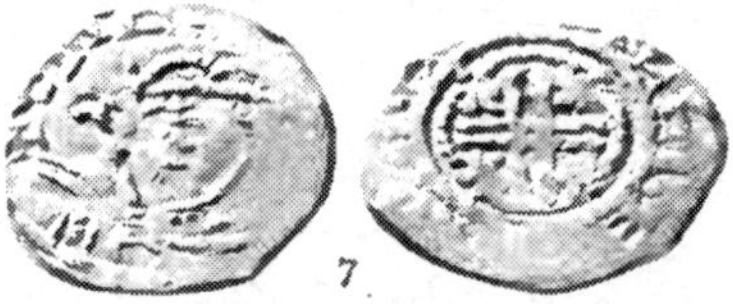

7

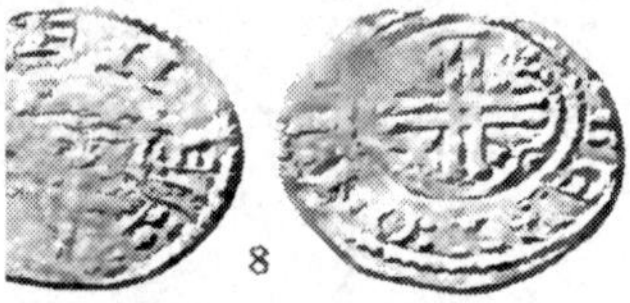

8

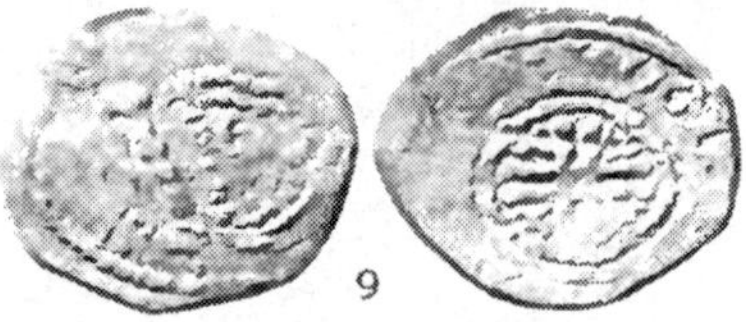

9

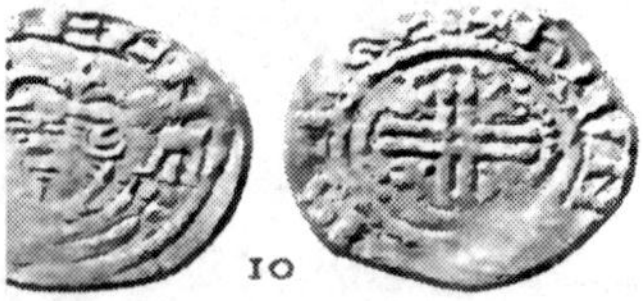

10

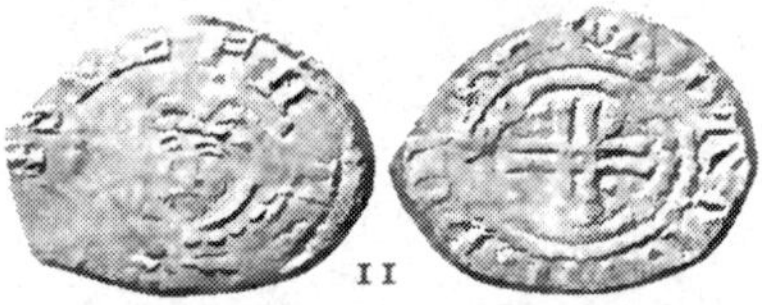

11

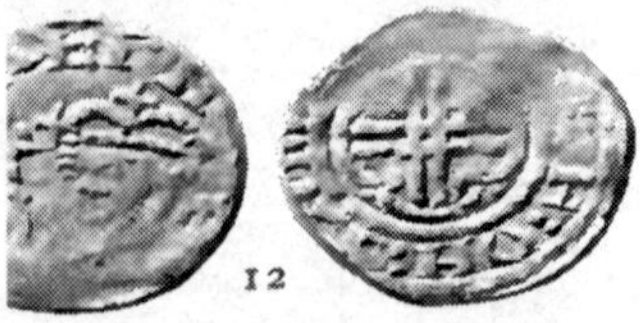

12

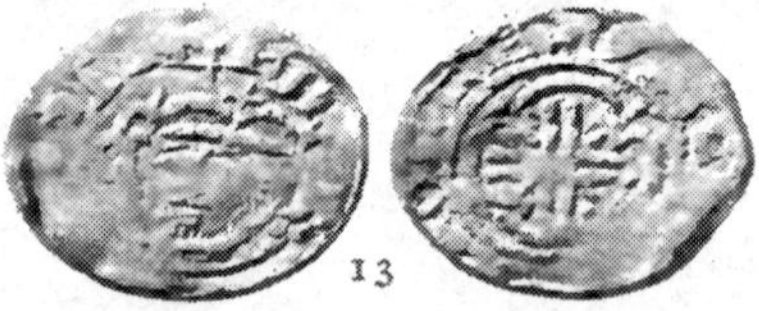

13

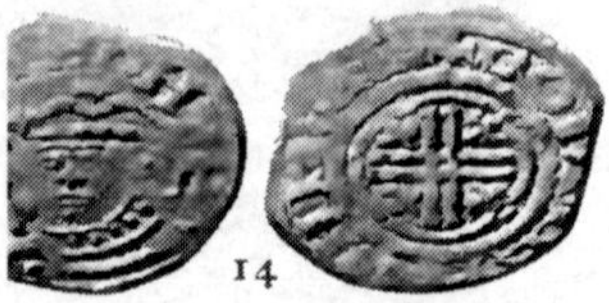

14

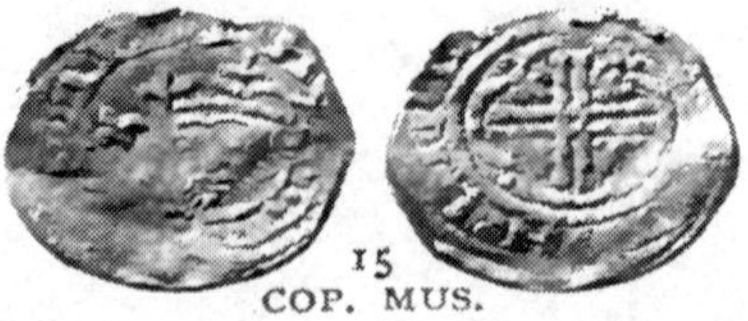

15
COP. MUS.

STEPHEN. TYPES V, VI, VII.

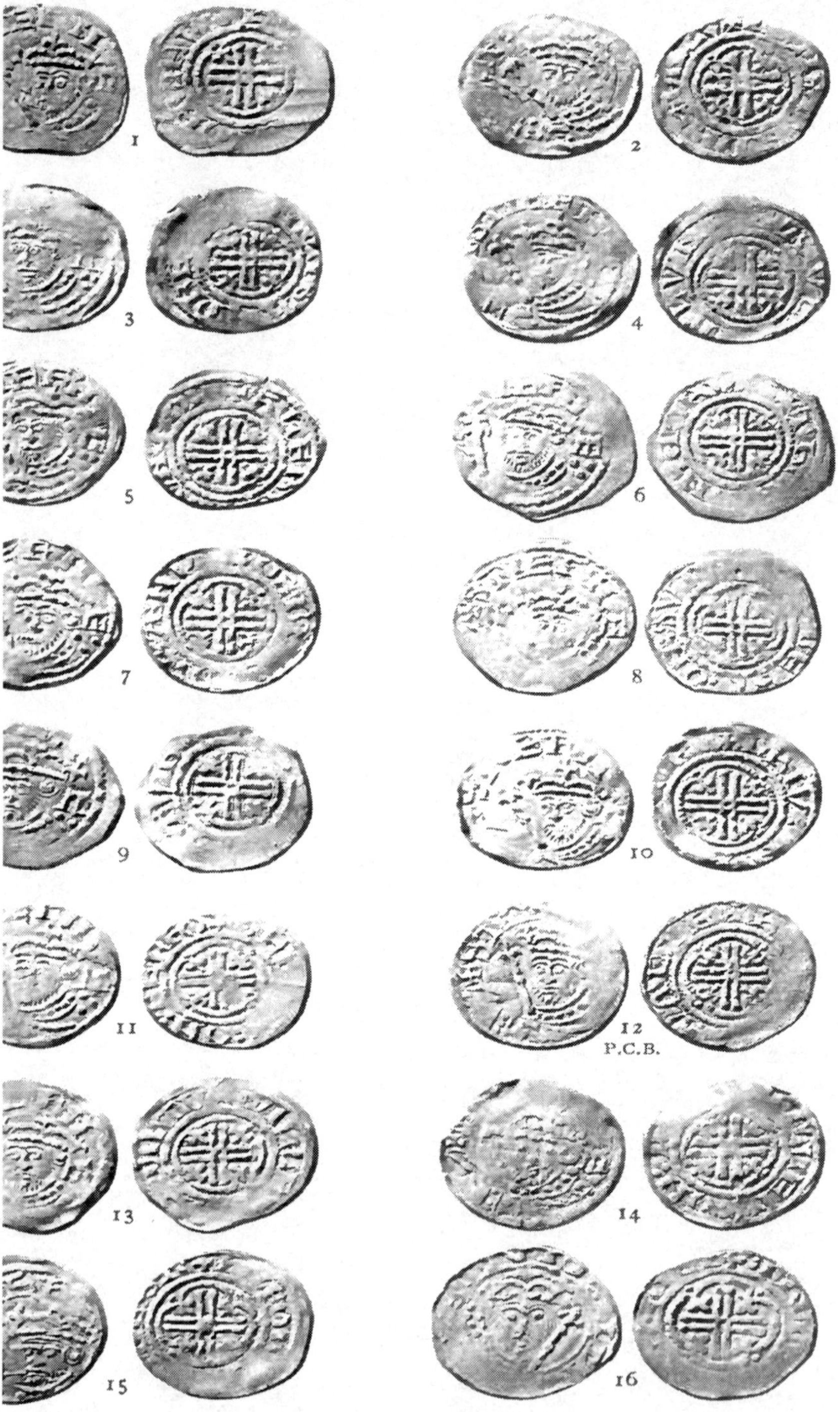
1
2
3
4
5
6
7
8
9
10
11
12
P.C.B.
13
14
15
16

STEPHEN. TYPE VII.

STEPHEN. COINS FROM ERAZED DIES; COINS INSCRIBED PERERIC.

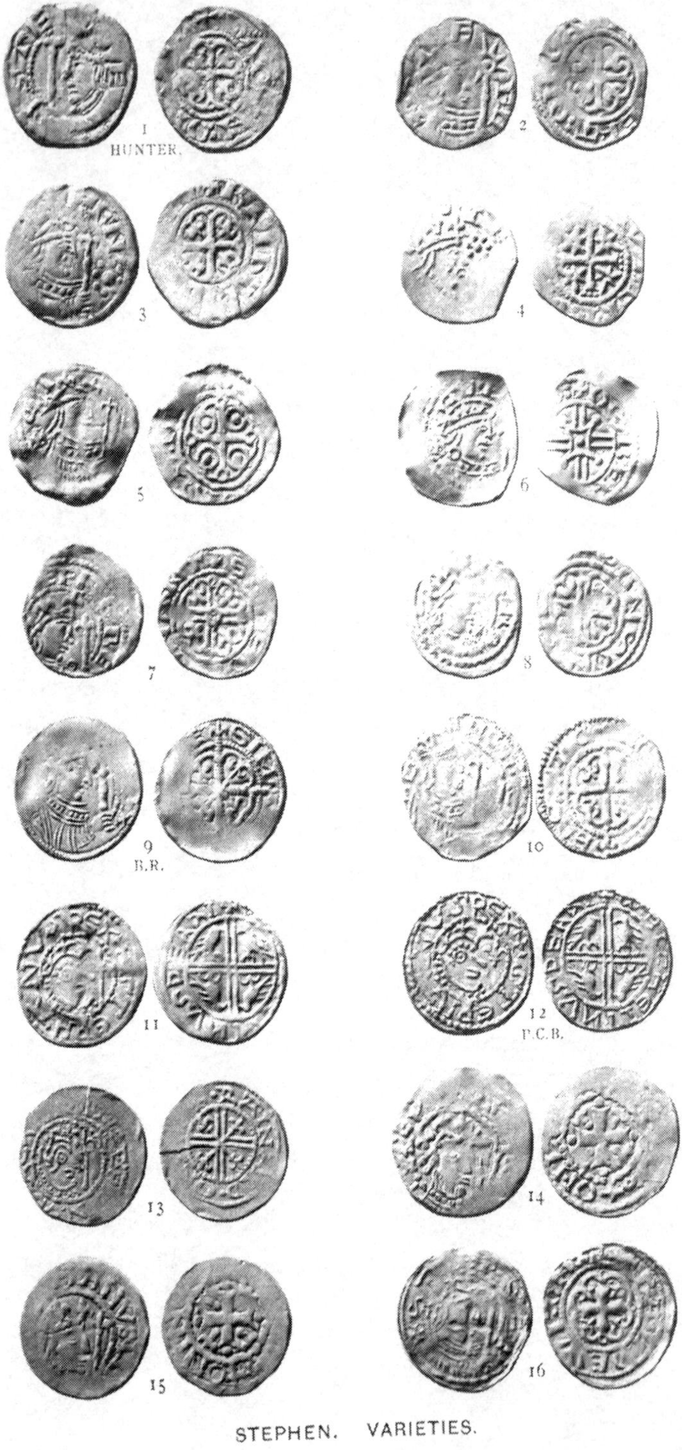
1
HUNTER.
2
3
4
5
6
7
8
9
B.R.
10
11
12
P.C.B.
13
14
15
16

STEPHEN. VARIETIES.

1
H.M.R.

2
H.M.R.

3

4

5

6

7
H.M.R.

8
H.M.R.

9

10

11

12

13

14

15

16
P.C.B.

STEPHEN.   VARIETIES.

QUEEN MATILDA AND EUSTACE (?);   EUSTACE, SON OF STEPHEN (?);
EUSTACE FITZJOHN;   ROBERT DE STUTEVILLE;   HENRY, BISHOP OF WINCHESTER.

1
P.C.B.

2
P.C.B.

3
B.R.

4
B.R.

5

6
B.R.

7

8
B.R.

9

10

11
B.R.

12

13

14

15

16
COP. MUS.

EMPRESS MATILDA; HENRY OF ANJOU.

HENRY OF ANJOU; ROBERT OF GLOUCESTER (?); WILLIAM OF GLOUCESTER (?);
BRIAN FITZCOUNT (?) AND UNCERTAIN BARONIAL.

ImTheStory.com

Lightning Source UK Ltd.
Milton Keynes UK
UKOW031811150812

197597UK00010B/96/P